TRANSFORMING
THE LEGACY

TRANSFORMING
THE LEGACY

COUPLE THERAPY WITH SURVIVORS
OF CHILDHOOD TRAUMA

Kathryn Karusaitis Basham
and Dennis Miehls

Columbia University Press   New York

Columbia University Press
Publishers Since 1893
New York   Chichester, West Sussex

Library of Congress Cataloging-in-Publication Data

Basham, Kathryn Karusaitis.
    Transforming the legacy : couple therapy with survivors of childhood trauma /
Kathryn Karusaitis Basham and Dennis Miehls.
        p.   cm.
    Includes bibliographical references and index.
    ISBN 0-231-12342-6 (cloth : alk. paper)
    1. Marital psychotherapy.   2. Psychic trauma in children.   I. Miehls,
Dennis.   II. Title.
    RC488.5.B365   2004
    616.89′1562—dc22   2004052788

∞ Columbia University Press books are printed on permanent
and durable acid-free paper.

Printed in the United States of America
c 10 9 8 7 6 5 4 3 2 1

: :   To Dr. Norma Steuerle, my valued friend and colleague, whose clinical wisdom and cheerful optimism continue to guide my practice

KATHRYN KARUSAITIS BASHAM

: :   To Beth, who instills confidence and the courage to change, and to James, who instills balance and hope

DENNIS MIEHLS

CONTENTS

List of Figures and Tables   ix

Preface   xi

Acknowledgments   xv

SECTION I :: CONTEXT

1   Introduction   3

2   Historical Review   15

SECTION II :: THEORETICAL FOUNDATIONS

3   Social Theory   37

4   Family Theory   51

5   Trauma Theory   70

6   Object Relations Theory   91

7   Attachment Theory   113

SECTION III :: COUPLE THERAPY PRACTICE

8   Biopsychosocial Assessment   133

9   Phase-Oriented Couple Therapy Model   154

10   Clinician Responses: Working with Traumatized Couples   212

11   Clinical Case Illustration   242

SECTION IV :: SPECIFIC CLINICAL ISSUES

12   Military Couples and Families   285

13   Gay/Lesbian//Bisexual/Transgendered Couples and Families   303

14   Immigrant and Refugee Couples and Families   315

References   331

Index   365

FIGURES AND TABLES

:: FIGURES

Figure 4.1   Genogram for Paula and Colette   67

Figure 5.1   Effects of Hyperarousal on Declarative Memory   77

Figure 8.1   Potential Countertransference Traps Influenced by the Victim–Victimizer–Bystander Scenario   141

Figure 11.1   Genogram for Rod and Yolanda   245

:: TABLES

Table 6.1   Couple Characteristics: Separation–Individuation Theory   101

Table 7.1   Child Attachment Classifications   117

Table 7.2   Correlation of Child/Adult Attachment Classifications   119

Table 8.1   Phase-Oriented Couple Therapy: Phases   135

Table 8.2   Phase-Oriented Couple Therapy: Biopsychosocial Assessment Factors   139

Table 10.1   Countertransference and Vicarious Traumatization: Similarities and Differences   237

Table 11.1   Phase-Oriented Couple Therapy: Biopsychosocial Assessment of Yolanda and Rod   248

Table 11.2   Phase-Oriented Couple Therapy: Treatment Phases with Yolanda and Rod   265

Table 14.1   Immigration by Source Area to Canada (1999–2001)   316

Table 14.2   Immigration by Source Area to the United States (1999–2001)   316

Table 14.3   Refugees by Source Area Now Living in Canada   317

Table 14.4   Refugees by Source Area Now Living in the United States   317

Before we proceed with the introduction to this text on couple therapy, we should address a few substantive and structural issues. An obvious question relates to our choice in writing about a couple therapy practice model specifically focused on survivors of childhood trauma. One may ask why each of us gravitated to this topic and how we decided to work together. Since there are many ways of coauthoring a text, the process we chose to follow also deserves attention. Finally we discuss some technical considerations regarding the use of clinical case material.

First we briefly describe how our professional interests in this topic were sparked. Since 1970, after the completion of my master's in clinical social work at the University of California at Berkeley, I (K.B.) have consistently practiced in a variety of mental health settings, with a wide range of culturally diverse clients with varying presenting issues. I first met Dr. Dennis Miehls as a colleague/classmate in 1985, when I returned to complete my Ph.D. in clinical social work at the Smith College School for Social Work. At the time, my academic and practice interests were grounded in psychodynamically oriented individual therapy as well as feminist-informed intergenerational and object relations couple and family therapy. Many years of intensive work with high-conflict divorcing couples drew me to focus on trauma theory as a useful theoretical lens for practice and research on child custody decisions, post-divorce. My fascination with synthesizing often disparate theoretical constructs peaked while I completed my clinical internship at the Department of Psychiatry at the George Washington University Medical Center. The department was the setting for ongoing debates as to the optimal practice models for use with individual clients diagnosed with characterological issues, many of whom had survived childhood trauma. Although psychoanalytic practice, based primarily on the work of Otto Kernberg, ultimately prevailed, ongoing critiques illuminated alternative perspectives for understanding the legacies of childhood trauma. A social constructionist stance allowed me to synthesize my psychodynamic training with trauma theories and immersion in couple and family therapy practice models. As my academic interests deepened, my clinical interests shifted to more couple, family, and individual therapy practice with survivors of childhood trauma. I continued to reflect, write, present locally and nationally, conduct research, and practice in this area.

In 1977, I (D.M.) completed my M.S.W. degree at Wilfrid Laurier University in Waterloo, Ontario. I was immersed in working with a range of couples and families in my first clinical position in London, Ontario. I worked in a United Way–funded agency, and my clients represented the range of sociocultural diversity in this southwestern Ontario urban community. I dealt primarily with what were termed, at that time, "multiproblem families," and in retrospect I realize that I was working with many dual-trauma couples. In keeping with the prevailing treatment mode of the time, I practiced as a systemic/structural family therapist. My interest in working in mental health peaked when I worked in large in-patient mental health settings in two health care centers. In addition to having serious and chronic mental health issues, many of my individual clients had experienced persistent and ongoing traumatic experiences. I began to look for practice models that would synthesize the biological, social, and psychological. Many clients had multiple diagnoses, and a single theoretical model was insufficient to prepare me to be a competent practitioner. Over time I expanded my training in psychodynamic theories and began to synthesize a range of theories. I had an avid interest in applying dynamic concepts to my couple and family work, and I developed expertise in couple therapy. My dissertation, completed at the Smith College School for Social Work in 1989, examined the impact of adult attachment factors on the beginning stages of intimate partnerships. In that project, I studied factors that promoted growth (resilience) within couples and laid the groundwork for the ongoing application of object relations, attachment, and family theories in my work with couples.

In the mid-1990s, we recognized that we shared similar interests in clinical practice with traumatized couples and started down our path of writing together. Since that time, we have each presented on aspects of couple therapy with trauma survivors in a range of clinical and academic settings, both nationally and internationally.

As we embarked on this book project, we entertained different approaches to writing. Early on, after consultation with the director of our college's writing center, we altered our shared inclination to co-write each chapter. Instead, we have approached the writing of this text by dividing the tasks involved. After we actively discussed the ideas, controversies, purpose, and structure for each chapter, one of us assumed primary responsibility for writing that chapter. We have regularly commented on and edited each other's writing. Each of us has also contributed clinical case material throughout all of the chapters.

The use of clinical vignettes or case studies warrants some review here. In using any clinical case material, authors must always thoughtfully consider how to balance the inclusion of illustrative material with the requirement to use confidential case material responsibly. We have followed the specific guidelines outlined by the American Psychological Association in its *Publication Manual*. Confidentiality is usually handled by one of two means. "One option is to prepare the descriptive case material, present it to the subject of the case report, and obtain written consent for its publication from the subject. The other option is to disguise some aspects of the case material so that neither the subject nor those who know the subject would be identifiable." Three main strategies have emerged to accomplish an effective disguise. They are "(a) altering specific characteristics, (b) limiting the description of specific characteristics, and (c) obfuscating case detail by adding extraneous material" (*APA Publication Manual*, 2001, p. 9).

We arrived at a mutually supportive yet intellectually challenging collaboration in which we both worked together actively to present this couple therapy practice model and also retained our individual writing voices. We shared responsibility for coauthoring Chapters 1 (Introduction) and 13 (Gay/Lesbian/Bisexual/Transgendered Couples and Families). Dennis Miehls assumed primary responsibility for Chapters 2 (Historical Review), 3 (Social Theory), 6 (Object Relations Theory), 7 (Attachment Theory), 10 (Clinician Responses), and 14 (Immigrant and Refugee Couples and Families). Kathryn Basham assumed primary responsibility for Chapters 4 (Family Theory), 5 (Trauma Theory), 8 (Biopsychosocial Assessment), 9 (Phase-Oriented

Couple Therapy Model), 11 (Clinical Case Illustration), and 12 (Military Couples and Families).

Although this project has demanded perseverance and rigor from each of us throughout the past two years, our collaboration has clearly enriched and strengthened our mutually respectful collegial connection.

ACKNOWLEDGMENTS

:: This book could not have been completed without the generosity and encouraging assistance offered by many people, whose contributions we thankfully acknowledge. We extend both admiration and gratitude to our clients, who taught us much about courage and perseverance while transforming their difficult legacies of childhood trauma into new directions in their lives. We have appreciated the collegial support of many individuals at the Smith College School for Social Work. Our writing and research efforts have been financially supported by the Brown Foundation and the Clinical Research Institute of Smith College. We thank our dean, Carolyn Jacobs, for interesting and thought-provoking dialogues that helped shape our ideas. Gerry Schamess has taught us a great deal about clinical practice and editing, skills that we have valued highly while working on this project.

We are especially indebted to our dear friend and colleague, Joan Berzoff, who spent considerable time and energy reading and rereading drafts of the manuscript. Joan is an exemplary role model in many ways: clinical writer, theorist, and teacher. We admire her productivity and her sharp wit. We also thank our resident and adjunct faculty colleagues at Smith College, who have consistently shown interest in and encouragement of this project. In particular, we thank Margery Daniel, Bill Etnyre, and Ziva Levite, who provided astute feedback on various chapters. We are indebted to our administrative support staff at the Smith College School for Social Work and thankful for their consistent professionalism.

We are especially grateful to AnnaMarie Russo, who edited and formatted the manuscript. We deeply appreciate her writing and editing acumen, her sense of balance, and her remarkable attention to detail. Her work so often went "above and beyond" her regular assignments. Last, we are indebted to our students, who have asked questions, provided critiques, and engaged us in thought-provoking dialogues. We thank our two research assistants, Julie Jacobs and Jen Babis, for their many hours of library assistance.

We thank E. Cherpanov, Ph.D., and H. Bui, M.S.W., of the Springfield, Massachusetts, Refugee and Immigrant Program (Child and Family Service of the Pioneer Valley, Inc.), who shared their clinical experiences with refugee and immigrant populations. In addition, we acknowledge email correspondence (February 2003) from our colleagues W. Gorman, Ph.D. (University of Illinois at Chicago) and I. Kira (Access Community Health and Research Center, Dearborn, Michigan), who offered insights about contemporary practice models with immigrant populations. These contributions are found in Chapter 14.

We also thank John Michel, our editor at Columbia University Press, and Ms. Jeanie Lu, editorial assistant, who ably moved us through the various stages of this project.

KATHRYN KARUSAITIS BASHAM AND DENNIS MIEHLS

: : I owe a special debt of gratitude to my parents, Dr. Vincent and Vera Karusaitis, who by the nature of their example, taught me appreciation for rigorously committing their lives to work with others. I have dedicated this book to my esteemed colleague, Dr. Norma Steuerle, who worked with me as a valued colleague/clinical psychologist, friend, and partner in clinical practice for eighteen years. Her sharp clinical acumen, unwavering optimism, and integrity of character have always guided my practice, and they continue to do so even after her tragic death in the September 11, 2001, terrorist attacks. Her presence, as a friend and professional colleague, is missed deeply yet reflected in the lives of those fortunate to have known her.

I extend gratitude to my family and friends. In particular, I thank my sister, Ann Karus Meeropol, and my brother-in-law, Michael Meeropol, for their steadfast, compassionate support of my writing ventures; my niece Ivy, for excelling in her creative and original filmmaking; and my nephew, Greg, whose adventuresome spirit and dedication to work with high-risk adolescents serve as inspiration. To my dear friends, Andrea and Norma, I thank you for the depth of our shared friendship. Many thanks to Beth Miehls for her steadfast encouragement and friendship. I extend many thanks to my dear friends Rebecca and Jorge Pulles, who have provided anchoring encouragement and constructive "nudging" to complete the project. I extend my gratitude to my long-term friend, Sheila Wolfe, for her keen sense of humor and generous support.

Throughout the years I have been fortunate to work with a number of exceptional clinical supervisors, consultants, and colleagues. I thank Dr. Sheila Gray, Dr. Joyce Everett, Dr. Susan Donner, Dr. Phebe Sessions, Ms. Dorothy Miller, Ms. Audrey Walker, Ms. Brenda Twyner Robinson, Ms. Khalilah Karim-Rushdan, Ms. Liz Carole Walton, Dr. Kathleen Mosby, Dr. Fred Wamboldt, Dr. John Zinner, and Dr. Peter Steinglass, who have provided invaluable contributions to my professional development. I also extend my gratitude to the members of the Georgia, Washington, and South Carolina chapters of the National Federation of Clinical Social Workers and the staff of Jewish Family and Career Services in Atlanta, Georgia, who have provided useful feedback and generous support to my workshop presentations of the couple therapy practice model. Last, I thank my coauthor, Dennis Miehls, for demonstrating skillfully the art of cooperation and collaboration. I have admired and appreciated the depth of Dennis's clinical acumen, his exceptional discipline, and his impressive dedication to excellence in clinical social work practice, education, and writing. I also appreciate the fact that we were still able to laugh together while completing this difficult project. Thank you for the positive transformative changes that I have experienced in the course of coauthoring this text.

KATHRYN KARUSAITIS BASHAM

: :   I thank a number of others who have helped shape my personal, professional, and academic identities. I am indebted to Beth, who so often "carried" our household when I was immersed in this project. I am also indebted to James, who, as a ready and competent computer technician, saved me much time and frustration. Beth and James offered support in countless ways that facilitated our completion of this project. I will be always thankful for their presence in my life. I thank my parents, who helped me internalize the attitudes that value both hard work and relaxation. I thank Hugh and Janet Stevenson, my dear friends, whose experience and encouragement helped to shape my academic career. I thank Dr. Ken Moffatt for his collegiality and the opportunity to work and write together. I am grateful to Ken for having introduced me to postmodern writers.

I have also had the good fortune of working with many astute clinicians and supervisors during my professional practice career. I thank Drs. J.

Casselman, E. Hanna, D. Kligman, J. Lohrenz, and G. Truant, who all helped to shape my professional self. Many other colleagues at London Health Sciences Center, King's College, and Wilfrid Laurier University have also challenged me to be a clear thinker, supervisor, and teacher. Last, I thank my coauthor, Kathryn Basham, who has artfully encouraged me to strive for the highest standards in our work. I am grateful for Kathryn's intellectual giftedness, her clinical wisdom, her humor, her perseverance, and her on-going collegiality and friendship.

DENNIS MIEHLS

CONTEXT

The first chapter introduces the reader to the underpinnings of the conceptual framework of the book. Initially, we report the demographic data related to the incidence of childhood trauma in the United States. We recognize the timeliness of our contribution in developing a practice model for couples and families experiencing trauma, especially since the United States is actively engaged in a war in Iraq. Although emphasis is placed on the legacies of childhood traumatic events, attention is also paid to the effect of traumatic experiences in adult life. The first chapter introduces key constructs of our couple therapy model, grounded in a synthesis of psychological and social theories and attuned specifically to survivors of traumatic events.

Chapter 2 provides a historical overview of the place of trauma in the mental health field. We discuss how sociopolitical contexts influence both historical and contemporary practice issues, and we summarize the development of trauma theory throughout the past century. Finally we review both the historical and contemporary trends of trauma-based work with couples and families.

Introduction

We face an unfortunate reality of increasing numbers of individuals who have endured childhood trauma; who have survived interpersonal and domestic violence; or who, as refugees, have sought asylum from political violence, armed conflict, or torture. As clinical social work practitioners, we need to respond effectively to these individuals who request clinical services to assist in coping with trauma-related issues and symptomatology. In addition to the pathways that lead to posttraumatic stress disorder (PTSD) or complex PTSD syndrome, many Americans have experienced residual effects in the aftermath of the September 11, 2001, terrorist attacks. With certainty, we are aware that many American citizens suffer ongoing, debilitating fears concerning further terrorist activity, including biological and chemical warfare. This climate of heightened anxiety is fueled by ever-increasing rates of violence and child maltreatment and by the ravages of poverty.

The demographic data regarding childhood trauma in the United States are quite alarming. The National Clearinghouse on Child Abuse and Neglect Information (2004) reported that in 2001 approximately 903,000 children were found to be victims of child maltreatment, a figure that represents 12.4 per 1,000 children in the population. In 1996, the third national incidence study of child abuse and neglect, based on reports from Child Protective Services, revealed substantial increases in the incidence of child abuse and neglect as compared with the data gathered from the prior national study completed ten years earlier (Sedlak & Broadhurst, 1996). Rates of physical abuse nearly doubled, those of sexual abuse more than doubled, and incidents of emotional abuse and neglect were two and one half times higher than the earlier levels. Contrary to stereotypical cultural assumptions, the data revealed no significant differences according to race. However, children from the lowest income families were eighteen times more likely to be sexually abused, almost fifty-six times more likely to be educationally neglected, and twenty-two times more likely to be seriously maltreated or neglected as compared with children from higher income families. Girls are abused sexually three times more often than boys. Although child abuse is sometimes underreported, it appears that low socioeconomic status and female gender are major risk factors in child maltreatment.

As this book goes to press, U.S. military forces are actively engaged in war in Iraq and at the same time facing increasing threats of terrorist activity with chemical, biological, or mass-destruction weapons. The impact on military personnel and their families will undoubtedly be life changing. Some military personnel who return to the United States from Iraq will require interventions from clinical social work practitioners.

Within this sociopolitical context, we propose a couple therapy model grounded in a synthesis of psychological and social theories and attuned to the survivors of traumatic experiences. Although emphasis is placed on the legacies of childhood traumatic events, attention is also paid to the effects of traumatic experiences in adult life. The rationale for writing this text emerges from each of our extensive clinical experiences, respectively, with a diverse range of individuals, couples, and families who have wrestled with the legacies of trauma.

:: THE COUPLE THERAPY PRACTICE MODEL

Without question, legacies of childhood trauma often affect adults in both elusive and fairly direct manners. Although some survivors of childhood trauma approach their adult lives with a unique zestful resilience, others experience difficulties in their capacities for attachment and intimacy (Rutter, 1993). Pain and distress may occur not only on an internal or intrapsychic level, but in interactions with other people as well. As many adults strive to maintain satisfying and productive partnerships, the majority of adult trauma survivors find themselves in relationships that require active work. In addition to issues of intimacy, trust, and control in decision making in these partnerships, parenting also assumes primary importance for many survivors. Although some researchers suggest a low incidence of intergenerational transmission of abusive behaviors from parents who had been abused as children, there is also a population of adults who were abused as children who actively struggle to use the most effective, nonabusive disciplinary methods with their children (Higgins, 1994; Kaufman & Zigler, 1987).

In spite of what we, as clinicians, see as an increasing prevalence of violence and traumatic events in our society, an accompanying backlash movement reinforced by false memory syndrome proponents is evident (Loftus, 1993; Loftus, Polonsky, & Fullilove, 1994). Major litigation directed against clinicians who have either allegedly or deliberately induced traumatic memories in the course of therapy has further undermined the veracity of some clients' reports. Denial and dissociation remain powerful defenses, not only for clients, but for clinicians as well. As one client who survived the Holocaust as a child stated very directly, "No one can bear to imagine the enormity of the torture and abuses inflicted by one human to another, and so there is a strong pull to minimize and avoid the reality of such abuses."

Although opponents of the mental health system often accuse mental health practitioners of serving only the "worried well," the real world of contemporary practice involves a vast number of adults who have experienced childhood abuse. It is imperative therefore that, in the midst of a political climate that denigrates relationship-based psychotherapy while overvaluing productivity and rapid behaviorally defined progress, we continue to advocate for culturally informed, theoretically grounded, relationship-based clinical social work practice. In our efforts to challenge denials of childhood abuse, it is equally important to avoid the opposite extreme. Here, the risk of problematizing the situation and amplifying aftereffects of trauma could obscure the transformative experiences and positive adaptations for many trauma survivors.

In the field of traumatic stress, treatment has typically focused on individual and group psychotherapy modalities as well as psychopharmacology (Briere, 1996; Courtois, 1999; Figley, 1988; Krystal et al., 1996; Pearlman & Saakvitne, 1995; Shapiro & Appelgate, 2000; van der Kolk, 1996, 2003). Within the past few decades, a number of cognitive–behavioral clinicians have developed psychoeducational couple and family therapy practice models aimed at supporting the family members of a traumatized individual client (Compton & Follette, 1998; Riggs, 2000). In particular, a number of feminist-informed clinicians have developed empowerment therapy models to help the partners and families of trauma survivors (Bass & Davis, 1988; Gil, 1992; Miller, 1994; Walker, 1979). More recently, eye movement desensitization reprocessing (EMDR) and dialectical behavioral therapy (DBT) have been popular and useful models for some clients (Linehan, 1993; Shapiro, 1995; Shapiro & Maxfield, 2003). Yet, once again, the primary therapy goals have involved working through individual aftereffects of traumatic events.

Several important questions arise in working with couples where one or both partners may have experienced childhood trauma. First, in what ways do trauma-related aftereffects influence an individual's capacity for a partnership? Second, in what ways do these trauma-related aftereffects influence the relationship itself? Third, in what ways do these couples present issues that are relevant for many adults, in particular, in what ways are their concerns directly related to the sequelae of childhood trauma? Fourth, in what ways are these couples unique?

Aftereffects of trauma are not restricted to the individual. In fact, family members are not only affected by the legacies of childhood trauma, but they also influence, both positively and negatively, the survivor's experience. As a result, it is important to pay attention to the role of couple therapy with adult survivors of childhood trauma that relies on social, psychological, and neurobiological theories as a way of understanding the multiple influences affecting a couple (Basham & Miehls, 1998a, 1998b). The range of influences is organized around institutional, interactional, and intrapersonal factors.

Constructs of Trauma

Before continuing with a discussion related to the legacies of childhood trauma, the constructs of trauma need to be defined. Although social constructionists posit a relativistic view of trauma based on the sociocultural context at a given moment in time, this fluid approach points to a range of meanings offered by researchers and clinicians in their definitions of trauma.

Figley's (1988, 1995) definition of trauma is useful in a general way. He refers to trauma as an emotional state of discomfort and stress resulting from memories of an extraordinary, catastrophic experience that shatters a survivor's sense of invulnerability to harm, rendering him or her acutely vulnerable to stressors. Herman (1992) discusses how traumatic events overwhelm an ordinary system of care that gives people a sense of control, connection, and meaning in the world.

This couple therapy practice model focuses primarily on type II trauma, the sequelae of childhood sexual, physical, and/or emotional abuse (Terr, 1999). However, in the context of reenactments of a trauma scenario, some adult trauma survivors also find themselves in domestic violence situations in adulthood that qualify as type II traumatic experiences of a chronic, repetitive nature. Regrettably, many adults who have experienced childhood trauma have also experienced type I traumatic events throughout their lives. Examples of these type I discrete traumatic events include natural disaster, accident, rape, or terrorist attack.

Different definitions are proposed for type III trauma. Kira (2002) discusses a wraparound treatment approach for survivors of torture. He defines this torture trauma as a modified model of complex PTSD or cumulative trauma disorders that specifically describe the effects of torture. Torture is viewed as "any systematic act by which severe pain or suffering, whether physical, emotional or mental, is intentionally inflicted on a person for any reason, by or at the instigation of or with the consent or acquiescence of a public official or another person acting in an official capacity" (Kira, 2002, p. 23). Clearly massive psychic traumatization also resulted from the horrific genocidal, often tortuous, acts inflicted during the Holocaust and, more recently, in Rwanda and Bosnia.

A number of researchers, social scientists, and clinicians propose another definition of type III traumatic experience. They tentatively propose the nosology of type III trauma as related to the chronic repetitive insults inflicted on individuals who are marginalized based on race, disability, sexual orientation, or religion. Allen (1998), Daniel (1994), Pinderhughes (1998), and Pouissant and Alexander (2000) assert that day-to-day racist assaults inflicted on people of color perpetuate the legacies of slavery and colonization. In addition, they believe strongly that such racist practices should also be understood as potentially harmful and traumatic. The cultural devastation resulting from the internment of Japanese Americans during World War II and the disenfranchisement of First Nations peoples in the United States are two other examples of culturally sanctioned trauma (Daniel, 1994). The heightened surveillance of Muslim adults and families at this time has led to culturally sanctioned traumatic events as well. (In this text, when we refer to type III trauma, we are considering the latter definition that relates to the cumulative daily culturally sanctioned abuses inflicted on marginalized populations. When we refer to the effects of torture, we will note this clearly as such.)

Each clinician must be mindful of the effects and legacies of type I, II, and III traumatic events on the lives of his or her clients. Although many children demonstrate extraordinary resilience in withstanding the pernicious effects of catastrophic events and do not suffer PTSD symptomatology, many experience derailments and interference in their identity development and relatedness to others. The severity of aftereffects are generally related to six factors: (1) the degree of violence, (2) the degree of physical violation, (3) the duration and frequency of abuse, (4) the relationship of the victim to the offender, (5) the age of the child when abusive events occur, and (6) the innate constitution of the child (Terr, 1999). When abuse occurs during infancy, the emergence of basic trust, a sense of cohesive identity, and the capacity for secure attachment are undermined. However, if abuse occurs after a child has developed a sense of cohesive self with object constancy, the aftereffects may lead to a DSM-IV-TR diagnosis of PTSD or the diagnosis of complex posttraumatic syndrome or disorders of extreme stress not otherwise specified (DESNOS) (APA, 2001; Friedman & Marsella, 1996; Herman, 1992; Mock, 1998). These latter diagnoses are more useful in understanding the complex processes of identity formation, including distortions in identity and dissociative phenomena that are more prevalent among clients with a history of repetitive maltreatment.

The "victim–victimizer–bystander" scenario is a central construct that warrants review (Herman, 1992; Miller, 1994; Staub, 1989, 2003). Children who have been subjected to physical, sexual, and/or emotional abuse have experienced victimization at the hands of an offender (or victimizer). At the time, a bystander either remained detached and failed to help, or else interrupted the abuse directly or through dramatic rescue efforts. Not only has a survivor of childhood trauma related to other people with these different roles, but she has also internalized a "victim–victimizer–bystander" template that guides her worldview. As individuals are perceived in the "victim," "victimizer," or "bystander" role, the earlier trauma scenario is reenacted in adolescent and adult life. Through the process of projective identification, the unconscious internalized conflict is projected outward through enactments of various roles. For example, a trauma survivor might alternately adopt a victim stance, with an overzealous-rescuing "bystander" role, while disowning her internal aggressive "victimizer" role. This "victim–victimizer–bystander" relationship template is vitally important in understanding intricate interpersonal processes as well as intrapersonal processes. However, we must be mindful to use this knowledge constructively to enhance our understanding about patterns of abuse rather than using the reenactments of the trauma scenario to justify blaming a victim of real maltreatment.

The Cultural Relativity of a PTSD Diagnosis

The exploration of the legacies of childhood trauma raises the controversy surrounding the increasing popularity of the DSM-IV-TR diagnosis of PTSD (APA, 2001; Keane, Weathers, & Foa, 2000). Although the heuristic nosology of a PTSD diagnosis provides a useful way to understand the impact of trauma among diverse cultural groups, the culture-boundedness of the model limits a universal generalizability (Friedman & Marsella, 1996; Mock, 1998).

A discussion of different constructs of trauma is incomplete without acknowledgment of the major role of resilience in mediating the impact of traumatic events. Various research projects have discovered a range of findings related to the absence, or presence, of the development of PTSD syndrome following a traumatic event. Not surprisingly, many studies report that children who live in violent communities are at higher risk for developing PTSD symptomatology (McCloskey & Walker, 2000; Pynoos, Steinberg, & Wraith, 1995). However, rather than presuming that PTSD is an inevitable response to horrific events, Allen (1998) found that a majority of African American individuals demonstrated distinct resilience following a traumatic event without developing PTSD symptoms. It is important to stress that such findings should remind us of the potential resilience of all individuals exposed to maltreatment and violence. However, it is equally important to guard against an assumption that certain people who have been marginalized, whether by racism, ablism, classism, or homophobia, are somewhat inured to trauma. Such an attitude would perpetuate a racial bias.

Cultural anthropologist, Judith Zur (1996) conducted a research study that explored perceptions of the Quiche, a group of indigenous Guatemalans, during their civil war. As this conflict involved genocidal activity, a Western viewpoint might predict PTSD among survivors. Instead, this researcher pointed out the absence of the social context in assessing PTSD, and concentrated on two elements of social context. First, the Quiche study participants held a belief that fate is responsible for acts of violence. Such a stance relieves the offenders of responsibility for their actions. Second, they valued emotional constraint as the optimal way of coping with their bereavement. Because overt grief is tolerated only for nine days as a cultural prescription, these families experienced the ongoing loss of a loved one as an economic, rather than a personal, loss. Finally, disturbing dreams, typically viewed as PTSD symptomatology, were instead interpreted by the Quiche as valuable portents from the dead and provided a source of relief. For those trauma survivors who suffered from political genocide, research data suggest the importance of evaluating the cultural meanings of trauma-related phenomena before prematurely recommending a treatment regimen for PTSD or complex PTSD. As the number of refugees from war-torn countries seeking sanctuary in the United States and Canada increases, it is imperative for clinicians to react in a culturally responsive manner to these couples and families in crisis.

:: SYNTHESIS OR INTEGRATION?

To design an effective culturally responsive couple therapy practice model, it is essential to attend to institutional, interactional, and intrapersonal factors affecting adult survivors of childhood abuses. Although family issues are often discussed in couple therapy, the unit of focus for this model is the dyad (i.e., the couple), when one or both partners have survived experiences of maltreatment in childhood. We will refer to these couples as either single-trauma or dual-trauma couples. For these couples, the presenting problems range from parenting concerns, relationship ruptures, conflict surrounding roles and responsibilities, sex and intimacy, financial strains, spiritual ennui, and adaptations to a new culture. However, if physical violence exists as one of the presenting problems, couple therapy, as a modality, is contraindicated. Instead, an advocacy approach is recommended to help the victim first access safety. In treating any couple, it is useful to rely on a range of biological, psychological, and social theories to assess a couple from different perspectives. Changes in the couple's capacities and needs may also call for continuing flexibility from the clinician in formulating assessments and treatment plans.

Many integrative couple therapy models aim to incorporate different theoretical models into a whole, through a blending or melding of constructs (Balcolm, 1996; Horowitz, 1998; Riggs, 2000). Instead, we propose a process of synthesis by combining discrete, and, at times contradictory constructs into a unified entity. Such an approach has usually been equated with eclecticism, an often-devalued approach in social work. Negative stereotypes are often hurled needlessly at eclectic practitioners who weather accusations of randomly constructing a potpourri of unassimilated theoretical constructs. A more accurate definition of eclecticism refers to a choice of the best elements of all systems.

Still, this definition differs from synthesis, which aims to build a unified plan with disparate constructs. A serendipitous benefit of such a practice model is the high value placed on the flexible use of different lenses to understand the uniqueness of the couple. Metaphor is helpful in describing this stance. If you visualize staring through a crystal, you may see differences in the texture and color of an object depending on what part of the multifaceted glass you are observing. Similarly, the fabric of this theoretical synthesis shifts color and shape over time during the course of different phases of couple therapy.

In a similar fashion, a case-specific practice model changes the synthesis of theoretical models depending on the unique features and needs assessed for each couple. Therefore, the assessment and therapy process sustains a continuing dynamic flow of theory models that advance to the foreground while other theoretical models momentarily remain in place in the background. This phase-oriented couple therapy practice model attends differentially to the centrality of the presenting issues. Important decision-tree processes occur at the initial contact with the couple, during the assessment phase, and during the course of the phase-oriented treatment.

Although a range of psychological and social theories are available in the knowledge base of the clinician at any given moment, data forthcoming from the couple's presenting concerns determine which set of theoretical lenses advance to the foreground. Certain theoretical models, however, are used from the onset of treatment. For example, since a relationship base provides the foundation for the practice model, it is essential to understand relationship patterns through the lenses of object relations and attachment theories (Kudler, Blank, & Krupnick, 2000; Lindy, 1996; Scharff & Scharff, 1987). In addition, social constructionist, racial identity, and feminist theories shed clarity on the family's social context (Manson, 1997; Marsella, Friedman, Gerrity, & Scurfield, 1996; Pouissant & Alexander, 2000). As a couple reveals their shared narrative, the presenting issues further signal which theoretical approaches may be especially relevant.

Stated concerns about interactional patterns in a couple's relationship call for the use of an historical family perspective to explore family patterns, rituals, or paradigms. A narrative family perspective may also illuminate the multiple and unique meanings of the trauma narrative(s) (Sheinberg & Fraenkel, 2001; Trepper & Barrett, 1989; White, 1995; White & Epston, 1990). Symptoms of clinical depression may signal the need to employ a cognitive–behavioral lens to explore affect regulation and cognitive distortions. In general, a review of the cognitive, affective, and behavioral functioning of each partner addresses mastery, coping, and adaptation (Compton & Follette, 1998). Finally, in the individual arena, trauma theory focuses on the short- and long-term neurophysiological effects of trauma on brain function, particularly memory and affect regulation (Krystal et al., 1996; Schore, 2001a, 2001b; Shapiro & Appelgate, 2000; van der Kolk, 1996, 2003). Although an assessment of each partner's trauma history is necessary in all cases, trauma theory may recede in centrality if an assessment reveals the absence of traumatic events. However, in situations in which one or both partners suffered maltreatment in childhood or adult life, trauma theory should remain one of the central theoretical lenses situated in the foreground of couple therapy. In particular case situations, it becomes clear how all of the social and psychological theory lenses are present concurrently from the onset and throughout the course of therapy. However, one or more theoretical lenses may advance to the foreground during the therapy, when that perspective may be relevant to a particular pressing issue at hand.

In summary, this synthesis of neurophysiological, social, and psychological theoretical models informs the biopsychosocial assessment that subsequently guides the direction of practice. A compelling image shared by our dean, Carolyn Jacobs, captures the dynamic process metaphorically (Jacobs, personal communication, 2003). While reflecting on a journey taken several years ago through the Serengeti Plain, she commented on her observations. Struck by a spectacularly beautiful and vast landscape, she was initially aware of the vivid range of primary and muted shades of red, brown, beige, and yellow painting the undulating landscape. After some time, the guide pointed in a particular direction toward the distant horizon. Very slowly, with a steady gaze, it was possible to see the distant detail of lions, hyenas, wild dogs, and flocks of varied birds revealing themselves. As she stared ahead, the scene changed continually, with different perceptions shifting dynamically back and forth. It was possible, however, to observe and hold the movement of the fauna and flora in the context of the broader background vista. In a similar process, holding the tensions of multiple, often contradictory theoretical perspectives requires flexibility in perception, understanding, and action on the part of the clinician. Knowledgeability about these varied models and perceptiveness is also an essential requirement to sustain this ephemeral yet solid stance.

:: ORGANIZATION OF THE TEXT

The book is organized in four sections: Context, Theoretical Foundations, Couple Therapy Practice, and Specific Clinical Issues. The first section, Context, provides the sociopolitical and historical context for the couple therapy practice model for adult survivors of childhood trauma. Chapter 1 offers an introduction to the text, including a rationale for the couple therapy practice model along with an explication and deconstruction of the range of definitions associated with trauma. In Chapter 2, a thorough and substantive historical review of the traumatology literature highlights the shifts over time in theory and practice within their sociopolitical contexts. Shifts from individual and group treatment models to a focus on practice modalities with couples and families are traced as well.

The second section, Theoretical Foundations, consists of five chapters that provide the theoretical scaffolding for the couple therapy practice model. They include Chapter 3: Social Theory, Chapter 4: Family Theory, Chapter 5: Trauma Theory, Chapter 6: Object Relations Theory, and Chapter 7: Attachment Theory.

The third section, Couple Therapy Practice, contains four chapters devoted to the explication of the phase-oriented couple therapy practice model. In Chapter 8: Biopsychosocial Assessment, the relevant institutional, interactional, and intrapersonal factors are reviewed that contribute to the completion of a thorough biopsychosocial assessment of the couple. In Chapter 9: Phase-Oriented Couple Therapy Model, we describe how the biopsychosocial assessment guides the creation of a treatment plan. Decision-making processes are included along with a discussion of the ways to build a facilitative therapeutic alliance. The phases of the therapy model are reviewed in detail. They include Phase I: Safety, Stabilization, and Establishment of a Context for Change; Phase II: Reflection on the Trauma Narrative; and Phase III: Consolidation of New Perspectives, Attitudes, and Behavior. Practice themes that are central for all traumatized couples in therapy are addressed. They include (1) composition of a "couple," (2) the role of violence, (3) parenting, (4) sexuality, (5) affairs, (6) dual diagnoses (i.e., substance abuse/addictions and complex PTSD), and (7) dissociation. In Chapter 10: Clinician Responses, we focus on the range of emotional, cognitive, and behavioral responses for the clinician working with traumatized couples in a couple therapy frame. Although we understand the intersubjective nature of the therapeutic alliance, efforts are made to tease out elements of personal, cultural, and objective countertransferential responses. The influences of vicarious traumatization and racial identity development are also explored. In Chapter 11: Clinical Case Illustration, we feature the case example of Rod and Yolanda, which illuminates the use of the couple therapy practice model.

The final section of the book, Specific Clinical Issues, focuses on specific clinical issues with particular client populations. They include Chapter 12: Military Couples and Families, Chapter 13: Gay/Lesbian/Bisexual/Transgendered Couples and Families, and Chapter 14: Immigrant and Refugee Couples and Families.

We now turn our attention to the historical view of couple and family therapy practice models designed for couples who choose to transform the legacies of their traumatic experiences from their childhood and adult lives.

Historical Review

At the outset of the twenty-first century, many individuals are experiencing traumatic events on a regular basis; too often, unfortunately, these are a daily occurrence. They include various forms of sexual, physical, and emotional childhood abuses; family violence, including elder abuse; war and political terrorism, necessitating adaptations of individuals, both combatants and civilians, and communities; community and societal violence such as inner-city crime, shootings, and racist attacks; and natural disasters. At this time it appears that many individuals who seek mental health treatment for relief of debilitating symptoms are experiencing the aftereffects of trauma. The broadening understanding of the impact of trauma on individuals has the potential, paradoxically, of numbing the responses of professionals and others to the aftereffects of trauma. Although it appears that many mental health issues can be related to trauma, an overemphasis on the effects of trauma could potentially dilute the specificity and resulting clinical understanding of trauma-related syndromes. In addition, many who experience trauma are resilient and do not seek assistance from the mental health system.

This chapter offers a historical overview of the place of trauma in the mental health field. First, we discuss how sociopolitical contexts impact both historical and contemporary issues. Next, we provide a brief synopsis of the development of trauma theory over the past century. Then, we summarize the historical trends of trauma-based work with couples and families. Finally, current implications of couple and family work with trauma survivors are posited.

:: SOCIOPOLITICAL CONTEXT OF TRAUMA
THEORY DEVELOPMENT

Historical Evolution of Concepts in Psychiatry

Herman (1992) comments, "The study of psychological trauma has a curious history—one of episodic amnesia" (p. 7). Here, she asserts that public consciousness of trauma has varied during the past century, and she proposes that this oscillation in interest has been related to larger contextual and political forces. Citing that our understanding of trauma has been informed by three lines of inquiry—hysteria, combat neurosis, and sexual and domestic violence—Herman asserts that the study of trauma was legitimized only after it was determined that some Vietnam combat veterans were exhibiting symptoms of posttraumatic stress disorder (PTSD).

The feminist movement validated and encouraged women to speak out and demand action(s) that would thwart the damaging effects of domestic violence. However, although feminist voices (Herman & Hirschman, 1977; Schechter, 1982; Walker, 1979) influenced some aspects of the therapeutic community, there have been continuous attempts within the profession to discredit the importance of family violence research that works toward the amelioration of familial abuse. Some professionals, fundamentally grounded in conservative and patriarchal influences, challenge the incidence of familial interpersonal violence. Gelinas (1995) comments that some, such as Richard Ofshe, claim that therapists can influence clients to manufacture memories of abuse (the false memory syndrome). In addition, one diagnostic category often traced to childhood abuse—dissociative identity disorder—is discredited, at times, as being either nonexistent or exaggerated in incidence (Merskey, 1995; Piper, 1995). These examples underscore Herman's (1992) comments that societal, primarily political, arenas influence which lines of inquiry are legitimized in the trauma field.

Currently, the study of trauma is proliferating in many areas. In fact, van der Kolk (1996, 2003) contends that the study of traumatic stress is potentially moving the field of psychiatry away from the compulsive activity of serializing and listing symptoms as the primary vehicle for making meaning of human responses. Rather, he comments that "The development of posttraumatic stress disorder (PTSD) as a diagnosis has created an organized framework for understanding how people's biology, conceptions of the world, and personalities are inextricably intertwined and shaped by experience" (p. 4).

The fact that not all individuals develop symptoms following similar difficult experiences speaks to the inherent differences in the psychological makeup of individuals. For example, Werner-Wilson, Zimmerman, and Whalen (2000) studied factors that demonstrated resilience in women who had been battered in their intimate partnerships. In addition to having social support, the resilient women in this study demonstrated a combination of personal strengths and perseverance, characteristics that facilitated their break with abusive partners (p. 179). Understanding the resilience of some individuals (O'Connell-Higgins, 1994; Rutter, 1985, 1987; Ryff, Singer, Dienberg-Love, & Essex, 1998) prompts a more expansive and thorough understanding of the factors that contribute to the development of PTSD for others. Long-debated questions continue to be the foci of current studies and to contribute to our understanding of trauma. For example, is trauma primarily a biological or a psychological disorder? Is it the event or the interpretation of the event that influences outcome? Do some individuals have preexisting vulnerabilities that influence outcome? What factors offer protective elements to individuals?

Ethnocultural Factors

In contemporary conceptualizations within the field of trauma, the impact of ethnocultural and anthropological studies should not be minimized. In their edited text, Marsella, Friedman, Gerrity, and Scurfield (1996) have published information that questions the universality of the concepts related to PTSD. The text brings together authors who question whether the use of this diagnosis is meaningful across cultures and ethnic groups. The editors contend that those who study PTSD must "eventually confront the role of ethnocultural factors in the etiology, distribution, expression, course, outcome, and treatment" (p. 1). As an example, Friedman and Marsella (1996) comment that cultural and religious beliefs will influence the understanding and lived experience of the trauma. They comment, "A terrifying physical ordeal might be appraised as a rite of passage in one cultural setting and as a traumatic event in another" (p. 24). Differential emphasis on symptoms, attributions and meaning of symptoms, and community concern over symptoms vary from culture to culture (Wilson & Keane, 1997).

Bracken (1998) suggests that non-Western countries do not necessarily rely on a cognitive approach in treatment of trauma. Rather, healing is likely to be more spiritually based with an emphasis on mutual aid. Nader, Dubrow, and Stamm (1999) comment that conceptualizing trauma through a narrow lens can create difficulties in working with a broad base of cultural groups. Western thinking tends to individualize aspects of trauma. Nader et al. argue that treatment models addressing the impact of war-related trauma need to integrate interventions with families and communities. Likewise, one needs to contextualize social issues when treating the psychological sequalae of trauma. These authors assert that "Failure to situate problems historically may lead to oversimplification, diagnostic problems, and the misdirection of resources" (p. xix). Jenkins (1996) suggests that any researcher studying PTSD needs to integrate aspects of gender and the sociopolitical environment in which an individual resides or from which he or she has originated (p. 178). DiNicola (1996) argues that a cultural family therapy model that synthesizes transcultural psychiatry with family therapy is imperative if clinicians are to appreciate the complexity of the interface of culture with trauma-related incidents. He says that cultural family therapy "allows one to examine culturally sanctioned definitions of self and the family and what constitutes a problem and what constitutes a solution" (p. 409). He suggests that this is particularly relevant when dealing with traumatized children. It is clear that the contemporary study of trauma will be enriched as the ethnocentric bias of Western symptomatology is challenged by more ethnocultural views.

Neurobiological Factors

Central to the current debate in the trauma field are investigations into the linkages that exist among trauma, neuroscience, and affect regulation (Allen, 2001; Krystal et al., 1996; Shapiro & Applegate, 2000; Siegel, 2003; van der Kolk, 1996; Yehuda & McFarlane, 1999). Theorists hypothesize that children who suffer early and prolonged trauma experience alterations in the development of brain functions and, consequently, have difficulty in regulation of internal affective states (Perry, 1997; van der Kolk et al.,

1996). As noted by Shapiro and Applegate (2000), a defining feature of resiliency or susceptibility is likely related to one's ability to modulate emotional arousal. Van der Kolk (1996) notes that intense affective experiences often influence or distort evaluation and categorization of traumatic experiences. Preexisting strengths or vulnerabilities impact the extent that events influence one's ability to modulate intense affect.

Perry (1997) asserts that although not all emotionally neglected children demonstrate signs of violence as adults, many do demonstrate antisocial behaviors and attitudes toward others. He argues that the decreasing impact of the impulse-modulating control of the cortical section of the human brain contributes to a generalized attitude of devaluation of others. Here, Perry argues that ongoing neglect and persistent, repetitive trauma impair the development of higher level brain functions (cortical and limbic systems); this influence potentially leads to poor impulse control and the consequent inability to modulate emotional arousal. Van der Kolk et al. (1996) also concur that individuals who suffer with PTSD are prone to have difficulties in modulating anger, as well as self-destructive, suicidal, and acting out behaviors that can all be understood as difficulties with affect regulation. (The psychophysiological aspects of PTSD are explored further in subsequent chapters.)

The relevance of this information to couple therapy is readily apparent. Many adults who have experienced PTSD will have difficulties in modulating their affective states, and this will have direct bearing on the ability of these individuals to partner successfully with another. Modell (1998) makes the point that individuals who experience affect dysregulation will experience anxiety in adult relationships. He comments, "The individual may feel flooded and overwhelmed by intense feeling and hence avoid human contact. These are people who cannot stand to be physically and/or emotionally touched. In some cases intense feelings such as sexual arousal may lead to the fear that the self will disintegrate" (p. 63). The development of goals in couple therapy must integrate methods that address the physiological outcomes of repetitive exposure to trauma. Some individuals will have experienced trauma that has had an impact on key aspects of brain development, especially the neocortex. The resultant consequences of this developmental deficit will often have a major impact on interpersonal functioning. In couple relationships, then, the difficulty in affect regulation will wield enormous influence in the management of anger and aggression, in the ability to be emotionally and sexually intimate with a partner, and in problem-solving abilities. Before further examining trends in couple therapy, a brief synopsis of the evolution of trauma theory over the past century is presented.

:: EVOLUTION OF TRAUMA THEORY

Early Theorizing

Young (1995) comments, "As far back as we know, people have been tormented by memories that filled them with feelings of sadness and remorse, the sense of irreparable loss, and the sensations of fright and horror" (p. 3). However, PTSD did not become part of the nosology of the American Psychiatric Association's *Diagnostic and Statistical Manual of Mental Disorders* until publication of the third edition in 1980. Since that time, the diagnostic category has captured the attention of many clinicians, researchers, and theorists throughout the world.

John Erichsen was one of the first physicians to study a "syndrome" related to trauma. In the 1860s, he treated individuals who had been involved in railway accidents. Coining the term "railway spine," he associated neurological symptoms suffered by these individuals with the aftereffects of the trauma they experiences. He elaborated the theory that the effects of violence on one part of the body may be transmitted to other parts of the body or internal organs. Here, physicians began to make the connection that "Traumatic shock has the effect of exciting or irritating nerves to the point of exhaustion" (Young, 1995, p. 15).

Based on clinical observations, Charcot, Janet, and Freud (Young, 1995) began to make associations between the development of traumatic symptoms and the experience of psychological trauma. They linked hysteria to incidences of trauma. Inherent in their thinking was the supposition that individuals experience an event as traumatic when fear and other emotional reactions are felt at the time of the event. Affective arousal, they posited, often impacts the integration of the experience into memory schemata (van der Kolk, 1996). Charcot believed that overwhelming fright could produce a traumatic response in an individual. Gelinas (1995) comments that Janet challenged the conventional wisdom of the time. Rather than assuming that rest periods would simply remedy individuals who were feeling overwhelmed, "Janet noted that the effects of experiences did not always dissipate with time . . . this feeling of being overwhelmed did not end when the overwhelming event ended" (p. 183). Janet elaborated the mechanisms of memory and articulated that individuals may be unable to integrate events into existing cognitive schemas (dissociation) or may remember events with intense clarity and vividness.

In his initial conceptualizations about trauma, Freud identified it as related to childhood sexual abuse. As Freud (1896) introduced the etiological factors of hysteria, he offered, "I put forward the proposition, therefore, that at the bottom of every case of hysteria will be found one or more experiences of premature sexual experience, belonging to the first years of childhood, experiences that may be reproduced by analytic work though whole decades have intervened" (p. 198). Freud clearly believed that it was possible for one part of the mind to keep secrets from itself (Young, 1995). At the end of the twentieth century, then, two separate scientific pathways intersected that influenced ideas about trauma. Young comments that individuals such as Erichsen were tracing the evolution of somatized traumatic memory while Charcot, Janet, and Freud were developing ideas related to psychologized traumatic memory. Viewed by some as a type of parasite, traumatic memory was thought to ravage the mind and affect the body. While medical men felt that they had privileged access to the meanings of these parasitic-like secrets, there was some common understanding that traumatic neuroses were produced by memories of events and that these memories often concealed ideas and urges that individuals could not face or act on (p. 39).

The Impact of World Wars I and II

While there was some interest in traumatic memory at the end of the nineteenth century, it was not until the outbreak of World War I that this interest was renewed with the development of treatment methods for traumatized veterans. The sheer numbers of men who were adversely affected while in combat could not be ignored. Herman (1992) comments that the illusion of honor and glory associated with war was challenged. She says, "Confined and rendered helpless, subjected to constant threat of annihilation, and forced to witness the mutilation and death of their comrades without any hope of reprieve, many soldiers began to act like hysterical women. They screamed and wept uncontrollably. They froze and could not move" (p. 20). Following the lead of pioneers such as W. H. R. Rivers, the Royal Army Medical Corps (RAMC) developed a system of classification of war-related neuroses that comprised four possible diagnoses: shell shock, hysteria, neurasthenia, and disordered action of the heart. In effect, these war neuroses rendered the victim ineffective as a frontline soldier. Young (1995) comments that RAMC classified these conditions as functional rather than organic disorders (p. 53).

After World War I, these disorders did not receive much attention from the medical or military community. The next significant influence in trauma conceptualizations came in 1941 with the publication of Abram Kardiner's *The Traumatic Neuroses of War.* This publication is largely accepted as the foundation to the classification system of posttraumatic stress disorder found in *DSM-III* (Gelinas, 1995; van der Kolk, 1996; Young, 1995).

Recognizing the link between physiological components and traumatic-based symptoms, Kardiner classified the disorder as physioneurosis (Gelinas, 1995). According to Kardiner, as noted by Young (1995), "Traumatic events create levels of excitation that the organism is incapable of mastering, and a severe blow is dealt to the total ego organization . . . the ego is now thrown into a perpetual struggle to regain mastery" (pp. 89–90). Kardiner's ideas influenced the treatment of trauma-induced war casualties during World War II. Grinker and Spiegel (1945) noted five separate categories of combat stress reactions: generalized anxiety states, phobic states, conversion states, psychosomatic reactions, and depressive states (van der Kolk et al., 1996). It was during World War II that American psychiatrists began to question the protective benefit of close attachments in the experience of combat stressors. Citing Grinker and Speigel, Herman (1992) notes that it had been observed "that the strongest protection against psychological breakdown was the morale and leadership of the small fighting unit" (p. 25). The American Army Medical Corps then began to treat soldiers for combat stress reaction as close to the fighting line as possible. Treatment consisted of reassurance, persuasion, rest, and relaxation (Young, 1995). Difficult cases would be sent to a base camp to receive more intensive intervention. As in World War I, this treatment was based on the idea that abreaction about the traumatic events would offer some symptom relief to the affected combatant.

Influence of the Vietnam War

Similar to the aftermath of World War I, the armistice of World War II contributed to a hiatus of professional interest in the field of trauma.

Then, in the 1970s, in response to veterans of the Vietnam war, a huge interest in posttraumatic stress responses developed in the United States. An organization called Vietnam Veterans Against the War began to encourage veterans to form mutual aid/support groups to engage in "rap sessions." According to Herman (1992), "The Vietnam veterans retold and relived the traumatic experiences of the war . . . to give solace to individual veterans who had suffered psychological trauma, and to raise awareness about the effects of the war" (pp. 26–27). The antiwar efforts politically influenced the eventual adoption of the American Psychiatric Association's (1980) diagnosis of the posttraumatic stress disorder. For further elaboration of the development of couple and family interventions post–Vietnam war, refer to the next section of this chapter.

Impact of Contemporary War and Terrorism

During the past twenty years an ever-increasing interest in the study of trauma has become evident. The Gulf War of 1990 and the Iraqi war of 2003 have added further information about the impact of war on both combatants and their families. The quick escalation of the Gulf War and the threat of chemical and biological warfare heightened anticipatory anxiety about traumatic events. Although chemical and biological warfare was not instituted during this period, the possibility of this enactment increased the severity of trauma for soldiers and their families. Yerkes and Holloway (1996) note that "Service members in the Gulf War were warned of the terrible weapons that would be deployed against them. They were given vaccines to protect them against biological agents that, as it turned out, were not used" (p. 40). Complicating the response of those back home was the heavy influence of the media reports during the Gulf War crisis. While the Vietnam conflict had been depicted as a television war, Norwood and Ursano (1996) argue that "The Gulf War, then, was the first war that was televised 'live'" (p. 11). The impact of this war on family members was immediate and ongoing as the war was repetitively shown on live television.

Television coverage of the horrific events of September 11, 2001, undoubtedly contributed to the development and maintenance of complex PTSD symptoms for many individuals. Repetitive images of the collapse of the Twin Towers in New York City and the attack on the Pentagon in Washington, D.C., were powerfully encoded in observers' memories. The continued threat of terrorist attacks, the persistent impact of biological threats, such as anthrax, and the development of the U.S. Homeland Security Office all contribute to an ongoing uneasiness about the future. The insidious nature of living with sustained "low-level" anxiety about one's safety is being demonstrated by many individuals in a range of clinical settings.

Like the Gulf War of 1990, the Iraqi war that began in 2003 has intensified worries about weapons of mass destruction, chemical warfare, and potential retaliatory terrorist attacks against citizens and icons of the United States. We do not yet know the nature of the complex PTSD symptoms that individuals or families will face in response to this armed conflict. To be sure, the incidence of complex PTSD and related disorders will increase as people respond to ongoing threats and real experiences of political unrest that may lead to further terrorist activities.

Conclusion

Certainly, war efforts seem to spark professional interest in the development of refined assessment and treatment tools for PTSD. As noted earlier, the feminist movement has also been consistently influential in theory development. As a positive example of this changing trend, Herman (1992) encourages therapists to conceptualize trauma responses as being best formulated as complex PTSD, rather than posttraumatic stress disorder. Feminist scholars and researchers underscore the usefulness of moving away from a categorization of "pathology" and turning toward a conceptual model that appreciates the complexity, the adaptation, and the resilience of trauma survivors. The next section of this chapter turns to specific trends in couple therapy with trauma survivors and their partners.

:: COUPLE THERAPY FOR SURVIVORS OF TRAUMA

The practice of couple therapy for trauma survivors is a somewhat underdeveloped field. The aftermath in the United States of the Vietnam war effort prompted some professional interest in PTSD with strategies to assist combat veterans who were readjusting to their couple and family relationships (Hogancamp & Figley, 1983; Johnson, Feldman, & Lubin, 1995; Nelson & Wright, 1996; Rabin & Nardi, 1991; Riggs, Byrne, Weathers, &

Litz, 1998; Solomon, 1988). Authors have documented that trauma survivors experience relationship and/or sexual difficulties with their partners (Balcolm, 1996; Barrett & Stone-Fish, 1991; Basham & Miehls, 1998a, 1998b; Compton & Follette, 1998; Courtois, 1997a; Johnson & Williams-Keeler, 1998; Maltz, 1988; Miehls, 1997; Nadelson & Polonsky, 1991; Pistorello & Follette, 1998; Riggs et al., 1998; Solomon, 1988; Wilson & Keane, 1997). Although some descriptions of the impact of trauma on couple systems exist, there is less agreement as to the psychotherapy modality of choice for the couple or family systems of trauma survivors.

Indications for Couple Therapy

Referring specifically to sexual abuse survivors, there seems to be some consensus that couple therapy is indicated only when certain parameters have been met. Although it is acknowledged that survivors often do benefit from having a relationship with a supportive partner, many treatment modalities emphasize the individual dynamics of survivors while ignoring the current relationship status or dynamic of those being treated. Treatment for sexual abuse survivors often involves a combination of individual and group therapies (Bergart, 1986; Briere, 1996; Courtois, 1999; Deighton & McPeek, 1985; Drauker, 1992; Herman & Lawrence, 1994; Paddison, Einbender, Maker, & Strain, 1993). Harris (1998) uses an empowerment model when working with poor women who have a history of trauma and substance abuse. The literature advocating a combination of individual and couple therapy or a progression from individual to couple or family treatment has been less extensive. In fact, some authors suggest that individual treatment is a necessary precursor to engaging survivors in couple therapy (Busby, Steggel, Genn, & Adamson, 1993; Feinauer, 1989; Matsakis, 1994). One critical guideline before engaging in couple therapy is to ensure that couples are not at risk for physical violence (Follette, 1991).

Couple Therapy Models

A number of approaches to couple therapy of trauma survivors are described in the literature. Approaches that target partners in self-help programs often elaborate the supportive role of partners in the healing process of survivors (Bass & Davis, 1988; Davis, 1991; Gil, 1992; Heiman, 1986; Karpel, 1995; Maltz, 1991). This literature tends to encourage the partner of the survivor to participate in psychoeducation about complex PTSD. In fact, couple therapy with trauma survivors has largely been influenced by utilizing methods geared toward psychoeducation of survivors and their partners. The working assumption is that intellectual understanding of the signs, symptoms, aftereffects, and ongoing manifestations of complex PTSD will help alleviate some of the relationship difficulties that these couples often experience.

Psychoeducational Approach to Couple and Family Therapy

Brende (1994) discusses his approach to psychoeducation for survivors and their partners, a program designed to assist Vietnam veterans and formulated to accommodate an in-patient hospitalization treatment program. Initially conceived to complement a three-month hospital stay, he has adapted the program to serve individuals in a briefer period. Covering twelve themes that are common conflict areas of veterans, the program is aimed to aid adjustment of survivors and their partners. Many participants go on to complete a twelve-step recovery with Combat Veterans Anonymous, and the author proposes, "The advantage of this modality is that it provides a structure and cognitive approach to understanding posttraumatic symptoms and the main elements of recovery" (p. 433).

Rabin and Nardi (1991) report on a psychoeducational program that they initiated with partners of Israeli veterans who had served in combat in Lebanon. The veterans were involved in a program called Ko'ach, which was formulated to assist the veterans to develop more competent coping behavior in the face of their posttraumatic stress symptoms. The wives of these veterans took part in an educational program that was specifically designed to address issues of relationship difficulties, which were viewed as being secondary to the trauma that their partners had experienced in combat. Wives were given information on the treatment that their husbands were receiving. In addition, they were educated about some aspects of family systems theory, change theory, the impact of crisis on systems, and role change (p. 216). Group training facilitated further understanding of interpersonal dynamics, communication principles, and assertiveness skills. Finally, the couples were brought together for couples groups, with the goal of training the couples in problem-solving behavior. The authors note that "An educational group and self-help model of work with this population of couples is more appropriate and more accessible than is couples' therapy" (p. 222). They claim that couples in the group format are "able to serve as a powerful resource for each other and are able to break through the isolation, shame, and secrecy that characterize these couples" (p. 222).

Nelson and Wright (1996) discuss aspects of working with female partners of veterans who demonstrate symptoms of PTSD. They postulate that a combination of individual, couple, and family treatment is often indicated in working with these systems. In addition, they discuss the efficacy of psychoeducational groups for veterans and their families (p. 462). Williams and Williams (1987) point out that educating veterans' families can often lead to increased communication skills, clarification of roles and values, and the development of mutual support for the couples. Family interventions for family systems impacted by the Gulf War have also assisted veterans and their partners in dealing with the discipline problems of their children. Norwood and Ursano (1996) reported that between 42% and 64% of children between the ages of three and twelve years were sad or tearful and often in need of treatment (p. 5).

The psychoeducational approach to working with trauma survivors and their partners has had a wider application than working with veterans and partners (Bolen, 1993; Chauncey, 1994; Davis, 1991; Maltz, 1988). In fact, Balcolm (1996) notes that many of the initial efforts in couple therapy were geared toward "helping the partner understand and adapt to the trauma survivor's changing symptoms and needs over the course of treatment" (p. 433).

However, the psychoeducational approach to doing couples work with trauma survivors is problematic in at least two ways. First, this approach presumes that partners of traumatized individuals will have the ego strength to be able to utilize cognition to intellectually understand their partner's interpersonal issues. It is clear that this ability may be compromised if the partner's interpersonal style is to be aggressive or further traumatizing to the survivor (Jehu, 1988), or does not respect personal boundaries or limits in the intimate partnership (Talmadge & Wallace, 1991). Increasingly, clinical practice demonstrates that partners of survivors may also have experienced trauma in their background (Balcolm, 1996; Basham & Miehls, 1998b). Often each individual in the partnership has experienced multiple traumas (Matsakis, 1994).

A second problem area in the exclusive use of psychoeducational approaches to couple therapy is the implicit positioning of the survivor as the identified patient in a system. If one engages the partner as a potential ally in the treatment of the survivor, through the use of psychoeducational measures and adaptations based on these measures, the survivor all too often is pathologized in the system (Miehls, 1997). This can further cast the survivor as the person "to blame" or the one who is responsible for the interpersonal difficulties in the couple system (Follette, 1991; Verbosky & Ryan, 1988). Unfortunately, many survivors are only too willing to accept the role of the disturbed one in partnerships, and thus the myth of their culpability in relationship issues is reinforced.

Sex Therapy for Survivors of Trauma

Sex therapy with trauma survivors is a field that has developed clear guidelines for intervention. Arising from the clinical experiences of working with sexual abuse survivors and their partners, a number of authors (Courtois, 1997a; Graber, 1991; Jehu, 1988; Maltz, 1988; Miehls, 1997; Westerlund, 1992) have developed methods of working with sexual issues in the context of couple therapy. Maltz identifies four conditions as indicators of couple readiness to engage in sexual therapy. The couple must have a strong commitment, a mutual desire for change, a general lifestyle compatibility, and a comfort level with nonsexual touch (p. 149). She postulates an approach to sexual therapy that, in the presence of these factors, formulates a stage model of intervention. Maltz comments that flexibility is important. Dependent on emergent themes and responses, the therapist needs to potentially shift modalities and, at times, to offer individual treatment to either partner. A stage model of treatment that combines educative, supportive, and psychotherapeutic techniques follows problem identification and assessment. The method includes aspects of dealing with symptoms related to trauma, such as flashback experiences. Couples need to have clear relationship boundaries. In addition, it is important that the partner's attempts to align with the therapist to "cure" the survivor are thwarted by the therapist (p. 167).

Miehls (1997) uses an object relational couple treatment approach in assisting couples to work through sexual difficulties. He encourages therapists to broaden their definitions of partners of trauma survivors. Rather than viewing partners as either benevolent helper-allies in treatment or potentially retraumatizing abusers, Miehls suggests that partners "demonstrate a continuum of dynamics which are multidetermined, complex, and which have specific purposes in the management of the partner's object relational world"

(p. 8). Rather than positioning the survivor as the identified patient in the system, Miehls demonstrates a model of intervention that utilizes the projective identification patterns of the couple as the potential vehicle for insight and interpersonal change. The intent of the object relational work is to prompt the individuals in the couple system to alter one's internal world.

Courtois (1997a) emphasizes that sex therapy for trauma survivors is indicated only when some preliminary psychotherapeutic work has been accomplished. She suggests that alliance-building stabilization techniques and ego-enhancing work are all prerequisites to conducting this specific therapy. In addition, other interpersonal issues are addressed before the initiation of sex therapy. Even when survivors demonstrate their readiness to pursue sex therapy, transference responses often occur and "The survivor may experience the therapeutic attempts to resolve the sexuality issues as coercive and out of her control" (p. 304). Courtois emphasizes that the sexual healing needs to happen at the pace of the survivor and that goals need to be individualized.

With these conditions and influences in mind, Courtois (1997a) encourages the survivor to take control of the work and to be the person who, ultimately, paces the sexual healing. Often education and cognitive techniques are useful in assisting the survivor to challenge distorted beliefs about sexuality. It is also useful to determine what conditioned responses the survivor experiences when she becomes engaged in sexual activity. As expected, many survivors have developed automatic responses of numbing or dissociation in the face of sexual stimuli, and the treatment needs to facilitate a broadening of survivor's responses. To become more fully present in current sexual activities, survivors "must be gently and persistently challenged to separate past from present" (p. 306). Clients often begin to explore their responses to sexual stimuli and need to reclaim or reconfigure aspects of their sexuality. To move away from the internalized sexual self that is often thought of as bad or dirty, survivors examine behaviors that may be unhealthy or dangerous. Sadomasochistic patterns will often surface and need to be examined and often altered (Maltz, 1991; Miehls, 1997).

Courtois (1997a) emphasizes that survivors often need several months to alter attitudes and sexual behaviors that were first formed and utilized in the face of traumatic experiences. The specific challenges to sexuality will have been largely determined as a result of the type of abuse the survivor experienced as a young child or adolescent. Gradual reintegration of what the survivor would consider healthy attitudes will determine the course of specific behavioral shifts in the sexual relationship. The ability to experience pleasure and satisfaction from the sexual relationship is a step that is often difficult for survivors to achieve. The pacing of the couple work needs to be determined by the survivor without a further positioning of the survivor as the "sick one" in the system.

Other Contemporary Couple Therapy Models

In addition to a psychoeducational and sex therapy approach in working with couples, a few other therapy approaches are worth considering as examples of current treatment modalities (Basham & Miehls, 1998a, 1998b; Compton & Follette, 1998; Johnson & Williams-Keeler, 1998; Sheehan, 1994). These provide the backdrop to the last section of this chapter, which considers current issues and further trends in the field of couple therapy with survivors of trauma.

Sheehan (1994) links concepts of intimacy to aftereffects of trauma as experienced by Vietnam veterans. Although she notes that intimacy is a broad concept, she discusses five areas associated with intimacy that are often problematic for veterans: fear of merger, fear of abandonment, fear of exposure, fear of attack, and fear of one's own destructive impulses (pp. 95–97). Sheehan explicates how trauma survivors manifest these particular fears, noting that many veterans would consciously or unconsciously sabotage more traditional methods of couple therapy. Thus, she "developed a treatment protocol that included several indirect approaches and metaphors that focused on healing the fears of intimacy" (p. 101). Her contention is that the use of metaphor helps couples to bypass resistance and to take ownership for the pacing of their healing journey. As the couple is able to use metaphor to initiate their healing, they will be better able to integrate aspects of more traditional couple therapy such as communication techniques and reframing, as examples.

Compton and Follette (1998) propose treatment strategies that are largely based on cognitive behavioral principles. The initial focus of the treatment is to encourage the participants to generate lists of behaviors that they feel would likely serve as reinforcers for their partner's choice of change behaviors. These behaviors are chosen with the focus on enhanced relationship satisfaction for both. The authors contend that this sort of behavioral exchange leads to increased trust within the system and sets the foundation for other work in problem-solving and enhancement in communication skills (p. 339). Potentially volatile issues need to be addressed in a gradual, stepwise fashion, and the therapist needs to be alert to potential avoidance strategies employed by the couple. Behaviors that reflect avoidance need to be addressed directly and integrated into the overall treatment plan. The authors propose externalizing problem areas as an "it" outside of the couple system; they propose that this minimizes blaming exchanges between the couple (p. 340). Finally, they propose a strategy of self-care as a way of getting relationship needs met both inside and outside of the dyad. The legitimization of expressing one's needs is reinforced and, they contend, problem-solving is enhanced.

Johnson and Williams-Keeler (1998) discuss their use of emotionally focused marital therapy in their work with traumatized couples. Emotionally focused therapy for couples (Greenberg & Johnson, 1988) is essentially a treatment model that attempts to facilitate secure attachment within couple systems. The focus of treatment is often the reprocessing of emotional responses specifically related to attachment behavior. The level of the work is both at the intrapsychic and interpersonal levels. In addition to assisting the couple to access and reprocess painful affective experiences, the therapist also helps to shape new interactions. The new interactions are shaped in such a way as to enhance emotional connection and compassion between the couple. Emotionally focused couple therapy follows nine steps that progress from the delineation of conflict issues, identification of the negative interaction cycle, and accessing unacknowledged feelings and interactional positions. Following this, problems are redefined in terms of underlying feelings. Individuals are encouraged to identify with disowned aspects of self, and partners are encouraged to accept their partner's experience. Participants are encouraged to express their needs and wants to the partners. Arising from this, there is an emergence of new solutions, and finally, treatment interventions are geared to the consolidation of new positions of interaction (Greenberg & Johnson, 1988; Johnson, 2002).

Johnson suggests that emotionally focused therapy is particularly relevant in working with traumatized couples, as it pays specific attention to how one processes, regulates, and integrates affect in the couple relationship. Johnson and Williams-Keeler (1998) suggest that the nine steps of emotionally focused therapy can be delineated to parallel a stage model of trauma treatment. Stabilization efforts encompass the first four steps of emotionally focused therapy. In their identification of patterns, trauma survivors arrive at an integrated understanding, "Not just understanding the cycles of their relationship and how their ways of coping with affect feed those cycles, but also understanding the nature of trauma and how it has affected each of the partners and defined the relationship" (p. 29). The middle stage of treatment builds self and relational capacities; partners co-create the relationship in such a way that each can feel safe in confronting fears and processing shame, anger, and grief. Finally, enhanced coping strategies facilitate changed interpersonal styles, paralleling integration in individual treatment.

Basham and Miehls (1998a, 1998b) also put forward a model of couple therapy that parallels a stage model of individual treatment for trauma survivors. Here, the authors integrate object relations theory with Judith Herman's (1992) individual treatment stage model of trauma therapy. Couples may work on stage I tasks of safety and stabilization; stage II tasks of reflecting on the trauma narrative; or stage III tasks of consolidating new perspectives. Basham and Miehls argue that a differential assessment of couple systems is necessary to facilitate the specificity of discrete treatment plans. Basham and Miehls (1998b) conclude, "The integration of object relations theory with complex PTSD theory in couple therapy enhances differential assessment and clinical interventions with survivors of childhood trauma" (p. 78).

:: CURRENT ISSUES AND FUTURE TRENDS
IN COUPLE THERAPY

As mentioned at the beginning of this chapter, the field of trauma, as an area of study, is currently expanding. As noted, the impact of trauma on neurobiological aspects of one's development is currently receiving much attention. This area offers much promise in increasing our understanding of the complexity of affect regulation. The interplay of affect regulation with couple treatment issues is a promising area for further inquiry. Because the persistent effects of trauma often compromise one's ability to partner successfully, efforts aimed toward enhancing couple therapy will prove to be a valuable focus of study.

Cross-cultural studies will further our understanding of resistance and individual differences in response to traumatic events. For example, clinical work with refugee and immigrant populations underscores the necessity of moving away from a Eurocentric bias of working definitions of trauma. We intend to highlight resilience in this text. Examining the specificity of differences across culture in adaptation to trauma will certainly enrich our understanding of resilience. Of importance, Miller (2003) describes a contemporary shift in theorizing aspects of trauma that challenges the notion that "victim" and "survivor" designations are permanent. Rather, she suggests that every emotional state (including the aftereffects of trauma) is impermanent and can be transformed (p. 32). Further integration and synthesis of psychological and social theory will enhance therapy approaches in couple and family work.

At the present time, couple therapy models with trauma survivors appear to be underdeveloped. Although much work has been offered that describes a psychoeducational approach to couple work, there has been less development in couple psychotherapy aimed at promoting intrapsychic change that will influence the interpersonal relationships of survivors. A biopsychosocial model of practice that synthesizes different theory bases furthers one's ability to respond to the complexity of circumstances confronting clinical practitioners. Creativity in selecting different practice approaches, focused on a wide range of presenting concerns, is demonstrated in succeeding chapters. Next, however, the theoretical scaffolding of the couple therapy practice model is introduced. Sociocultural/institutional, interactional, and intrapersonal perspectives are understood through the theoretical lenses of social theory, family theory, trauma theory, object relations theory, and attachment theory, respectively.

THEORETICAL FOUNDATIONS

The following five chapters summarize key theoretical constructs that inform the couple theory practice model, which is discussed in Section III of the text. In Chapter 3, we discuss certain tenets of social theory. Aspects of identity, including racial identity development, shame, and stigmatization are discussed. This analysis illustrates how social and institutional factors influence clinicians and couples as they embark on a course of couple therapy that addresses the legacies of childhood traumatic experiences.

The next chapter of this section, Family Theory (Chapter 4), is pivotal in offering an understanding of interactional factors that characterize the couple's relationship patterns. Areas of focus include the victim–victimizer–bystander dynamic, power and control issues, distancing and distrust, sexuality issues, and boundaries and communication patterns between the couple.

The last three chapters of this section—Trauma Theory, Object Relations Theory, and Attachment Theory—focus on the individual dimensions of the practice model. The chapter on trauma theory (Chapter 5) emphasizes the neurobiological responses to traumatic events that persistently influence the affect, cognition, and behavior of adult survivors. In this chapter, readers are informed of research findings in the field of traumatology.

In Chapter 6, we summarize concepts from both American and British object relations theorists. Constructs from the

American school highlight relevant themes related to separation individuation that affect traumatized couples. Constructs from the British object relations theorists highlight concepts related to the relationally based practice model. Last, in Chapter 7, we discuss the burgeoning influence of attachment theories on, and linkages with, contemporary trauma theories.

Social Theory

This chapter explores the constructs of self and identity, as these are manifest individually and in society for survivors of trauma. We discuss identity as a social construction and illustrate how identity is formed, recursively, in interaction with societal norms and expectations. In addition, we examine the role of stigma and shame in the formation of survivor identity. So often shrouded in secrecy and threat, survivors of childhood trauma internalize a sense of self that is tainted. Again, societal attitudes reinforce the internalized sense of shame. After examining theories related to social construction of identity and stigma, we give a detailed description of racial identity development theory. Then, we briefly introduce the reader to sociocultural factors that influence identity formation. Here, key issues related to social identity are summarized. In the assessment chapter that follows, we include detailed questions that will assist the reader to complete culturally sensitive assessments of the multiple identities of partners when they engage in couple therapy. In addition, the treatment chapter illustrates culturally sound practice interventions that honor the range of identities of both client and clinician. In the clinical case example of Rod and Yolanda (Chapter 11), we demonstrate the importance of racial identity in cross-cultural couple therapy practice. One implicit goal of therapy is that each partner embarks on an identity change trajectory that encourages a shift from thinking about oneself as victim to seeing oneself as a survivor, and then as a transcender of trauma.

Before moving to the theories, it is important for the reader to anticipate that the institutional factors of the assessment model, to be expanded in the next section of the text, include the responses of both clinicians and clients. More detailed information illustrating the range of therapists' responses can be found in the assessment chapter and in the chapter covering clinician responses. To contextualize this chapter, it is important to note that a culturally responsive clinician who works with culturally diverse clients approaches the assessment process with an attitude of openness that values the idea that identity is influenced by multiple factors. Postmodern writers (Akamatsu, 1998; Falicov, 1998; Laird, 1998; Tatum, 2000) suggest that individuals are influenced by multiple factors in the formation of identity. Identity is fluid, with different parts of one's identity becoming salient at different times, dependent on the context of the interaction (Laird, 1998).

:: THE SOCIAL CONSTRUCTION OF IDENTITY

To accommodate the influence of multiple identities for client and clinician, the culturally responsive practitioner allows for dissonance within oneself (Dyche & Zayas, 2001; King Keenan, 2001; Miehls & Moffatt, 2000) that facilitates the possibility of exploration of multiple meanings of behavior within an individual and in interpersonal interactions. Dyche and Zayas (1995) suggest that workers can form treatment alliances with a range of clients if they approach clients with a cultural naiveté that demonstrates their willingness to honor the culture of the client. Adams (2000) asserts that to be culturally competent, it is important for the therapist to have undergone some self-exploration. McGoldrick (1998) notes that developing "cultural competence requires us to go beyond the dominant values and explore the complexity of culture and cultural identity . . . without accepting unquestionably our society's definitions of these culturally determined categories" (p. 8). Guided by theories of intersubjectivity (Aron, 1996a, 1996b; Benjamin, 1998a, 1998b; Bowles, 1999; McMahon, 1997; Miehls, 1999; Noonan, 1999; Trop, 1997), culturally responsive clinicians are open to the mutual influence of the clients' and clinicians' identities in the therapeutic process, and as such, honor and value differences between themselves and clients. Perez-Foster (1998) underscores that the clinician's awareness of potential cultural countertransference "cannot be more vital than in the treatment of patients whose culture, race, or class markedly differs from that of the therapist" (p. 255). Cohen (1998) suggests that cultural rules influence human thought and behavior and consequently limit one's perceptions. Cohen notes that "cultural rules act as blinders to keep us looking in the correct (i.e., the agreed on) directions. These rules inhibit our freedom far more than political coercion does" (p. 73). The clinician and the couple, then, often need to deconstruct certain aspects of behavior that are embedded in the cultural consciousness of all participants. The clinician will need to assist the couple in making unconscious cultural attitudes transparent. Even though cultural practices commonly function in a way that promotes integrity and coherence within the group, partners in a dyad may challenge the socially constructed axioms of the group. For example, Liu and Chan (1996) comment that East Asian cultural practices often discourage the open discussion of sexuality. They argue that the discussion of same-sex relationships is particularly difficult. They note, "Same-sex sexual behavior, awareness, and identification are shrouded in secrecy, stigma, and the sometimes overwhelming power of cultural expectations" (p. 137). One can then imagine the multiple levels of cultural tradition that are challenged by East Asian individuals when they disclose their gay, lesbian, or bisexual identities to their families. Cultural traditions, in this instance, then, do not function to provide a sense of integrity. Rather, for the gay, lesbian, or bisexual individual, cultural traditions exacerbate her or his lived experience as being "outside" of culture. The clinician also needs to make transparent the cultural attitudes that influence the couple in the negotiation of power (gender roles) and privilege (authority within the system). Postulating a balanced approach to issues of difference, Hare-Mustin (1989) offers a useful conceptualization of "alpha–beta" biases. Essentially, she cautions clinicians to neither minimize difference when one is clearly observable (beta bias) nor to exaggerate difference at unnecessary times (alpha bias). By this she means that clinicians tend to want to see everyone as either "the same" or "different" based on culture, gender, race, or other cultural signifiers.

:: SELF, IDENTITY, SHAME, AND STIGMA

As noted, identity is a fluid concept that is shaped by myriad factors including intrapsychic, interpersonal, and societal processes. Knowledge of oneself and the formation of self and identity are co-constructed recursively from particular points in history and from particular social locations (Chambon, 1999; Gergen, 1985). Thus, the identity of any survivor of trauma is shaped through the cultural practices and attitudes of the larger community in which one lives. Certain practices and values are privileged, while others marginalize the position and identity of the survivor (Laird, 1998;

Moffatt, 2001). A survivor of childhood trauma, a political refugee, or a survivor of domestic violence are all positioned, in contemporary North American society, as marginalized, pathologized, and "less than" those who hold power and privilege in the cultural group. For example, in instances of interpersonal violence, the survivor needs to contend with the implied message that she is responsible for the abuse and that somehow she invited the aggression of the perpetrator.

Burkitt (1994) challenges the notion of the self-contained individual who has an essential inner being and argues that "the 'individual' with whom psychology is concerned should be seen as a construction of various discourses in society, which produce both the image and the capacities of such a subject" (p. 9). Christopher (2001) suggests that culture serves as an internal guide that brings meaning to our daily actions and discernment about self and others. He clearly links internal processes to the social experience. Danaher, Schiratz, and Webb (2000) and Foucault (1980) note that (disciplinary) power and resistance operate in a recursive relationship between knowledge and power. In other words, certain attitudes and practices concerning survivors of trauma become validated in society while other knowledge becomes marginalized or excluded. For example, the recursive process of the trauma narrative often labels trauma survivors as victims, needy, or even mentally ill. Foucault's (1979) concept of disciplinary power can be utilized to illustrate how survivors of trauma are positioned as problem-saturated individuals who come under the scrutinizing power strategies of observation, examination, normalizing judgment, and documentation by family members, as well as the legal, health, and mental health systems. Foucault (1979), King Keenan (2001), and Moffatt (1999) demonstrate how the structured and repetitive use of these power strategies contribute to the process in which certain factors in a recursive process are underscored, while other factors are systematically ignored or devalued. Many systems overemphasize the individual symptoms and responses of the survivor of trauma. Factors such as inequitable social relations, gender, or privilege of perpetrators or certain caregiving systems are exempted as subjects of enquiry. The resulting process leads to a devaluation of the survivor's strength or resilience and a further abdication of responsibility of other more powerful forces in the professional or personal communities.

So, the survivor of childhood trauma is scrutinized and positioned as "deviant" both within one's family and even in the larger community. The great sense of shame that survivors of trauma carry is often profound. Survivors of torture and of physical or sexual abuse are often repeatedly and explicitly warned not to talk about their experiences (Akhtar, 1999; Elsass, 1997). The element of secrecy contributes to an internalized sense of shame. The stigmatized individual loses his sense of dignity, self-respect, and self-acceptance. Goffman (1963) noted that a stigmatized individual feels he has a "spoiled" self, an identity that is imperfect. Lewis (1998) comments that "the degree to which stigmatized persons can blame themselves or are blamed by others for their condition reflects their degree of shame. The idea of responsibility and perceived responsibility is central to stigma and shame" (p. 127).

Lansky (1991) underscores how shame contributes to interpersonal difficulties and potential fragmentation in couple systems. He describes the narcissistic vulnerability of partners when their relationship needs are frustrated and when "the shame generated by continued exposure of these needs is not acknowledged" (p. 17). Balcolm, Lee, and Tager (1995) demonstrate that shame interactions between partners become recursive so that "shame becomes imbedded in the system, is expressed by each member, and becomes both causal and consequential" (p. 55). Vogel and Lazare (1990) also demonstrate that victim–victimizer interactions between partners lead to an internalized sense of humiliation and stigma within individuals.

It is clear that the survivor of trauma, his or her family, and his or her community contribute to the recursive pattern that positions survivors as problem individuals. As noted, the clinician needs to be aware of the way that identity is constructed in society, that certain practices are privileged, and that a deep sense of shame and humiliation profoundly affects the sense of self of the survivor. At this point, we offer a detailed description of racial identity developmental theory, and then discuss the interface of social identities in the assessment and treatment process. Carter (1995) and Wilkinson (1997) contend that in the United States race is the most salient factor that shapes identity. Our own clinical experience demonstrates that race is often a central factor in identity development; consequently, we start with a more detailed review of the process of racial identity development. As mentioned, this will be followed by a brief general introduction of additional factors related to social identity. The reader is encouraged to appreciate that sociocultural factors such as gender, race, ethnicity, and so forth coexist within each individual and that these multiple factors intersect with each other to contribute to the identity of each partner. In each instance, it is important as well for the clinician to be self-evaluative about his or her own attitudes and identity with regard to sociocultural factors. Clinical vignettes highlight the issues. As noted in the preceding, these themes are expanded in the treatment section later in the text.

:: RACIAL IDENTITY DEVELOPMENT

The intersection of the racial identity development of the clinician and of the partners in the couple dyad provides a fertile ground for understanding the influence of race in the couple relationship. It is imperative that the clinician has a sense of his or her racial identity development so that countertransference responses can be understood within this conceptual framework. Similarly, the interpersonal relationship of the couple is impacted by the racial identity development of each partner. Racial identity development theories (Cross, 1991; Helms, 1995; Helms & Cook, 1999) describe the transformative processes that individuals undergo to achieve a sense of racial "maturity" or racial self-actualization. Tatum (1997) argues, "It is assumed that in a society where racial group membership is emphasized, the development of a racial identity will occur in some form in everyone" (p. 93).

However, people of color and white individuals experience different pathways of racial identity development (Helms & Cook, 1999). Tatum (1992) proposes that white individuals experience societal privileges that influence the experience and process of racial identity development. For people of color, the racial identity development process is influenced by the internalization of societal attitudes that suggest "white is right" and "black is wrong." Similarly, Americans of European descent are socialized to think that "black is bad"; consequently, the projection of bad traits onto African Americans and other people of color is a process that is often sanctioned in the United States. The power differential between those from the dominant culture and racially oppressed individuals further inflates the grandiosity and sense of privilege of many European Americans. Miliora (2000) suggests that cultural racism is experienced as a narcissistic trauma that erodes a person of color's normative grandiosity and sense of self. Daniel (2000) notes that ongoing incidents of racialized assaults can be conceptualized as an ongoing form of trauma. As noted, then, these and other contributing factors alter the pathways of racial identity development for people of color and for white people.

Helms and Cook (1999) offer the following model of ego schemas of racial identity development that influences the information processing strategies for people of color. The model integrates the experiences of Asians, Africans, Latinos/Latinas, and Native Americans (p. 85). They suggest that people of color often begin in a status of "Conformity" in which white people and their culture are idealized. From there, people of color move to a status of "Dissonance." Here, there is an internal cognitive shift that moves from a position of complicity or denial of difference to the recognition that, as a person of color, one is a member of a targeted and oppressed group. Characterized by feelings of confusion and uncertainty, the person of color has not yet acquired a schema that honors the experiences of his or her own group.

People of color attempt to maintain stability in their sense of self by adopting their own group's values. This involves immersion in their race and culture, a process by which they may idealize, somewhat naively, all aspects that are considered to be inherent to their racial and cultural background. Denigration of the "white world" is a part of this status, known as "Immersion." Similarly, there is a push toward developing characteristics that affirm the solidarity of one's own group, and this is referred to as "Emersion." Here, there is a great deal of shared pleasure when recognizing the achievements of others who are identified with one's own racial group. Helms and Cook (1999) describe the next stage of racial identity development as "Internalization," in which people of color use more abstract thinking processes that allow for an informed assessment and integration of complex information about race. Here, one is more objective about the meaning of behavior within one's own group and about the meaning of behavior of white individuals. Flexibility of identities facilitates self-reflection, which moves the individual to an "Integrated Awareness" schema, the most complex of these ego statuses. At this level, a person of color can maintain a positive sense of a racial self and has the ego strength to identify and resist social practices that undermine the positive integration of group identity. Here, there is sufficient fluidity to accept certain aspects of oneself that may be deemed to have origins in other socioracial or cultural groups. There is the ability to recognize the complexity in others, and there is often a thirst to be in a multicultural environment that fosters the benefits of potential growth for both people of color and white individuals. Miehls (2001) asserts that racial identity development can be viewed as one aspect of identity complexity.

For white individuals, Helms and Cook (1999) suggest that experiencing privilege or being associated with groups that experience privilege leads to a conscious or unconscious sense of entitlement. To maintain the privilege afforded to white individuals, the white group often exercises power in ways that are used to dominate people of color. Consequently, white individuals who become more aware of their racial identity development depart from the normative strategies of white people (p. 89). Helms and Cook suggest that white individuals start from a place of "Contact." In this status, individuals deny the reality of racism. White individuals do not initially acknowledge their white privilege (McIntosh, 2001) and do not understand the benefits they accrue as a result of white privilege.

When white individuals begin to have some consciousness about racial inequalities and the privileged status that they experience, there is a period of "Disintegration" during which the individual experiences anxiety, discomfort, and confusion. When the individual begins to challenge the status quo of white privilege, there may be fears of ridicule from the dominant group. Anticipating possible marginalization, many individuals adapt by experiencing a status that is termed "Reintegration." In this schema, white individuals try to reach a homeostatic balance by once again identifying with the predominant values of their own racial reference group. As opposed to taking individual responsibility for racism, individuals tend to idealize their own socioracial group while simultaneously denigrating those from other groups. Perceptions are distorted so less anxiety or confusion is experienced.

In the "Pseudo-Independence" ego status, white individuals intellectually criticize some members of the group who are blatant racists. There is recognition that some "good" white individuals are not racist. In making this demarcation, the individual can rationalize that he or she is a "good" white individual; however, the individual has not yet done sufficient self-examination to recognize his or her personal responsibility for racial oppression. In the "Immersion" status, white individuals attempt to recognize and alter previously held distortions about race. Relevant and accurate information about racism is sought so that one can examine one's own schema. Often the individual is hypervigilant about issues of race and may become an activist to try to stop racism. During the "Emersion" phase, individuals seek out other white individuals who have progressed in their racial identity status. There is an attempt to feel a sense of belonging with other like-minded white individuals. Lastly, white individuals may reach a status termed "Autonomy." Helms and Cook (1999) suggest that this "schema permits flexible analytic self-expression and responses to racial material" (p. 93).

It is important to note that while these statuses of racial identity development are elaborated in a stepwise fashion, most do not proceed in a linear fashion through "stages" of development. Rather, individuals typically revisit racial identity statuses and themes at different points in their development. Each time, a slightly different perspective is gained.

In the assessment process, then, it is important for the clinician to be aware of his or her own racial identity status. Particularly when working in cross-racialized therapy, it is necessary for the clinician to discern barriers that might impact a sound working alliance. It is important to discern if the members of the dyad are at somewhat similar or discrepant places, in terms of their racial identity, and how these differences impact the couple relationship. The following example highlights this issue.

I once worked with a couple that identified as Japanese Canadian. The husband of the heterosexual partnership was a professional man who felt that his success was based on his identification with white culture and values. In terms of his racial identity, he clearly was at the Conformity schema. He insisted that his partner adjust her behavior to fully be in line with white traditions. His partner was at a more integrated status of racial identity development and wished to honor her familial traditions while integrating some aspects of Western culture in her own behavior. This issue would be hotly contested between the two, especially as it influenced the couple's decision-making around how to entertain the husband's corporate clients. However, in the process of therapy, the impact of the racial identity discrepancies became more overt when the couple was making decisions related to the inclusion of Japanese traditions with their two Canadian born children. An explicit discussion about the partners' differences in racial identity facilitated their ability to reach some compromises that honored each person's racially and culturally determined values.

In summary, we recognize that racial identity development in both clients and the clinician fundamentally influences interactions in the therapeutic process. Other sociocultural factors shaping social identities will now be briefly highlighted. Specific questions that capture the multiple identities of participants follow in Chapter 9 on treatment.

:: OTHER SOCIAL IDENTITY FACTORS

The following material highlights specific aspects of biopsychosocial assessment as influenced by sociocultural factors. It is important to recognize that these social factors are intertwined with each other. Multiple factors come together to shape the couple interaction that informs a biopsychosocial assessment. For example, aspects of ethnicity and gender are often interconnected. Influences of socioeconomic class, sexual orientation, religion, disability, and age also need to be considered when the clinician is completing the biopsychosocial assessment. In addition, it is important to assess the interaction between social and intrapsychic factors. There is often a confluence of social factors and internal factors that determine a person's identity.

Ethnicity

Definitions of ethnicity vary, and different authors emphasize certain constructs to illustrate ethnicity (Cornell & Hartmann, 1998). Among the factors in their analysis of ethnicity, Cornell and Hartmann mention that "ethnic groups are self-conscious populations; they see themselves as distinct" (p. 19). Ethnicity, then, recognizes some unique characteristics within the group and implies that some kinship, common history, and shared symbols are understood by members of that ethnic group. Winkelman (2001) suggests that ethnic groups are distinctive groups with salient differences from other groups in society. He notes that the distinctiveness can be based on "geographical isolation, in-group marriage, a distinctive cultural heritage or national background, a specific language, common values and beliefs including religion, specific social roles and behavioral patterns" (p. 283). Partnered individuals may have different views of what constitutes trauma, dependent on ethnic understandings. In couple systems, then, conflict can emerge between partners who have dissimilar ethnic backgrounds. In our experience, it is often most difficult for partners to accept differences in their partners if each has presumed that the other partner shared the same ethnic characteristics. Ethnicity is often a source of pride for individuals and many celebrate their ethnic origins within their families and communities.

Religion/Spirituality

The relevance of religion or spirituality in the dynamics of each couple is variable. Although many individuals were raised in families that practiced some formal religion, as adults they make different choices in terms of their own religious practice. In fact, many trauma survivors abandon their religious beliefs, blaming God for failing to protect them from perpetrators. However, others rely, either consciously or unconsciously, on basic fundamental beliefs to help them make meaning in times of crisis. For some, religious affiliation and beliefs increase the risk of oppression. Kaye/Kantrowitz (2000) comments that many Jewish individuals experience bigotry as a result of their "religion"; she also suggests that Jews carry the historical legacy of a people who survived attempted extermination. Similarly, she makes the point that we need to "help make visible the cultural war against all non-Christians" (p. 141). This is particularly relevant after the events of September 11, 2001, as we have increasing documentation of discriminatory acts and attitudes toward Muslim individuals and families. It is important to recognize that many individuals experience solace and hope as they practice spirituality. Finally, Northcut (2000) comments that psychodynamic theories have often been ambivalent about the inclusion of religion in psychotherapy. As such, clinicians need to self-examine their own views about religion and spirituality and to guard against countertransference responses or dismissive attitudes concerning faith practices.

Socioeconomic Class

Differences and biases related to socioeconomic class are often hidden during the assessment and treatment of couples. Langston (2001) notes that there are many myths in the United States related to socioeconomic class. One predominant myth is that the United States is a classless society. This often contributes to the hidden dimension of socioeconomic class in couple interactions. Ehrenreich (2001) notes that working class individuals are subject to discriminatory attitudes. She comments, "Even deeper-rooted than the stereotype of the hard-hat bigot is the middle-class suspicion that the working class is dumb, inarticulate, and mindlessly loyal to old-fashioned values" (p. 145). Privileged individuals often question the ambition and intelligence of working class individuals (Langston, 2001, p. 126). Higginbotham and Weber (2001) recognize that "upward mobility is a process that requires sustained effort and emotion and cognitive, as well as financial support" (p. 166).

For survivors of childhood trauma, the hidden dimensions of class oppression intersect with the secretive, "tainted" sense of self that was associated with being victimized. The survivor's sense of shame is multidetermined and some working-class survivors report that others position them as immoral or even promiscuous. Immigrant and refugee couples often lose their class status when they emigrate to North America (Akhtar, 1999).

Gender

Gender is often thought to be an extremely powerful part of identity that influences interpersonal behavior. Simply put, women are often viewed as inferior to men. Ortner (1996) writes, "I would flatly assert that we find women subordinated to men in every known society. The search for a genuinely egalitarian, let alone matriarchal, culture has proved fruitless" (p. 24). Men and women internalize attitudes and stereotypes about gender that are based on patriarchy, power, and the privileging of men. Powerful rules about gender shape interpersonal behavior and communication between men and women. Lorber (2000) notes, "Gender signs and signals are so ubiquitous that we usually fail to note them—unless they are missing or ambiguous" (p. 204).

Greene (2000) comments, "African American men and women who have internalized the racism, sexism, and heterosexism inherent in the patriarchal values of Western culture may scapegoat any strong women, that is, any women who defy traditional gender role norms" (pp. 93–94). Goldner (1989) notes that "Gender and the gendering of power are not secondary mediating variables *affecting* family life; they *construct* family life in the deepest sense" (p. 56; italics in the original). Survivors of childhood sexual abuse know too well the power that their (male) perpetrators wielded in their families of origin. Often these survivors were clearly viewed as the male's property who could be mistreated without consequence. Likewise, many refugee women have been brutalized in their home countries.

These authors illustrate the fundamental belief that contemporary North American culture is a patriarchal culture. As such, men and women internalize values that legitimize the experience and power of men while systematically devaluing the experience of women. In fact, women are often blamed for causing family problems. Even though feminist thinking has now defined women's subordination to men as morally unacceptable, in practice, it still exists (Goldner, 1989). In summary, gender inequities exist in devaluing attitudes, imbalances in financial compensation for employment, and disparity in division of family responsibilities. The inequities related to patriarchy mirror and reinforce the unequal trauma-related power dynamics. For a more thorough analysis of gender, from a feminist perspective, refer to Chapter 4 on family theory.

Issues of Ability/Disability

The assessment of issues of ability and disability, and the impact of physical, psychological, and/or learning disabilities are important to understanding the couple's dynamics. Here, the clinician needs to be aware of his response to disabled individuals, and Stromwall (2002) prompts social workers to consider their biases. The couple therapist needs to counter the reality that media and society, as a whole, ignore the real experiences of many disabled individuals. Piastro (1999) notes, "The media did not reflect new perspectives, such as the independent living and disability rights movement's way of interpreting society" (p. 43).

Although an acute disability may temporarily shift role functions in a couple relationship (Rolland, 1994), it is useful to deconstruct the attitude that the "disabled" partner is the needy partner. This stereotype is damaging to the ego of the disabled person and needs to be challenged. As Fine and Asch (2000) note, "It is assumed that the person with the disability is in constant need of help and support, rather than being a victim of the nondisabled persons' projections or fantasies" (p. 335). Rather, the reciprocal roles of the couple need to be kept in perspective. It is useful to have the couple highlight how their relationship is, indeed, complementary in terms of caretaker/patient. It is also important to recognize that the disability of one partner may have nothing to do with the changing patterns in the couple system. Many individuals with disability have a remarkable capacity for resilience and these strengths of the client need to be noted and honored.

Sexual Orientation

Individuals who identify as lesbian, gay, bisexual, or transgendered experience discrimination as a result of marginalization by the dominant society (Laird & Green, 1996). A later chapter more fully discusses issues related to lesbian, gay, bisexual, and transgendered individuals. Here, only a brief synopsis is given. As in other areas, the influence of sexual orientation intersects with other social factors that determine identity. For example, Greene (2000) discusses historical and contemporary reasons why it is particularly difficult for African-American lesbians to openly acknowledge their sexual orientations to their families. She comments that "The message put forth is that lesbian sexual orientation, unlike racial identity, is something that can and should be concealed" (p. 101). Heterosexist attitudes often shape the "standard" to which lesbian, gay, bisexual, or transgendered individuals measure themselves. In addition, many clinicians carry biases, based on myths or misconceptions, when treating this population. Clinicians and clients may have internalized homophobic attitudes. However, a focus on negative attitudes about homosexuality potentially diminish the pride that many gay, lesbian, bisexual and transgendered individuals experience.

:: CONCLUSION

In summary, then, a full biopsychosocial couple assessment fully integrates aspects of sociocultural factors that influence the development of identity. Having to mediate the persistent presence of shame and stigma, many survivors of childhood trauma feel that they are damaged individuals who are somehow "mentally ill." During the therapy, the clinician encourages survivors to challenge internalized beliefs that they are pathological individuals. Rather, understanding complex posttraumatic stress syndrome as a normative, adaptive response to trauma, the survivor begins to reclaim a sense of identity that transcends the status of "victim." Close attention to the sociocultural factors that influence identity development equips the clinician with valuable information that facilitates therapeutic process. These factors are clearly illustrated in the treatment section to follow. Our next chapter focuses on family theory, in which the influence of feminist principles is expanded.

Family Theory

This chapter explores how family theories lend clarity to our understanding of the interactional and intergenerational influences affecting adults who have navigated traumatic experiences during childhood. As an overarching framework, a social constructivist stance aims to support the importance of multiple views. In particular, feminist, intergenerational, and narrative family theories provide vital perspectives toward understanding the legacies of childhood trauma evident in the couple and family relationships forged by these adult trauma survivors.

To reiterate a central frame for this discussion, a social constructionist position values multiple perspectives and supports a "both/and" stance as opposed to "either/or" dichotomized thinking (Laird, 1998). A focus on resilience is also crucial in countering reified, problem-saturated views. White and Epston (1990) describe deconstructionism as procedures that question taken-for-granted realities and practices, those "truths" that hide their biases and prejudices and subjugate persons' lives. Although attention to the subjective meaning of a client's situation is important, such a postmodern stance is often critiqued by feminists. They worry that a challenge to "grand narratives" designed to prescribe certain "objective truths" can be threatening to the reality of actual abuse and to issues of social justice. As Hare-Mustin and Maracek (1994) assert, feminists are concerned with "postmodernism's seemingly endless fascination with words and texts to the exclusion of material reality . . . potentially ignoring women's lived experiences by retreating into arcane theory" (p. 15).

:: FEMINIST FAMILY THEORY

A feminist perspective is grounded in what Foucault (1980) describes as the insurrection of subjugated knowledge. More specifically, a feminist family therapy perspective aims to tease out and challenge gender assumptions that direct a family's ways of interacting (Sheinberg, 1992). For many, feminism highlights a need to enlarge the influence of social justice, fairness, and equality as core values in family relationships (Hare-Mustin & Maracek, 1994; McNay, 1992), while dismantling a patriarchal power structure. Because a universal confrontation of patriarchy may contradict social work values of self-determination and respect for all religions and cultures, such a rigid politicized stance is contraindicated in clinical practice. However, a feminist-informed clinical practice allows for exploration of the meaning attached to gender beliefs as well as advocating for the rights of women and children when safety is an issue.

Emergence of Feminist Family Therapy

Throughout the past few decades, several feminist family therapists began to critique the prevailing theory models of the time, most notably systems and psychodynamic theories (Goldner, 1999; Hare-Mustin & Maracek, 1994; Hartman, 1996; McGoldrick, 1998). Since systemic models at that time paid little, if any, attention to issues of gender, race, class, or sexual orientation, feminist social workers argued that mothers were overrepresented as the causes of psychopathology. An overvaluation of the constructs of "autonomy" and "differentiation" led to a privileging of cognition and separateness over connection. In gendered terms, the stereotypic notions of male psychology were exalted. As patriarchal societal influences have shaped our notions of couple and family in both the United States and Canada, feminists were mindful of the social injustices inherent in a system that privileges the "father" legally and relationally. Such a reality translates into the subordination of women in the family, with diminished value attached to women's contributions. Especially useful themes and practices from feminist family therapy are (1) the impact of gendered beliefs and socialization on relationships, (2) effects of inequalities embedded in patriarchy, and (3) holding an "offending" person responsible for his or her abuse.

Balancing Gendered Beliefs and Roles

Hare-Mustin (1994) offers a useful method to modulate gender biases. She notes that an alpha bias is created by exaggerating differences in a way that stereotypes and reifies an aspect of that difference. For example, an alpha-biased perspective on gender differences suggests that most men are more cognitively and instrumentally focused, while most women behave in affective, relationally determined ways. Although this statement might be accurate for some men and women, the glaring generalizations signal alpha-biased stereotyping. On the other hand, a beta bias presumes that there are no differences at all between individuals related to a particular factor. For example, if a clinician presumes that there are no biological, cultural, and societal differences between men and women, it would follow that we are all similar based on a shared humanity. Ignoring gender differences in such a glaring way reflects a strong beta-biased position. With reference to any aspect of diversity, whether it is gender, race, ethnicity, sexual identity, socioeconomic class, disability, or age, it is important to be mindful of how biases may shape the discourse about differences and commonalties. It is equally important to minimize both alpha- and beta-biased positions. The following clinical vignette reveals some pitfalls in a beta-biased position expressed by one couple.

MARGARET AND PETER ∷ Margaret, a thirty-two-year-old Caucasian epidemiologist, a survivor of childhood sexual abuse, met her prospective husband Peter, a thirty-one-year-old Polish-American biostatistician, twelve years earlier while pursuing graduate studies. She was immediately infatuated with Peter's charisma as he addressed the local feminist alliance, enthralling the audience with a rousing speech about men who batter. Their early bond was forged around a shared political and social justice consciousness. Both partners espoused profeminist political beliefs.

After ten years of marriage, they sought couple therapy to address their harsh daily arguments over a fair division of labor. Although they shared beliefs about an equal partnership and a fifty–fifty division of all responsibilities, Margaret resented Peter's withdrawal from cooking and shopping. Indignantly, Peter claimed that he was more skillful in caring for the cars, the yard, and the bills. Bitter battles over decision-making and power issues ensued. Who was in charge of what? Who fulfilled or shirked her or his responsibility? Who should feel shame? Guilt? Because both partners had convinced themselves that they differed from their respective families of origin by espousing a more equitable relationship, they were convinced that a cognitive readjustment would effectively shift their dynamic. They were completely stunned to discover they had sunk into stereotypical gender roles.

To understand this derailment, I explored with this couple what role expectations were held for men and women in their families of origin. This discussion led to an intriguing dialogue about the conflicting messages received for both partners. Although stereotypical gender roles were enacted, yet verbally challenged by both sets of parents, both Margaret and Peter had internalized their families' paradigms. On the one hand, it was important to fulfill stereotypical gender roles while, on the other hand, challenging them. Inevitably, internal and external conflict arose with these contradictory messages. Only as the presence of these family "ghosts" was acknowledged could this couple directly address how their relationship might change.

Soon, Margaret and Peter started to recognize how their rigid "politically correct" beliefs straightjacketed them as harshly as the oppressive patriarchal gender roles that they challenged. As each partner assumed a moral high ground, the other partner was rendered powerless. After several months of painful yet freeing self-reflections, both partners recognized, with some humor, how exhausting their "value policing" had become. In fact, Peter joked that metaphorically "his legs were very worn out by continually trying to climb up to Margaret's higher moral ground." Rather than defend and protect herself immediately, Margaret also shared some bemusement that she, too, was fatigued with their Victimology Olympics. Each partner tired of his or her relentless victimized suffering in response to the other partner's alleged insensitivity. Most compelling was the realization that the unequal power dynamics further perpetuated their "victim–victimizer–bystander" dynamic originated in their respective families of origin.

Unequal Power in Couple Relationships

Although feminism clearly purports to challenge and eradicate an unfair patriarchal power structure, imposing such a strong political position as a clinician contradicts a basic social work value of self-determination. However, as stated earlier, a feminist-informed couple therapy allows for exploration of the meanings attached to gender beliefs, as well as advocates for

the rights of women, children, and men when safety is an issue. The imposition of a value system that dismantles unequal power relationships may also
interfere with certain religious and cultural beliefs firmly held by a couple.
Many religions and ethnic groups support the privileging of male power,
along with the subordination of women. How then does a feminist-informed
clinician deal with a client's value system that supports inequality and social
injustice? On the one hand, insisting on one's own politics represents an
abuse of power or unethical practice. On the other hand, failing to question
the origin and meanings of a couple's gendered assumptions may be clinically and ethically irresponsible. Once again, is there a way to balance
the reality of one's own political and cultural beliefs while respecting the
religious/cultural beliefs of the couple?

BRAD AND FRANCES :: A young dual-trauma Jehovah's Witness couple
sought therapy because they fought unrelentingly and threatened each other
with divorce. Since they desperately wanted to restore their marriage within
the dogma of their religious community, they formulated goals that involved
greater stabilization of their unequal stereotypically gendered roles. As both
Brad and Frances realized that their discontent related to their constant devaluation of the other, they recognized the value and positive features in their
family roles. By the end of therapy, this couple had reestablished a harmonious
unequal relationship bolstered by their religious beliefs. However, they were
now able to integrate a questioning stance about how best to fulfill these roles
with some individual creativity, rather than experiencing total subjugation.

PELIM AND DOROTHY :: Pelim and Dorothy, a dual-trauma intercultural
couple, had met in graduate school, where they studied anthropology. They
had been intrigued by each other's respect for cultural diversity. After ten years
of marriage, Pelim, a thirty-six-year-old Muslim Pakistani immigrant, and
Dorothy, a thirty-two-year-old fifth-generation African-American Baptist
teacher, a survivor of childhood sexual abuse, worried that their marriage
would end in divorce. Although this couple had agreed to rear their two children in the Islam faith and Muslim culture, Dorothy failed to recognize the
suppressed resentment and grief suffered by renouncing her faith. As both
partners discussed the importance of their respective religious and cultural beliefs with regard to child-rearing practices, they negotiated a more equitable
relationship. Although they agreed to continue to rear their children as Muslim, Dorothy rejected the cultural expectations of regularly providing domes-

tic service to her husband. She reconnected with her Christian religion, choosing a Methodist Church described as more inclusive and tolerant, as compared with her original childhood church community. Once again, this couple aimed to reclaim a level of mutual respect and deference to each other's central cultural beliefs; however, equality in all spheres of life was not sought.

Holding the Offending Person Responsible

With the acknowledgment of actual trauma or abuse, a social constructionist approach should be suspended, as one could always question the perception or experience of an event. However, in the realm of violence and abuse, it is important to shift into an either/or position, momentarily, to ascertain who is responsible for inflicting the abuse. A danger of systemic family theory has been to explore circular causality involved in family systems that foster the continuation of the cycle of violence. Even though these patterns might be vividly evident, it is still imperative to hold the offending person accountable (Goldner, 1993).

Once again, the use of language is critical. Rather than referring to the legalistic language of the "perpetrator," "perp," "victimizer," or the "offender," it is preferable to talk about a person or individual who has offended. In this way, the person's entire identity is not defined exclusively by the abuse.

:: INTERGENERATIONAL FAMILY THEORY

An intergenerational family perspective grounded in systems thinking originated several decades ago with talk of fusion, differentiation, and intergenerational transmission of family patterns through interlocking triangles (Alexander, 1985; Bowen, 1974). Although current systemic thinking has shifted away from a mechanistic perspective of these processes, understanding the role of triangles as well as meaning-making in conveying intergenerational processes is still relevant (Basham, 1999a; Falicov, 1998; McGoldrick, 1998; Pinderhughes, 1998).

Extensive literature related to the adaptation of survivors of warfare, armed conflict, historical trauma, and political genocide sheds further clarity on the intergenerational effects of trauma. Not only should we pay careful attention to the experiences of our immigrant, refugee, and veteran populations, but we should also be mindful of the intergenerational legacies of trauma for our U.S. and Canadian citizens who are wrestling with the aftermath of relational childhood abuses as well as collective trauma. Themes that are particularly relevant in discussing intergenerational family theory are (1) intergenerational transmission processes, including triangles; (2) family loyalties and secrets; and (3) rituals.

Intergenerational Transmission Processes

Parenting

Although many adult survivors of childhood trauma approach their lives with unique resilience and zest, other adult survivors experience difficulties in their parenting capacities. Several research studies have suggested a low incidence of intergenerational transmission of abusive behaviors among parents who were abused as children, but there is also a population of adult survivors who struggle with ways to use nonabusive modes of discipline with their children (Figley, 1989; Kaufman & Zigler, 1987; Main & Goldwyn, 1984; O'Connell-Higgins, 1994; Trepper & Neidner, 1996; Walsh, 1998). Child welfare social policy advocates and direct service clinicians are eager to find more effective ways to interrupt intergenerational patterns of child maltreatment. Because the theme of parenting is so important in couple and family therapy with survivors of childhood trauma, this topic will be covered in more depth in the chapter devoted to treatment processes.

Aftereffects of War, Armed Conflict, and Genocide

Considerable attention has been paid to the intergenerational trauma for survivors of war, armed conflict, and genocide. The literature related to intergenerational trauma uses various terms to define the processes. They include intergenerational trauma and grief, cross-generational trauma, cumulative trauma, collective trauma, intergenerational posttraumatic stress, soul wound, or historical trauma (Bar-On, 1998; Danieli, 1998; Felson, 1998; Hardtmann, 1998; Sigal, 1989; Solomon, 1998; Yellow Horse Brave Heart-Jordan, 1995). As these terms are not completely interchangeable, I will refer to intergenerational transmission processes for purposes of this chapter. More specifically, research with second- and third-generation Holocaust survivors, American Indian survivors of rampant genocide, and collective trauma inflicted on African Americans all point to areas of resilience as well an unresolved grief and trauma-related symptomatology (Danieli, 1998; Pinderhughes, 1998).

Although clinical studies have reported particular problems in the off-spring between Holocaust survivors and their children (Bar-On, 1998; Danieli, 1998; Felsen, 1998), more recent empirical studies have produced more contradictory information (Kellerman, 2001; Solomon, 1998). For example, Felsen (1998) reports that although second-generation survivors often report heightened anxiety, survivor guilt, depression, difficulties with managing aggression, and reduced self-differentiation, they do not as a group qualify for classification within DSM-IV-TR psychopathology. More recent studies of second- and third-generation survivors point to strong family loyalties and a compelling drive from the offspring to keep the memory of the genocide alive in the public eye.

Reports from research studies following veterans of World War II reveal some important findings regarding the relational aftereffects of their experiences. Bernstein (1998) reports on a study of 150 ex-prisoners of war who report distinct problems adjusting to family life, with patterns of social withdrawal, and compulsive immersion in work as a way to cope with unresolved guilt feelings around capture. Another effect of World War II tragedies includes the impact on the third-generation (Sansei) children of former Japanese Americans who were interned during the war. Nagata (1998) published results of a survey research project in which 799 Sansei-generation offspring revealed a continuing "felt experience" of their parents' internment, evidenced in family communication breakdowns, grief, identity conflicts, and ambiguity regarding civil rights.

Another disturbing finding from a research study of Vietnam war veterans suggested that veterans whose fathers served in combat experienced an increased risk of posttraumatic stress disorder (PTSD) and other postwar adjustment problems as compared with other Vietnam veterans. In fact, the stressors associated with a Vietnam veteran's return home to an inhospitable welcome and the intergenerational effects of the father's combat-related trauma combined to exacerbate the son's emerging PTSD symptomatology (Rosenheck & Fontana, 1998). Another interesting study approached from a clinical perspective uncovered several mechanisms of transmission, including silence, overdisclosure, identification, and reenactment (Ancharoff, Munroe, & Fisher, 1998).

The holocausts experienced by Alaskan Native tribes as well as indigenous American Indian tribes have further resulted in distinct evidence of resilience as well as unresolved trauma and grief passed down to subsequent populations (Cashin, 2000; Graves, 2004; Yellow Horse Brave Heart-Jordan, 1995). Such historical trauma that inflicts cumulative emotional and psychological wounding over a life span and across generations derives from massive group catastrophes (Yellow Horse Brave Heart-Jordan, 1995).

Finally, the research related to the intergenerational transmission of the effects of slavery reveal both positive and functional, as well as self-defeating patterns established after four hundred years of slavery. In an interesting paper, Cross (1998) differentiates the complex adjustment patterns linked to slavery from aspects of black psychology that are the product of contemporary racism and economic neglect. Along similar lines, Pinderhughes (1998) continues to trace intergenerational patterns among African-American families in terms of both resilience and the sequelae of unresolved grief and trauma. Positive coping skills have emerged, placing strong value on education and religion; in marked contrast, negative aftereffects are characterized by the intergenerational transmission of internalized oppression. These negative effects often surface in attitudes about skin color and racial self-identification.

In summary, the pernicious aftereffects of war and armed conflict have been more systematically documented in terms of the potential for transmission of positive and negative effects of these experiences intergenerationally. However, the impact of historical and collective trauma imposed on populations exposed to extremes of political torture and maltreatment in other countries, as well as within the United States and Canada, demand equal attention in terms of immediate acuity as well as the long-term intergenerational effects. With this perspective in mind, a central goal in couple therapy should focus on reinforcing the positive adaptive features of these intergenerational experiences as well as interrupting destructive family relational patterns. A clinical vignette may illuminate these complex phenomena.

RACHEL, SETH, AND BEN :: Seth, a forty-two-year-old Jewish trombonist and his forty-two-year-old wife, Rachel, an attorney, sought couple/family therapy. Initially, they were distressed about the condition of their sixteen-year-old son, Ben. Although intellectually gifted and talented musically, Ben failed to submit any work at school yet still enjoyed playing his clarinet. After continual suspensions from high school, Ben retreated to the solitude of his basement home, until one day he showed his parents the fruition of his "art project." For seven days, Ben had been systematically cutting incisions in his chest with a razor blade, creating a bloody tattoo of a heart. The word DEATH was boldly inscribed in the center. After expressing a shared horror, Ben's parents escorted Ben to a psychiatric emergency room, where he was promptly admitted. While in the hospital, staff earnestly pursued any sources of precipitating stressors for clinical depression. Their conclusions pointed to the rejection from a girlfriend, who had rebuffed him the week before, and feelings of being "lost" and "drifting" since school was so "boring."

Following discharge, I interviewed the family together and each member separately as well, promising limited confidentiality to avoid triangulation. Information emerged from Ben that exactly one year ago, his maternal grandfather died suddenly from a pulmonary embolism. There was no funeral, no sitting shiva, and no shared grieving among the family about his death. Slowly, Ben revealed very strong love and deep loyalty toward his grandfather, who he admired deeply for having survived six months of hiding in Hungary during World War II while family members were systematically captured and ultimately killed. No one had ever talked about these wartime experiences although the suppressed grief and distress were enormous. When Ben and his parents shared that they never talk about his grandfather, Ben yelled to his parents, "How loud do I have to get before somebody else cries out?" He went on to talk about the brutal silence at home. In sessions with Rachel and Seth, Rachel expressed her fears of sharing any emotions, as she was steeling herself to deal with the fairly recent revelation of her husband's affair. Seth had distanced himself from his wife with a brief romantic interlude, similarly avoiding any expression of grief. As a survivor of physical abuse inflicted by her father, Rachel had learned quiet acquiescence.

Barely audible, Ben muttered in one meeting that he wanted his "memorial tattoo" to stay with him at all times to remember his grandfather. As no one else in the family openly grieved his grandfather's loss, Ben became the living personification of his memorial. He wanted to acknowledge the goodness and tortuous tribulations suffered by his beloved grandfather. As words replaced symbolic self-mutilation, Ben talked and talked and talked about his grandfather in both group and family psychotherapy sessions. He shared his pride, his sadness, his rage, his worry, and, ultimately, his desire to connect with his parents, who he felt had betrayed him with their silence. Ultimately, as Seth and Rachel worked through their feelings of betrayal and distrust surrounding the affair, they were more emotionally available to support Ben with his grief. Collectively, Ben and his parents were better able as a family to talk about Ben's grandfather. With these efforts, the family was able to interrupt a tenacious intergenerational pattern of unresolved grief and trauma.

Family Loyalties and Secrecy

This poignant clinical vignette conveys an important feature in couple and family therapy with survivors of childhood trauma. In spite of horrific neglect or abusive treatment, many children and adults continue to hold on to their insecure attachments to their caregivers. When all logic disappears, this connection must be understood in terms of invisible loyalties (Bozmormenyi-Nagy & Spark, 1973). Secrecy occurs frequently in abusive families, protecting the culpability of the offending family member as well as sustaining a "shame-based" identity for the victim(s). When an adult survivor of childhood trauma confronts the reality and impact of abuse, she or he often unearths secrets developed in response to terror and/or shame.

For Ben and his parents, unresolved grief and trauma were transmitted intergenerationally through unconscious processes that relegated these issues to the world of silent secrecy. The intergenerational triangle formed by maternal grandfather, Rachel, and Ben perpetuated unresolved grief and trauma-related symptomatology. Another triangle, consisting of Ben and his parents, intensified the anxiety and stress in the entire family as it mirrored the pattern of intense overprotectiveness grounded in fear with a detached bystander. Intergenerational triangles reflecting the "victim–victimizer–bystander" scenario prevailed. Even so, strong family loyalty fueled Ben's driving need to memorialize his grandfather in a concrete, corporal expression. Paradoxically, his artistic tribute combined both a positive tribute to his beloved grandfather as well as a behavioral reenactment of aggression, now turned against himself. Such self-harm was reminiscent not only of his grandfather's suffering, but also a behavioral expression of his inherited self-punishment fueled by survivor guilt.

In the course of couple/family therapy with survivors of childhood trauma, it is extremely important to be mindful of the existence of secrets and invisible loyalties. However, it is equally important to avoid intrusive questioning in these areas because retraumatization could hurt family members further. A reasonable balance involves benign questioning that allows the couple to set the pace for the revelation of any secrets or shame-based recollections.

Rituals

Family therapists generally share strong convictions that rituals serve an important adaptive function in enabling families to cope with what are considered ordinary life cycle transitions as well as idiosyncratic events (Imber-Black, Roberts, & Whiting, 1998). Since social conventions often determine which transitions call for rituals, we, as clinicians, need to be carefully attuned to those significant events, especially those that are stigmatized or marginalized that are also vitally important to our clients. There are openly prescribed rituals for many ordinary life occurrences such as births, deaths, marriages, birthdays, "coming-of-age," or graduations. There are fewer, if any, prescribed transitional rituals for marginalized events. The following transitions or life events clearly deserve acknowledgment, but generally require creative efforts by family members to craft a ritual. They include the following examples: commitment, marriage, and dissolution ceremonies for gay, bisexual, lesbian, or transgendered couples; divorce; remarriage; immigration; adoption; foster home placement; or a move to a nursing home or an assisted living facility.

ALEX AND IVAN :: Many adult survivors often report horrific tales of disrupted family gatherings. One second-generation Russian Orthodox sexual abuse survivor, Alex, tried to describe to her husband, Ivan, how devastated she and her siblings felt on one occasion when her abusive father, disinhibited by a drunken state, threw a Christmas turkey across the living room. It knocked the tree to the floor and shattered all of the decorations. Since then, she hated celebrating Christmas in her home, creating considerable friction with her husband, who loved the holidays. Only as she was able to express her despair over this debacle could her husband empathize with her profound hurt.

Regrettably, this example is one among many in which family rituals have been destroyed rather than used to draw the family together.

Since childhood trauma has often robbed adult survivors of some joys and innocence while growing up, their recovery typically includes some grieving for their damaged childhoods. While recognizing the positives in their earlier years, it is also essential for them to grapple with grieving their losses. In these situations, the creation of a healing ritual helps to promote connections within the family.

RACHEL, SETH, AND BEN (continued) :: After several months of talking together, Rachel, Seth, and Ben decided to plan a memorial service for Ben's grandfather. They decided that Seth and Ben would play chamber music pieces that Ben's grandfather especially enjoyed. As Rachel and Ben harnessed their respective artistic talents, they created a photo collage of grandfather's history, including one baby picture, several pictures obtained during the Holocaust years, and many photos of him with his family after he emigrated to the United States. The capacity to pay tribute to this beloved man, as well as affirming the horrific events of the Holocaust, provided an essential healing function for this family. The ritual further helped Rachel to remember her father as a complex man who loved her and his family deeply, while also imposing harsh physical punishment that shattered her sense of well-being.

:: NARRATIVE THEORY AND THERAPY

Narrative theory and therapy, in general, focus on the importance of a person's narrative, defined as the accounts that persons tell themselves and others, and/or that are told to them about their experiences. In this way, the meaning of events, experiences, self-views, and interactions are all described and explicated (Freedman & Combs, 1996; Laird, 1998; Neal, Zimmerman, & Dickerson, 1999; Sheinberg & Fraenkel, 2001). It follows that problem-focused language leads to the establishment of problem-saturated narratives that reify problems and interfere with possibilities for changing fixed patterns. In reference to the legacies of childhood trauma, a narrative therapy approach aims to alter "the story of shame" associated with the abuse (White, 1995). A re-storying of the narrative leads to a new narrative grounded in resilience and pride in one's positive features. Major risks of focusing exclusively on strengths with adult survivors of childhood trauma are of trivializing or actually denying the heinousness of the traumatic experiences. Major themes relevant to narrative theory and therapy include (1) multiple perspectives, (2) "both/and" thinking, (3) the use of language, and (4) transforming a problem narrative to a strengths-based narrative.

Multiple Perspectives

Although the notion of multiple perspectives seems obvious in terms of approaching a couple and family, it is important to stress the importance of valuing each person's perspective (Weingarten, 1991). Rather than trying to ascertain one primary "truth" or "reality," it is important to consider the views of all parties concerned. No one perspective is inherently better than another; instead, all perspectives need to be considered in order to arrive at an overall impression of similarities and differences in views. Some narrative therapists conclude that a clinician's view is not inherently better than those of families; however, the societally sanctioned power ascribed to professionals who can diagnose often prioritizes those perspectives (Sheinberg & Fraenkel, 2001, p. 54). In practical application to couple therapy, it is important to explore the multiple meanings and outlooks experienced by each partner, even if the clinician holds a different viewpoint. Honoring and valuing multiple perspectives does not necessarily translate into agreement with an opposite point of view. Instead, it highlights the continuing importance of deferring to the client's view of their situation as well as their notion of a preferred reality.

Valuing Complexity, Ambiguity, and "Both/And" Thinking

The ongoing tension involved in holding discrepant views or bearing seemingly contradictory thoughts, perceptions, and feelings leads to a self-view that is composed of many strands of meaning and complex identity (Sheinberg & Fraenkel, 2001). Gergen (1991) describes the "fluid self" as flexibly shaped by social context and community, in contrast to a uniform essentialist self that remains the same across all situations. A "both/and" stance encourages the recognition and acceptance of a broad spectrum of feelings, thoughts, and values that may shift, given different situations, yet still embody some core consistencies as well.

Working with this flexible stance is quite important for trauma survivors, who often cast their self-views in a rigid and polarized manner. Often, the internal identity is a shame-based negative, doomed, and powerless self. Dynamics of relational trauma establish and, then, reinforce the dichotomized "either/or" thinking that fuels a rigid, essentialist self-view. At the moment when childhood abuse occurs, there is, in fact, a person who is offending, while there is a child-victim who is being mistreated. Although there is a clear, concrete dynamic involving a victim, victimizer, and bystander in this trauma scenario, complexity emerges when we realize that the victim might be experiencing aggressive victimizer feelings, while the offender might, at the time, be experiencing a sense of victimized powerlessness. For purposes of holding the offending person responsible, we need to remain clear in our "either/or" thinking. However, in terms of helping trauma survivors with their recovery, they need to understand that their loving attachment feelings toward their offender might be quite ordinary. In summary, a "both/and" stance always serves to maintain complexity while an "either/or" position is essential to ensure accountability.

Use of Language

The use of language is central to narrative theory and therapy; ways in which accounts of events are told to oneself and others or are told to others determine the meaning attached to these particular events (Andolfi, Angelo, & Nichilo, 1989; Eron & Lund, 1999; Fraenkel et al., 1998; Rampage, 1991; Zimmerman & Dickerson, 1994). Inevitably, language that is negative or problem saturated tends to reify problems and interfere with a person or couple's capacity to change. How often in couple therapy do we hear nasty harangues from partners who assault each other with unrelenting name-calling? It is clearly not uncommon for distressed couples to refer to their partners with negative attributions that exacerbate existing tensions.

Language that is used in the mental health and social work field carries considerable influence as well. For example, an outgrowth of the feminist movement revealed a change in the language for women who had been sexually abused as children. The term "survivor" replaced the more frequently used term "victim." As women claimed some agency in coping with their traumatic experiences, their language for self-definition reflected an empowerment message. At the present time, many trauma survivors actually prefer to self-identify as "transcenders," "overcomers," or "thrivers," all self-identifications that are not narrowly defined through their traumatic experiences.

Transforming a Problem Narrative to a Strengths-Based Narrative

The basic guidelines of valuing multiple perspectives, maintaining complexity of a "both/and" position, and recognizing the powerful influence of language all combine to provide a solid foundation for a narrative therapist. Since sexual abuse, and in many cases, physical and emotional abuse, involves a "story of shame," one goal of couple therapy is to elicit conversations about "stories of pride" (Sheinberg & Fraenkel, 2001, p. 52). A working assumption is that partners may have multiple coexisting narratives. Each partner, as well as the couple, might have a self-perception of having lived a "story of abuse" while at the same time living and continuing to live other, more positive stories of pride. Once again, it bears repeating that a goal is to hold the complexity of positive and negative experiences, rather than having a strengths-based outlook magically erase the impact of trauma.

Externalization of the problem begins with the exploration of each partner's experience of the problem. In this way, a narrative postmodern approach enables us to make visible the negative effects of the problem on the partners and on the couple relationship. Rather than asking why a person feels a certain way, the clinician pursues what the problem does to the couple. It is also imperative to address the links between culture, power, and relationships. Additional central themes of the work include (1) transparency and situating oneself as the clinician, (2) exploring preferred experiences of self, (3) co-constructing a coherent narrative truth, and (4) reauthoring practices relating preferred experiences to preferred narratives (Neal, Zimmerman, & Dickerson, 1999, p. 392). The following clinical vignette features a single-trauma lesbian couple, Paula and Colette, who have been partners for five years. Figure 4.1 shows the genogram for Paula and Colette.

PAULA AND COLETTE :: Paula, age thirty-seven, completed a college education and now works as an administrator in a high pressured consulting organization that markets controversial military contracts, while Colette, age thirty-seven, also a college graduate, works as a healthcare professional. After five years of partnership, Paula initiated a call for help, as she felt despairing about the future of the relationship. She complained of sadness and tearfulness, reporting that she was also isolated at home most of the time, lethargic, and profoundly sad.

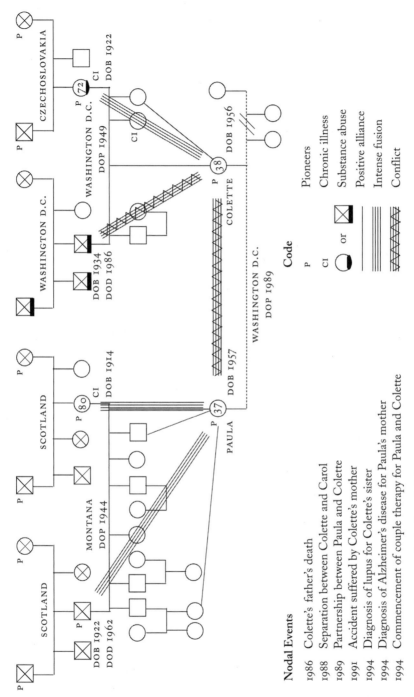

Code

P	Pioneers
CI	Chronic illness
⬚ or ⬛	Substance abuse
‖‖‖	Positive alliance
⫴⫴⫴	Intense fusion
⨯⨯⨯	Conflict

Nodal Events

1986 Colette's father's death
1988 Separation between Colette and Carol
1989 Partnership between Paula and Colette
1991 Accident suffered by Colette's mother
1994 Diagnosis of lupus for Colette's sister
1994 Diagnosis of Alzheimer's disease for Paula's mother
1994 Commencement of couple therapy for Paula and Colette

FIGURE 4.1 :: Genogram for Paula and Colette.

Paula, the youngest of seven children, was reared in poverty in a midwestern farming community by a widowed mother of Scottish ancestry. Her father, reared on a Lakota reservation, died suddenly of a heart attack when Paula was five, leaving the task of child rearing exclusively to her mother. Paula reports her early childhood as carefree and loving, only to be interrupted by many years of isolation, painful loss, and poverty. Paula's mother had recently been diagnosed with Alzheimer's disease, forcing her to lean on her children as a result of her increasing frailty and deteriorating cognitive abilities. Colette is the second of four children born to a Catholic Slovak family. Both parents drank heavily during Colette's childhood, during which time she was sexually molested by an uncle on several occasions. When Colette initially came out to her family during college, after an initial crisis characterized by accusations of sinfulness, each family member developed an accepting attitude toward Colette's sexual orientation. Three years earlier, her mother suffered an alcohol-related accident, which resulted in her paraplegia. Only one month ago, Colette's younger sister was diagnosed with lupus.

As both Paula and Colette argued about each other's unavailability, neither partner had discussed the emotional burden of their respective family members' illnesses. To contextualize their lives, questions were explored about Paula and Colette's families of origin. (See Figure 4.1, genogram for Paula and Colette.) Paula described her mother as a victim of a health tragedy and of tragic circumstances in losing her husband. Similarly, she referred to herself as a victim of her sister's and societal homophobic bigotries, insensitivity at her workplace, and of a lack of appreciation from Colette. Colette similarly described herself as a victim of her parents' alcoholism and of the sexual abuse inflicted by her uncle. When each partner recognized the major exhaustion associated with worrying and providing caretaking for their respective family members, she started to recognize the positive features in their caregiving capacities. When they saw that the impact of sexism rendered them as women expected to provide caregiving for frail family members, their collective fatigue and depressed states made much more sense. Ultimately, Paula was able to see the phenomenal strengths in her mother's survivorship and iconoclastic spirit. Not only did she cope effectively with losing her husband, but managed with minimal education to support all seven of her children by piecing together several different jobs. In discussing her father's life, she also reclaimed some of the cultural traditions valued by the Lakota tribe. In this case, the centrality of family was highlighted and reowned or "re-membered" in connection with her father.

Colette, who had always viewed herself as "unlucky" and "inevitably burdened," states that she attributed her victim stance to her abusive uncle, chaotic family, and oppressive society. As she talked about her experiences growing up, her narrative was enriched by stories of joyful times sharing camping and sewing with her mother. She also recalled inspiring talks with her father, who always read her stories. As both partners shared their tales of their growing up years, each partner listened attentively. She recalled how her independent, curious spirit was encouraged by several important people. Hence, what felt continually like a powerless victimized role altered with new elements of adventure.

With increasing capacity for empathy, each partner was able to "re-story" their narratives in such a way that many positive qualities entered center stage. They included courage, adventure, curiosity, iconoclasticism, resilience, compassion, independence, and competencies. These qualities did not erase the pain suffered by each woman, nor did they dismantle societal homophobia or misogyny. However, they fortified the women's self-identities by enriching their self-views. During the course of Phase II and III of their couple therapy, Paula and Colette changed their self-definitions from "victim," to "survivor," and then, ultimately, to "pioneer."

Now that the salient themes grounded in feminist-informed, intergenerational, and narrative family theories and therapy have been introduced in couple therapy with survivors of childhood trauma, we will shift from an interactional and intergenerational perspective to an individual perspective, reviewing the relevance of trauma theory in understanding the neurophysiological impact of traumatic experiences on an individual's and couple's emotional, cognitive, and behavioral functioning.

． ． ． ．
． ． ． ．
． ． ． ．
． ． ． 5

Trauma Theory

This chapter addresses the groundbreaking developments in the field of neurobiology, neuropsychology, and traumatology during the past decade that have challenged the mental health community to expand its knowledge base. Based on research data from several investigators, positron emission tomography (PET) and magnetic resonance imaging (MRI) have revealed direct connections between relational and nonrelational trauma, with associated effects on the human brain and body (Putnam & Trickett, 1997; Pynoos, Steinberg, Ornitz, & Goenjian, 1997; Siegel, 1999; Spiegel, 1997; van der Kolk, Burbridge, & Suzuki, 1997). Because the aftereffects of trauma clearly influence an individual's neurobiological and neuropsychological status, this chapter focuses attention on individual phenomena, as differentiated from interpersonal interactions between the couple or exchanges within their families or community.

The chapter reviews (1) research data related to the neurobiological effects and aftereffects on adults who suffered relational trauma during childhood, (2) research data more specifically related to the effects of relational trauma on right brain development and affect regulation in infant mental health, (3) some of the neurobiological effects and aftereffects of trauma on memory, and (4) the clinical implications for couple and family therapy.

:: RESEARCH RELATED TO NEUROBIOLOGICAL
   EFFECTS AND AFTEREFFECTS OF CHILDHOOD
   RELATIONAL TRAUMA

Research studies exploring the impact of trauma on infants have yielded data that explicate behavioral, developmental, neurobiological, and psychobiological responses. Several studies have established that relational or social stressors are far more "detrimental" to child development than are non-relational assaults, such as an accidental fall (Sgoifo et al., 1999). For this reason, relational trauma is the focus of this discussion (Schore, 2000, p. 206).

The neurophysiological status of an infant is based on a combination of factors, including genetic constitutional predisposition and environmental or psychosocial stressors. Many studies have demonstrated how dysfunctional maternal behavior negatively affects fetal development, particularly in the hypothalamic–pituitary–adrenocortical (HPA) axis. For example, the effects of maternal use of alcohol (Streissguth et al., 1994), drugs (Espy, Kaufman, & Glisky, 1999), and tobacco (Fergusson, Woodward, & Horwood, 1998) may interfere with the fetus's cognitive and physical development. However, these maternal behaviors are not usually referred to as traumatic.

Abuse and neglect from an early caregiver, however, do qualify as relational traumas. Clearly, caregiver-induced trauma is "qualitatively and quantitatively more psychopathogenic than any other social or physical stressor (aside from those directly targeting the developing brain)" (Schore, 2000, p. 207). In one pivotal study, Perry, Pollard, Blakely, Baker, and Vigilante (1995) reported two separate psychobiological responses to trauma experienced by an abused infant. With the initial threat, an alarm or startle reaction was activated, resulting in increased heart rate, blood pressure, respiration, and muscle tone. Hypervigilance emerged, followed by crying, and, ultimately, screaming.

Beebe (2000) vividly describes a "mutually escalating overarousal" characterized by a continuing lack of empathic attunement from the caregiver (p. 436). Even after the infant expresses extreme distress, including complete head aversion, arching away, or screaming, the mother continues, unrelentingly, with poorly attuned responses, failing to soothe the infant. The limbic areas are stimulated with excessive levels of the major stress hormone corticotropin releasing factor (CRF), which regulates catecholamine activity in the sympathetic nervous system. Both noradrenaline and adrenaline levels increase rapidly. In such "kindling states" (Post, Weiss, Smith, Li, & McCann, 1997), large amounts of CRF and glutamate are emitted. The latter is a major innervating excitatory neurotransmitter in the brain (Schore, 2000). This sympathetic regulatory response can be described metaphorically as the "agitator," a force that excites the amygdala, the brain's "alarm system," which mobilizes to defend and protect the child from harm. The amygdala is one of the limbic structures of the brain that evaluates the emotional meaning of incoming stimuli. It assigns free-floating feelings of significance to sensory input, which the neocortex then further elaborates with personal meaning. The amygdala guides emotional responses in connection with the hypothalamus, the basal forebrain, and the hippocampus. When stimuli overwhelm, the amygdala underfunctions in this regulation of sensory-laden information. The hippocampus, the brain's "filing system," is a limbic structure that categorizes experience in spatial maps and stores cognitive memory. A well-functioning hippocampus is essential for the retention of explicit, logical, or declarative memory (van der Kolk, 1994). When the amygdala (the "alarm system") is overwhelmed, the hippocampus (the "filing system") ceases to function effectively.

Perry et al. (1995) also describe, in addition to this early forming excitatory state, a second, later-forming reaction by the infant to trauma. Here, the child withdraws into her internal world and dissociates. A state of withdrawal, compliance, restricted affect, and numbness often occurs. Schore states that this is a parasympathetic regulatory mechanism whereby the individual strives to "avoid attention and be unseen" (Schore, 2000, p. 10). A metaphoric image of this adaptive response is a "reclusive hermit." During a passive state, in which the infant attempts to detach from an intolerable situation, levels of blunting endogenous opiates are elevated, contributing to the numbness. Other physiological changes include an increase in cortisol levels and an increase in vagal tone, resulting in decreased blood pressure and heart rate, despite increases in circulating adrenaline. This increased parasympathetic hypoarousal allows the infant to establish homeostasis in the face of the emerging state of sympathetic hyperarousal. Paradoxically, these contradictory sympathetic energy-expending and parasympathetic energy-conserving components of the child's autonomic nervous system are both hyperactivated, creating a toxic neurochemistry in the developing brain (Schore, 2000, p. 11). In anthropomorphized terms, both the "agitator" (sympathetic regulatory mechanism) and the "reclusive hermit" (parasympathetic regulatory system) activate in order to protect and regulate intense affects.

Without the mediating reparative influences of sound caregiving, these stress-induced responses start to organize the neural system, resulting in enduring aftereffects. As a result, permanent shifts in the affective centers of the limbic system may result, which ultimately influence affect regulation and the attachment pattern for the child, the adolescent, and the adult trauma survivor. Post, Weiss, and Leverich (1994) suggest "early adverse experiences may leave behind a permanent physiological reactivity in the limbic area of the brain" (p. 800). The infant posttraumatic stress reactions of hyperarousal and dissociation may well set the template for symptomatology in later life, including adult posttraumatic stress disorder (PTSD) and complex PTSD. Nijenhuis, Vanderlinden, and Spinhoven (1998) add that when infants express stress responses to threatening stimuli, their immature brain processes are appropriate "fight/flight" responses. However, adults who have been traumatized as children retain these immature responses to stress. As a result, when confronted with severe stress in adult life, the adult brain will then regress to an infantile state. Thus, the physiological activation of a regressed infantile state, or a state of retraumatization based on trauma-related aftereffects, is especially pronounced among adults who experienced trauma during childhood because of the consequent alterations in their brain neurophysiology.

:: EARLY RELATIONAL TRAUMA, AFFECT
REGULATION, AND RIGHT-BRAIN DISRUPTION

Since the effects of early relational trauma on infant development are so key to the understanding of child, adolescent, and adult development, this section devotes particular attention to Schore's (2000) infant research. An infant's capacity to shift between the dual states of interactions with others and solitude depends on a secure attachment relationship, which facilitates right brain development. Such a relationship promotes efficient affect regulation and fosters adaptive infant mental health. In contrast, it is important to note the effects of "traumatic attachment experiences on the development of brain regulatory systems, the neuropsychology of a disorganized/disoriented attachment pattern, the inhibitory effects of early trauma on the development of control systems involved in affect regulation and the connections between traumatic attachment and enduring right brain hemisphere dysfunction" (Schore, 2000, p. 204).

It is widely understood that early trauma alters the development of the infant's right brain, the hemisphere that is responsible for processing socioemotional information, attachment functions, and bodily states. The right hemisphere, more so than the left, is involved with the limbic system and the sympathetic and parasympathetic components of the autonomic nervous system. Therefore, it plays a central role in the components of emotional processing, on cognitive as well as physiological levels. In addition, the right hemisphere is specialized for the secretion of stress hormones, the human stress response, and vital functions that support survival. The orbitofrontal system, which is expanded into the right hemisphere, exerts executive control function for the entire right brain. Since this right prefrontal cortex is critical in processing affect and self-functions, any intense and unregulated stress induces heightened negative affect, chaotic biochemical reactions, and a developmentally immature defective right brain. Needless to say, there are serious long-term effects that bear scrutiny. Individuals with extreme right frontal activation often react negatively to a very low intensity negative elicitor and have trouble terminating a negative emotion once begun (Wheeler, Davidson, & Tomarken, 1993). Persinger and Makarec (1991) report more frequent negative affects and lower self-esteem among adult trauma survivors with more pronounced right brain hemisphericity.

Perry et al. (1995) state that early traumatic environments that disrupt normal patterns of neural activity interfere with the organization of the cortical–limbic areas. They compromise brain-mediated functions of attachment and empathy, as well as affect regulation. In fact, Teicher, Ito, and Glod (1996) report that children who suffered early physical and sexual abuse revealed electroencephalographic (EEG) abnormalities in frontotemporal and anterior brain regions. Such alterations affect prefrontal development, especially the prefrontolimbic system. Apparently, the pernicious effects of early trauma and neglect create deficits in the efficiency of the frontal subcortical system, leading to problems in attachment and affect regulation.

In fact, current neurobiological research on PTSD reveals dysfunctioning frontal–subcortical systems (Sutker, Vasterling, Brailey, & Allain, 1995) as well as altered functioning in the orbitofrontal region (Bremner et al., 1997; Shin et al., 1999) and in the amygdala (Rauch et al., 1996).

An outgrowth of an inefficient orbitofrontal reparative function is difficulty with self-soothing at times of stress. In a study using functional MRI equipment, Hairi, Bookheimer, and Mazziota (2000) identified the inability of the orbitofrontal areas to modulate the hyperexcited amygdala's fear response. The higher right brain frontal network, referred to colloquially as the "worry circuit," which usually mediates such emotional stimuli, is dysfunctional as a result of early relational trauma and "type D" disorganized/disoriented attachments. Not only are "type-D" attachments associated with

PTSD syndrome, they are also associated with hostile aggressive behavior (Lyons-Ruth, Alpern, & Repoacholi 1993). The leading research on attachment theory is discussed thoroughly in Chapter 7.

The usual constraints imposed on hypothalmic sites by the orbitofrontal cortex are absent when rage erupts. In addition, there are high correlations between PTSD and borderline diagnoses (Herman, Perry, & van der Kolk, 1989). There are also similarities in affect dysregulation, disturbances in impulse control, interpersonal difficulties, self-integration, and a tendency to dissociate under stress. Neurobiological studies further reveal altered amygdala functioning in clients with borderline personality organizations (Corrigan, Davidson, & Heard, 2000).

Other clients who exhibit violent behavior are often diagnosed with sociopathic personality disorder. Once again, through brain imaging research, these individuals have been found to have decreased orbitofrontal metabolism leading to angry eruptions (Siegel, 1999). Interestingly, stimulation of the prefrontal cortex is also purported to block the emergence of these aggressive attacks. Schore (2000) notes how the "type D disorganized/ disoriented attachment style and the orbitofrontal pruning are associated with the affective aggression of various levels of borderline personality disorders and the predatory and stalking type of aggression of sociopathic personality disorders" (p. 230).

Now that the direct connections between relational trauma and right brain development have been established, the discussion turns to a neurobiology of dissociation. It is important to stress here how dissociation involves a self-protective stance for those children who use it in response to cumulative relational trauma. A child may severely restrict overt expressions for attachment to defend against abuse and neglect. The social interactive regulatory modes are replaced by less complex autoregulatory modes. Thus, the habitual use of dissociation as a defense often is associated with type D attachment styles in later life. On a neurophysiological level, the orbitofrontal system of the child connects to the body via direct connections to the autonomic system. When there is extensive thinning of synaptic connections in this process, the central nervous system can no longer efficiently regulate the autonomic system. In fact, the loss of activity means that under stress, a balance between the sympathetic (excitatory) and parasympathetic (inhibitory) components of the autonomic nervous system is absent. When cardiac activity is both stimulated and inhibited, a freeze response occurs. Metaphorically this is like riding the gas and the brake at the same time. This familiar state translates into the blank, dazed look of a traumatized child, or the frozen watchfulness of a traumatized adult. Frozen states and speechless terror are often reported by trauma survivors as affective and neurophysiological legacies from their childhood trauma that fuel rapid shifts in moods. Dissociation often surfaces to inhibit the vegetative vagal system, while providing a state of surrender. In the process, dissociation serves a protective function while interfering with social interactions and expression of affect. In fact, while this psychically deadening defense regulates stress, it compromises mature emotional learning because this basal state is characterized by an avoidance of emotional contacts.

:: NEUROBIOLOGY OF TRAUMA: MULTIPLE
   EFFECTS AND AFTEREFFECTS

For more than a century, researchers have acknowledged the ways in which overwhelming traumatic experiences are stored in somatic memory and expressed with significant changes to the body. Typically, the symptomatology of PTSD or complex PTSD syndrome occurs after exposure to events that are intensely distressing. Many research studies have supported the biological changes co-occurring with the stress syndrome (Bremner, 2002; Rothschild, 2000; Siegel, 1999, 2003; van der Kolk, 1994, 2003). They include (1) psychophysiological changes, (2) shifts in neurotransmitter activity, (3) changes in the HPA hormones, (4) possible traumatic nightmares, (5) possible decreased hippocampal volume, (6) possible impairment to psychoimmunologic functioning, and (7) changes in memory (van der Kolk, 1994, p. 256). To convey the complexity of these responses, each area (see Figure 5.1) is described in fuller detail.

First, the psychophysiological effects following trauma include extreme autonomic responses that are reminiscent of the actual trauma. Alternating patterns of hyperarousal and numbness plague trauma survivors, who are disturbed regularly by startle responses, lowered thresholds to sound intensities, and a reduced electrical pattern in cortical events. Second, changes in neurotransmitter functions include shifts in noradrenergic and serotonergic functioning along with an increase in endogenous opioids. Third, to be more specific, extreme stress produces an elevation in norepinephrine, decreased glucocorticoid levels, decreased serotonin activity, and alterations in mem-

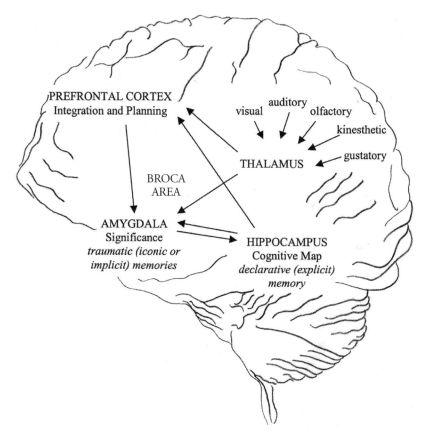

FIGURE 5.1 :: Effects of hyperarousal on declarative memory. Adapted from van der Kolk (1994).

ory. Fourth, memories are generally encoded as iconic or sensorimotor images rather than semantic or declarative content. Amnesias and hypermnesia may occur while traumatic memories are often stirred in response to noradrenergic stimulation and/or physiological arousal. Disturbing nightmares or daymares might plague the individual as their traumatic memories are reactivated. Fifth, changes in neuroanatomy include a decreased size in the hippocampus (the portion of the brain that provides a cognitive map while storing explicit declarative memory) and activation of the amygdala and connected structures during flashbacks. Sixth, there is a distinct, decreased activation of the Broca area (i.e., the speech region) during flashbacks resulting in silence, speechless terror, and, at times, mutism. Seventh, there is marked right-hemispheric lateralization, which diminishes the cognitive oversight of the prefrontal cortical region of the brain.

As discussed earlier, a structural limitation of the right brain affects an individual's capacity to regulate affect. Schore (2000, 2003) suggests that early trauma and neglect significantly alter early right brain development, which is reflected in a type D disorganized/disoriented attachment style (Main & Solomon, 1986). Consequently, this severe right brain attachment disturbance is associated with a high risk for PTSD (Schore, 1997, 1998, 2000) and a predisposition to relational violence (Lyons-Ruth & Jacobvitz, 1999; Schore, 1999, 2003).

To understand thoroughly the full complexity of trauma-related after-effects, a more detailed focus on memory is crucial to comprehend the inner worlds of traumatized adults. According to van der Kolk (1994), there are several interlocking processes in which victims of trauma experience: (1) an alteration in neurobiological processes affecting stimulus discrimination expressed as heightened arousal and decreased attention, (2) the acquisition of conditioned fear responses to trauma-related stimuli, and (3) altered cognitive schemata and social apprehension. Inevitably, these processes determine the encoding of declarative or iconic memories. Declarative (or explicit) memory refers to a conscious awareness of facts or events that have happened to an individual. This form of memory functioning is seriously affected by lesions to the frontal lobe and hippocampus in traumatized adults. On the other hand, nondeclarative, iconic (implicit) memory refers to memories of skills and habits, emotional responses, reflexive actions, and classically conditioned responses. Most researchers refer to traumatic memories as examples of iconic (implicit) memory. Thus, impairments that emerge following trauma generally lead to the organization of memory on sensorimotor or iconic levels. In more popular lexicon, theoreticians and clinicians refer to these recollections as "body memories."

One of the greatest difficulties in communicating about trauma memories may be a total or partial absence of explicit verbally encoded memories. Instead, memories have been organized on an implicit, perceptual level, without any accompanying verbal, cognitive narrative. In neuroimaging studies of people with PTSD, symptom provocation supports this clinical observation. For example, during the restimulation of traumatic memories, there is a decrease in the activation of the Broca area, the part of the brain most central to the transformation of subjective experiences into speech.

quickly questioning Maureen about the intensity of her reaction. Maureen stopped talking and settled into mutism. While Alice retreated to her garden for safety from any further verbal attack, Maureen retreated for an hour to reflect on her reaction. In her solitary state, she began to realize that the smell of the antiseptic solution reminded her of the smells that permeated her childhood home. Her association led to memories of the many cuts and wounds inflicted on her by a wildly rageful father, who tyrannized her when she was a young child. He regularly struck her with sticks and his belt, inflicting reddening welts and cuts infected by filthy splinters. After witnessing such abuse, without any active protest or direct intervention, Maureen's mother usually tended to her daughter's injuries by applying antiseptic fluid and creams. At other times, she would fastidiously cleanse the house, in a zealous effort to purge the house of shaming dirt and blood. Without any means of fighting back or rescuing her daughter from this horrendous physical abuse, both mother and daughter repetitively cleansed the wounds. Although still terrified by the abusive exchanges, Maureen felt strangely comforted by the nursing attention from her mother.

On that quiet afternoon, when Maureen smelled the antiseptic cleaning fluid, a sensorimotor memory from her childhood was immediately triggered. As she smelled the substance that was associated both with her healing and the concealment of her abuse history, her "fight/flight" response was triggered. At that moment, her experience of attack seemed as real to her as it had when she was eight years old, and, although Maureen's rational side understood that her partner was not abusive, for a fleeting moment, she perceived Alice as an abusive offender.

Maureen had always been keenly aware of her "defender" mode in response to abusive treatment to real and/or perceived criticism. However, this event taught her how powerfully the early physical abuse had been encoded in her iconic body memory. The physical abuse she suffered from ages eight to ten predisposed her to respond to olfactory stimuli that were reminiscent of those childhood traumatic events. In the language of neurophysiology, her low threshold to stimuli rendered her susceptible to an overstimulation of the thalamus, calling forth distinct sensorimotor memories of the early trauma. Consequently, full-blown retraumatization hurtled her backward to a regressive, traumatized state. Only after she had reestablished an affective equilibrium was she able to approach her partner, Alice, and discuss her emotional response.

This is most pronounced in the phenomena called "alexithymia" or "no words for feelings" that is a common symptom for trauma survivors (Schore, 2000, p. 24). Simultaneously, the areas in the right hemisphere that process intense affect, emotions, and visual images show heightened activation, particularly in the amygdala.

To bring these phenomena alive and experience-near, let me describe the typical process for information processing and memory encoding. Usually information is registered by the various senses and transmitted to the thalamus (the central relay system) and then onward to the neocortex (the "thinking" brain). Information is typically organized and assigned appropriate meaning after being ferried to the limbic system, which triggers the appropriate emotional response. In this scenario, the emotions are accommodators for the neocortex. By contrast, in a reactivated trauma scenario, an adult responds to visual, auditory, tactile, or olfactory stimuli. When this information is experienced as dangerous, given associations to an earlier iconic memory, a "fight/flight" stress response surfaces. At this point, the amygdala is activated and hijacks the process, broadcasting distress and disaster, thus triggering cascading effects of physiological responses. The person is alerted to confront danger, alternately shifting from a state of internal agitation to a phase of numbness and paralysis. Emotional reactivity, rage outbursts, "freezing," and emotional/physical paralysis may occur.

Iconic Memory

A case illustration demonstrates the dramatic phenomenon of iconic (sensorimotor) memory.

MAUREEN AND ALICE :: Maureen, a forty-year-old mental health professional, committed to couple therapy to restore her somewhat fragile fifteen-year lesbian partnership. She reported similar incidents of feeling overwhelmed by her hypervigilant, hyperalert "fighting" stance. In the midst of a calm, restful Sunday afternoon, she reported smelling strong antiseptic cleaning fluid. Her partner, Alice, expected to be thanked for her efforts to initiate a spring-cleaning spree. Instead, Maureen launched into a rageful harangue of verbal assaults, questioning how Alice could be "so unbelievably insensitive to her physical health." She wondered: Why is she trying to make me so sick? Why is Alice trying to kill me? Alice was stunned by her partner's response,

:: CLINICAL IMPLICATIONS FOR COUPLE THERAPY

An obvious question arises as to why (if at all) these neuro-psychological legacies of childhood trauma have any bearing on couple therapy. Earlier in this chapter knowledge was established that affect dysreg-ulation, startle response, and psychophysiological symptoms are prevalent aftereffects of childhood trauma that are evident among adult trauma sur-vivors. Because most of these cognitive, affective, and behavioral effects are grounded in neurophysiological changes, effective treatment might then in-clude the following adjunctive therapy approaches: psychopharmocology, cognitive–behavioral therapies (Compton & Follette, 1998), body–mind ap-proaches (Atkinson, 1999, 2002; Ogden & Minton, 2000), eye movement desensitization and reprocessing (EMDR) (Shapiro, 2001; Shapiro & Max-field, 2003), dialectical behavioral therapy (DBT) (Linehan, 1995), hypno-therapy (Brown, 1990), and various expressive therapies (e.g., drama, art, and poetry). All of these therapeutic approaches typically may be introduced in Phase I of couple therapy. However, many of these adjunctive therapies are also very useful during Phases II and III of couple therapy as well.

To explicate the couple therapy practice implications in this next section, clinical interventions are introduced that remediate several of the most cen-tral neurophysiological and neuropsychological aftereffects of childhood trauma. Once again, a complete biopsychosocial assessment will guide the de-sign of a couple therapy plan that addresses these key aftereffects. These issues include (1) affect dysregulation, (2) the pendulum of hyperarousal versus numbness, and (3) dissociation with iconic memories. Brief clinical vignettes situated in couple therapy with Nancy and Ed will illuminate these practice interventions, evident in Phase I work of their eight-month course of therapy. To deal with this couple's affect dysregulation, dissociative phenomena, and psychophysiological symptoms, a range of techniques grounded in cognitive–behavioral therapy, psychopharmacology, body–mind approaches, and psycho-education were utilized.

NANCY AND ED :: A dual-trauma couple consisting of Ed, age thirty-four, and Nancy, age thirty-five, engaged in a course of eight months of couple ther-apy. Both of these working-class, heterosexual, Caucasian marital partners of ten years had been reared in second-generation families of origin who pledged strong allegiance to their Eastern European Catholic heritages. Ed suffered

childhood physical and emotional abuse from age eighteen months throughout his childhood at the hands of his older siblings and his parents. For example, Ed regularly reported vague recollections from his preschool years of
being thrown down the stairs, along with two of his brothers, and smacked
across the head and face, under the guise of ordinary punishment. His siblings
also recall chaos in the family home that resulted in parental neglect of Ed during the first several years of his life. Shortly after Ed's younger brother was
born, his ten-year-old sister was recruited to care for him. Given her young
age and immaturity, Ed's sister often treated her baby brother like a cherished,
yet hated, doll. While dressing Ed, she frequently pinned his shirt or pants to
the toddler's skin until Ed cried uncontrollably. No adult intervened. Ed
adapted to this physical abuse by relying on dissociative defenses that were
intermittently interrupted by rage storms.

Nancy, on the other hand, adapted to sexual abuse between the ages of ten
and twelve imposed by a maternal uncle, with loud outbursts of yelling, compulsive eating, and clinical depression that persisted into adulthood. In their
marriage, Ed and Nancy regularly engaged in brutal, vicious fighting, without physical abuse. More specifically, Ed often erupted in rage storms while
Nancy hurled verbal harangues with steadfast tenacity. Overall, affect dysregulation ruled their relationship.

Affect Dysregulation and Rebalancing Affects

Before describing the specific manifestations of affect dysregulation for Ed and Nancy, a summary of some general information is indicated.
By definition, affect dysregulation manifests in a shifting pattern of affective
states from numbness to hyperarousal. As emotions are both intense and extreme, an individual has greater difficulty regulating the balance of these affective states. When more adaptive measures of coping, such as sublimation,
intellectualization, and rationalization, fail to mediate the strong affective
shifts, many survivors seek less functional adaptations. For example, many
trauma survivors turn to substance use and abuse to regulate their affects,
which, in many cases, leads to addiction. Drugs of choice may include
alcohol, benzodiazapenes, opiates, barbiturates, hallucinogenic substances,
and/or stimulants to regulate affect, by stimulating the states of numbness,
only to be followed by a need to calm hyperarousal. Compulsive behaviors
such as overeating, binging and purging food, anorexia, compulsive gam-

bling, and shopping might also serve to regulate these affective states. Other self-destructive parasuicidal behaviors, such as cutting, burning, and other modes of injuring oneself, at times, function to arouse internal stimuli while releasing opiates for a trauma survivor who is devoid of emotions. Hypo- and hypersexuality may also play important roles in regulating sexual drives and yearnings.

Another important byproduct of affect dysregulation is the eruption of "rage storms," an explosive emergence of intense anger and rage accompanied by a heightened adrenergic physical state. In contrast, an opposite stance is dissociation, where affects are isolated from the experience of the event at hand or an historical event that is being recalled. Other psychophysiological responses, such as startle responses or physical symptoms, may also occur.

In couple therapy sessions, efforts that encourage talking during "rage storms" typically fail miserably. In fact, many couple therapists who practice cognitive–behavioral approaches to promote communication or conflict resolution skills building have discovered that talking during a rage state is counterproductive. At those times, the amygdala has hijacked the client and the therapy process. Instead, a therapy plan that involves "affect-balancing" for each individual is recommended before any further verbal exchanges are undertaken. In this situation, a central therapy goal is to promote neural relaxation. More specific goals include (1) reflection on the psychophysiological buildup of sensations without talking about feelings, (2) mindfulness focus on physical sensations and affect, (3) deep breathing exercises based on relaxation training methods or Eastern spiritual techniques (e.g., yoga or meditation), and (4) activation of the "nurture-sorrow" neural circuits after the balancing of the rageful feelings (Atkinson, 2002; Ogden & Minton, 2000). This last approach suggests that when the amygdala calms following neural relaxation, an individual accesses a broader range of affects, including tenderness and sadness, that can prepare the individual for connection. From a cognitive–behavioral perspective, greater integration occurred in the integration of the affective/cognitive split, while distortions in "faulty attributions" were clarified (Basham, 1999b, p. 145; Compton & Follette, 1998).

More specifically, each partner is encouraged to identify the psychophysiological buildup, while attuning her- or himself to physical and emotional sensations. While focusing and maintaining mindfulness of physical sensations, each partner is asked to move to a state of balancing calm through the use of a body–mind technique of the client's choice. One particular clinician describes "pragmatic experiential" therapy in which he helps his clients to reach an equilibrium where one or both partners have calmed their rage responses, but then move toward accessing their vulnerabilities by activating the "nurture-sorrow" neural circuits (Atkinson, 1999, p. 31). To depathologize the adaptive function of the rage storms, he anthropomorphizes the protective "fight/flight" physiological response by referring to it as "the protector," the "scout," or the "defender." Only when affective equilibrium has been reached can each partner talk about, reflect on the symbolic meaning of the event, and reduce "faulty attributions." In this way, the neocortical functioning for each partner is activated in an effort to provide a cognitive balance to the right-brain-dominated rage eruption.

Balancing the Rage Storm

NANCY AND ED (continued) :: A return to Nancy and Ed's ongoing couple therapy journey sheds clarity on this complicated process. One day, Ed and Nancy arrived for their session in ebullient moods, talking animatedly about their enjoyment of rollerblading the day before. Within seconds, Nancy shifted to reporting a disturbing event two days earlier, which involved clearing out her work area to allow Ed more space. In their move to a new home, no particular personal area had yet been carved out for Ed. In an effort to integrate Ed's belongings into the room, Nancy started to unpack and merge some of Ed's compact discs and papers into her desk, without having involved Ed in the plan. Later in the day, when Ed unsuccessfully searched for a car registration statement, he fumbled through Nancy's desk. While digging for his receipt, Ed became increasingly furious. When Nancy arrived home, he screamed loudly that she "had no right to touch his things," followed by many vicious expletives. In the next couple therapy session, as Nancy anxiously started to describe this happening, Ed's face reddened, the volume of his voice rose steadily, his fists tightened, and he started to move frenetically back and forth in his chair.

Having witnessed a similar rage storm on other occasions, I commented to both Nancy and Ed that I observed the beginnings of an emotional escalation. Nancy remarked, "Yeah, he's at it again, misrepresenting and exaggerating what I did. I was only trying to help. He is such an ingrate!" Having received permission at the beginning of treatment to interrupt any nonproductive and/or abusive exchanges, I interrupted. "Excuse me, may I please interrupt? I hear blaming comments from you (Nancy), and I see that you (Ed) are wrestling with some very strong emotions. Are you each willing to turn away from each other for the time being? I think it is important for each of you to focus on ways that you can balance your feelings right now." Nancy turned quickly one hundred eighty degrees away from Ed and toward the wall, quietly commencing her breathing exercises. I turned to Ed, who was literally jumping up and down in his seat. I asked, "Are you willing to describe your physical sensations right now while looking directly at me?" Ed replied with agitation, speaking very loudly, and tentatively scanning me with visible fear on his face. He offered, "My hands and upper legs are trembling. I feel hot. I hate Nancy." I replied, "You started to describe your sensations and then shifted to your feelings about Nancy. For the time being, are you willing to focus on your physical sensations?" Ed replied, "There is energy pulsating through my skin. It is pressing against my legs, my stomach, and my back. I feel a lot of pressure on my back." I wondered and asked, "What do you need to do to balance your feelings?" Two minutes of silence lapsed, while Ed's legs continued to tremble. I asked, "Are you able to breathe deeply as you are experiencing your energy in your legs, your stomach, and your back?"

"Yes, I am trying," he responded quietly.

I continued, "Do you sense any reduction in tension and pressure?" Slowly, minute after minute, with long, deep, slower breaths, Ed's facial color lightened and he stared directly at me, a gaze that helped to ground his unsteady mood state.

In the meantime, Nancy had been deeply engrossed in her own self-reflection. I asked for each of them to alert me when they thought they had achieved sufficient balance in their feelings to resume talking together. After five minutes, Nancy said that she was ready. Since Ed was still struggling to balance his affect, I asked if she was willing to wait five more minutes, and I would check with Ed. After five more minutes, Ed volunteered that he would talk with Nancy and me again. While Ed reflected on feeling attacked and responding, in his words, "primitively," he stated that he needed "to fight back for survival when Nancy mistreated him." As I affirmed that Ed's protective "defender" was activated when he experienced a threat from Nancy, he acknowledged that he had felt terrified, "even though it does not make sense!" Ed offered that when Nancy moved his possession, the paper receipt, he was reminded of how ignored and neglected he was as a young child when his needs were overlooked. When Ed yelled that his "integrity" was threatened, it initially did not make sense. It became quite clear though that Ed's rage was initially triggered in the midst of a traumatic reenactment where he experienced Nancy's handling of his possession as a boundary transgression. His sense of psychological and physical integrity was violated in ways that were reminiscent of the physical abuse that his sisters and parents had inflicted on him in early childhood. Ed's augmented rage response signaled retraumatization in process, based on early childhood abuse and neglect.

However, when Ed was overwhelmed by his rage, a therapy approach that attended to cognitive and verbal exchanges would have been inappropriate. Instead, it was imperative to call a "time out" to the verbal dialogue and allow each partner to rebalance their neurophysiological states before proceeding with any discussion. Only after the "rage storm" had subsided could this neocortical reflection on the retraumatization experience be helpful. Both partners gained understanding about the event, while empathy between the partners strengthened. In the language of cognitive–behavioral therapy, Ed's distorted thinking or "faulty attributions" of the retraumatization were ultimately understood more clearly without emotional reactivity. However, this could occur only after Ed and Nancy were able to find ways to balance their affect. In this process, both partners were also able to achieve greater integration of their splitting in affect and cognition.

Dissociative Phenomena

Another typical neurophysiological response expressed by trauma survivors is dissociation. Since this defense serves to protect an individual from experiencing the full emotional intensity of a given event, such an adaptation serves to titrate the direct expression of affect between partners in a couple. The clinical vignette of Nancy and Ed demonstrates the use of psychoeducational interventions to reduce misunderstanding and anxiety related to dissociative phenomena.

NANCY AND ED (continued) :: Nancy frequently criticized Ed because he had difficulty remembering and following through on promises that he had made to her about planning for social events or general household chores. A small criticism often ballooned into a litany of complaints about Ed's "alleged bad memory." In the meantime, Nancy prided herself on completing lists and plans to compensate for what she saw as Ed's problems with concentration and attentiveness. What emerged in one couple therapy session was a typical dynamic of the alternating "victim–victimizer–bystander" dynamic, with Nancy launching into a victimizing role by criticizing Ed for his "poor memory," and Ed then retaliating in a victimizing stance about what he views as Nancy's "abject intolerance." Ed then shut down or remained silent for several minutes. Nancy attacked him for being "cowardly and unwilling to engage in a discussion."

On one occasion, during a discussion about the sequelae of childhood trauma, we talked about the phenomena of dissociation as a protective adaptation. While discussing how dissociation creates divisions between content and affect, while also interrupting memory and a sense of time, Nancy's indignant demeanor softened. She felt increasing empathy toward Ed as she started to understand that the legacies of his childhood trauma interfered with his capacities to plan for the future, while also enjoying the present. Ed sighed with tremendous relief as he noted that maybe "forgetting" has something to do with his coping, rather than being evidence of his "unworthiness and deficiencies." Because Ed's shutdowns from talking were so pronounced, we discussed the physiological responses of the deactivated Broca area of the brain in the midst of a stress response. Rather than seeing Ed as morally defective, both partners understood that, at those moments of mutism, Ed was experiencing trauma-related alexithymia. Although Nancy had compensated with what appeared to be some depression-related symptomatology such as concentration and attention problems, she acknowledged that she took antidepressant medications to alleviate trauma-related symptoms of clinical depression. In the end, rather than vilifying Ed for memory gaps, both partners shared ways that each of them might understand and compensate for these symptoms and behaviors.

Psychophysiological Responses

As discussed earlier in this chapter, many survivors of childhood trauma experience a wide range of physiological symptoms and sensations, including startle responses, hyperarousal, numbness, and somatic memories. Clinical interventions that are grounded in cognitive–behavioral therapy, body–mind approaches, and psychoeducation are typically useful here.

NANCY AND ED (continued) :: A return to Ed and Nancy's clinical journey brings us to various neurophysiological symptoms that each partner reported in the course of treatment. This couple's sexual relationship had dete-
riorated in the past two years, in part, exacerbated by heightened stress related
to the death of Nancy's mother and the divorce of Ed's parents. Their interactional pattern, rooted in the "victim–victimizer–bystander" dynamic, intensified with increased emotional abuse, power conflicts, and distancing.
Both partners complained that their sexual relationship had become a battleground, in which neither person chose to yield to the other's requests or needs.
When Nancy complained that her efforts to approach Ed were met with sharp
rejection, what unfolded was a description of Ed's hypervigilance and startle
response. During moments of occasional tenderness, Nancy would approach
Ed by caressing his neck and shoulders, in hopes of inspiring some reciprocation of physical affection. Instead, Ed startled abruptly, and yelled at Nancy,
"You should know I hate to be surprised. What is the matter with you?" Nancy
immediately felt hurt and wounded, sharp emotions that quickly converted
into rage and retaliative criticism. In one of our many psychoeducational discussions concerning the neurophysiological legacies of trauma, we talked
about a startle response as a signal to danger. At those moments, an historical
"fight/flight" response was activated that placed Ed's neural system on hyperalert. As Nancy and Ed understood the historical ghosts that plagued their intimate moments, Ed asked Nancy to speak to him first, rather than surpris-
ing him. He also asked her if she would be willing to touch him on the arm
when she reached out to him, rather than on the neck area. The region of his
neck was associated with vivid recollections of physical abuse when his older
sister grabbed him by the hair and neck, choking him until he complied with
her dictates. As a result, touching this area was met instantly with a startle response and mobilization of the "defender." An important feature in this clinical intervention was to maintain the locus of control with the client, in this
case, facilitating the empowerment of each partner to gain some control and
mastery over the couple's sexual relationship.

Nancy reported little interest in sex, expressing concern about what she described as a physical numbness as well as a heightened sensitivity to touch on
her arms and legs. Her shame about what she thought was her sexual inade-
quacy was reinforced by Ed's criticisms about her unresponsiveness. When it
became apparent that Nancy had adapted to her traumatic experiences of molestation by her uncle by generally "numbing out," in contrast, her physical

sensitivity on her arms and legs was heightened with reports that "her skin felt singed and burned." She experienced virtually no feeling at all in her clitoral/vaginal area. To enable both partners to appreciate each other's sexual wishes, as well as anxieties, discussion ensued about ways to enhance their sexual relationship. Because many trauma survivors are betrayed by "rules" set by offending adults, the notions of rules or contracts in the sexual arena are inevitably fraught with emotional upset. Instead, partners often find it useful to think about constructing parameters around what feels like comfortable, sensual, and erotic touch, as compared with uncomfortable or frightening touch. Both Ed and Nancy talked about how they were interested in enhancing the sensuality in their relationship first, before they attempted to resume intercourse or oral sex, activities that had receded from their sexual lives in the past two years. They agreed that they would experiment with some sensate focus exercises (Cole & Rothblum, 1988; Kaplan, 1974; LoPiccolo & LoPiccolo, 1978; Maltz, 1994; McCarthy, 1990; Schnarch, 1991; Wilson & James, 1992) to enhance their physical sensations, starting with nonerogenous zones. Typically, they agreed ahead of time about a set of parameters regarding touch. They also agreed that before embarking on any sensual or sexual activity, they would check with each other to see if each partner was in accord. Gradually, Nancy and Ed were able to reflect on, enjoy, and, ultimately, talk about what their various sensual experiences were like for them. With increasing physical sensitivity and emotional trust, they chose to expand their parameters to erogenous zones as well.

Since Nancy reported "electrical sensations" in her arms and legs, she and Ed experimented with massaging those areas while in water. She found that the soothing touch of water with bath oils tempered the heightened sensitivity of her skin and enabled her to relax. As she regained some level of sensual feeling in her arms, she recalled early traumatic memories. Recollections of intense pain surfaced reminiscent of the time when her uncle forced her to submit to intercourse, while pinning her arms and legs against the bed. In those early years, her body had encoded these terrifying memories in her skin, a human being's usual protective external boundary from threats. In Nancy's case, her skin signaled danger and high alert during these horrific childhood experiences.

In summary, the combination of psychoeducation, body–mind approaches, psychopharmacology, and cognitive–behavioral interventions enabled Ed and Nancy to develop a more mutually caring, respectful, and nonabusive relationship. Both partners were tentatively able to strengthen empathy toward the other while renewing their love and sexual satisfaction. However, the paths toward this positive change included careful attention to the appropriate timing of body–mind and cognitive–behavioral verbal approaches to couple therapy. Clearly, the extensive literature on the neurophysiology and neuropsychology of trauma has taught us that neural relaxation of rage responses and psychophysiological symptoms should precede the increased understanding that occurs with psychoeducation and use of cognitive–behavioral methods.

In line with our focus on the individual aftereffects or legacies of childhood traumatic experiences, our focus now shifts from the neurophysiological effects on individuals to an exploration of the inner world through the theoretical lenses of object relations and attachment theories. Although these perspectives primarily address intrapsychic phenomena, the effects on the couple relationship are also explored.

6

Object Relations Theory

        This chapter elaborates the key object relations theories that we utilize when we assess and treat couples. We recognize that object relations theory is broadly defined and originates from many sources. We begin this chapter with a brief overview of object relations theorists. Then, we focus our discussion on the object relations theories of Mahler, Pine, and Bergman (1975), Fairbairn (1952a, 1952b, 1963), and Winnicott (1956, 1958), which have particular utility in our work with survivors of childhood trauma, and we highlight aspects of their theories that address the role of trauma.

First, we discuss the contributions of Mahler, Pine, and Bergman. Their conceptualizations of separation–individuation theory have become the starting point for many object relations formulations that have been applied to couple systems (Bader & Pearson, 1988; Basham & Miehls, 1998a; Lachkar, 1992; Scharff & Savege Scharff, 1991; Sharpe, 2000). As such, their ideas form a foundation for the following discussion concerning the assessment of object constancy of the individuals in the couple system. We view the individual developmental achievement of object constancy to be a key factor that needs to be determined for each partner of the couple system. The clinician is able to engage couples in Phase II (reflection of trauma narrative) and Phase III (consolidation of new perspectives, attitudes, and behaviors) work that involves titrated affective reexperiencing when the partners are able to hold complex images of each other, even when their needs are frustrated. This is a central component of object constancy. As discussed in the treatment section of the book, Phase I work is useful with all couples. Phase II and Phase III therapeutic work involves a cognitive reflection on the trauma narrative, with ego supportive interventions. In some instances, it is clinically indicated to utilize object relations theory to promote insight in the couple system, through clarification of projective identification processes. This type of introspection is best suited for couples who possess object constancy. In general, object relations theories inform the clinical interventions at different phases of treatment, whether they are aimed toward ego support and/or insight. Clearly, a major strength of object relations theory is the focus on relationship issues.

Second, the conceptualizations of W. R. D. Fairbairn (1952) are highlighted as another relevant theoretical framework for understanding the process in which individuals appear to seek relationships that reenact earlier traumatic experiences. Fairbairn's concept of the internal saboteur (Fairbairn, 1952; Greenberg & Mitchell, 1983) explicates the motivations of individuals who seek out relationships with others who are fundamentally hostile and rejecting.

Third, D. W. Winnicott's (1956, 1992) concepts of the holding environment, good-enough mothering, the capacity to be alone, and the ability to use objects to modulate aggression are also woven into both assessment and treatment of couples who are survivors of childhood trauma. Given the central importance of and linkage to object relations theory, attachment theory (Ainsworth, Blehar, Waters, & Wall, 1978; Bowlby, 1969; Fonagy, 2001; Johnson, 2002; Main, 1995) will be discussed thoroughly in the following chapter of the text.

:: A BRIEF SYNOPSIS OF OBJECT
   RELATIONS THEORY

Greenberg and Mitchell (1983) note that all psychoanalytic theories contain theories of object relations (p. 14), and as such, we recognize the utility of providing a broad generalized description of object relations. According to these authors, "The term thus designates theories, or aspects of theories, concerned with exploring the relationship between real, external people and internal images and residues of relations with them, and the significance of these residues for psychic functioning" (p. 12). While there is no singular definition that can adequately capture the complexity of theorizing about object relations, it is our working definition that every person forms an internal sense of self and other that has been shaped largely by one's interactions with primary caretakers. In turn, these conscious and unconscious views of self and other influence our perceptions of others and our behavior toward others. In other words, object relations fundamentally affect how one behaves in interpersonal relationships. As such, the intimate couple relationship is often viewed as a relationship in which the object relational world of each partner is fundamentally and urgently activated (Basham & Miehls, 1998a; Catherall, 1992; Lachkar, 1992; Sharpe, 2000; Siegel, 1991; Willi, 1982). Miehls (1997) suggests that "Object relations theory underscores that an individual is dramatically influenced and shaped by the interpersonal exchange(s) with an intimate partner" (p. 9). Object relations theorists also suggest that individuals will unconsciously couple with an "other" who holds the promise of providing a corrective emotional experience for them (Bader & Pearson, 1988; Solomon, 1989).

Object relations theorists are often broadly grouped into two schools, the American and the British (Melano Flanagan, 1996). The American school of object relations theorists furthered the thinking of ego psychologists such as Hartmann (1939), who essentially viewed object relations as one specific function of the ego. Ego psychologists, for the most part, "retained Freud's instinctual and mechanistic emphasis and . . . tended to minimize the more personal impact of the caretaking and social environment" (Goldstein, 2001, p. 22). However, based on the observations of direct mother–child interactions, authors such as Jacobson and Mahler focused more on the developing infant and how one builds up an internalized representation of self and other. While these theoreticians attempted to stay true to some of Freud's dual instinct and structural theories, Goldstein asserts, "Jacobson and Mahler usually are credited with building object relations thinking into ego psychology" (p. 22). Another theorist from the American school, Otto Kernberg (1975, 1976), wrote extensively about the integration of drive theory with object relations theory. He wrote about individuals diagnosed with personality disorders.

The British school of object relations has shaped our current views of object relations. Mitchell and Black (1995) note that Melanie Klein was the theorist who provided the bridge between Freudian theory and contemporary British object relations theories. They note that Klein redefined "the nature of 'drive' to include built-in human objects" (p. 113) and that she "portrayed a distinctly human infant from the start" (p. 113). Goldstein (2001) notes that "like Freud, Klein emphasized the power of the instincts, particularly the aggressive drive, but unlike him, she argued that the goal of life was relationships with others (objects) rather than instinctual gratification" (p. 31). Klein's views were controversial and contributed to a schism within the

British Psychoanalytic Society. While some analysts supported her theorizing, others remained loyal to more traditional Freudian concepts, including a group headed by Anna Freud. In addition, a third or independent group began to articulate theories that became known as the British object relations school.

Mitchell and Black (1995) note, "The major figures in this middle group, W. R. D. Fairbairn, D. W. Winnicott, Michael Balint, John Bowlby, and Harry Guntrip, all built on Klein's vision of an infant wired for human interaction" (p. 113). However, these authors moved away from Klein's ideas that infants have innate aggression that fuels their interactions with others. These middle group authors recognized that infant development was crucially influenced by the quality of the parenting that individuals experienced. Impingements that obscure a positive connection between parent and child are, at times, experienced as traumatic by the infant. Fundamentally, it is this group of authors who held to the notion that infant's object relations are shaped by the interaction between infant and caretaker. In their writings, these authors emphasized that the fundamental *drive* in object relations theory is the child's drive for attachment or relationship with another person.

:: SEPARATION–INDIVIDUATION THEORY:
MAHLER, PINE, AND BERGMAN

Mahler, a pediatrician and child analyst, moved to the United States from Hungary in the late 1930s. She initially studied emotionally disturbed children, which led her to formulations of childhood autism and symbiosis (Mahler, 1968). In New York City, Mahler and her colleagues established a center that functioned as a research laboratory. They invited young mothers and their children to attend their center. In this setting, the mothers benefited from socialization and support with other new mothers while the research team made observations of mother–child interaction that shaped the foundation theory of the separation–individuation process. Mahler et al. (1975) explicated this process in their groundbreaking text, *The Psychological Birth of the Infant: Symbiosis and Individuation*. The theory is essential to understanding how an individual develops a separate, individuated, and autonomous self out of the early mother–child matrix.

Two main critiques of separation–individuation theory need to be voiced. First, this theory privileges autonomy and independence as highly valued developmental achievements. The values of individualism and separation are culture bound and most aptly described as a "Western, white middle class, male belief system of mental health" (Melano Flanagan, 1996, p. 158). Separation–individuation theory is not universally relevant cross-culturally. Second, as this theory postulates *stages* of development, it is often seen as a linear model of development that has definitive fixed points of maturation. In fact, separation–individuation theory provides a template of development that has variability. Pine (1985) suggests that rather than a fixed linear development, individuals experience "developmental moments" in which the themes and work of each stage of development predominate. In other words, when a child is considered to be in a symbiotic stage of development, maturation will center on symbiotic themes. However, this does not mean that the child is characterized only by tasks of that particular stage at that particular rigid time period. Rather, Pine notes that individuals will achieve development throughout one's maturation; he recognizes that complex individuals cannot be reduced to mechanistic accomplishments of a certain stage of development. Similarly for couples, partners do not move through stages of separation–individuation development in a stepwise fashion. Couple systems also have dominant themes that are highlighted at different moments in treatment. With these two critiques in mind, we now briefly describe the developmental trajectory that Mahler et al. (1975) termed separation–individuation theory.

These authors suggested that newborn infants are born into a period of autism in which they are immersed in their own orbit and unaware of their surroundings. Mahler proposed that the newborn lacks the capacity to be aware of external objects and that the newborn's activities are centered on keeping a sense of physiological homeostasis. Summarizing Mahler, Greenberg and Mitchell (1983) say, "The infant is concerned only with the satisfaction of its needs, with tension reduction, and operates according to the principle of hallucinatory wish fulfillment rather than locating possible sources of satisfaction in the external world" (p. 274). St. Clair (1996) says, "In terms of object relations, this first stage is objectless" (p. 113). However, more current infant researchers present different views concerning autism. Beebe and Lachman (1988) and Stern (1985) fundamentally challenge the concept of normal autism that Mahler, Bergman, and Pine proposed. Stern suggests that infants do not ever have a time period in which they lack awareness of people in their environment. Stern notes, "In autism there is a generally selective lack of interest in or avoidance of human stimuli. That is never the case with normal infants" (p. 234). Stern acknowledges that infants develop an increasing capacity for social relatedness, but comments, "The infant never was autistic and cannot become less so. The process is rather the continuous unfolding of an intrinsically determined social nature" (p. 234). In fact, Stern notes that Mahler updated her own view of normal autism and conveyed to him that the initial phase might have been called "awakening" (p. 235). Stern contends that the infant is ready at birth to engage in interactions with others.

Mahler, Bergman, and Pine, however, saw the emergence from the autistic state as a crucial process that enables the infant to develop a symbiosis or delusion of a common boundary when he or she begins to appreciate that there is another person who is assisting in his/her ability to reduce tension. Symbiosis is conceptualized as a normative process in which the infant experiences a sense of merger with the caretaking person. During this time (from four to six weeks to four to six months), the child develops a basic sense of security and safety. At this point, the infant's experience is one of fusion with the caregiver. As such, the infant operates as if she and the caretaking person are psychologically one unit. The infant begins to organize experiences with caregivers as either "good" (responsive) or "bad" (frustrating), and these set the template for further psychological integration of these early experiences that split the responses of caregivers into these rigid categories. If the infant does not experience an adequate symbiosis and is unable to maintain a delusion of a common boundary, she would likely experience some aspects of annihilation anxiety. A ruptured symbiosis will leave the child feeling panicked, traumatized, and fearful that psychological and/or physical survival is unattainable. Termed annihilation anxiety, an infant will feel overwhelmed when the delusion of the common boundary is ruptured. An infant will not be able to develop a basic sense of trust if she is traumatized in this early phase of development. Rather, she will approach relationships with suspicion and fear.

Physiological and psychological maturation propel the infant into the beginning phases of separation–individuation proper. The child moves through phases of differentiation, practicing, rapprochement, and on-the-way-to-object-constancy. Again, there is some variability, but generally, children are thought to develop the capacity for object constancy at approximately age three. This theory, then, is considered a "pre-oedipal" theory, with the emphasis on achievement of early development. Goldstein (2001) notes that new treatments for depression and borderline and narcissistic pathology were formulated as a result of separation–individuation theory (p. 28). Horner (1984) illustrates the application of separation–individuation theory to individual psychotherapy with a range of individuals. In couple systems, an assessment of separation–individuation themes elucidates the partners' capacity to engage in increasingly complex interpersonal relationships.

During differentiation, a child begins to develop the capacity to perceive differences in her experience with that of her caretaking person. Physically, the child is no longer satisfied with complete molding with the caretaker, and increasingly finds ways to begin to separate from her. The child may arch her back or show other indications of wanting to have physical space between herself and her caretaker. She begins to explore differences and develops an acute interest in cataloguing body parts as either yours or mine. When infants explore a caregiver's hair, nose, or eyeglasses, the intent is to begin to establish a sense of inner and outer reality and to begin to discern what is part of me and what is part of the other.

The practicing subphase is a highly exploratory time for the child. Characterized as having a "love affair with the world" (Greenacre, 1957), or experiencing the "world as its oyster" (Mahler et al., 1975), the child is at the height of her grandiosity and takes increasing pleasure in her explorations and accomplishments. The child is also able to experience pleasure in seeking out objects other than her primary caretaker and seems to operate with a sense of invulnerability. This invulnerability is fueled by the child's confusion of what aspects of her caretaker she carries inside of herself. While the child has some recognition that her caretaker is not the same physical person, there is still a belief that the child and caretaker are psychologically fused. Thus, behaviors that might seem reckless, such as running to the edge of the ocean without any recognition of danger, are understood as a demonstration of the child's inadequate recognition of what is herself and what is mother.

In fact, when the child becomes aware that the caretaker is not physically or psychologically joined with her, she experiences a period of confusion and apprehension for the toddler. Often a painful and difficult time for both the child and the caretaker, the toddler experiences a "rapprochement crisis," becoming aware that indeed the world is not her oyster and that she is vulnerable and still needs further connection with her caregiver. The child's needs

oscillate between an intense clingy approach and an equally intense opposi-
tional stance to the caretaker. Termed "ambitendency," this phase is characterized by the toddler's wish to be close and the wish to be separate; these
contrasting wishes fuel two enduring fears—the fear of engulfment and the
fear of abandonment (Mahler et al., 1975; Melano Flanagan, 1996, p. 162).
The toddler attempts to reconcile the notions that one does not need to be
psychologically taken over by closeness with another, or that some psychological distance between two people does not necessarily lead to unbearable
isolation. These issues are often activated within an intimate couple relationship. Traumatic experiences during this phase of development often
cripple the survivor with a view of others as being both torturously available
and/or torturously unavailable.

The last phase of separation–individuation theory is termed "on-the-way-
to-object-constancy" (Melano Flanagan, 1996, p. 164) or "libidinal object
constancy" (Greenberg & Mitchell, 1983, p. 279). During this phase of development, which is chronologically observed to occur during and through
the child's third year of life, "the child must attain a sense of his own indi-
viduality, as well as a sense of the other as an internal, positively cathected
presence" (p. 279). Here, the child's task is to continue to view the caretaker
as a good person even while one's needs are being frustrated. Melano Flanagan says it is "the capacity to retain belief in the goodness of the object even
when it is not being gratifying in the moment" (p. 164). When the child (or
an adult who has not attained object constancy) is unable to maintain these
contradictory states, she will use splitting as a defense mechanism. This cat-
egorizing of oneself or others as either "all good" or "all bad" is often witnessed in dyads with object relational impairments.

We now describe how separation–individuation theory is utilized in assessment and treatment of couple systems. Key to this process is the clinician's assessment of whether or not the individuals have the capacity for object constancy. Also important is to note the use of projective identification,
another commonly used defense mechanism utilized in couple systems,
which will be elaborated.

Separation–Individuation Theory and Couple Systems

When individuals have achieved object constancy, there is an opportunity to develop increasingly satisfying intimate couple partnerships

(Bader & Pearson, 1988; Cashdan, 1988; Mitchell, 1988, 1993; Sharpe, 2000; St. Clair, 1996). Scharff and Savege Scharff (1991) point out that there is a dynamic interplay between one's intrapersonal world and one's interpersonal relationships. A number of theorists suggest that individuals often consciously or unconsciously hope that their partners will provide a relationship opportunity for a corrective experience to ameliorate earlier developmental frustrations (Lachkar, 1992; Miehls, 1993; Sharpe, 2000; Solomon, 1989). Each person's internal world in part determines the felt satisfaction or dissatisfaction he or she derives from the interpersonal relationship. Object relations theories appreciate a fundamental dialectic in couple relationships—that each individual's intrapsychic world influences the couple relationship dynamic while the couple relationship affects the individual intrapsychic world of both partners.

As noted in the assessment chapter, the clinician scrutinizes a number of object relational capacities to determine the level of intervention that might benefit the couple. Determinations of level of anxieties and the attainment of object constancy are crucial factors in making treatment decisions. Object relations theories explicate different levels of anxiety that coincide with developmental achievement. Schamess (1996) outlines the levels of anxiety:

- Annihilation anxiety: a pervasive sense of not being able to survive if one is not psychologically connected to another person. The individual feels that she will "fall apart," "go crazy," or disintegrate if the relationship becomes troubled. Subjectively, the individual feels overwhelming terror. This anxiety is initially experienced in the first year of life.
- Loss of object anxiety (abandonment anxiety): a pervasive sense that one will be left alone to manage internal and external threats. For children, it is originally experienced in the second and third years of life. Adults who experience this anxiety may demonstrate clingy, dependent behavior in their relationships or conversely may act out by pretending that they do not need connection with others.
- Loss of love of the object anxiety: a pervasive sense that one will be disapproved of or not loved by primary caregivers. For children, it is usually experienced in the third and fourth years of life. Adults who experience this anxiety are very conscious of what others think of them and often seek unconditional approval from others.

- Fear of bodily harm anxiety (castration anxiety): a pervasive fear that one's mental or physical capacities will be lost if there is a rupture in the relationship. For children, it is experienced at ages four to six and is predicated on the belief that the parent will punish the child for having hostile wishes against the parent.

In object relations theory, the clinician always assesses whether a person has the capacity to see the other as a "whole" object, or a part object, viewing the other as simply a need gratifier. If partners use each other as part-objects, how does the couple enact this? Is this way of interacting mixed with a repetition of a sexual abuse history in addition to object relations impairment? Some individuals have experienced childhood trauma that further exacerbates earlier object relations disruptions. While many couples may show an ability to be empathically attuned to each other when the relationship is going smoothly, is this capacity present during times of conflict? If so, to what extent does the conflict challenge the strength of the couple's object constancy? Table 6.1 summarizes characteristics of couples at different development levels. A narrative description of separation–individuation theory applied to couples follows.

Separation–Individuation Themes in Couple Systems

Bader and Pearson (1988) and Sharpe (2000) apply Mahler's theory of separation–individuation to the developmental processes that many couples experience. As individuals, couples do not move through phases of development in a linear fashion. Rather, we listen for themes that reflect evidence of symbiotic, practicing, or rapprochement issues in the couple's interaction. The questions in the following subsections aim to assess a couple's possible symbiotic merger.

Symbiotic Themes

Does this couple demonstrate a sense of enmeshment that seems to be related to a wish for a symbiotic merger with each other? Is either partner threatened if his or her partner attempts to initiate any aspects of differentiation? Is there an unspoken injunction that the couple needs to stay symbiotically attached? At times, couples enact a pattern of hostile–dependent interactions. In these couple systems, the main theme is the inability to live together coupled with the inability to live separately. In these systems, the

TABLE 6.1 :: Couple Characteristics: Separation–Individuation Theory

Phase of Development	Developmental Themes	Interpersonal Style	Intervention Strategies
Symbiosis/merger	Wish for enmeshment or emotional isolation Annihilation anxiety Need gratification prevails	Discouragement of partner differentiation Hostile–dependent (victim–victimizer exchanges) Unconscious projective identification patterns with affects and conflicts projected onto partner	Establishment of safety/security Cognitive/behavioral interventions Affect regulation Encouragement of beginning differentiation
Practicing themes	Wish for exploration Narcissistic pursuit of goals Abandonment anxiety	Partner as impediment to self-development Narcissistic envy/rage	Legitimizing individual pursuits while staying in relationship Management of rage responses
Rapprochement themes	Ambitendency/ ambivalence Approach/avoidance conflicts Domination/control issues Loss of love of the object Anxiety	Partner becomes repository of closeness/distance issues. Minimal empathy Conscious projective identification of negative affects and conflicts onto partner Splitting as a defense	Furthering stability/ security Cognitive–behavioral interventions Diffusing power struggles Developing beginning capacity for empathy and beginning clarification of projective identification patterns
Object constancy	Capacity to hold complex understanding of relationship, even when frustrated Ability to hold on to internal images of self and other	Ambivalent views of partner do not threaten relationship Ability to delay needs Ability to empathize	Attaching insight to projective identification patterns Re-storying of trauma narrative

verbalized mantra would sound something like, "I can't live with him, but I can't live without him." Couples with trauma histories may reenact "victim–victimizer–bystander" exchanges and may be vulnerable to physically acting out against each other. What is the primary anxiety experienced in this couple system? Is it largely abandonment anxiety, or is there a more regressive pull toward annihilation anxiety for either partner when the symbiosis is threatened? Can the partners engage in any activities that are separate from each other, or is there an injunction to always be together? In short, can either partner tolerate any expression of difference in the areas of thoughts, feelings, or behaviors?

Practicing Themes

Here, one member of the dyad may become more exploratory and decide to pursue individual interests, regardless of the response of his or her partner. Concern for the partner's wishes is not considered, and one or both partners may have an unbridled enthusiasm for new activities. Within the couple system, individuals who are experiencing wishes for a "love affair with the world" may indeed have initiated a love affair with another person. Is there a sense that the commitment to the relationship is being challenged by one partner's grandiosity or narcissism? At times of stress, do the individuals experience abandonment anxiety, or is the primary anxiety a loss of love of the object? What is the level of empathy within the system? Is there the ability to empathize, even cognitively, with the partner's trauma story? Or is there a lack of empathic connection (Lansky, 1986; Miehls, 1993; Solomon, 1989)? Narcissistic envy may also precipitate competition and agitation if one partner feels that his partner is being viewed by the outside world as more successful than he. We often observe that highly successful couples become vindictive and arrogant toward each other. This demonstrates a failure of object constancy along with a tendency to become narcissistically rageful if one perceives his partner as standing in the way of individual pursuits and ambitions.

Rapprochement Themes

Ambitendency about the relationship often characterizes the emotional tone of a couple that wrestles with rapprochement themes. The capacity to hold a coherent sense of self is challenged in these systems when either one or both partners have dynamic conflicts in the area of closeness/distance. Does the couple demonstrate severe oscillations between closeness and distance? Is there increased anxiety when one partner pushes for emotional closeness? Rather than suffering annihilation anxiety, couples experiencing rapprochement issues will likely experience anxiety as loss of love at times of conflict. Is there a capacity to share angry or rageful feelings toward the partner without symbolically destroying him (Benjamin, 1992; Miehls, 1999; Winnicott, 1971)?

In addition to these developmental themes, we assess a couple's use of projective identification in the system. Intimate partnerships that are characterized by closeness, intensity, and repetitive interactions often become characterized by exchanges that are punctuated with patterns of mutual projective identification. Klein (1948) initially described projective identification as a process in which an individual projected a disowned aspect of self onto another, without the other person's participation. We find Ogden's (1982) working definition to be useful, clinically. Ogden (1982) comments that projective identification serves four functions in the process of individual psychotherapy. Projective identification often means that the therapist feels some disavowed affect of the client, about which the client is unaware. This dynamic occurs regularly among couples. First, it is "a type of defense by which one can distance oneself from an unwanted or internally dangerous part of the self" (p. 36). Second, he also views it as a type of communication in which the person who projects is trying to increase the empathic attunement of the recipient to the projector. Third, Ogden states that projective identification is a type of object-relatedness in which the person who is projecting maintains some separate sense of self from the recipient so that the recipient can be viewed as a receptor of the projector's feelings but also is "sufficiently undifferentiated to maintain the illusion of literally sharing the projector's feeling" (p. 37). Lastly, Ogden sees projective identification as a potential pathway for psychological change. If the recipient of a projection can process the psychological material in a manner that is not distorted or feared, as is the case of the originator of the feeling, then there is the possibility that the recipient can serve as an object of identification and potential "teacher." In other words, the person with unwanted and disavowed feelings may witness new and healthier ways of dealing with feared and discarded feelings, given that the recipient of the projection demonstrates that it is possible to manage these feelings or psychological processes in adaptive and growth-promoting ways.

Couple systems, through exchanges of multiple projective identification processes, can be viewed as interactional systems that provide a potential opportunity for individual growth for each partner. The unconscious wish that one's partner will offer some aspect of corrective experiences has been previously noted. For example, Miehls (1997) suggests, "The dynamic interplay of intimate partners offers the opportunity for the system to take a mutual responsibility in finding a solution to the psychological dilemma" (p. 10). Object relations theorists note that each individual in a couple often uses projective identification to attempt to maintain balance in his/her own intrapsychic world (Catherall, 1992; Miehls, 1997; Sharpe, 2000; Siegel, 1991; Solomon, 1997; Zinner & Shapiro, 1972). Describing the reciprocal nature of the interactions, Sharpe (1997) says that "*Mutual projective identification* occurs when two persons, either patient and therapist or both partners of the couple, engage in this activity" (p. 41; italics in the original). Siegel also describes the attempts of individuals in intimate partnerships to shape each other through projective identification mechanisms. As projective identification can occur on either an unconscious or conscious level, it is important to appreciate that disavowed internal conflicts are often projected onto one's partner, followed by an attempt to engage the partner behaviorally in such a way that she feels compelled to enact some aspect of the projector's disowned conflict.

As couples often share different dimensions of dynamic conflicts, it is difficult to discern which partner owns, in his internal world, the projection. Indeed, it is often therapeutic for each partner to understand cognitively what his part of the conflict is, to affectively reprocess the dynamic in therapy and to reinternalize an updated and more adaptive response to the dynamic issue. Careful examination of the therapist's personal experience with any particular couple can aid in the understanding of the couple's projective identification patterns. Are you, as therapist, compelled to take in the projections of one or both partners? Are you aware of feeling compelled to work outside of your usual therapeutic frame? If so, is this as a result of falling into a countertransference trap (Chu, 1988) that is reflective of a projective identification process between the couple and the clinician?

It is challenging to work with and unravel projective identifications in the therapeutic endeavor, especially as it can be difficult and anxiety producing. Individuals who have not achieved any measure of object constancy will not be able to tolerate this sort of exploratory therapeutic work affectively.

To complete an object relational assessment of the couple system, it is useful to look at a number of parameters that strengthen a differential assessment of each partner's object relational capacity. There are three main vehicles to complete an object relations assessment of the couple system. With cross-confirmation in the following three domains, the validity of the object relations assessment is strengthened. First, the therapist should clearly be able to discern the relational themes in the couple's interactional patterns. Second, speculations about object relations are possible by gathering a thorough history of family-of-origin patterns. Speculations about the stability of the family-of-origin contribute to the clinician's understanding of the individuals. Last, the manner in which each partner positions him- or herself with the therapist provides additional data about the partner's object relational capacity and achievements.

:: W. R. D. FAIRBAIRN

As previously mentioned, our assessment model and intervention strategies are also influenced by the work of W. R. D. Fairbairn, a Scottish analyst who maintained close connections with the British Psychoanalytic Society. Fairbairn elaborated a model of object relations theory that clearly emphasizes that individuals are driven to be connected to another person (Goldstein, 2001; Greenberg & Mitchell, 1983; Mitchell & Black, 1995; St. Clair, 1996). Fairbairn challenged Freudian theory and envisioned "a unitary, integral ego with its own libidinal energy, seeking relations with real external objects" (Greenberg & Mitchell, p. 163). His basic premise is that each individual's ego seeks relationships with real people who are external to him- or herself. He proposed that the ego stays whole or intact as long as these external relationships are satisfactory. However, if the individual is frustrated, rejected, or disappointed by the external object, the ego splits into three different parts; this splitting is viewed as the ego's adaptation to the rejection by the external other. St. Clair notes, "In short, the ego's frustrating relationships with objects becomes internal, and these inner objects become active structures within the psyche" (p. 57).

Fairbairn's "endopsychic structure," as it is called, is determined by the individual necessity to find homeostatic responses to frustrating objects. In fact, Fairbairn suggests that when real relationships are satisfying, the infant/child has no need to internalize good aspects of the caretaker. His theory, then, is often characterized as a theory of "pathology"; he did not explicitly propose a theory of "normative" development in which individuals internalize both good and bad aspects of the interpersonal interaction (Greenberg & Mitchell, 1983; Mitchell & Black, 1995; St. Clair, 1996). Fairbairn observed the responses of traumatized children and formulated his ideas based on these observations. He noted that abused children often characterize their abusive parents as good; he came to conceptualize this as the ego's adaptation to the abuse. Helpless to change an abusive parent, the "only power a child has to change or improve a terrible problem in that environment is to change him- or herself. The child attempts to control the troublesome object in his world by mentally splitting the object into good and bad aspects and then taking or internalizing the bad aspect" (p. 56). Fairbairn emphasized that the internalization process is characterized by multiple structures of interactions that have the capacity to act as independent agencies within the ego. This notion underscores that the ego can have multiple parts or characteristics that seem to be at odds with each other. Fairbairn suggests that there are three internal objects that are separated out in the ego, and these are characterized as "the ideal object (the gratifying aspects of the mother); the exciting object (the promising and enticing aspects of the mother); and the rejecting object (the depriving, withholding aspects of the abuser)" (Greenberg & Mitchell, p. 164).

The ego is split to accommodate to different experiences with caretakers. As a result, the ego is at risk for conflict within itself. The part of the ego that continues to hope for positive contact and relatedness to the exciting object is termed the "libidinal ego." The part that stays connected to the rejecting object is termed the "anti-libidinal ego," or "internal saboteur." Lastly, the "central ego," which adapts to the external world, is available for interpersonal relations with real people in the outside world, and relates to the frustrating parent as an idealized figure (Goldstein, 2001; Greenberg & Mitchell, 1983). Fairbairn recognized that an individual's libidinal ego, fundamentally motivated by hope for better relationships, is often in direct conflict with the internal saboteur of the ego.

These internal conflicts are often, then, enacted in troubled partnerships. Each partner has often internalized split-off parts of his or her ego as a result of earlier relationship frustrations. Dicks (1967) articulated the confusion of partners when each is influenced by the competing aspects of Fairbairn's "egos." It is possible therefore for one partner to perceive the other as a hateful rejecting object (anti-libidinal ego) or as a wished for object who will be gratifying, supportive, and loving (the libidinal ego). In fact, the anti-libidinal ego part of an individual may indeed sabotage the potential change and benefits of couple therapy. We illustrate this process in the clinical vignette that follows.

In summary, then, Fairbairn puts forward a model of objects relations theory in which one can have competing forces within the structures of the ego. As a result of unsatisfying relationships with primary caregivers, individuals split off certain aspects of themselves and of their relationships; this serves a defensive purpose and is predicated on the idea that individuals internalize "negative" or destructive aspects of traumatizing or rejecting relationships. As such, an individual may simultaneously be hopeful that his or her partner will be a person who can alleviate past relationship fractures (libidinal ego), and at the same time may enact self-sabotaging behaviors in relationships (internal saboteur). As noted by Goldstein (2001), "The child, and later the adult, cannot relinquish or escape from the control of internal bad objects that sabotage the ability to get one's needs met" (p. 74). The internal saboteur will reject new relationships that might be loving or caring. This split-off part of one's ego needs to be made transparent in couple therapy. Otherwise, the client is often doomed to repeat patterns in which any hopeful attitudes about relationship possibilities are dismissed. Greenberg and Mitchell (1983) note that "The anti-libidinal ego is the enemy of hope, particularly of hope for anything meaningful with other people" (p. 166).

PAUL AND JANET :: Paul and Janet were referred for couple therapy with the explicit understanding on the part of each that they were on the brink of separation. During the assessment interviews, the couple shared a pattern of interpersonal dynamics that was very destructive. Paul admitted that he often spurned Janet's attempts to be emotionally connected. Janet acknowledged that while she attempted to stay connected to Paul, she found herself increasingly avoiding contact with him. Janet acknowledged that she had become increasingly worn down by Paul's continuous assaults on her character. She noted that whenever she did *anything* nice for Paul, he would accuse her of trying to hide something from him. In fact, he would suggest that she was being nice to him as a way of assuaging her guilt about having an affair.

Paul expressed his confusion. He recognized that he was attracted to Janet because he saw her as a loving person. However, he commented that he often perceived her behavior toward him as manipulative and calculated. He perceived that Janet was using him to achieve financial gain. Although other issues emerged in the beginning sessions of this couple treatment, the dynamic of Paul's internal saboteur became readily transparent in the fifth session.

Prior to this session, the couple had agreed to go out to dinner with Paul's parents. When Janet and Paul arrived at the designated meeting place, Paul reported that he became apprehensive when he saw his mother enter the restaurant. In the session, he commented that he saw "that look in her eyes," and went on to explain that he could see that she was under the influence of alcohol. Paul disclosed that his mother had actually had a long-standing alcohol and prescription drug problem and that when she was incapacitated, she would often physically beat Paul. Janet acknowledged that she had wondered how severe the beatings had been, as Paul's sisters had hinted that Paul certainly "got the worst of it" from their mother.

The couple reported that the dinner was a painful experience, with Paul's mother belittling him for not spending enough time with her and his father. His father abruptly left the restaurant, and Paul and Janet were left behind with Paul's drunk and abusive mother and their two small children. Paul drove his mother home in her vehicle and took a cab back to the couple's home. Later in the evening, when Janet met Paul with an understanding welcome, he exploded at her. He told Janet that he could take care of himself, that his mother's behavior was not that bad, and that Janet always exaggerated her responses to these minor events. Janet was able to extricate herself from the dialogue, as she anticipated that Paul would further position her as the bad guy. In brief, I was able to point out the pattern of the couple's interaction. Paul had enough ego strength to hear the comment of the therapist when he said, "It is confusing to me how Janet's loving behaviors get experienced as assaults to you, Paul."

Over time, the couple was able to work with these dynamics and the therapist was grateful to have Fairbairn's concept of internal saboteur in mind as interventions moved between Phase I (safety and stabilization) and Phase II (reflection on the trauma narrative) work with Paul and Janet. In this instance, Janet and Paul had sufficient ego strength that permitted each the open exploration of the dynamic. Again, it was imperative to have assessed that each partner has some ability to hold ambivalent affects toward the other. This achievement became the focus of the work with Janet and Paul. As expected, Janet's own insecurities about not being a "good-enough" partner also emerged and were worked through. The primary issue, though, of assisting Paul to understand better his own internal saboteur formed the foundation of his beginning restorying of his trauma history.

:: D. W. WINNICOTT

Also a member of the middle school of British object relations theorists, Winnicott was initially trained as a pediatrician, a specialization that clearly influenced his theory development as a psychoanalyst. His theory about normative development and clinical process is increasingly recognized as highly relevant to clinical practice (Applegate, 1996; Goldstein, 2001; Greenberg & Mitchell, 1983; Grolnick, 1990). Winnicott (1992) emphasized the importance of the mother–infant bond in normative development. His emphasis on early development and the importance of environmental influences are compatible with development across diverse cultural groups. His theory has relevance for a range of family systems, although his focus on the mother–infant dyad unfortunately reinforces the patriarchal notion that mothers are solely responsible for child "psychopathology."

Winnicott noted that a pregnant woman develops a primary maternal preoccupation in her later stages of pregnancy. He describes that pregnant women become completely in tune to their developing baby, especially as the time of delivery of the infant approaches. This preoccupation sets the emotional tone for the development of the mother–infant bond. In fact, Mashud Khan (1992) notes that Winnicott said during a discussion of the British Psychoanalytic Society, "*There is no such thing as an infant,* meaning, of course, that whenever one finds an infant one finds maternal care, and without maternal care there would be no infant" (p. xxxvii; italics in the original). This clearly states Winnicott's ideas about the intensity of the relationship between mother and infant child. Emerging from this dynamic, the mother provides a relationship that is secure and calming. In this "holding environment," the infant's physiological and emotional needs are contained and met. These beginning interactions form the fundamental sense of self for the infant. In other words, if the infant has a reasonably secure interaction with a good-enough mother, a cohesive sense of self is initiated.

When the mother is able to respond to the child's needs, there is a "moment of illusion" (Greenberg & Mitchell, 1983; Grolnick, 1990) in which the infant believes that the baby has magically created the object. The infant's capacity to experience these illusory moments contributes to the infant's sense of a core self. These early experiences are crucial for healthy development. Optimally, the mother is sufficiently in tune to the infant's early needs. However, as the infant matures, there is less demand for the mother to be perfect and then, Winnicott emphasized, that "good-enough" mothering is required to contribute to healthy development (Brandell, 1997; Mitchell, 1988). In fact, the infant does need to integrate the reality that she is unable to truly control the object (other) in her world. Greenberg and Mitchell say, "As the mother recovers from her maternal preoccupation and becomes interested once again in other areas of her life, the child is forced to come to terms with what he cannot do, cannot create, cannot make happen" (p. 193). In other words, the infant has an increasing capacity to become differentiated and to recognize her- or himself as separate from other people or objects in her or his world.

In addition to the graduated failure of adaptation by the mother, the infant's sense of self is enhanced when she is able to explore her autonomy while in the presence of the mother. Winnicott believed that the capacity to be alone is a crucial developmental achievement that also contributes to the development of a healthy sense of self. He discusses the importance of the mother being present, but not intrusive, when the infant is exploring certain aspects of development. Emerging from the state of complete un-integration, the infant begins to develop a capacity for spontaneous gestures and behavior. While in the mother's presence, the infant experiences a state of what Winnicott termed "going-on-being" (Greenberg & Mitchell, 1983). Here, the capacity of the infant to feel the nonintrusive presence of the mother allows, in a paradoxical way, the development of the capacity to be alone. In other words, the felt presence of the mother permits the exploration of separateness by the infant.

The child also develops a further sense of self when she integrates her aggression in relationship to others. Winnicott made a distinction between "object relating" and "object usage." In the former, the infant at first feels the object is under her illusory control. Greenberg and Mitchell (1983) note that "object-usage is the perception of and interaction with the other as independent and real, outside of the infant's omnipotent control" (p. 196). Object usage, normatively, involves two steps. Initially, the infant perceives she is destroying the object with her rage. She feels the object is under her control. However, when the caregiver withstands the child's aggression, and does not withdraw from the child, the child's development is enhanced. The process aids the infant in seeing that there are resilient others outside of her own control and that the parent is a person in her own right. The caregiver serves the function of containment of the infant's affect, certainly a function that many therapists perform when they act as containers for clients' highly charged affect states.

Winnicott's three concepts (primary maternal preoccupation and the holding environment, the capacity to be alone, and the distinction between "object-relating" and "object-usage") are important to the assessment and treatment of couples who are survivors of childhood trauma.

Couple Therapy and Winnicott's Principles

The interface of the therapist and the couple presents a number of opportunities for the application of Winnicottian principles in therapy. First, the clinician clearly establishes the therapeutic relationship with the intent of creating a holding environment and by providing a containment function. Not only is the clinician in tune to the individual needs of each partner, but it is also important to recognize that the couple looks to each other to provide a holding environment. In fact, each partner unconsciously or consciously hopes that the other will provide a holding environment in which one can feel safe to develop a sound sense of self. In addition, the holding environment of the couple facilitates each partner's sense of self that is complex and differentiated. A holding environment allows experiences of closeness and enhanced autonomy. The clinician has responsibility for creating a safe, viable working environment that enhances the therapeutic goals of the couple.

The capacity to be alone, in the presence of the other, is a crucial developmental achievement for many. One client, Jay, commented on his sense of calm when he knew that his partner, Tom, was in the couple's home in another room. The couple was working on aspects of closeness/distance in their emotional worlds, and Jay poetically described his comfort in exploring his interests when he knew that Tom was nearby in their home. Often, individuals have not developed the capacity to be alone, and consequently vehemently oppose any sort of differentiation that the partner may initiate.

As noted in the preceding, healthy development occurs when a child acknowledges that she does not have omnipotent control over the (m)other and recognizes the importance of the other as a subject in her own right. Winnicott (1971) describes the other as truly having value for the child when the caregiver can survive the destructive intentions of the infant. This has direct application to a couple system. To move to a complex understanding of one's partner, especially in relationship to feelings of aggression and rage, each partner needs to be able to directly express aggression toward the other, without the partner retaliating or recoiling from the interaction. It is unconsciously frightening for an individual to feel that he or she can destroy the partner with aggression. It is equally frightening if the clients feel that their clinician will be destroyed if they express aggression. As Winnicott noted, it is useful to recognize that one can use an object to aid in differentiation and management of aggressive affects. Often, couples need to be encouraged to express their aggression in direct ways. In doing so, the clinician can highlight that each member can survive the open expression of aggression. In addition, the clinician can underscore the viability of the individuals and the system when facing direct expression of aggression to each other.

:: CONCLUSION

In conclusion, this chapter demonstrates the utility of object relations theory in working with couples with trauma histories. The assessment of object relational capacities, especially object constancy, is an important factor to determine in all couple systems. Likewise, the identification of interpersonal patterns that appear to be self-defeating and self-sabotaging is useful. The provision of a therapeutic holding environment can further the couple's abilities to explore efforts toward independence and autonomy as each partner develops a capacity to be alone. Finally, the capacity to verbalize aggression constructively toward one's partner aids in the development of a fluid, complex self that is not reduced to dichotomous roles of sadist and masochist or as victim and victimizer. The next chapter explicates how attachment theory is synthesized into the couple therapy practice model.

7

Attachment Theory

This chapter explores how one's attachment history and internal working models of self and other, as formed from attachment interactions, influence an intimate couple relationship. Adult attachment patterns are increasingly viewed as key elements that influence the development of intimate partnerships (Berman, Marcus, & Berman, 1994; Collins & Feeney, 2000; Dutton, Saunders, Starzomski, & Bartholomew, 1994; Fisher & Crandell, 1997; Hazan & Shaver, 1987; Johnson, 2002; Johnson, Makinen, & Millikin, 2001; Kobak & Hazan, 1991). Ample literature demonstrates that trauma histories influence the attachment experiences and classification of children, adolescents, and adults (Alexander, 1992; Alexander et al., 1998; Allen, 2001; Fonagy, 1998, 1999; Fonagy, Gergely, Jurist, & Target, 2002; Lyons-Ruth & Block, 1996; Roche, Runtz, & Hunter, 1999; Schore, 2000, 2001a, 2001b; Shapiro & Levendosky, 1999). Consistent with other developmental theories, attachment theory emphasizes that early relationships fundamentally influence the formation of interpersonal and intrapersonal dimensions of self and other. Attachment theory is readily applied to diverse communities. Bowlby (1980) speaks to the supposition that one's attachment needs are lifelong when he says, "Intimate attachments to other human beings are the hub around which a person's life revolves, not only when he is an infant or a toddler or a schoolchild, but throughout his adolescence and his years of maturity as well, and on into old age" (p. 442).

Adults generally form attachment relationships with peers as opposed to caretakers, although these peers are felt to have unique importance. "The peers may be perceived as sources of strength, but they need not be perceived this way; they may instead be perceived as fostering the attached individual's own capacity for mastering challenge" (Weiss, 1982, p. 173). Johnson (2002) says that attachment theorists describe three elements of adult attachment: attachment, caring, and sexuality (p. 44). Although she posits that most couples transform romantic affiliations into full attachment bonds over a period of approximately two years, cross-cultural variability in this process can occur.

In this chapter, we outline the foundation concepts of attachment theory. A description of child and adult attachment classification systems frames the specific examination of how childhood trauma influences the attachment styles of children and adults. To better understand couple dynamics related to attachment constructs, we examine the functions of adult attachment in more detail. We discuss how the internalization of attachment relationships impacts an individual's ability to (1) regulate affect, (2) enhance mentalization, and (3) develop secure partnerships that foster intimacy and mutuality. A clinical vignette illustrates an effective use of attachment theory principles when working with a couple with extensive histories of childhood trauma.

:: FOUNDATION CONCEPTS OF ATTACHMENT THEORY

Bowlby's (1958, 1969, 1973, 1980, 1988) early formulations of attachment theory were influenced by his observations of the ill effects of hospital and institutional care on infants and young children. Bowlby synthesized elements of ethology, control systems theory, cognitive science, and psychoanalytic principles in his theory that suggests that infants have a biologically based predisposition for social interaction. This social interaction eventually becomes focused on a particular adult. As Bowlby observed, children seek closeness and contact with the attachment figure (Thompson & Lamb, 1986, p. 6). Attachment, as conceptualized by Bowlby, was not meant to apply to all aspects of parent–child relationships, nor was it conceptualized as being only a social bond. Rather, an attachment behavioral system is thought of as only one of many behavioral systems operative within infants, while attachment behaviors are conceptualized as serving the biological function of protecting the attached individual from physical and psychological harm. Drawing from ethological principles, Bowlby (1958, 1969) postulates that one's attachment behavioral system serves the protective function of species survival; he notes the relatively long period of human infantile helplessness and the consequent and necessary seeking out of a protective figure for purposes of survival (Ainsworth, Blehar, Waters, & Wall, 1978). Similarly, attachment in the face of a situation that is novel, fearful, or strange is thought of as a "part of a group of behavioral systems whose function it is to maintain a relatively steady state between an individual and his or her own environment" (Brethreton, 1985, p. 7).

Attachment behaviors are activated within infants as they evaluate the environmental signals that result in feelings of security or insecurity. Because the end goal of the attachment system is to experience a sense of security, the ability to regulate one's own emotional reactions becomes a central developmental achievement of securely attached individuals. As individuals are not born with a capacity to regulate emotions, a "dyadic regulatory system evolves where the infant's signals of moment-to-moment changes in his state are understood and responded to by the caregiver, thereby achieving this regulation" (Fonagy et al., 2002, p. 37). Allen (2001) notes that "attachment is the foundation for distress regulation" and that attachment "interactions generate mental representations that underpin subsequent interactions. This propagation of representations is intergenerational as well as developmental, passed on from one generation to the next as well as evolving from childhood into adulthood" (p. 44). Bowlby proposed that working models of attachment provide prototypes for subsequent relationships. These models operate at an unconscious level and thus are resistant to quick or easy change. Each partner brings his or her internal working model of self and other into the intimate partnership.

Child Attachment Classifications

Using Bowlby's theoretical foundation, Ainsworth (1973) initiated studies of mother–child interaction. Ainsworth et al. (1978) gathered data by observing a number of mothers and infants and developed a research methodology that is widely known as the Strange Situation Experiments (Alexander, 1992; Alexander & Anderson, 1997; Bretherton, 1985; Lyons-Ruth & Block, 1996; Osofsky, 1988). Initially, the research methodology facilitated three classifications of toddlers' attachment patterns: secure, avoidant, and ambivalent attachment. The researchers observed and recorded patterns of infants and toddlers when they were reunited with their mothers after a prescribed, uniform separation from them. Subsequently, Ainsworth

(1982) and Main and Solomon (1986, 1990) showed four categories of child attachment manifest in the research paradigm. In addition to attachment classifications of secure, avoidant, and ambivalent, some children are rated disorganized/disoriented in their attachment internal working model.

Securely attached toddlers are thought to have confidence in the availability of parenting figures. In addition, the parents of securely attached toddlers are thought to be able to assist their infants in modulating their affect and to be used as objects for mentalization (Fonagy et al., 2002). Avoidantly attached infants do not presume the availability of parenting figures and behave defensively to minimize affect and other emotions that would signal separation-related distress. The defensive posture of these infants gives the behavioral message that attachment is not important to them. Avoidant children are presumed to have had inadequate help from caregivers in managing their affective experiences; "therefore, they *overregulate* their affect and avoid situations that are likely to be distressing" (Fonagy et al., p. 38; italics in the original).

On the other hand, ambivalently attached infants tend to show distress when reunited with parents from whom they have been separated. They are unable to be calmed by caregivers and often escalate behavior that aims to ensure some continued contact with parents. Fonagy et al. (2002) note that these children "*underregulate*, heightening their expression of distress, possibly in an effort to elicit the expectable response of the caregiver" (p. 38; italics in the original). The child may be frustrated, even if the caregiver appears to be available to him or her.

Lastly, disorganized/disoriented toddlers demonstrate an unpredictable pattern of attachment when faced with separation from their parents. If they seek proximity to the caregiver, they behave in unpredictable, strange, and at times contradictory ways. These children have often been victims of traumatic experiences in childhood (Allen, 2001; Fonagy, 2001; Main & Solomon, 1990). Fonagy says that disorganized/disoriented attachment is secondary to the child's having experienced a frightened or frightening caregiver (p. 36). These infants paradoxically fear the caregivers from whom they seek solace. Allen notes that parents of disorganized children often have been recently traumatized, have an unresolved history of childhood trauma, or have unresolved loss of important figures through death (p. 52). Table 7.1 summarizes child attachment classifications describing behaviors of child and parent that contribute to the classification.

TABLE 7.1 :: Child Attachment Classifications

	Child Behavior	Caregiver Behavior
Secure attachment	Explores environment confidently	Emotionally available
	Seeks out caregiver when distressed	Helps to modulate affect
	Calmed by caregiver	Child-focused
Avoidant attachment	Fails to seek out caregiver when distressed	Emotionally unavailable
	Ignores caregiver's attempts to reconnect	Cannot modulate own affect aroused by separation
	Overregulates affect	Self-focused
Ambivalent attachment	Seeks and resists caregiver when distressed	Unable to read signals from child
	Cannot be calmed by caregiver	Alternates between emotional availability and unavailability
	Underregulates affect	
Disorganized/disoriented attachment	Behaves in strange stereotypical ways	Appears angry or frightening to child
	Adopts a frozen posture	Restimulated with traumatic memories when interacting with child
	Appears fearful of caregiver	

Adult Attachment Classifications

Main, Kaplan, and Cassidy (1985) examined adult behavior and reports of attachment history to develop a classification of adult attachment. Their Adult Attachment Interview gives investigators a tool that facilitates classification of adult internal working models of attachment. The semistructured interview is designed in such a way that respondents give a narrative that reflects their attachment histories. The probes of the interview are thought to unearth unconscious responses of attachment histories and experiences. A sophisticated rating system has been established that requires thorough training by researchers to utilize the classification method accurately. Essentially, raters look for coherence of attachment-related constructs in respondents' narratives. Those who are able to articulate the complexity of attachment in a coherent fashion are classified as secure in the adult attachment paradigm. Results of the Adult Attachment Interview yield four classifications: secure, dismissing, preoccupied, and disorganized attachment styles. These categories parallel the four classifications of infant/child Strange Situation attachment classifications.

Adults who are rated secure give coherent stories about their attachment experiences. They are able to describe attachment relationships with some sense of continuity and also integration of attachment experiences. These individuals have the ability to form sound attachment relationships with other adults and/or their children.

The first of three insecure patterns of adult attachment is "dismissing." These individuals minimize the importance of attachment relationships or, alternatively, have an idealized, unrealistic view of their attachment histories. The main interpersonal style for those who minimize attachment is to be self-reliant; they give the impression that they are immune to attachment-related phenomena in their interpersonal worlds. Kobak and Sceery (1988) comment that dismissive individuals "tended to devalue the importance of attachment relationships . . . or tended to discount their importance for present functioning" (p. 137). This rating parallels the rating of avoidant attachment in children.

A second pattern of insecurity is described as "preoccupied" with attachment; here, adults tend to be awkward in their attempts to form attachments. These individuals clearly seem to be concerned with attachment phenomena, but struggle or show ambivalence about some aspects of the attachment relationships. These individuals are able to recall childhood attachment experiences, but clearly have not integrated the events; they often have some sort of ongoing power struggle with their attachment figures. This category parallels the childhood classification of ambivalent attachment.

Finally, as mentioned previously, those adults who parallel the disorganized/disoriented childhood classification are thought of as having unresolved grief or loss issues, or a history of childhood trauma. We now turn to a fuller discussion of the correlation between childhood trauma history, which is often instrumental in forming the disorganized/disoriented child, and adult attachment classification. However, first see Table 7.2, which links child and adult attachment categories, and highlights Adult Attachment Interview characteristics.

Trauma and Disorganized Attachment in Children and Adults

As noted, disorganized behavior is linked to parent–child interactions that are in some way frightening for the child. Bereft, disorganized

TABLE 7.2 :: Correlation of Child/Adult Attachment Classifications

Child Classification	Adult Classification	Adult Attachment Interview Characteristics
Secure	Secure Has capacity for satisfying intimate relationships	Coherent, clear accounts of attachment relationships Capacity to appreciate complexity of parents Integrated loss and grief experiences
Avoidant	Dismissing Aloof, emotional distant Compulsive self-reliance Minimizing importance of attachment	Idealization of troubled or abusive parents Failure to provide clear, consistent examples of attachment experiences Contradictory descriptions of parents
Ambivalent	Preoccupied Desirous of relationships but conflicted about closeness/ distance Rageful when disappointed	Intense, unresolved anger toward parents Lack of coherence and consistency in descriptions of parents
Disorganized/disoriented	Disorganized/disoriented Emotionally chaotic in relationships Approach/avoidance style Potentially violent	Discussion of loss or abuse precipitates panic, fear, or dissociation Potentially prolonged silence(s) during interview

adults are often emotionally unresponsive to the attachment needs of their children. They may convey a sense of depression or emptiness to the child. The child does not have the capacity to understand fully the adult response and becomes overwhelmed. Fonagy (2001) notes, "The prevalence of attachment disorganization is strongly associated with the presence of family risk factors such as maltreatment, major depressive or bipolar disorder, and alcohol or other substance misuse" (p. 37). Depressed adults may miss or misunderstand the child's moment-to-moment changes in behavior. Consequently, shared interactions that facilitate secure attachment and the capacity of the infant to develop affect regulation and early mentalization processes are impeded (Fonagy et al., 2002). Disorganized attachment and trauma histories impact the child's regulation of affect and mentalization; these processes are related yet discrete developmental phenomena.

Because the attachment bond between parent and child is thought of, primarily, as an affective bond, the role of affect and affect regulation is central to attachment theory principles. Feeney (1998) suggests that attachment styles reflect the manner in which individuals deal with negative affect. Because attachment behavior is manifest at times of distress, the caregiver has the opportunity to help the child begin to modulate affect. Sroufe expanded Bowlby's views of emotional affects. Developmentally, the infant moves from a position of affective coregulation with the caregiver to a capacity for self-regulation. Sroufe (1996) comments that the second half of the first year of life marks a shift in the infant's ability to process affect. During that time, the infant develops the capacity to make interpretations about a caregiver's reliability and self-regulatory capacities, which influences the infant's self-esteem and ability to be self-reliant. According to Fonagy et al. (2002), "Self-regulation can be considered as a higher kind of affect regulation; in another sense, it constitutes a change in form. . . . Affect regulation on the second level is about the meaning that affects have for particular individuals" (p. 95).

Infants can rely only on their caregivers to help them identify, modulate, and, at age-appropriate times, express their affective experiences. Reliance on the caregiver is clear, as it is only through the experience of and interaction with an attachment figure that an infant learns the meanings associated with a range of internal states and affective experiences. Schore (2000) notes, "Emotional communications are rapidly transmitted back and forth between the infant's and mother's face, and in these transactions the caregiver acts as a regulator of the child's arousal levels" (p. 34).

Although maltreatment of the infant is one clear factor that contributes to disorganized classification, Fonagy (2001) reports that the caregiver's unresolved trauma history is also correlated with infant disorganization. Parents' unresolved grief experiences, past traumas, or more current traumas may impact their ability to provide a secure base for their children. Increasingly, disorganized attachment patterns are correlated with varied forms of child and adult psychopathology (Lyons-Ruth & Block, 1996; Lyons-Ruth & Jacobvitz, 1999; Sroufe, 1997). Fonagy purports that there is a strong link between disorganized attachment and violence in interpersonal relationships. In addition, he says that individuals with a borderline personality organization also likely fit with a disorganized attachment paradigm.

Traumatized children often become confused when they attempt to know and understand the meaning of abusive behaviors at the hands of their caregivers. In fact, some traumatized children will disavow reflection and mentalization processes, as the disavowal is an adaptation to the traumatic circumstance. Fonagy (2001) says, however, that "Although restriction of mentalization was originally adaptive, there is a clear and powerful link between this restricted capacity and the vulnerability to later trauma. The inability to reflect upon the mental state of the perpetrator, as well as the reaction of the self, may prevent the child from resolving the original traumatic experience or coping with subsequent assault" (p. 176). Further, he suggests that the lack of mentalization processes contributes to an impoverished or limited internal world, in that the circumstances of abusive reality cannot be fully integrated. Hence, the correlation of disorganized/ disoriented attachment classifications with difficulties in affect regulation and mentalization processes is quite high and repetitively demonstrated with traumatized children.

In this theory, then, mentalization is a broader category of experience that encompasses self-regulation. Further, regarding adults, mentalized affectivity "marks an adult capacity for affect regulation in which one is conscious of one's affects, while remaining within the affective state. Such affectivity denotes the capacity to fathom the meaning(s) of one's own affect states" (Fonagy et al., 2002, p. 96). These authors outline the impact of mentalization affectivity in individual adult psychotherapy. Later, we demonstrate how we utilize the concepts/processes of affect regulation and mentalized activity in couple therapy. Mentalization also encompasses the ability of the individual to discern or to anticipate the meaning of others' behavior and affects. Insecure attachment classifications correlate with difficulties in affect regulation and mentalization processes.

:: ATTACHMENT THEORY AND COUPLE SYSTEMS

The development of research methodologies (Bartholomew & Horowitz, 1991; George, Kaplan, & Main, 1985, unpublished manuscript; Hazan & Shaver, 1987) that permit the rating of adult attachment styles, individually or in relationships, has furthered the application of attachment theory to couple systems. In a general sense, individuals who have a secure attachment history develop secure internal working models of self and other. These individuals have relationship capacities that promote trust in partners, and secure individuals often report relationship satisfaction (Berman et al.,

1994; Bowlby, 1988; Fisher & Crandell, 1997; Hazan & Shaver, 1987; Johnson, 2002; Kobak & Hazan, 1991; West & Sheldon-Keller, 1994).

West and Sheldon-Keller (1994) suggest that individuals often look for a special and preferred other when they partner, so as to achieve a sense of security. Fisher and Crandell (1997) say that secure couple attachment "involves an ability to shift freely between the dependent and depended-on positions. . . . there is an open expression of the need for comfort and contact, as well as an open reception of that contact" (p. 216). They go on to say that these couples cognitively appreciate the benefit of the fluidity of being caregiver/receiver in the couple relationship. Kobak and Hazan (1991) note that spouses with secure working models have a better marital adjustment and are able to modulate emotion constructively in the relationship (p. 861). Hazan and Shaver (1987) purport that secure lovers are able to accept and empathize with their partners, despite their partners' shortcomings or deficiencies. They also say that securely attached partnerships endure longer than insecure partnerships (p. 515). Johnson (2002) says that more secure individuals have a capacity for reflective functioning that allows for meta-monitoring of interactional cycles (p. 52).

On the other hand, insecurely attached individuals are often viewed as inflexible and rigid in partner interactions (Fisher & Crandell, 1997, p. 216). Dutton et al. (1994) report that anger in intimate relationships and insecure attachments are often precursors of emotional or physical abuse between the partners. Insecure individuals, they contend, exert dominance in relationships and "emotional abuse is a product of attachment rage" (p. 1382). Fonagy (1999) also cites that male perpetrators of violence against women may be seen as an exaggerated response of a disorganized attachment system (p. 7). Hazan and Shaver (1987) report that avoidantly attached individuals often fear intimacy, are jealous partners, and are labile. They say that ambivalently attached individuals often are obsessive in their partnerships, and that they demand reciprocation in interactions (p. 515). Hindy and Schwarz (1994) characterize anxious romantic attachment as insecure, emotionally dependent, and clinging (p. 179).

Johnson et al. (2001) report that in couple therapy, couples experience an "attachment injury" when "one partner violates the expectation that the other will offer comfort and caring in times of danger or distress" (p. 145). They say that couples develop impasses in couple therapy when the origin of the attachment injury is hidden. In brief, resolution of attachment injury is a multistep process that names the site of the attachment injury, elaborates on the impact of the injury, offers opportunity to further articulate the complexity of the injury, and allows each partner to grieve the injury. The couple is moved to further empathy and connection where caring behaviors offer some restorative power that facilitates healing in the relationship (p. 153). Johnson et al. (2001) and Johnson (2002) presume that couples generally have capacity for insight and can empathically respond to each other. This is not always so, in our experience. We see many couples who do not have these object relational capacities, and the couple work, for these dyads, focuses on Phase I work and a cognitive approach to Phases II and III.

Solomon (2003) also presumes a couple's capacity for insight and mentalization, as she purports that couple therapy helps the partners acknowledge unresolved attachment vulnerabilities. She also encourages the couple to emotionally process their unresolved feelings. Neither Johnson nor Solomon discuss the potential damage that traumatized couples may experience, interpersonally, if they are prematurely encouraged to disclose affect or retrieve affectively laden traumatic memories. We are convinced that couples must engage in preparatory stabilization work before they begin to directly emote about and/or recall traumatic incidents.

At this time, we describe a segment of couple therapy that was partially guided by attachment theory tenets. Consistent with our couple therapy model, theoretical perspectives are used differentially, depending on the clinical data. The vignette illustrates a combination of Phase I and Phase II interventions with the therapist using his empathic attunement to create a holding environment. In addition, cognitive–behavioral techniques assisted the couple to:

- Regulate affect
- Enhance mentalization capacities
- Reflect on affect
- Enhance their interpersonal exchange devoid of blaming or projection

:: APPLIED THEORETICAL CONCEPTS

KEN AND JANET :: Ken and Janet, a dual-trauma couple, requested therapy when each indicated that the marriage was on the brink of dissolution.

Although they described that they had been soul mates during college, each reported increased dissatisfaction in the past two years of their twenty-five year relationship. Ken, age forty-five, is a real estate broker and Janet, age forty-four, is a successful restaurant owner. Both are from white, middle-class backgrounds. I had gleaned the following family histories.

Ken described his father as a harsh disciplinarian who regularly punished him for any behavior viewed as contrary to the family's Catholic tradition. For example, at the age of twelve, Ken was caught stealing some ammunition for his pellet gun from a hardware store. In addition to a severe beating, for a number of consecutive days, Ken's father forced Ken to stand, blindfolded, against a wall in the family garage. Ken's father periodically fired a number of shots from the pellet gun in Ken's direction. Ken was hit on a few occasions in the legs and buttocks area, but he describes his extreme panic when he would anticipate where, or if, the next pellet would hit him. Ken's father was a good marksman, and he would fire shots around Ken's head that would purposefully miss Ken. Understandably, Ken alternately experienced either hyper-arousal or numbing symptoms whenever he felt any beginning feelings of panic that restimulated these earlier traumatic experiences. Ken's mother had not protected Ken during these instances, and had adopted the stance that Ken and his father needed to work out their differences. She clearly adopted the bystander role in the "victim–victimizer–bystander" dynamic of this on-going trauma.

Janet's parents abused alcohol regularly and expected her to function as the mediator of their marital discord. At times, she actively resisted this role and would retreat into the solace of her own bedroom. However, as the eldest of three children, she felt some responsibility to be a caretaker in her family. Her parents coerced her, in many instances, into their emotional turmoil, and expected Janet to help them discharge their hostile and rageful affect. Behind the scenes, Janet orchestrated the day-to-day operation of the family; she was skilled at keeping her siblings safe and out of the line of the parents' abusive arguments. However, Janet would often be drawn into the parents' arguments, and her wish to take care of her siblings contributed to her taking some action in the family. Nonetheless, when able to extricate herself, Janet emotionally withdrew from her parents, in spite of their attempts to draw her into their emotional quagmire.

This essential history of each partner illuminates some potential reenactments between the couple. Ken often looked to Janet to help him regulate affect when he was troubled. Janet often withdrew in those moments, fearful that she would be overwhelmed with her own affective experience. In the next part of the vignette, we illustrate the importance of facilitating the attachment of the couple, while having each maintain some ability to prevent a reenactment of a previous attachment-related phenomenon. Although a formal assessment of adult attachment classification was not fully conducted, clinical impressions supported the idea that Janet had clearly not been able to utilize either of her parents as secure objects. She had internalized an avoidant sense of self that minimized the importance of close connection. She preferred to deal with her emotional world independently, and wished that Ken would deal with his world in a like fashion. Ken, at times, demonstrated characteristics of a disorganized form of attachment. He often became overwhelmed with affect related to any uncertainty in outcomes related to Janet's intentions around assertion.

Affect Regulation

Current disappointments often plunge couples into affective storms that are difficult for them to manage. The clinician needs to adopt an active directive approach so as to prevent further interpersonal damage in the relationship. Often, an important Phase I first step is to encourage some form of affect regulation by enabling the partners to disengage from each other.

KEN AND JANET (continued) :: At the beginning of the session, Ken launched into an attacking monologue in which he raged at Janet for not understanding or helping him work through a difficult job-related situation. Ken bellowed that his business partner had publicly ridiculed him in a meeting. Ken accused Janet of withdrawing when he needed her; he angrily instructed me to make sure that she "stayed in the room," an expression that we had previously used in therapy interactions. I was aware of emotionally shutting down myself, as my own triggers around aggression were being stimulated. I became somewhat indifferent and had the thought that the two of them needed to work this out. Initially, in my helplessness to have Ken calm himself down, I had taken the bystander role. Like his mother, I left Ken to his own devices to deal with his "father figure," embodied in both his business and his relationship partners.

Although detached, I could see that Janet appeared frightened as Ken escalated his demands of her and me. She seemed to experience panic. I was aware that the couple had reenacted a central relationship dynamic. Ken felt panic because of the real or perceived threat from his work partner, reminiscent of his father. Janet felt panic because of her sense of helplessness in observing Ken's rage. Symbolically, Ken had become her raging, drunk parents who demanded that she calm everyone's feelings. I instructed the couple to turn away from each other's line of vision, and firmly instructed them to stop verbally engaging each other. Janet was relieved, and Ken became more agitated with these instructions.

Cognitive–Behavioral Interventions

In these instances, we encourage the couple to rely on previously acquired skills such as relaxation techniques of meditation or deep breathing. Some individuals are also able to begin to cognitively challenge their generalized, automatic, negative attributions of their partners (Basham, 1999b; Baucom & Epstein, 1990; Northcut, 1999). Refer to Chapter 5, Trauma Theory, for a further elaboration of these Phase I interventions. Janet clearly felt relieved to have some alone time, and immediately complied with my instruction. Ken, however, was unable to calm himself, and began to focus his rage in my direction.

Empathic Attunement and Beginning Mentalization Processes

Adults with internal working models characterized by an insecure attachment are not able to self-regulate affect. Rather, an injunction to "calm down" exacerbates their panic and sense of fragmentation. The clinician/caregiver needs to demonstrate that he can withstand their affect and can empathize with it. The empathic connection will be met with some relief and often an ability to allow the caregiver to help coregulate the affective storm.

KEN AND JANET (continued) :: I moved my chair closer to Ken and said that I could see how terribly frightened he was. I spoke purposefully about his sense of being alone in his panic. I noted that he was only asking for help in managing his feelings. I quietly commented on his fear that his business partner was going to discipline him, or even torture him, as his father had. As Ken became less angry, he began to sob uncontrollably. I stayed quiet during his crying, although I moved myself into his line of vision so that he could see, as well as feel, my presence. I encouraged him to experience his sadness as fully as possible. I said to him that Janet and I were there, and that he could count on our presence.

When I turned to Janet, I saw that she had physically curled herself into a self-protective ball. I commented on how frightened she was. I said that she was petrified that Ken was going to demand that she help him with his feelings. How could she do that when she was so terrified? She also began to cry, but did seem to stay engaged with my voice. I let her know that she did not have to do anything in that moment other than simply to reflect on her feelings.

Mentalization Processes—Reflection

Fonagy et al. (2002) argue that mentalized affectivity "directs us to appreciate new meanings in the same affects, not simply to create new affects" (p. 436). This ability is so important for survivors of childhood trauma. These individuals often need to create new narratives about their traumatic experiences so that they can develop more coherent, vibrant senses of self. However, this is not a process of uncovering or remembering repressed traumatic memories. Rather, the process of mentalized affectivity assists the individual to become a self-reflective agent who develops a sense of comfort with his own subjective experience. In other words, the ability to stay focused on the internal world, without trying to transform the feelings, allows one to capture the subtleties of the affective world. As well, the process promotes the inward expression of feelings that allows for an expanded repertoire during difficult affective experiences. Rather than having to express the full range of one's affect, an individual can reflect on his or her interior world, can become conscious of the feeling without trying to modulate it, and can aid his own capacity to regulate affect.

I asked the partners to recognize the complexity of their feelings in the moment. I quietly said that I could see that each had many feelings, and I asked them to reflect on what they needed at that time. We sat quietly for some time, and it was clear that I had been able to assist both partners to calm themselves. In these interactions, I was purposefully using my empathy to help Ken and Janet regulate their frightened and hostile affects. This technique is compatible with the "holding" and "containment" proposed in a Winnicott framework. However, it was also clear to me that their anger was infused with sadness and loss. After some time, I asked Ken if he could share his experience of the last few minutes. He spoke eloquently about how his terror had been exacerbated and how he frantically wanted Janet to ease his feelings. He acknowledged that my presence had been useful and that he had become aware, during the interaction, of how frightened Janet was. He usually had difficulty understanding why Janet would leave the room when he was emotional. In this session, he witnessed her self-protective position and said that he understood her inability to help him in those moments. He went on to say that he "stayed with his sadness," as I had encouraged him to do. He was relieved that he did not lose control of himself, and he noted that he did not feel a compulsion to share his emotions with Janet in that moment. He acknowledged that, in our presence, he had been able to reflect on his sadness.

Enhanced Interpersonal Exchange

When an individual develops the capacity to hold one's feelings in one's internal world—in essence, to express the feelings to oneself—there is less urgency to rid oneself of the feeling via projection or blaming statements. However, when partners are able to share their affective experience, in a nonblaming manner, communication is enhanced. Then, the secure individual recognizes the expression of affect as an invitation to dialogue as opposed to an attack from the other.

For example, Janet reported her fear that I was going to push her to try and comfort Ken during the exchange. She was well aware that the fear was related to her experiences in her family of origin. I let her know that, although it was good to have insight about the source of her feelings, she did not have to explain them away so quickly. She seemed confused but interested in this comment. I went on to say that I could understand if she chose to stay in her interior world when she was feeling so distressed. I said that I thought Ken would continue to develop his own ways of managing his feelings and that she did not have to engage him in those dialogues. Interestingly, she said that she thought she could have a dialogue with Ken, knowing that she did not have to be responsible for helping him to calm down or for fighting his battles for him.

In summary, assessment and treatment of traumatized couples are enhanced when the clinician utilizes key aspects of attachment theory constructs. It is particularly important that the clinician assess the signs of insecure, especially disorganized/disoriented, attachment working models of the partners. The clinician can listen for attachment themes during both the assessment and treatment phases with couples. As noted in the preceding, there are certain indicators that an individual is demonstrating insecure attachment patterns. While not completing a full Adult Attachment Interview, the astute clinician can listen for themes that reflect insecure attachment patterns (Hesse, Main, Abrams, & Rifkin, 2003). See Table 7.2 for a summary of relevant themes.

In treatment, affect regulation and the capacity for mentalization can be strengthened in partners who have insecure attachment. Affect regulation interventions assist a couple to stabilize and to become less damaging to each other, interpersonally. To enhance self-reflective processes and promote internalization of secure attachment representations, partners can be assisted to actively utilize mentalization processes that invite dialogue with each other.

In the clinical vignette, Ken and Janet each demonstrated some elements of insecure attachment in their internal worlds. Ken had trouble modulating affect, while Janet retreated from his injunction to help him manage his affect. First, in the previous exchange, Ken was able to identify, through self-reflective processes, the mixture of affects—anger, hurt, sadness, frustration, fear—that he was experiencing. Second, he was able to use the therapist to help calm himself; finally, he was able to stay with his affect and was able to express it in his interior world. With increased available choices, he was able to invite Janet into a conversation about his affect, as opposed to expecting her to alter his affect. Likewise, Janet was able to identify the range of her feeling. She also revealed some ability to use the therapist to calm herself. Last, she also was able to prepare herself to have a conversation with Ken about her feelings and his feelings.

The next section of the text demonstrates how these theories are synthesized in couple therapy. First, the biopsychosocial assessment guides and anchors the model. Then, the phase-oriented therapy model is elaborated. This is followed by a chapter that summarizes the responses of clinicians engaged with therapeutic work. Last, a detailed clinical case illustrates both assessment and treatment issues.

COUPLE THERAPY PRACTICE

This section contains four chapters that are devoted to the explication of the phase-oriented couple therapy approach. This practice model is grounded in a synthesis of social, family, trauma, object relations, and attachment theories, which have been reviewed separately in Section II (Theoretical Foundations). Throughout this third section, our effort is to demonstrate the coherence of this case-specific model, drawing from different theoretical perspectives that are useful at a particular phase of the work or in response to a specific presenting issue.

In Chapter 8, we focus on the biopsychosocial assessment. Because any assessment functions as an integral part of treatment, we initially provide a clear contextual frame by summarizing the salient features of the practice model. Then, we review the relevant institutional, interactional, and intrapersonal factors that contribute to a thorough biopsychosocial assessment.

In Chapter 9, we describe how the biopsychosocial assessment guides the creation of a treatment plan. Then, we discuss ways to build a facilitative therapeutic alliance, setting the stage for a detailed review of the therapy phases (i.e., Phase I: Safety, stabilization, and establishment of a context for change; Phase II: Reflection on the trauma narrative; and Phase III: Consolidation of new perspectives, attitudes, and behavior). Finally, we address specific practice themes that are central with all traumatized couples in therapy.

They include: (1) the composition of a "couple," (2) the role of violence, (3) parenting, (4) sexuality, (5) affairs, (6) dual diagnoses (i.e., substance abuse/addictions and complex posttraumatic stress disorder), and (7) dissociation.

Chapter 10 focuses on the clinician's responses in working with traumatized couples in a couple therapy frame. We explore the influences of vicarious traumatization, racial-identity development, countertransference phenomena, and the realm of intersubjectivity.

Finally, in Chapter 11, we feature a case example, the couple therapy with Rod and Yolanda, which illuminates the use of a phase-oriented couple therapy practice model. Our attention now turns to the crafting of a complete biopsychosocial assessment.

· · · ·
· · · ·
· · · ·
· · · 8

Biopsychosocial Assessment

In this chapter we review the relevant institutional, interactional, and individual factors that constitute a thorough biopsychosocial assessment. As we introduce the metaphoric image of couple therapy as a challenging journey, a biopsychosocial assessment should serve as both a compass that directs the course of the work and an anchor that stabilizes the focus. Undoubtedly, the assessment emerges as a central feature of any couple therapy venture that ultimately determines the direction and guides the movement of the work. However, before we embark on a detailed analysis of the assessment procedure, we will situate this process in the context of the phase-oriented couple therapy practice model, which is summarized in the next section. (A more detailed account of the treatment model is presented in Chapter 9.)

:: OVERVIEW OF PHASE-ORIENTED
   COUPLE THERAPY MODEL

The synthesis of theoretical models used in practice depends on the unique features and needs assessed for each couple. For example, as social constructionist, racial identity, and feminist theories serve to clarify the family's social context, these perspectives broaden the assessment (Marsella, Friedman, Gerrity, & Scurfield, 1996; Pouissant & Alexander, 2000).

Intergenerational and narrative family theories inform our understanding of intergenerational family assumptions, rituals, and unique multiple meanings (Sheinberg & Fraenkel, 2001; Trepper & Barret, 1989; White, 1995; White & Epston, 1990). Finally, in the individual arena, trauma theories focus on the short- and long-term neurophysiological effects of trauma on brain function, particularly memory and affect regulation (Krystal et al., 1996; Shapiro & Applegate, 2000; van der Kolk, 1996). To strengthen further an understanding of each partner's inner world, psychodynamic theories, more specifically object relations and attachment theories, shed light on the interplay of the inner and outer worlds (Kudler, Blank, & Krupnick, 2000; Pearlman & Saakvitne, 1995; Scharff & Scharff, 1987). They also provide an internal conceptual scaffolding for this practice model in all cases through understanding relational patterns and guiding reparative therapeutic experiences. Finally, a review of the cognitive and behavioral functioning of each partner also addresses mastery, coping, and adaptation (Compton & Follette, 1998). In summary, this synthesis of biological, social, and psychological theory models informs the biopsychosocial assessment that subsequently guides the direction of practice. The relational (i.e., object relations and attachment theory) and social theory models provide anchoring throughout the entire course of couple therapy. Other theoretical models advance to the foreground or recede into the background depending on the presenting issue at hand.

In spite of the creative variability that enters into each couple case assessment, some general guidelines are useful for all assessments and decision-making regarding the sequencing and choice of interventions. Overall, this couple therapy practice approach functions as a phase model that parallels many contemporary individual and group psychotherapy stage models with trauma survivors (Courtois, 1988; Herman, 1992; Miller, 1994). However, there are distinct commonalties and differences between these models. In general, stages are similar to phases in terms of identifying certain uniform challenges, yet traditional stage models presume essentialist sequential development. During the past ten years, greater emphasis has been placed on phase-oriented individual and group psychotherapy models (Chu, 1992, 1998; Courtois, 1999; Figley, 1988; Gelinas, 1995; Pearlman & Saakvitne, 1995). Our phase-oriented couple therapy model approximates these models more closely, anticipating that relevant themes may be revisited flexibly at different periods throughout the work. The phases of couple therapy include Phase I: Safety, stabilization, and establishment of a context for change; Phase II: Reflection on the trauma narrative; and Phase III: Consolidation of new perspectives, attitudes, and behaviors (see Table 8.1). This fluid process calls forth an image of a three-dimensional triple helix with continuously interconnecting themes that weave together in an animated tapestry.

TABLE 8.1 :: Phase-Oriented Couple Therapy: Phases

Phase I: Safety, Stabilization, and Establishment of Context for Change

1. Assessment of safety
2. Self-care
   • Physical health
   • Mental health (e.g., depression, anxiety, and unresolved grief)
   • Sleep, nutrition, and exercise
   • Substance use and abuse
   • Biobehavioral strategies for stress reduction and self-soothing
3. Relevant diversity themes
4. Support systems (e.g., religion/spirituality, family, and community)
5. Communication skills
6. Assessment of partnership status (i.e., continuation? stasis? dissolution?)

Phase II: Reflection on Trauma Narratives

1. Exploration of meaning of traumatic experiences
2. Intergenerational legacy of victim–victimizer–bystander pattern
3. Exploration of different meanings of intimacy
4. Creation of healing rituals
5. Clarification of projective identification processes (Only in cases in which each partner possesses the object relational capacities, sufficient ego strengths, and the ability to bear ambivalence will this intervention be indicated.)
6. Emergence of memories (Only in cases in which each partner possesses the object relational capacities and ego strengths to bear the retrieval of traumatic memories might the uncovering of memories be indicated. Congruence with cultural beliefs must exist as well.)

Phase III: Consolidation of New Perspectives, Attitudes, and Behaviors

1. Remediation of presenting issues
2. Increased empathy for resiliency and survivorship in partners' listening to each other's trauma narratives
3. Shifts in victim–victimizer–bystander dynamic leading toward equitable relating
4. Enhanced sexual relationship
5. Strengthened capacities for self-differentiation, object constancy, and self-care
6. Self-definition that moves beyond survivorship identity
7. Changes in parenting style
8. Strengthened social identities (e.g., gender, race/ethnicity, sexual orientation, age, disability, religion, class, etc.)
9. Shift in social consciousness

Phase I: Safety, Stabilization, and Establishment of Context for Change

Phase I tasks are relevant for most, if not all traumatized couples in therapy. Here, it is essential to determine if the couple has secured basic safety in terms of food, shelter, and freedom from domestic or external violence. As mentioned earlier, an advocacy role is assumed to ensure safety for a victim if physical violence is detected. A couple therapy modality is contraindicated at such times as it often inflames an incendiary dynamic.

Assessment of self-care is strengthened by psychoeducational support about posttraumatic stress disorder (PTSD) and complex PTSD symptomatology. The clinician explores how well each partner cares for his or her basic physical and mental health needs. After reviewing the safety of the external environment along with efficacy of self-care, the clinician needs to assess the extent of interpersonal supports among family, friends, and colleagues.

In general, this phase involves a full range of psychoeducational, cognitive–behavioral, body–mind, spiritual, and ego-supportive interventions that promote adaptation and coping. Collaboration with relevant support systems such as school, treatment professionals, Department of Social Services (DSS), and probation officers is often crucial during this phase as well. Many couples are content to end their therapeutic work after completing these Phase I tasks, if the major presenting issues have been resolved. Such cognitive–behavioral changes can positively influence a couple over a sustained period and can readily be accomplished within a brief time frame. Many couples may choose to move along to Phase II or III work, which involves a reflection on and restorying of the trauma narrative. However, not all couples need to follow such a course of therapy in order to establish new and more equitable ways of relating.

Phase II: Reflection on the Trauma Narratives

Phase II involves sharing original perspectives on the childhood trauma experiences while restorying the narratives with a new focus on resiliency and adaptation. Since there has been so much controversy about the utility of uncovering traumatic memories, many couples benefit, instead, from a reflective sharing of their traumatic experiences without full affective reexperiencing. Instead, an integration of affect, cognition, and memory emerges as a distinct therapy goal. In addition, increased capacity for empathic attunement often occurs during this sharing of experiences.

Congruence with sociocultural influences may also determine the usefulness of uncovering of traumatic memories. If such a path promotes flooding or decompensation, uncovering work is clearly contraindicated. In addition, when there are distinct cultural prohibitions against catharsis, such affective reexperiencing is also contraindicated. For example, I worked with a couple who fled as political refugees from a Central American country; both partners had suffered torture and imprisonment from caregivers and prison guards during their respective childhoods. Cultural, religious, and political forces joined together to create a shared worldview that valued containment, while devaluing expressiveness of intense affect. In this case, a cognitive reflection of the aftereffects of trauma and the "victim–victimizer–bystander" dynamic helped this couple. Retrieval of memories was clearly contraindicated.

Finally, object relational and attachment capacities also determine the efficacy of uncovering traumatic memories. If partners have not yet attained object constancy and lack the capacity to sustain ambivalence in intimate relationships, then, once again, uncovering of traumatic memories would be contraindicated.

An important point to revisit is that we, as clinical social workers, continue to overvalue the importance of the uncovering of traumatic memories under the guise of privileging an insight-oriented psychotherapy frame. Even when cultural congruence and object relational capacities exist, it remains preferable to focus on safety and stabilization work if the couple reports satisfaction with their Phase I progress. If continued work is indicated, Phase II tasks would then focus on reflecting on, and through this process, restorying the trauma narrative. With cultural congruence and object relational capacities intact, these couples may then benefit from clarification of their projective identification processes.

Phase III: Consolidation of New Perspectives, Attitudes, and Behaviors

Phase III tasks involve a focus on family of origin work along with further strengthening of family and community relationships. Couples at this point often report less shame, stigma, and isolation. They often move beyond self-definitions as "survivors" to "overcomers," "transcenders," or "thrivers." To shift from a self-definition exclusively as survivor, the partner(s) explore their feelings associated with the experience of victim or bystander, which occurs fairly easily, as well as the aggressive feelings associated with their victimizing parts, which is more difficult. When each partner develops the capacity to own each of the "victim–victimizer–bystander" roles, he or she is better able to sublimate aggression into more proactive and creative activities. This transition often involves an abandoning of a rigid self-definition, which is linked exclusively to the traumatic experiences. During this phase, parenting can become less problematic, and couples may express a greater sense of mastery, vitality, and joy. Couples may also engage themselves in political and social action as a way to advocate for safer childhoods. Resolution of the tasks undertaken during these phases of couple therapy does not follow a sequential developmental line. Instead, a more realistic path involves a revisiting of different phases throughout the course of the work.

An example is the case of a dual-trauma couple, discussed in the chapter on military couples, which consists of Johnnie, a forty-two-year-old Vietnam veteran helicopter pilot, and Jeannie, a forty-one-year-old thrice-married beautician. Both partners wrestled with the sequelae of childhood physical and sexual abuses and chronic, repetitive trauma in their adult lives. After five months of couple therapy focused primarily on physical safety, self-care, remediation of psychiatric symptomatology, relapse prevention, and strengthening of support networks, both partners were ready to discuss repair work with their respective families of origin, using their understanding of the "victim–victimizer–bystander" dynamics (Phase II and Phase III work). Although some progress was noteworthy, Johnnie failed to attend his twelve-step meetings, and Jeannie regressed to self-mutilative cutting. When these symptomatic behaviors surfaced, the harm reduction and stabilization measures embedded in Phase I work were revisited until criteria were met sufficiently once again to address interpersonal issues. In contrast to following a steady, sequential path in therapy, a couple more typically vacillates back and forth between the assessment phase and Phases I, II, and III of the couple therapy model.

:: GUIDELINES FOR BIOPSYCHOSOCIAL
   ASSESSMENT

A central reciprocal question arises: In what ways do the aftereffects of trauma influence individual capacities for a partnership, and in what ways do these aftereffects influence the relationship itself? Since each couple is unique and complex, it is necessary to engage a couple in a thorough biopsychosocial assessment that guides careful decision-making regarding sequencing and choices of practice interventions. Each clinician is urged to identify both strengths as well as possible vulnerabilities in each of the sections of the assessment outline (i.e., the institutional, interactional, and individual) (see Table 8.2). Inevitably, various questions arise that explore the strengths and vulnerabilities within each partner and within the couple relationship.

TABLE 8.2 :: Phase-Oriented Couple Therapy: Biopsychosocial Assessment Factors

---

I. INSTITUTIONAL (grounded in social constructionist, feminist, and racial identity development theories)

1. Clinician attitudes and responses (racial identity, vicarious traumatization, countertransference)
2. Extended family and community support
3. Service delivery context (social policies, finances, political contexts)
4. Previous and current mental health treatment
5. Diversity (race, ethnicity, religion, socioeconomic status, disability, sexual orientation, gender)

II. INTERACTIONAL (grounded in intergenerational and narrative family theories)

1. Victim–victimizer–bystander dynamic
2. Power and control struggles
3. Distancing and distrust
4. Boundaries
5. Sexuality and physical touch
6. Communication
7. Dearth of rituals
8. Meaning of trauma narrative
9. Intergenerational patterns

III. INTRAPERSONAL

A. Individual, cognitive, affective, and behavioral functioning (grounded in trauma theories)
   1. Areas of resilience
   2. Complex PTSD symptomatology
      F ears (nightmares, flashbacks, intrusive thoughts)
      E go fragmentation (dissociation, identity distortion)
      A ffective changes/addictions and compulsive behaviors/antisocial behavior
      R eenactment
      S uicidality/somatization (insomnia, hypervigilance, numbness vs. hyperarousal, startle response, bodily complaints)
B. Intrapsychic (grounded in object relations and attachment theories)
   1. Capacity for whole-, part-, or merged-object relations (Mahler/Horner)
   2. Themes of symbiosis, differentiation, practicing, rapprochement, and "on the road to object constancy" (Mahler/Horner)
   3. Internalized victim–victimizer–bystander dynamic
   4. Role of projective identification
   5. Attachment patterns: secure or insecure (preoccupied, dismissive, or disorganized)
   6. Role of "internal saboteur" (Fairbairn)
   7. Capacity for concern, object use, and aloneness (Winnicott)

Institutional Factors

A review of institutional factors notes how the influences of clinician responses, extended family, neighborhood, the agency context, network of helpers, faith-based community, and the political climate may exacerbate or mediate the aftereffects of trauma. Relevant diversity themes (i.e., race, ethnicity, socioeconomic status, religion, age, gender, sexual orientation, and disability) also require a central focus, as they affect both the incidence and aftereffects of childhood trauma.

Clinician Responses

Personal and professional values shape our attitudes, beliefs, and biases toward clients. Although our clinical practice is guided by ethical standards of care established by our professional organization (NASW, 2000), we are also mindful of the contributions of distinguished practitioners/researchers in the traumatology field who have devised working guidelines for the treatment of adults abused or possibly abused as children (Courtois, 1997b; Wilson, Friedman, & Lindy, 2001). Ongoing self-reflection is necessary for all clinicians to monitor the influences imposed by any incongruence between personal values and professional ethics.

Not only must a clinician be mindful of countertransference responses, but she must also be aware of the impact of vicarious traumatization and re-traumatization (Chu, 1992; Francis, 1997; Pearlman & Saakvitne, 1995). The realm of intersubjectivity raises the question of how each couple and clinician affect each other, both cognitively and affectively, in the ongoing work. How are these various influences recognized and addressed? Especially in the realm of cross-cultural couple therapy, what assumptions and cultural biases does each individual bring to the work? How does the clinician's racial identity development inform and influence attitudes and clinical interventions? What is the effect of different statuses in racial identity development for the couple and the clinician?

In most couple therapy situations with trauma survivors, there are a number of predictable countertransference traps (see Figure 8.1). As many trauma survivors possess an internalized relational template that involves the "victim–victimizer–bystander" pattern, this drama may be regularly externalized through projective identification. As a result, each partner may engage the other, as well as the clinician, in these projective identification dances. Of course, the clinician's unresolved personal issues factor into this equation as well. If the clinician has suffered her or his own traumatic experiences, attention to these personal countertransference responses is crucial in maintaining balance both as the clinician and as the trauma survivor.

For example, the first potential countertransference trap involves slipping into a passive and indifferent bystander stance that mirrors the couple's numbness and detachment. Another trap leads to helpless victimization, or not knowing how to proceed. When a clinician finds herself extending the boundaries of sessions, losing clarity around professional role and financial

Aggression

Passive indifference

Detachment

Helplessness

Ambiguity regarding boundaries

Eroticized response

Reaction formation

Idiosyncratic responses based on uniqueness of clinician

FIGURE 8.1 :: Potential countertransference traps influenced by the victim–victimizer–bystander scenario.

compensation, or generally trying to become the quintessential omnipotent helper, she may be succumbing to a rescuer enactment. An eroticized countertransference trap is common as well, where a range of sexualized feelings may be activated toward either partner. Understandably, caution is recommended to avoid eroticized reenactments that recapitulate the earlier childhood traumas. Behaving aggressively toward the couple may be another countertransference enactment when identifying with the victimizer role. Finally, reaction formation represents a trap in which the clinician, while disavowing anger, acts in a false and overly solicitous manner.

In summary, enactments on the part of the clinician are inevitable. However, it is essential that the clinician understand the nature of the countertransference enactments both to strengthen the empathic connection with the client and to minimize the occurrence of these missteps as much as possible. Without this level of self-scrutiny, the validity of the biopsychosocial assessment of the couple could be sharply undermined.

Diversity Themes

Now that the clinician responses have been introduced, let us focus on the range of diversity themes that require attention in every biopsychosocial assessment. In this section, questions are posed that explore the influences of race, ethnicity, religion, gender, sexual orientation, disability, and socioeconomic status for the couple (Allen, 1998; Friedman & Marsella, 1996; Kersky & Miller, 1996). Although the questions are primarily focused on the couple, it is equally important for the clinician to be cognizant of the influences of his or her own social identities within the intersubjective realm of the couple therapy.

First, does each partner express a racial identity connected to a marginalized racial group or to the dominant culture? What is the degree of privilege or oppression experienced by each partner? What has been the nature and duration of racist or bigoted experiences? Does either partner identify with a racial group that places her at high risk for trauma? In what ways is racial identity a source of positive and/or negative identification? What is the nature of each partner's racial identity development? Is there an intersection with other marginalized identities? Is there evidence of internalized racism? If so, is internalized racism projected onto the partner?

Second, how does each partner define ethnicity? How does ethnicity affect attitudes regarding family? Gender roles? Child-rearing practices? Definition of childhood physical, sexual, or emotional abuses? Definition of physical discipline? In what ways does ethnicity provide for positive or negative identification? Are there intergenerational legacies of interethnic conflict influencing this couple?

Third, how does each partner identify religious/spiritual beliefs? In what ways does religion provide support? In what ways, if any, does religion reinforce denial of abuses? Is there involvement in a supportive faith community? If there has been a lack of adherence to family-of-origin religious beliefs, is there a resulting sense of shame or guilt? Has the couple integrated shared spirituality or religious practices? Are there intergenerational legacies of interreligious conflict? Has either partner suffered abusive treatment based on religious identity?

Fourth, what gender role assumptions were learned in the family of origin? What gender role assumptions operate in the current partnership? Where are the legacies of patriarchy in gender relations? Who exerted the most power in decision-making in the family of origin? In the current partnership? Are there unequal or inequitable patterns of relating in the partnership? How do these factors influence parenting? Do patriarchal, inequitable patterns of relating lead to physical, emotional, and sexual abusive behavior? Is there physical violence apparent?

Fifth, how does each partner describe his or her sexual orientation? Is sexual orientation an area of concern personally? Or, in response to homophobia? And heterosexism? If gay, bisexual, lesbian, or transgendered, what degree of comfort is there with "coming out" with friends, family, and work? Has either partner been treated abusively because of sexual identity? What supports exist for this partnership? Is one partner more comfortable with being "out" in the larger community? How does the couple handle difference in terms of "passing" in the heterosexual community?

Sixth, at what age did the trauma occur? In what ways did the traumatic experiences influence developmental tasks of that particular age cohort? Is age an issue now in terms of enhanced vulnerability? For example, many elders who had abused their children in earlier years often suffer abuses in their later years at the hands of their own adult children as well as employed caregivers. Sadly, but predictably, adult trauma survivors frequently reenact their own childhood trauma scenario by abusing the elderly parent.

Seventh, do either or both partners live with a current physical, learning, or emotional disability? Did the disability have some bearing on the trauma that occurred? For example, hard-of-hearing and deaf clients are often at high risk for childhood abuses both in their family homes and residential schools.

Eight, are socioeconomic statuses comparable for each partner? If not, is there tension related to this difference? What is the nature of the couple's financial situation? Are there financial pressures? Does the couple receive public assistance? Does poverty place this couple at risk for witnessing or being victimized by violence?

In summary, the full range of sociocultural and institutional factors must be reviewed thoroughly to provide a contextual framework for understanding each couple. In the context of intersubjectivity, a clinician may use her countertransferential responses and enactments as a victim, victimizer, or bystander to enrich further the assessment of the couple's dynamics. Understanding how various social identities influence the clinician and the couple in therapy is very important as well.

Interactional Factors

The interactional factors that surface that have particular relevance to survivors of childhood trauma include the interplay of the "victim–victimizer–bystander" paradigm, intimacy, power and control, communication, sexuality, and boundaries (Miller, 1994; Staub, 1989, 1994). Since survivors of childhood trauma have been subjected to abuses of power from adults designated as their caregivers, such violations set the stage for a sense of betrayal and distrust. Subsequently, these individuals find themselves in relationships during adulthood where the dynamics of a "victim–victimizer–bystander" pattern are reenacted. Not only might a survivor relate to other people with this pattern, but she also internalizes a "victim–victimizer–bystander" template that guides a vision of the world. Each adult survivor has experienced situations of victimization at the hands of a victimizer. Usually, a bystander, who either failed to help, remained detached or uninvolved, or responded as a rescuer to interrupt the abuse, appears in the lives of trauma survivors through reenactment. Having experienced the various feelings associated with traumatization, an inner template of the "victim–victimizer–bystander" is internalized. (A more detailed discussion of this process will follow in the section on individual factors.)

Let us return to the review of important interactional factors relevant for most trauma survivors in couple therapy. First, the "victim–victimizer–bystander" scenario is based on an internal template that influences the trauma survivor on a day-to-day basis to view the world in terms of a trauma scenario. People at times are experienced as victimizers (even when there is no objective reality present), or there may be an augmentation of affect in response to a hurtful or insensitive remark. In couples, either partner may shift between the roles as victimizer, victim, and bystander. This tendency is very common among trauma survivors and sets the stage for inequitable patterns of relating where partners shift in terms of one-up and one-down positioning. Polarizations in thought, affect, and behavior often occur where couples argue in dichotomous ways about who is right or wrong or good or bad. The capacity to tolerate disappointment and ambivalence in relationships titrates the extreme polarizations of this relational pattern. Although these interactional patterns are important in understanding the escalation of violence, we remain very clear that victims of violence should not be held responsible for activating violent behavior in the partner.

A clinical example of this "victim–victimizer–bystander" paradigm will be elaborated at length in Chapter 11. Featured is a dual-trauma African-American couple, Rod and Yolanda. At the beginning of couple therapy, each partner was bitterly engaged in destructive verbal battles characterized by alternating roles as victim, victimizer, and bystander. During the course of their therapeutic journey, both partners moved toward resolving multiple oppressions related to childhood abuses and racialized maltreatment. Throughout the work, they gradually recognized the compounding effects of abuses of power within their intimate relationship, their respective families of origin, and society.

A second interactional pattern common among dual- or single-trauma couples is the battle for power and control. Once again, the alternating "victim–victimizer–bystander" pattern sets the stage for many struggles. Partners complain of domination or subjugation by the other during unrelenting quarrels about who will gain power to make decisions. For example, during the height of their intense fighting, Rod and Yolanda battled regularly about who was the better caregiver, parent, or financial planner.

A third interactional pattern is distancing. Although an interplay of pursuing and distancing is common for most couples, distrust related to childhood abuses leads to heightened wariness, tentativeness, and withdrawal. As a result, the nature of distancing needs to be clarified for a couple. For example, Jane, who survived childhood physical and sexual abuse, immerses herself in homebuilding and architectural design, finding no time for any conversation with her partner, Maria. As a survivor of childhood sexual abuse, Maria maintains distance by providing overly zealous caretaking for relatives and friends, taking her away from home and from her partner. Although each partner expressed extreme withdrawal from the other, culturally based explanations were offered. Their different ethnic backgrounds were significant, in fact, in understanding differences in family values, but this did not fully explain the augmented trauma-related distancing responses.

Fourth, boundary ruptures are common among trauma survivors. A middle-aged, dual-trauma Eastern European Jewish couple experienced difficulty with establishing flexible boundaries. When the couple moved to a new home, there was no individual space for either person. Ultimately, Rebecca asserted a need for a private sanctuary. A tiny converted closet became the safe place where she could retreat to read, reflect, and collect herself without the risk of intrusions. Harry learned to respect her privacy and recognized a need for his own solitude as well.

Another example concerns a second-generation Italian-American female trauma survivor who shrieked in distress whenever her male partner playfully surprised her. After reporting that this teasing was reminiscent of earlier childhood sexual abuse when her father unexpectedly appeared in her bedroom, he understood her fears and no longer personalized the rejections. Each partner could develop more empathy toward the other; only then were the couple able to change their behavior. A female probation officer, in treatment with her male partner, had survived physical and sexual childhood abuses. She described her road rage when a driver cut into her lane that led to a screaming, threatening chase of this man's car until she careened to a stop. Having experienced this intrusion as a retraumatizing boundary violation, she reacted with augmented rage, terrifying her husband, who was an unsuspecting passenger.

Fifth, the sexual arena for trauma survivors may be fraught with distrust and fearfulness around sensual and sexual touch. Defenses of dissociation, repression, isolation of affect, and suppression fuel inhibited sexual desire. Often survivors need to discover ways of relating sexually that do not trigger specific traumatic memories. In other situations, they need to desensitize themselves to the globally negative feelings of shame and guilt often associated with sexual feelings and behavior. At times, behavioral management of physiologically based sexual avoidant patterns needs to be instituted. For example, a heterosexual dual-trauma couple established verbal "rules" that provided each partner with a sense of predictability around which areas of their bodies were "safe" for sensual touching. Since each partner had experienced violating, nonconsensual sex, both needed to confirm verbally with each other that neither partner felt coerced or intimidated into an agreement before any sexual activity could ensue. Another common trauma-related pattern is hypersexuality, which one female trauma survivor described as a "compulsive driving pressure."

Sixth, communication can often be difficult if a partner was encouraged to suppress all talking about feelings surrounding the childhood abuse, or for that matter, any other issue. "No hear, no see, and no talk" is a common motto among trauma survivors. Destructive, often abusive, verbal exchanges are also common as enactments of the "victim–victimizer–bystander" scenario.

Seventh, a paucity of rituals surfaces as another important interactional factor. In the presence of physical, emotional, or sexual abuse during childhood, many families lived with chaos and violence on a regular basis. It is not uncommon that such trauma is associated with a high incidence of substance abuse and addictions. A consequence of such unpredictability is a paucity of healing, celebratory, and mourning rituals. Needless to say, when holiday times arrive, family chaos often interferes with any healing ritual that could help families to celebrate their meaningful connections. For example, a middle-aged Polish Catholic trauma survivor recalled that most Thanksgiving holidays during her childhood were characterized by random drunkenness and rageful outbursts from her alcoholic, abusive father, who threw the festive turkey across the dining room on more than one occasion. To the dismay of her husband, she had always refused to cook a turkey. He finally understood her reluctance after listening attentively to her family stories. Given the possibility of horrific family gatherings, it is important to explore the use and meaning of family rituals both in the present as well as during the past.

Eighth, the unique meaning of a trauma narrative emerges as another important interactional theme. Each partner relates her trauma narrative with a full range of idiosyncratic, affectively laden associations. Early on in couple therapy, self-definitions frequently refer to the powerless "victim" role, which is later supplanted by a more complex view that describes an adaptive, resilient "victim-survivor." Throughout the course of therapy, the individual and collective narratives often shift in words and meaning. However, as individuals may not change at the same pace, the unevenness in movement needs to be addressed.

Ninth, intergenerational patterns of relational styles, modes of coping, family paradigms, as well as unresolved grief, loss, and trauma exist as important interactional themes that provide an historical context to the couple's presenting issue. These patterns contain both positive and negative features. For example, couple therapy with a dual-trauma couple revealed the female partner, Nokai's, expressions of deep sadness in response to her husband's rage storms. As each partner explored the paradigms symbolically inherited from their families of origin, Nokai talked about the dehumanizing treatment that her parents suffered in Japanese internment camps during World War II. Edward felt compassion for Nokai's burden as a carrier of intergenerational trauma and grief. However, only in lengthy discussions about his own childhood did Edward recall that his father, a World War II veteran who was involved in the bombing of Dresden, had refused to discuss his wartime experiences. Instead, Edward understood that his own depression and PTSD-related irritability existed in the context of an elaborate intergenerational projection process as well.

In summary, while the resilience and perseverance of many trauma survivors can often fortify relationships, there are risks of reenacting the trauma scenario of the "victim–victimizer–bystander" dynamic in their intimate coupling as well as in other relationships. To assess the full functioning of the couple, the degree of intimacy, distancing, boundary ruptures, sexuality, communication, and ritual all require careful exploration.

Intrapersonal Factors

Now that the interactional factors have been explored, the individual factors, both biological and neurophysiological, as well as the intrapsychic factors deserve exploration. Important influences include the neurophysiological effects of trauma, including PTSD and complex PTSD symptomatology (Dansky et al., 1996; Krystal et al., 1996; Rothschild, 2000; Shapiro & Applegate, 2000; van der Kolk, 1996, 2003). A review of each partner's physical health should include any illnesses, hospitalizations, history of treatment, and current functioning. In addition, self-care themes are very important. They include nutrition; exercise; sleep and eating patterns; substance use, abuse, or addictions; and biobehavioral strategies for self-soothing. Since many trauma-related and addiction-related symptoms mimic underlying physical conditions, a thorough physical examination is indicated at the onset of any couple therapy. For example, a female partner in a single-trauma couple continually attributed her rage storms to the legacies of trauma. After I recommended, on three occasions, that she pursue a medical examination, her endocrinologist diagnosed a severe thyroid condition that explained much of this emotional lability.

Intrapsychic factors focus on each partner's object relational and attachment capacities, as well as the role of projective identification (Kudler, Blank, & Krupnick, 2000; Lindy, 1996; Miehls, 1997; Prior, 1996; Scharff & Scharff, 1987).

Individual Factors

First, complex PTSD symptomatology needs to be evaluated to determine the presence or absence of a range of trauma-related symptoms and behaviors (APA, 2000). Although there are a number of assessment tools available to review PTSD symptomatology, such as the Structured Clinical Interview for DSM (SCID), the Clinician-Administered PTSD scale (CAPS), self-report questionnaires, and psychophysiological measures, an extensive clinical interview is recommended as providing the most valid and reliable data (Keane, Weathers, & Foa, 2000).

F-E-A-R-S, the mnemonic device proposed by Jean Goodwin (1990), summarizes the most salient features of this complex PTSD syndrome (see Table 8.2). F-E-A-R-S refers to the sequelae of childhood trauma, and includes (1) *F*ears, as manifested in nightmares, flashbacks, and intrusive thoughts; (2) *E*go fragmentation, as manifested in dissociation and identity distortions; (3) *A*ffective changes, addictions, antisocial behavior and compulsive behaviors; (4) *R*eenactments; and (5) *S*uicidality/*S*omatization, as manifested in insomnia, hypervigilance, numbness versus hyperarousal, hypersexuality, inhibited sexual arousal, startle responses, and/or bodily complaints. Exploration of the full range of these symptoms must be completed for both partners, especially when the power of denial prevents many trauma survivors from recognizing or reporting these difficulties.

We briefly highlight the specific assessment of four of these factor—affect regulation, physical health, dissociation, and substance abuse/addictions—since they are so central for all traumatized couples. Traumatic experiences that occur both in childhood and adult life sharply invade a person's ordinary balance of affects and emotions. As elaborated in the chapter on trauma theories, traumatic events disrupt a body's neurophysiological balance. This leads to mood lability and instability, along with a predilection to swing from numbness (or deadening of affect) to a state of hyperarousal, accompanied by an augmentation of emotions. Rage storms are common for individuals during the initial traumatization and retraumatization experiences. At those moments, clients report an escalating buildup of tension and anger that erupts in a split-second rage reaction. A complete fight/flight response is activated with the emergence of powerful adrenergic responses. Since affective instability occurs regularly, it is important to assess parasuicidal and suicidal tendencies of each partner.

Another phenomenon that deserves special attention is dissociation. This term has been applied extensively to an entire range of conditions, including dissociative states, dissociative defenses, and dissociative disorders. For our purposes, we will rely on a working definition of dissociation as a disruption in the usually integrated functions of consciousness, memory, identity, or perception of the environment (APA, 2000). Research data have supported strong associations between diagnoses of PTSD and dissociative disorders (Allen, 2001; Brenner, 2001; Courtois, 1993, 1999; van der Kolk et al., 1996). Kluft (1992), who describes dissociation as "a defense in which an overwhelmed individual cannot escape what assails him or her by taking meaningful action or successful flight, and escapes instead by altering his internal organization i.e. by inward flight" (p. 143). He continues on to describe two key components of dissociation as detachment and compartmentalization. Each partner should be assessed on a continuum of detachment to see if she or he is mildly or moderately detached, involving some level of depersonalization (feeling an unreality related to the internal world) and derealization (experiencing the external world as unreal). Reports of haziness, cloudiness, floating, and feeling spacey are common descriptors for dissociation. More extreme detachment can be quite profound. Examples include the occasion when a client may fail to account for hours of activity and lose contact with the passage of time. At other times, extreme cases of tonic immobility can lead to a catatonic state.

When compartmentalization occurs, the client fails to integrate or connect different aspects of conscious experiences. A dramatic form of compartmentalization occurs with the emergence of dissociative identity disorder, in which an occurrence of two or more distinct identities or personality states influences the person's behavior. Although there has been considerable controversy in the past decade about the existence of this condition (Piper, 1994; Putnam, 1995a, 1995b; Spanos, 1996), there is persuasive evidence that many individuals with trauma histories describe switching between and among distinct behavioral states (Allen, 2001; Brenner, 2001; Cohen, Berzoff, & Elin, 1995). A major error committed by mental professionals occurs when "alters" are viewed as separate people with a reification of separate identities. Instead, these different states may well represent different aspects of a poorly integrated identity. When couples understand that everyone has various states of mind and emotions, compartmentalization is normalized. The existence of these distinct mental states is therefore not the problem. Instead, the rigidity around compartmentalization causes ruptures in memory and integrative functioning. Because these phenomena are so complex, it is often helpful to use a standardized measure, such as the Dissociative Experiences Scale (Waller, Putnam, & Carlson, 1996) or the BASS model (assessment of behavior, affect sensation, and knowledge) (Braun, 1988) to assess a partner's tendency toward dissociation.

There are strong associations between the incidence of PTSD and substance abuse and addictions. Early studies on male combat veterans, typically treated in Veterans Administration (VA) settings (Keane & Wolfe, 1990), established this connection. Within the past ten years, mixed gender studies with more diverse samples have revealed estimated rates of PTSD from 12% to 34% (Grice et al., 1995). Even more stunning findings have been revealed for women. For example, studies of women in the general population, without considering substance abuse, estimate lifetime trauma rates of 36% to 51% (Najavits, Weiss, & Shaw, 1997). Women in substance abuse treatment programs also show higher trauma rates than women in the general population, with rates ranging from 55% to 99% (Najavits et al., 1997, 85%; and Fullilove et al., 1993, 99%).

Without doubt, the syndromes of PTSD, complex PTSD, and substance abuse are strongly associated (Evans & Sullivan, 1995; Ruzek, Polusny, & Abueg, 1998). The presence of trauma has been associated with the emergence of substance abuse, supporting the "traumatogenic" theory of substance abuse disorders or "self-medication" (O'Donohue & Elliott, 1992). Since there are such strong connections between substance abuse and PTSD, we, as clinicians, must be thorough in our assessment of substance use. This inquiry can be conducted either in the couple therapy session or in concurrent individual sessions with each partner. A range of useful assessment instruments may be helpful as well, such as the CAGE questions related to drinking (Ewing, 1984) or Substance Abuse Subtle Screening Inventory (SASSI) (Evans & Sullivan, 1995; Levin & Weiss, 1994).

Very often, survivors of childhood trauma who abuse or are dependent on chemicals present symptoms that mimic a range of psychiatric conditions, including major depression, generalized anxiety, substance abuse psychoses, somatic complaints, or cognitive confusion. These symptoms may be directly caused by the substance abuse, or they may be evidence of an underlying psychiatric or medical disorder. Since so many substance abuse–related symptoms are identical to trauma-related symptomatology, it is commonplace for a clinician to overlook a careful differential diagnosis. The risk involved in such an oversight leads to an incorrect treatment plan with accompanying negative consequences.

Evans and Sullivan (1995, p. 101) have devised an important dual diagnosis assessment tool that aims to tease out this differential diagnosis. To establish if a client who is abusing or dependent on chemicals may also have a coexisting psychiatric disorder, the following questions are raised: (1) Did the client have symptoms of the psychiatric disorder prior to extensive involvement with chemicals? (2) Do the psychiatric symptoms continue or worsen during a four-week or longer period of abstinence? (3) Do the client's responses to interview questions, his or her observed behaviors, or the result of psychological testing indicate that the symptoms and problems are substantially more intense than those typically seen in cases of substance abuse of dependence? (4) Does the family history, genetic or otherwise, indicate possible familial transmission of a coexisting disorder? (5) Is there a history of a positive response to psychotropic medication or other specific psychiatric treatment? (6) Is there a history of multiple chemical dependency treatment failures and has the client tried to work a twelve-step program of recovery? The greater number of affirmative responses points to the likelihood of a coexisting psychiatric disorder. Such a coexisting diagnosis of major depression, bipolar disorder, dissociative disorder, or panic disorder would signal a need for a more thorough psychiatric evaluation with the possible inclusion of psychotropic medications.

Intrapsychic Factors

Now that the biological and neurophysiological factors have been explored, we turn to the assessment of each partner's intrapsychic, or internal, world. To understand the nature of each partner's inner world, it is important to first document the full range of ego strengths and evidence of resilience. Since the object relational world of each partner has significant bearing on the nature of the partnership, it is important to ascertain if each person has the capacity for whole, part-object, or merged object relations. According to American object relations theory, in particular that of Margaret Mahler, it is useful to determine if relational patterns suggest themes associated with symbiosis, differentiation, practicing, and rapprochement (Horner, 1984; Mahler, Pine, & Bergman, 1975). The biopsychosocial assessment aims to understand the inner object world of each partner, including ways in which the "victim–victimizer–bystander" dynamic has been internalized. As projective identification occurs either on an unconscious or conscious level, certain disavowed internal conflicts are regularly projected outward, followed by the occasional engagement of the partner in the externalized drama of the other partner's inner world (Ogden, 1982). Questions must be explored as to how the mutual projective identification processes operate between the couple and between the couple and the clinician.

For example, in the case of Rod and Yolanda mentioned earlier, Yolanda behaved in ways that irritated and angered Rod, who then distanced from her, reactivating in him an intrapsychic conflict related to desiring connection yet fearing abandonment. Rod then enacted an abusive, abandoning role, similar to the roles assumed by her father and uncle. In turn, Rod externalized his internal conflicts about connection and abandonment by failing to follow through on agreements, which aroused the ire and harsh criticalness of Yolanda. In this way, Yolanda would then be experienced as the victimizer(s) of his early life. The clinician regularly needed to restrain or repair an enactment related to a victimizing role of Yolanda when she was critical or a rescuer/bystander role toward Rod when persecuted by his wife. Needless to say, the mutual projective identificatory processes required constant monitoring.

Additional questions related to the internal world need to be raised. For example, do the interpersonal dynamics reflect themes of need gratification, domination and control, or competitiveness? To explore the construct of Fairbairn's (1952a, 1952b) "internal saboteur," questions should be raised to determine the nature of the individual's tie to the abuser, especially when the connection is maintained by self-hatred rather than through hatred of the abuser. According to Winnicott's theoretical formulations, it is important to assess each partner's capacity for care or concern, object use, and being alone (Winnicott, 1956, 1958). Klein's (1948) construct of the "paranoid-schizoid" position is important as well. When a partner feels hurt and destroyed, she may attack her partner, only to then experience the partner as validating her perception of the world as dangerous, bad, or poisonous. Questions should be raised to determine each partner's worldview in this regard. To determine the nature of attachment style, questions need to address whether the primary attachment bond is secure or insecure (i.e., preoccupied, dismissive, or disorganized).

In summary, an understanding of the couple's inner world(s) involves a thorough exploration of the full range of neurophysiological factors associated with complex PTSD syndrome, object relational capacities, attachment styles, and ego strengths. This view of each partner's internal world combined with an evaluation of interactional and institutional factors converges to create a complex biopsychosocial assessment of the couple's competencies and vulnerabilities. This detailed assessment may then be used as a constructive tool to design a dynamic phase-oriented couple therapy treatment that attends differentially to the centrality of the presenting issues. In response to the expressed concerns, the assessment serves as both a compass and an anchor while navigating the course of couple therapy with a particular focus in place. When stabilization or resolution has been achieved, the couple and the clinician may move along to another focus of attention.

Phase-Oriented Couple Therapy Model

This chapter introduces a phase-oriented couple therapy practice model grounded in a synthesis of social, psychological, and trauma theories. Although the focus of attention is the dyadic couple relationship, this approach deals with family issues as well. First, the model is described in depth, stressing the general principles that undergird the practice approach. Next, the three treatment phases include Phase I: Safety, stabilization, and establishment of context for change; Phase II: Reflection on trauma narratives; and Phase III: Consolidation of new perspectives, attitudes, and behaviors (see also Table 8.1). Rationales for decision-making processes then unfold as we describe how a clinician employs the biopsychosocial assessment to forge a treatment plan and craft goals that guide choices for clinical interventions. In keeping with the metaphoric image of a therapeutic venture as a sailing journey, a thorough assessment functions both as a compass for directing the work and as a stabilizing anchor.

Second, specific relevant themes that are central in most couple therapy situations are then reviewed. They include: (1) composition of a "couple" (e.g., What is a "couple"? Is this a dual-trauma or single-trauma couple? Do the partners self-identify as heterosexual, bisexual, homosexual, or transgendered? Is this an interreligious or intercultural couple?); (2) interpersonal violence; (3) parenting; (4) sexuality; (5) affairs; (6) coexisting trauma-related disorders (including substance abuse and addictions, affective disorders, and characterological issues); and (7) dissociation.

:: THE PHASE-ORIENTED COUPLE THERAPY MODEL

This phase-oriented couple therapy practice model for survivors of childhood trauma is based on several organizing principles and guided by ethical standards of care that provide a solid foundation for all clinical work. They include: (1) relationship-based foundation in the therapeutic alliance, (2) empowerment with the locus of control situated with the client, (3) the centrality of resilience, (4) the integral influence of diversity variables and the sociocultural context, (5) a synthesis of psychological and social theoretical lenses, (6) a social justice consciousness, and (7) a flexible use of one's professional self (NASW, 2000).

Although a range of social, psychological, and trauma theories are available in the knowledge base of the clinician at any given moment, data forthcoming from the couple's presenting concerns determine which set of theoretical lenses advance to the foreground. However, certain theoretical models are used from the onset of treatment. For example, because a relationship base provides the foundation for the practice model, we must understand how trauma in childhood has shaped ways of relating, and how it influences the current relationship template. The lenses of object relations and attachment theories inform how these early relational patterns influence later relationships in adulthood (Kudler, Blank, & Krupnick, 2000; Lindy, 1996). In addition, social constructivist, racial identity, and feminist theories help to clarify the family's social context (Manson, 1997; Marsella, Friedman, Gerrity, & Scurfield, 1996; Pouissant & Alexander, 2000).

As the couple reveals their shared narrative, the presenting issues further signal which theoretical approaches might be especially relevant. Stated concerns about relationships and social interactions signal the need for an intergenerational family perspective so as to explore family patterns, rituals, and paradigms across generations (Danieli, 1998). A narrative family perspective may also illuminate the multiple and unique meanings of the trauma narrative (Merscham, 2000; Sheinberg & Fraenkel, 2001; Trepper & Barrett, 1989; White, 1995; White & Epston, 1990). Symptoms of clinical depression may signal the need to employ a cognitive–behavioral lens or a biological lens to explore affect regulation and cognitive distortions. In general, an assessment of the cognitive, affective, and behavioral functioning of each partner also addresses coping and adaptation (Compton & Follette, 1998). Finally, in the individual arena, trauma theories focus on the short- and long-term neurophysiological effects of trauma on brain function, particularly memory and affect regulation (Allen, 2001; Krystal et al., 1996; Schore, 2001a, 2001b; Shapiro & Applegate, 2000; van der Kolk, 1996, 2003). These theories also explain the complex effects of substance abuse or addictions and trauma-related disorders (Evans & Sullivan, 1995).

Although an assessment of each partner's trauma history is necessary in all cases, trauma theory may recede to the background if the assessment reveals the absence of trauma. However, in situations in which one or both partners has suffered trauma during childhood or adult life, trauma theory should remain one of the central theoretical lenses situated in the foreground of the couple therapy. In particular case situations, it becomes clear how all of the social and psychological theoretical lenses are present concurrently from the onset and throughout the course of therapy. However, one or more theoretical lenses may advance to the foreground in the couple therapy, when that perspective may be relevant to a particular presenting issue at hand.

This synthesis of biological, social, and psychological theory models informs the biopsychosocial assessment that subsequently guides the direction of practice. Holding the tension of multiple, often contradictory, theoretical perspectives while seeing the broader view requires flexibility in perception, understanding, and action on the part of the clinician. Knowledgeability and perceptiveness about these varied models are also essential requirements to sustain a questioning, flexible, yet grounded stance.

In contrast to sequential, essentialist stage models, a phase-oriented couple therapy treatment model assumes that diverse themes may be revisited at different periods throughout the work. In summary, the phases of couple therapy include Phase I: Safety, stabilization, and establishment of context for change; Phase II: Reflection on the trauma narrative; and Phase III: Consolidation of new perspectives, attitudes, and behaviors (Basham & Miehls, 2002). A metaphoric image of a dynamic three-dimensional triple helix comes to mind, where interconnected themes continually shift and weave together in a tapestry of new dimensions and perspectives.

Decision-Making Processes

To determine the treatment plan and goals for an individual couple, the clinician considers several central factors. Decision-making regarding a course of phase-oriented couple therapy will consequently be informed by the biopsychosocial assessment, with specific attention paid to cultural congruence, object relational capacity, and the dimension of time.

Cultural Congruence

First, the nature of "fit" between cultural congruence and a psychotherapy process needs to be assessed. If the couple expresses culturally defined attitudes that preclude a focus on introspection, self-reflection, and/or exploration of affect-laden psychological phenomena, then couple therapy should focus primarily on Phase I issues. In such a clinical case, Phase II work would involve a cognitive reflection of how the childhood traumatic experiences affect here-and-now interactions. Phase III tasks would focus on a consolidation of gains revealed in improved functioning, symptom relief, and cognitive understanding of the legacies of childhood trauma. A major asset of this particular course of couple therapy is the compatibility with a brief time frame for treatment.

Even when there is cultural congruence, object relational capacities, and sufficient time to deal with issues in more depth, many couples, on completion of Phase I tasks, decide to approach the tasks involved in Phases II and III in a cognitive framework. We do not encourage the retrieval of childhood traumatic memories. Instead, we counter a popular belief still held by many clinicians supporting a full affective reexperiencing of childhood traumatic memories. When clinicians privilege an insight-oriented therapy frame, while devaluing ego supportive and cognitive–behavioral interventions, couples might experience their progress as "not good enough." As a result, it seems very important to value the centrality of Phase I tasks, along with a cognitive perspective on Phases II and III, when appropriate.

Object Relations and Attachment Style

Object relational capacity and attachment style are central factors in shaping the direction of a couple therapy treatment plan, especially in Phases II and III. As mentioned earlier, Phase I tasks are recommended for all couples. Only when criteria are met for completion of these Phase I tasks is it appropriate to progress to Phase II. If couples choose to explore, in depth, the relational aftereffects of the legacies of childhood trauma, then Phase II work is recommended. For partners who have attained object constancy, emerging secure attachments, and some capacity to sustain ambivalence in the face of disappointment in intimate relationships, a reflection on the trauma narrative may involve a titrated reexperiencing of the traumatic memories, including restorying of the trauma narrative. These couples may also benefit from clarification of their projective identification processes. However, if couples lack sound object relational capacities and operate with disorganized attachment styles, then a cognitive reflection on the aftereffects of childhood trauma is more appropriate. In those situations, the partners might not possess sufficient ego and object relational strengths to withstand the emergence of intense affect related to the traumatic memories. Instead, couple therapy should start with a psychoeducational approach, encouraging cognitive reflection on how the "victim–victimizer–bystander" relationship template affects here-and-now relationships.

Phase III of the couple therapy model also takes a different shape, depending on the object relational and attachment capacities of the couple. This phase focuses on consolidation of new perspectives, attitudes, and behaviors. Typically, couples also actively evaluate the course of therapy, assessing areas of progress and areas for potential work. At this point in the couple therapy, the "victim–victimizer–bystander" scenario has been introduced on a psychoeducational level for all couples. However, in Phase III, the couple focuses more consistently on the recapitulation of this dynamic in their everyday interactions as well as on their interactions with other key relationships in their lives. This awareness might occur on a strictly cognitive level when therapy is time limited or when couples function with disorganized, part-object relational styles. Once again, rather than assuming that all change must occur through insight, behavioral and cognitive shifts may occur in interpersonal relationships after there has been sufficient cognitive reflection on the trauma narrative.

Yet those couples who possess sound object relations and relatively secure attachment styles may benefit from an insight-oriented method that clarifies the reowning of projected conflicts through projective identification processes. In these clinical situations, shifts may also be accompanied by affective and structural changes. Progress toward more equitable, mutual modes of relating are evident in day-to-day relationships, problem-solving, parenting approaches, and the sexual relationship.

These partners experience the type of Phase II work in which a restorying of the trauma narrative involves affective reexperiencing as well as an internalization of disowned projections. These couples often report awareness and shifts in both their understanding and experience with intergenerational influences, leading to real changes in attitude and interactions with important people in their lives. Couples often report a strengthening of social identities that varies in complexity, depending on the depth of the exploration. For example, although either or both partners may change a self-identification from "survivor" to "thriver" or "transcender" with regard to their childhood trauma, they often report greater cohesiveness in their gender, racial, ethnic, and/or sexual identities as well. In addition, during Phase III, some couples express a desire to engage in political advocacy to transform their adversity into positive action by challenging social injustices. Again, the degree of such changes in the areas of multiple social and psychological identities usually depends on both the object relational and attachment capacities for each partner, as well the availability of ample time to accomplish these therapy goals.

Time

After the completion of a thorough biopsychosocial assessment, the clinician gauges what treatment plan is recommended, based on the couple's unique set of issues. Finally, the limitation of time enters into decision-making. If there are requirements for a short-term contract (anywhere from one to twelve sessions) imposed by an agency, organization, or insurance carrier, then the clinician needs to assess with the couple what plan seems feasible, given the time constraints. Generally, emphasis is placed on Phase I tasks. If there is latitude to propose a couple therapy plan that extends beyond this three-month point, then a more thorough working through of Phase II and III tasks may be accommodated and recommended, if appropriate. All goals should be co-created by the clinician and client, paying attention at all times to sustaining the locus of control with the client.

In summary, Phase I tasks look similar in couple therapy with all clients. Two different paths occur for Phases II and III, depending on object relational and attachment capacities, cultural congruence, and the limitations of time. If there is cultural incongruence with a titrated affective reexperiencing, a time limitation, and/or unstable object relations or insecure/disorganized attachment patterns, Phases II and III rely on a cognitive reflection on the tasks. On the other hand, in the absence of time limitations and in the presence of relatively secure object relations and cultural congruence, Phase II and III tasks will involve a modulated affective reexperiencing of the trauma narrative and more in-depth attention will be paid to the intergenerational and family of origin relational influences on the couple's day-to-day relationships. The work also focuses intensively on how the legacies of childhood trauma affect parenting, sexuality, and identity development.

Relationship Building and the "Holding Environment"

Couple therapy begins with the establishment of the therapeutic alliance. Many trauma survivors have experienced violations of rules, and they carry memories of betrayal and insidious quid pro quo deals with their abusive offenders. As a result, the language of "contracts" or "rules" in couple therapy can often be fraught with "triggers" of these early betrayals. We find it useful to explore what language is more neutral for a couple. For example, creating a therapy frame by setting flexible "parameters" or "guidelines" may provide couples with less emotionally charged language to support the work.

Winnicott's (1965) concept of the holding environment is applicable for all psychotherapy settings, but is especially useful in designing a couple therapy frame for traumatized couples. Certain factors are pivotal in establishing a "safe-enough therapeutic holding environment." They include: (1) a professional stance as "container" and "good-enough" clinician (Applegate, 1995); (2) clarity of structure around safety, payment, and confidentiality; and (3) collaboration with helping professionals and funding sources.

Professional Stance and Use of Self

A clinical stance that conveys respectful curiosity, reliability, and cultural sensitivity is important from the onset. In approaching any issue of difference, the principles of alpha and beta bias are useful in attuning to commonalities and differences (Hare-Mustin, 1989). With this lens, we approach any issue of difference with an awareness of what unique experiences are shaped by differences in sociocultural factors (e.g., race, religion, or ethnicity) without slipping into polarized stereotypical alpha-biased thinking. On the other hand, the presumption of universality and commonality, although promoting global harmony, smacks of a beta-biased trivializing of important and salient differences. Maintaining a balance between alpha- and beta-biased assumptions is critical throughout the course of couple therapy as we address many differences and similarities. Since many couple therapy situations involve a cross-cultural therapeutic alliance, a clinician must be prepared to explore the full range of beliefs and attitudes regarding differences in worldview, social identities, family of origin influences, and intrapsychic conflict (Pérez-Foster, 1998).

As the realm of intersubjectivity within the context of the therapeutic relationship demands attention to the similarities, differences, and mutual interconnections between the client (the couple) and the clinician, ongoing self-reflection is imperative. Just as object relations and attachment theories help clinicians to understand the compelling force of transference–counter-transference phenomena, social theories, such as feminist and racial identity development models, enable the clinician to explore social identities for the client as well as for herself. To engage in this important self-reflective process, the clinician may borrow the useful construct of reflexivity to review these multiple interconnecting factors (Kondrat, 1999).

As mentioned earlier, the establishment of therapeutic exchanges and structure starts immediately, at the time of the first contact. Likewise, the development of a biopsychosocial assessment starts with the first contact and continues throughout the entire couple therapy as the process unfolds. For example, in scheduling an initial meeting with a couple, it is often helpful to talk first on the telephone with one or both partners and then to offer to meet for a consultation session. The couple is informed in the following language:

> The initial consultation meeting should hopefully provide each of you with an opportunity to express your concerns. I (as the clinician) will be able to hear in-depth the nature of each of your concerns. Then, I will be in a more informed position to offer you recommendations. The meeting should also provide both of you with the opportunity to meet me and make your decision about how you might like to proceed.

This intervention is deliberately aimed toward maintaining the locus of control and decision-making with the couple. Such an empowerment intervention is useful in all couple therapy, yet is especially important for trauma survivors who have been disempowered by their abusive offenders. By encouraging commitment to only one consultation meeting, rather than an expectation of open-ended therapy, distrust is acknowledged and emotional intensity is titrated.

After the consultation session(s), recommendations should be offered regarding an anticipated treatment plan, including the optimal frequency of meetings, setting of fees, cancellation policy, and accessibility via phone or email correspondence. Clinicians vary the frequency and length of sessions, with a typical span ranging from fifty- to sixty- or ninety-minute sessions on a weekly or biweekly basis. During the active phases of the couple therapy model, we propose an optimal frequency of meeting on a weekly or biweekly basis, with sessions that typically last one and one-half hours. This length of time allows a couple time to review the previous session and to comment on both their noteworthy gains as well as areas for focus and agenda setting. At least one hour is available, then, to focus in depth on the specific issues identified for the session, with at least fifteen minutes available afterward for remobilizing a balanced emotional state and planning for the upcoming week. In the event of crises, more frequent sessions are indicated. Following the end of the therapy course, couples often choose to continue to meet on a monthly or bimonthly basis, so as to reinforce their progress. One dual-trauma couple refers to their intermittent meetings as "tune-ups" for reinforcing their relational skills and "keeping the historical ghosts in check."

Clarity of Structure

A variety of agreements and parameters for couple therapy are useful in establishing a secure foundation in the early sessions. First, it is important to ask partners for permission to interrupt any abusive verbal exchanges. With prior permission in place, a clinician can ensure a baseline of safety during sessions, for both the couple and the clinician, by interrupting potentially destructive comments and volatile exchanges. Second, safety agreements from both partners ensure a plan to refrain from any physical expression of anger, including self-harm, both inside and outside of the session.

Third, discussion about the fee and mode of payment can often be riddled with trauma-related associations. Financial bribes and extortion are common among survivors of childhood trauma who were coerced to submit to abusive treatment in exchange for money. Boundary violations were often followed by financial payment, when an abuser tried to offer reparation for the maltreatment. For example, Angela, an adult trauma survivor, recalled many occasions in which her father slipped a ten-dollar bill under her bedroom door before he entered the room, as a hoped for enticement (or bribe) for Angela to comply with his sexual violations. Any effort by her partner to gift Angela with a financial present was met with intense rage, understood only much later in couple therapy as an example of a complex post-traumatic stress disorder (PTSD)–related enactment. As a result of such experiences, many clinicians find themselves sinking into "victim–victimizer–bystander" countertransference enactments as they try to negotiate fee setting and a payment schedule. As a result, the exchange of money between the couple and the clinician is a potentially fertile ground for "victim–victimizer–bystander" reenactments. Establishing clear guidelines about the amount charged and expectations for timeliness of payment are important as additional structural beams to support the emerging scaffolding of the therapeutic holding environment.

Fourth, limited confidentiality is another important parameter. Although many couples anticipate complete confidentiality, based on an individual psychotherapy framework, they need to be educated that the clinician maintains limited confidentiality. This translates into maintaining confidentiality vis-à-vis external sources, unless there is written permission. However, information and secrets are not held from either partner. This method ensures potential impartiality and fairness from the clinician, and conforms to the Health Insurance Portability and Accountability Act (HIPAA) requirements for privacy protection. It also allows freedom to meet with either partner in occasional individual consultation sessions, when indicated.

Collaboration with Adjunctive Professions and Funding Sources

Externalization of the "victim–victimizer–bystander" dynamic frequently yields rampant splitting and polarizations among key helping professionals who are involved with the couple. A fairly common phenomenon is the open warring among clinicians about their often contradictory treatment recommendations. Such intense dichotomized emotional debates mirror the couple's internal and external worlds dominated by the "victim–victimizer–bystander" template. Rather than recognizing the parallel process and interrupting the collective enactments, many professional teams continue on this futile path, unrelentingly. Inevitably, staff and clients are placed in rigid, categorical positions as the injured victim, the insensitive victimizers, the idealized rescuer, or the impotent, helpless bystander. When such divisiveness continues, the traumatized couple typically suffers because of the lack of effective coordination. Given these potential tensions, relationships with insurance companies or with Medicaid/Medicare providers should be approached cautiously as well. Full disclosure about the implications of reporting mental health information should always be discussed with the couple. Since many trauma survivors have difficulty protecting themselves, they may expose their private issues in a potentially hazardous manner. On the other hand, some trauma survivors might be obsessively worried about global retaliation from such providers, and may withhold information. Fueled by visceral fears, augmented by historical trauma-related terrors, these individuals often fear disclosure of personal information. However, in some cases, the unwillingness to disclose information might undermine the couple's therapy, if there is limited access to other professionals or financial supports.

Overall, the stability and predictability of a sound therapeutic holding environment enable the couple to gradually establish a workable level of trust and thus engage in the beginning phase of couple therapy. All clinicians working with traumatized couples are challenged to reflect regularly on multiple responses of a personal, objective, and cultural nature, as a way to monitor potential biases and understand both the couple's world and the intersubjective space within the therapeutic relationship. The clarity of structure for the phase-oriented couple therapy work includes agreements around (1) constructive, nonabusive communication; (2) safety; (3) fee setting and payment scheduling; and (4) limited confidentiality. Finally, clinicians must assume responsibility for assessing the organizational processes on the team, within the agency, and between professionals, and for changing these if they undermine the coherence of the couple's therapy. Instead, clinicians need to promote collaboration and tolerance of complex and, at times, contradictory beliefs and opinions.

Couple Therapy Phases

In this section, the three phases of the couple therapy model are described in detail (see also Table 8.1). The specific tasks associated with each phase are presented along with clinical vignettes that illuminate the various clinical issues.

Phase I: Safety, Stabilization, and Establishment of Context for Change

Phase I tasks are relevant for most, if not all, traumatized couples in therapy. These tasks include a full range of themes that aim to ensure (1) a basic sense of physical, psychological, and social safety; (2) stabilization, both individually as well as interpersonally; and (3) the establishment of a context for change, which involves clarifying relevant diversity themes and partnership status, as well as developing effective communication skills. This phase involves a full range of psychoeducational, cognitive–behavioral, body–mind, spiritual, and ego supportive interventions that promote adaptation and coping. Collaboration with relevant support systems such as schools, mental health and health professionals, Department of Social Services (DSS), and probation officers is often crucial during this phase as well.

Based on these objectives, object relations and attachment theories are useful at the onset to establish a therapeutic alliance (Winnicott, 1965). Guided by perspectives that are grounded in feminist, social constructionist, and racial-identity developmental theories, the clinician approaches the initial encounter and relationship building with an awareness of the social context (Pérez-Foster, 1998). Building a therapeutic alliance through an empathic connection enables the couple to discuss self-care and stabilization. Specific goals related to safety, self-care, and stabilization might best be met with clinical interventions that are grounded in ego psychology, cognitive–behavioral, and trauma theories. While completing a thorough biopsychosocial assessment that highlights areas for goal setting, the couple and the clinician may start to embark on Phase I tasks. We now review each of these Phase I couple therapy tasks.

Safety   It is essential to determine if the couple has secured basic safety in terms of food, shelter, and freedom from external or domestic violence. When physical violence exists, the clinician must advocate to ensure safety for a victim. At such times, a couple therapy modality is contraindicated, as it generally inflames an already incendiary dynamic.

Self-Care   The topic of self-care covers the areas of physical health, mental health, sleep, nutrition and exercise, substance use/abuse, and strategies for stress reduction and self-soothing. In this initial phase, we offer psychoeducational support about PTSD and complex PTSD (Allen, 2001). For example, clients are taught about the symptomatology associated with PTSD and complex PTSD, including a discussion of mood alterations, flashbacks, dissociation, and hypervigilance versus numbness. When appropriate, the neurophysiological effects of trauma are discussed to help couples understand certain behaviors through the lens of trauma theory. For example, a neurophysiological explanation of a startle response challenges an inaccurate interpretation of interpersonal rejection. Forgetfulness and "poor memory" may be related to dissociation, while rage storms can be explained in terms of a traumatic stress-induced "fight/flight" response.

Within this psychoeducational framework, the theoretical construct of the "victim–victimizer–bystander" scenario, grounded in trauma and intergenerational family theories, is also introduced as an internalized relationship template that affects all interpersonal relationships to some extent. Object relations theory is useful in understanding the complex internal world of "all-bad," "all-good," and "ambivalently held" objects (Basham & Miehls, 1998a, 1998b; Scharff & Scarff, 1991; Siegel, 1991; Zinner, 1989).

Based on the high incidence of co-occurring mental health diagnoses, various psychometric measures are used to arrive at a differential diagnosis between PTSD, complex PTSD, affective disorders, psychotic disorders, eating disorders, other compulsive disorders, substance use/abuse, and characterological issues (Wilson & Keane, 1997). Referrals for psychiatric consultation and/or medical consultation are crucial here if clinicians lack specialized education in psychiatry and medicine.

Since many of the legacies of childhood trauma involve neurophysiological responses, attention should be paid to strategies for stress reduction and self-soothing. As discussed in the chapter on trauma theories, many survivors have difficulty regulating affect and balancing the pendulum of hyperarousal to hypervigilance. In this arena, certain body–mind approaches are very useful for clients to find ways to reduce stress, meditate, and self-soothe. Depending on the particular couple and the respective partners, the following approaches may be effective for stress reduction, symptom relief, and skills training: yoga, biofeedback, relaxation exercises, meditation, hypnosis for affect regulation, massage, acupuncture/acupressure, dialectical behavioral therapy, and cognitive–behavioral interventions (Basham, 1999b; Compton & Follette, 1998; Gottman, 1999). Current thinking in the traumatology field discourages clinicians from promoting abreaction or the uncovering of early traumatic memories. Although considered an effective approach in earlier years, such cathartic methods are currently critiqued for promoting decompensation and regression. One notable exception that integrates cognitive–behavioral and neurophysiologically informed clinical interventions with affective reexperiencing of the traumatic event is eye movement desensitization reprocessing (EMDR) (Shapiro, 1995; Shapiro & Maxfield, 2003). Although this therapeutic method has received mixed reviews in terms of efficacy for type II traumatic events, it has been especially useful with discrete traumatic events.

Physical Health   It is important to explore each partner's physical health and her or his level of participation in monitoring physical self-care. Many survivors of childhood trauma experience trauma-related responses to the management of their physical and medical health care. Because childhood physical, sexual, and emotional abuse often leads to problems with body image and the relationship one has to one's body, numbness and detachment, as well as failure to seek medical consultation, are often problems. Failure to comply with treatment recommendations is also common, when trauma survivors undermine their care by self-medicating or neglecting all care. In contrast, trauma survivors who experience psychophysiological symptoms, related to stored iconic memories, may seek frequent support from the health care system. At the same time, they often engage in destructive behavior characterized by enactments of the "victim–victimizer–bystander" scenario. This may include parasuicidal or suicidal behavior, in which the client threatens to, or actually does, inflict self-harm. In the face of helplessness, some health professionals victimize these trauma survivors, complaining that they are malingering or hypochondriacal. In either situation, trauma survivors are often subjected to rebuke and humiliation.

ROSA AND JOAN :: Rose, a thirty-two-year-old Latino client educated as a nurse practitioner, was involved in couple therapy because of intense fighting over her many undiagnosed psychophysiological symptoms. Her thirty-year-old lesbian partner, Joan, neglected her symptoms of clinical depression. This ten-year partnership had been haunted by legacies from both women's traumatic childhood histories within their respective families of origin. Rosa claimed that she did not need to seek medical care as she was already trained in the field. After many discussions about her fears of potential retraumatization from the physical examination, Rosa finally mobilized her courage to meet with an internist. When type 2 diabetes was diagnosed, Rosa felt doomed. She promptly reported to Joan and me that all of the clinicians were incompetent. Joan promptly commented that Rosa's complaints sounded like a reenactment of the "victim–victimizer–bystander" scenario, with Rosa cast as the mistreated victim, and all of the clinicians as the insensitive victimizers. After several couple therapy sessions, Rosa recognized the pernicious effects of her traumatic reenactment and decided to engage more responsibly with her health care providers.

The phenomenon of overly zealous adaptations (i.e., either avoidance or stress-induced overutilization of services) can occur in the realm of mental health services as well. Although various therapy modalities are often recommended to trauma survivors to deal with the range of psychological and medical difficulties, this complex network sets the stage for multiple projections of the "victim–victimizer–bystander" scenario.

An example is the case of a dual-trauma heterosexual couple who were struggling with the aftermath of an affair initiated by the female partner, who works as an attorney. The male partner, also employed as an attorney, had been meeting with two individual therapists concurrently, until he recognized, in a couple therapy session, that he was symbolically retaliating toward his wife by choosing two supportive partners. However, in the spirit of splitting and projection, he proceeded to cast one therapist as the all-good nurturing clinician while the other was the all-bad withholding, mysterious (i.e., secretive) therapist. In this case, each partner's object relational tendencies toward splitting were augmented by the polarizations around power and control issues evident in the "victim–victimizer–bystander" dynamic. The arena of litigation, which values charging and convicting a victimizer, only reinforces the emotional intensity of this trauma scenario.

As couple therapists who work with trauma survivors, we each find extensive opportunities to collaborate with a range of helping professionals. Thus, it is imperative to remain mindful of the process of splitting. Indeed, it is very important to avoid slipping into a countertransference trap that reinforces polarized devaluations and idealization.

Substance Use/Abuse   Because the potential for substance abuse is so high for survivors of childhood trauma, a detailed discussion of treatment implications is deferred to a later section in this chapter.

Support Systems (Family, Community, and Religious/Spiritual Affiliation) Patterns of conflict and distance embedded in a "victim–victimizer–bystander" scenario often characterize the support systems surrounding an adult survivor of childhood trauma. For many dual- or single-trauma couples, rigid boundaries that serve a "defender" function constrict their lives through isolation. In an effort to protect themselves from emotional hurt, the couple, paradoxically, experiences emotional and social undernourishment. This leads to a state of internal hollowness that mirrors the barren landscape of their traumatic childhood years.

All aspects of the ecosystem should be addressed to assess the areas of strength and vulnerability in the couple's support network. Then, goals could be set to bring about possible changes in the network of extended family, friends, colleagues, neighbors, and community acquaintances. Connections to a faith-based community should also be examined, especially as a couple's religious and spiritual beliefs may be a source of comfort and meaning. The absence of such commitments may or may not contribute to a questioning of purpose. Because so many survivors of childhood trauma have perceived betrayal by God or a "higher power," each partner's relationship with spirituality or religion should be explored thoroughly. The recent crisis surrounding clergy abuse has stirred major doubts about the complicity of the Church hierarchy and a sense of betrayal for victims of these offenses. Vestiges of the "victim–victimizer–bystander" dynamic also surface in parenting approaches. As partners struggle with more empathic, fair, and nonabusive methods of parenting, they often challenge some of the harmful parenting practices experienced in their respective childhoods.

A common clinical error is to encourage trauma survivors to move rapidly toward healing emotional cutoffs with their families of origin by confronting the offender. These efforts are usually aimed at facilitating forgiveness and reparation. If, and when, such an approach might be clinically appropriate, it should occur only after the couple has established a sound therapeutic alliance and has completed all aspects of Phase I and II work. An important treatment guideline to consider involves avoiding simplistic solutions to conflictual, distanced, or absent relationships. Instead, the couple should be engaged in an intense review of their support system and encouraged to focus on relationships that they choose to strengthen. Only then can goals and a sound treatment plan be set.

> JOHNNIE AND JEANNIE :: The dual-trauma military couple, Johnnie and Jeannie, who were introduced in an earlier chapter, had distanced from virtually all support systems at the point of their marital crisis, to the extent of disconnecting all phone lines. In the course of their Phase I couple therapy work, an indicator of progress included practical steps to reconnect their phone and cable lines, thus reopening access to the outside world. Jeannie also resumed her attendance at her twelve-step Narcotics Anonymous home group, while Johnnie reconnected with his oldest son after a ten-year hiatus.

Opening up and extending these networks provide a couple with additional emotional and social supports as well as affirm their multiple identities vis-à-vis their family, community, and faith-based community. With increased safety and stabilization in place, the couple can reflect more effectively on their trauma narratives.

Communications Skills   A capacity to communicate effectively may often be influenced by childhood trauma–related aftereffects. As noted in Chapter 8 on assessment, the motto of "no hear, no see, and no speak" resounds loudly in many dual- or single-trauma couples. In addition to this psychological injunction to remain silent, the neurophysiological responses of alexythymia and subdued Broca area further contribute to the suppression of expression. Internal "victim–victimizer–bystander" scenarios also set the stage for verbally abusive exchanges and faulty attributions. Nonverbal communication can similarly convey a range of feelings including warmth, compassion, disappointment, and hatred.

This multilayered issue should be addressed with multilevel clinical interventions. First, the optimal cultural norms for communication need to be understood before particular treatment issues are defined (Marsella, Friedman, Gerrity, & Scurfield, 1996). The following questions should be posed: How do ethnic and cultural influences shape this couple's view of optimal communication styles? What value is attached to verbal or nonverbal expression? What value is attached to expressing thoughts and feelings about taboo topics?

Second, distinctions between abusive and nonabusive exchanges must be differentiated with the couple. As mentioned, couples are asked to provide permission to the clinician to interrupt any destructive exchanges in future sessions. When couples assent to this agreement at the beginning of therapy, the clinician can then call on this mediating influence in the midst of an emotionally escalating situation. The clinician's professional and personal values certainly play a vital role here in defining abuse. To minimize these biases, efforts should be made to discuss the particular types of exchanges that would be deemed abusive (i.e., intimidating, belittling, demeaning, attacking, judgmental, blaming, and denigrating language and behavior).

Although popular psychology culture still promotes an early introduction of psychoeducational models to remediate hurtful communication, this plan is frequently not helpful. As mentioned in Chapter 5 on trauma theories, the vast literature on the neurophysiology of trauma has taught us that neural relaxation of rage responses and psychophysiological symptoms should precede any practice of cognitive–behavioral methods to develop communication skills. Only when clients have tools to regulate their intense affects during dialogues should cognitive–behavioral techniques be introduced that promote active, empathic listening, conflict resolution, and "fair fighting" (Basham, 1999b; Compton & Follette, 1998; Gottman, 1999).

Assessment of Partnership Status   When couples enter therapy, they often arrive with expectations about what couple therapy provides and what they believe their goals and responses should be. With the emergence of couple therapy from the historical tradition of marital therapy or pastoral counseling, many couples continue to view a couple therapy modality as a directive, guidance approach, reminiscent of spiritual direction offered through religious affiliations (Northcut, 2000). In spite of the differentiation of secular couple therapy from church-based marital therapy, many couples still operate with these basic assumptions. From the onset of couple therapy, these issues need to be explored. The couple might be asked: What is your understanding about how couple therapy works? What would you like to accomplish? Do you have specific questions about the foundation or purpose of this approach? A psychoeducational approach often helps to clarify the purpose of couple therapy and the role of the clinician. In keeping with the metaphor of a journey, we usually suggest that the couple decide on a destination. Our role as clinical social workers is to provide navigational help to guide them toward their goal or destination.

Another misconception held by many couples is that engagement in couple therapy requires a distinct desire to work on the relationship as a prerequisite for participation. In fact, many couples use couple therapy to make a decision about the status of their partnership. At the onset of any consultation, four different paths are available. A couple may choose to (1) change and improve their relationship dynamics; (2) separate, divorce, or dissolve their partnership; (3) engage in a process that leads to a decision regarding the status of the partnership; or (4) decline couple therapy.

When a couple attending a couple therapy consultation is uncertain about the direction of the relationship, it is often helpful to pose a time-limited framework to assess the strengths and vulnerabilities of the relationship. During this evaluation process, the couple is in a better position to reach a decision regarding their future. Uncertainty frequently occurs when an affair has jolted a partnership into a state of instability. Sometimes, the aggrieved partner might respond reactively to hurt and anger by ending the relationship. On other occasions, the initiator of the affair pressures to dissolve the partnership in response to feelings of guilt or shame. However, when such actions are driven by impulse, the couple may then experience considerable regret. In such cases, crisis intervention that focuses on the aftermath of the affair is most useful with a time-limited frame. During this time period, plans for deciding about the future of the relationship are suspended. Once the crisis has abated, another time-limited agreement might focus on assessing the strengths and vulnerabilities of the relationship to help with a decision regarding future direction.

Phase II: Reflection on the Trauma Narrative

Phase II of this couple therapy model involves sharing perspectives on the traumatic childhood experiences while restorying the narratives with a new focus on resilience and adaptation. This particular treatment phase focuses on a number of themes. They include: (1) exploration of the meaning of the traumatic experiences, (2) exploration of different meanings of intimacy, (3) exploration of the intergenerational legacies of childhood trauma, and (4) creation of healing or transitional rituals.

Meaning of the Trauma Narrative   Given the current controversy regarding the uncovering of traumatic memories, it is important to note up front that most couples benefit from a reflective sharing of their traumatic experiences, either on a cognitive or a cognitive and titrated affective level, without full affective reexperiencing of early traumatic memories. As noted earlier in the section of this chapter on decision-making processes, Phase II work will be shaped differently according to the cultural congruence, flexibility of time, and the couple's object relational capacities. Where there is a time limitation restricting the clinical work, incongruence with cultural beliefs, and/or part-object relations, childhood trauma memories will be discussed in the context of the "here-and-now" expressions of these trauma-related legacies. Given this treatment situation, Phase II work should rely on clinical interventions that encourage the client to reflect on the effects and legacies of their childhood traumatic experiences in the present, recognizing the persisting influences of the "victim–victimizer–bystander" dynamic. Such an approach may draw from narrative and intergenerational family therapy approaches in which questions are posed regarding the meaning and influence of the trauma narrative along with the exploration and identification of trauma-related intergenerational family patterns (Danieli, 1998). Only when couples possess whole-object relational capacities and cultural congruence should there be a titrated affective uncovering of memories. In such a treatment situation, Phase II work may involve the clarification of projective identification processes (grounded in object relations theories) with couples who possess cultural congruence and reasonably secure attachment and sound object relational capacities (Bader & Pearson, 1988; Basham & Miehls, 1998a, 1998b; Scharff & Sharff, 1991; Sharpe, 2000).

Partners in dual- or single-trauma couples often deny or minimize the significance of their childhood traumatic experiences of sexual, physical, or emotional abuse. As a result, many couples seek treatment with a disguised presentation, revealing other presenting issues, such as divisive arguments or estrangement. In the course of questioning couples about how their cultural views and families of origin shaped their attitudes about coupling, family, intimacy, and parenting, clinicians often see narratives emerging that signal childhood maltreatment. With the ever-present risk of interpreting or suggesting the existence of childhood trauma, a clinician must tread carefully to avoid enacting an intrusive, judgmental "victimizing" stance of searching diligently for traumatic childhood memories, or an ineffectual "bystander" position of collusive blindness. Labeling childhood experiences as abusive or traumatic without sound confirmation from the client's experience qualifies as a "victimizing" countertransferential enactment. This assessment violates basic ethical standards of care in the field of traumatology.

As partners start to recognize the impact of these trauma-related childhood legacies on their day-to-day lives, they observe recurrent appearances of the "victim–victimizer–bystander" scenario. Gradually, both partners acknowledge the internalization of multiple roles, rather than solely assuming a one-dimensional "victim" role. Such a realization frees couples from entrenched interactional battles over who is right, who is in charge, or who gets his or her way.

For example, the lesbian couple Rosa and Joan, who battled regularly over power and control, started to see how each partner vied for "victim" status while each failed miserably at convincing the other of her victory. Indeed, each partner felt victimized regularly until the couple interrupted this destructive pattern.

Meaning of Intimacy As partners talk about the meaning of intimacy, the clinician needs to explore the messages and family paradigms learned from their families of origin. The following questions might be asked: In what ways did your family members express affection? Joy? Pride? Satisfaction/ dissatisfaction? Encouragement? Solace? Kindness? Respect? Typically, as partners share their recollections of these experiences, they begin to distinguish between verbal and nonverbal expressions. Not surprisingly, these modes of expression shaped by cultural, religious, and family beliefs are often incompatible between partners.

ROSA AND JOAN (continued) :: As Rosa associated affection with care-taking of other people devoid of any verbal conversation, Joan replied passionately, "Intimacy could be shared only with comforting and tender remarks," reminiscent of the caring comments she recalled given by her father and grandmother. Although each partner felt unappreciated for her demonstrations of affection, both started to understand how the projections of their internal conflicts prevented each woman from understanding her partner's meaning of intimacy. Bolstered by a stronger empathic connection, Rosa and Joan slowly learned to more graciously accept the other partner's displays of affection, while also trying to make slight modifications in the ways that affection could be expressed.

Intergenerational Pattern of "Victim–Victimizer–Bystander" Dynamic Not only are intergenerational patterns of expression passed along through generations, but patterns of conflict resolution are transmitted as well. When partners are asked to reflect on how negative feelings were expressed and how differences were managed in their respective families of origin, a range of responses emerge. Useful questions to facilitate this discussion might address: How did your family (nuclear, extended, and ancestral) express and deal with anger? Disappointment? Conflict? Disapproval? Sadness? Grief?

Once again, concerning Rosa and Joan, Rosa recalled her mother insisting on immediate compliance, prohibiting complaints from any of her six children. Joan, on the other hand, recalled loud verbal arguments that would last for hours without apparent resolution. Both partners learned extreme methods of regulating affect—that is, either total suppression, as in Rosa's family, or chaotic venting, as in Joan's family—resulting in a collective sense of victimized helplessness. Not surprisingly, a "victim–victimizer–bystander" dynamic was reenacted regularly with unrelenting tenacity. Embedded in this repetitive enactment, however, was a strong adaptive stance, demonstrating each partner's capacity to engage and struggle with difficult issues. In the course of the couple therapy, this "determined, fighting spirit" was redefined as a strength.

As noted earlier, clarification of projective identification processes can further illuminate enactments and promote restorying of the narrative. For Rosa and Joan, their intermittent capacities for sound object relations and cultural congruence enabled them to benefit from these interventions. An important step in identifying projective identification processes is to recognize strong polarities in thought or behavior. In this clinical example, Rosa and Joan continually battled about who was in charge or who was right. Polarizations prevailed! Joan viewed Rosa as emotionally labile and irresponsible, while Rosa viewed Joan as detached and rigidly tyrannical. As each partner railed against the other, neither partner felt understood, which only fueled anger and powerlessness. The enactment of the projective identification process involving the "victim–victimizer–bystander" template was complete. As these processes gradually unfolded, the projective identification surfaced vividly. When this occurs, each partner represses, splits off, and projects onto the partner the side of the internal dispute that is disowned. What are fought out are the problems that neither partner has been able to address internally. Thus, core issues emerge as a polarization of attributes, such as "over-responsible–under-responsible," or "expressive–detached." By maintaining a rigid view of these differences, each partner then recognizes the disavowed parts of self that have been projected onto the partner. Fighting over disowned projected parts of self then ensues.

Thus far, we have seen in Joan and Rosa only one aspect of the disavowed conflict, a disowned attribute. The behavior expressed by the clinician distinguishes this process as projective identification rather than projection, as the clinician enacts a part of the disavowed conflict. In this instance, the couple was fighting over who was more or less responsible, or who was more or less expressive. However, the underlying intrapsychic conflict related to the "victim–victimizer–bystander" template. The conflict embodied a wish for control versus a fear of loss of control that may be played out around any number of issues, in this case, responsibility and expressiveness. Each partner wrestles with this internal conflict shaped by her early childhood traumatic experiences of a loss of personal control and agency. It translates into the conflict over who abuses power (the victimizer), who is abused by power (the victim), and who stands by and ignores the situation (the bystander). As each partner projects this conflict outward, the other partner may enact one aspect of the conflict. For example, when Joan rages at Rosa, she enacts the victimizer role, leading to a sense of victimized powerlessness. When Rosa detaches, she enacts the passive bystander role by ignoring serious danger and recapitulating the earlier traumatic experiences. In the end, both Joan and Rosa alternately feel powerless and detached. To understand and transform this dynamic, each partner needs to recognize her agency in the process and refrain from enacting one of these roles. Instead, by focusing on individual responsibility, they can address each issue together, as a couple. Rather than blaming the other, each partner answers questions about ways each woman experiences her power and competence. Before each partner is capable of re-owning her projected conflicts, the clinician must be prepared to "hold" intense projected affects, functioning as a Winnicottian "container"(Winnicott, 1965). As Joan and Rosa wrestled with their conflicts, I wrestled internally with containing Joan's projected sense of emotional vulnerability while also containing Rosa's projected conflicts with control and helplessness. In time, both women reowned their projected conflicts and developed greater balance in their affect regulation and in shared responsibility.

Intergenerational patterns are important as well, as both positive and negative themes resonate from one generation to the next. To enable the couple to explore the meaning of and reshape their trauma narrative, unearthing intergenerational patterns adds an important dimension for the couple's understanding of their respective families of origin. For example, Rosa initially described herself and her mother as victims of circumstance, given the tragedy of her father's untimely death and the resulting financial hardship. As Rosa traced her family history, she discovered that her mother, maternal grandmother, and maternal great-aunt challenged some traditional roles for women in their Mexican villages, and immigrated to the United States. Rosa began to identify her iconoclastic lifestyle proudly with the pioneering spirit of her ancestors. Although she knew very little of her father's life, as she searched for information, she discovered that he had worked as a tradesman, yet always enjoyed playing the guitar. Even if there was no causal connection here, she felt a positive identification with his creative spirit while he was fighting his virulent cancer. As Joan explored information about her family, it yielded several generations of aunts, grandmother, and great-aunts on both the maternal and paternal sides who not only reared children but also worked as midwives. Although Joan often devalued her caregiving qualities, she recognized the intergenerational value placed on this important role. In fact, the extent of caregiving was the problem, not the valued quality in and of itself. An exploration of family paradigms and intergenerational patterns may reveal not only patterns of dysfunction, including the "victim–victimizer–bystander" scenario, but also areas of mastery and creativity that help the couple to restory their trauma narratives.

Transition/Healing Rituals   One final theme that is addressed in Phase II (reflection on the trauma narrative) of the couple therapy model relates to healing and family rituals. As noted in Chapter 8 on assessment, many adult survivors of childhood trauma have been reared in families in which a disorganized, chaotic environment or cloaks of secrecy prevented them from celebrating important events with an appropriate ritual (Imber-Black, 1989). As a result, couples may be thwarted in their efforts to move along with life's challenges. In many cases these rituals have been spoiled by abusive events during childhood, while at other times the rituals were completely absent. It is important therefore to explore with each couple how they acknowledge important events: How did they acknowledge their partnership? With a commitment ceremony? Wedding? How did they acknowledge other important nodal events, such as births? Deaths? Graduations? Retirement? Other nodal events that are less immediately associated with transitions or celebration rituals include foster care moves, adoption, miscarriage, infertility, emigration, geographic moves, and the end of life. Then there are the traumatic events that garner even less attention, as they often evoke disturbing feelings. For example, the clinician may ask: How often are you aware of transition or healing rituals that help individuals accept divorce? Dissolution of a relationship? Traumatic illnesses and deaths? Coming to terms with the legacies of childhood trauma? In recent years, some mental health practitioners have encouraged victims to confront their offenders, often involving pressing criminal charges. Such a path may or may not help as a healing ritual. Instead, a different path may promote healing during this transition period. For example, trauma survivors might be encouraged to chronicle in writing, drawing, sculpture, or any other art form an acknowledgment of their childhood traumatic experiences, emphasizing their resilience and triumphs as well as their suffering. Constructing this ritual, either alone or in the presence of witnesses, may bring significant closure to a difficult life chapter.

OLGA AND BORIS :: Olga, a twenty-nine-year-old Russian Catholic woman, and Boris, her thirty-one-year-old Russian Orthodox husband, ended their marriage of six years. During the couple therapy, this dual-trauma couple realized that they had gravitated to each other through traumatic bonding, and had proceeded to verbally abuse each other steadily for five years. As they moved toward divorce, the couple agreed to meet for a special visit together in a park where they had initially met. Here, they buried their wedding rings. After some tears, they expressed relief that they had finally stopped badgering each other, realizing that there was very little positive core to the marriage, other than mutual rescuing.

Then, after Olga had connected her "victim–victimizer–bystander" relational patterns as a legacy of her abusive childhood, she remembered how her father had abused her, both physically and sexually, during adolescence following the early, tragic death of her mother. Her father subsequently committed suicide, after a ten-year bout with untreated clinical depression. To affirm both the positives in her family life along with the tragic circumstances, Olga decided to celebrate her parents' lives. She also mourned their deaths, as well as the death of her innocence.

Olga wrote letters to both parents expressing gratitude, outrage related to her abuse and neglect, as well as hope for the future. Then she proceeded to head to northern Vermont in the springtime to visit her mother's grave. After an imaginary conversation with her mother, she buried the letter at her mother's tombstone and headed to the raging river nearby where her father had drowned himself several years before. His body had never been found. Anna knelt by the riverside, spoke to her father, and gently slipped the letter into the river. After a few months, she expressed a sense of calm and strong conviction about her fortitude in life. Both partners grieved multiple losses. With the aid of these healing rituals, they were able to move on.

In summary, as each partner expresses her or his trauma narrative to the partner, there is an opportunity to restory the narrative, accessing the strengths embedded in adaptation. In the process, depending on the object relational capacities of each partner, the partners are able to strengthen their capacities for empathy toward each other. With heightened awareness about the intergenerational transmission of the legacies of childhood trauma, the exploration of the "victim–victimizer–bystander" pattern and of how it affects both historical and current relationships strengthens the partnership, as well as each partner's individual recovery. Transitional healing rituals might also aid in facilitating this progress.

Phase III: Consolidation of New Perspectives, Attitudes, and Behaviors

Phase III tasks focus primarily on a consolidation of the family-of-origin work started in Phase II, along with further strengthening of family and community relationships. Once again, if there is a time limitation or part-object relating, this phase will focus primarily on the cognitive reflection of the "victim–victimizer–bystander" pattern in all areas of the couple's life. Couples at this point often report less shame, stigma, and isolation. Their parenting skills often broaden to include improved listening and the capacity to set firm yet benevolent limits. The couple may choose to focus on how the legacies of childhood trauma have affected their sexual relationship in terms of power inequities, distrust, and neurophysiological symptomatology.

If a couple is able to work within a longer-term framework and is supported by object relational and attachment capacities, they may benefit from continued insight-oriented interventions, developing greater capacity to tolerate the aggressive victimizing roles within themselves. Through this process, partners are more capable of sublimating their aggression into proactive and creative activities. This transition also involves abandoning a rigid self-definition that is linked exclusively to the traumatic experiences. During this phase, couples may express a greater sense of mastery, vitality, and joy. They often may move beyond self-definitions as survivors to self-definitions as "overcomers" or "transcenders." Although the legacies of childhood trauma remain vivid in memory, they no longer function as a primary definer of identity. During this process of shifting identities, partners often report positive shifts in the emergence of their racial, ethnic, sexual, and psychological identities. These couples may also engage themselves in political and social action as another way to advocate for safer childhoods. In the ending phase of couple therapy, one of the Phase III tasks involves evaluating the efficacy of the treatment. Couples are asked to review their therapy goals and comment on the progress or lack thereof. Relationship satisfaction should be evaluated. Remediation of presenting issues and overall relationship satisfaction likewise should be examined. In most cases in which couples have felt a sense of accomplishment, they describe a transformation of pain and loss into a renewed sense of hope in their relationship. When couples describe dissatisfaction with therapy, it often relates to a failure in progress with the stated goals or a rupture in the therapeutic alliance. In these situations, it is very important for the clinician to assess thoroughly any possible enactments of the "victim–victimizer–bystander" scenario.

In summary, this section has reviewed the decision-making processes that guide a couple therapy treatment plan and has explicated the relevant aspects of Phases I, II, and III of this phase-oriented couple therapy practice model. The next section elaborates central themes that command particular attention. They include: (1) the composition of a "couple," (2) the role of violence, (3) parenting, (4) sexuality, (5) affairs, (6) substance abuse/addictions, (7) multiple/dual diagnoses of trauma-related disorders, and (8) dissociation.

:: CENTRAL THEMES

Composition of the "Couple"

With increasing awareness that "health" or "normality" are socially constructed, couple and family therapists understand that worldviews and the larger sociocultural contexts influence expectations for optimal couple functioning. However, many family researchers continue to describe optimal couple functioning in terms of culture-bound definitions. The empirically based multidimensional Beavers Systems Model (Beavers & Hampson, 2003) focuses on family competence. The model is used to assess how well a family, as an interactional unit, performs the necessary and nurturing tasks of organizing and managing itself. Another widely used couple and family therapy model is referred to as the Circumplex Model (Olson, Russell, & Sprenkle, 1980). Optimal couple functioning here includes a balance of cohesiveness, flexibility, and communication. The researchers suggest that optimal communication involve the following skills: "Listening skills include empathy and attentive listening. Speaking skills include speaking for oneself and not speaking for others. Self-disclosure relates to sharing feelings about oneself and the relationship" (Olson & Gorall, 2003, p. 520). Along similar lines, Gottman's laboratory studies have lent clarity to couple interaction processes with data suggesting that "happy" couples must "sustain a level of positive interactions and conflict resolution to sustain a happy and stable relationship" (Driver, Tabares, Shapiro, Nahm, & Gottman, 2003, p. 499).

Although these studies provide useful theoretical constructs to assess optimal couple functioning, most of the norms have been based on middle-income, Caucasian, two-parent families. Given this limitation, definitions need to be expanded to accommodate a culturally diverse sample. Ironically, Walsh, who writes compellingly about the need to critique confining definitions of family or couple health, continues to espouse increased gender equality in families (Walsh, 2003). Although she argues for a feminist-informed understanding of coupling, the concept of an equitable relationship does not always apply in certain unions that privilege patriarchy or other inequitable modes of relating. For example, in certain Muslim and Orthodox Jewish families, religious dogma supports gender role inequities. An ethical question arises: Should a clinician work with the couple's value system or impose her own worldview of equitable partnership? Clashes between the personal and professional value systems of the clinician and the couple inevitably activate clinical dilemmas.

Along similar lines, rather than restricting the notion of coupling as confined to a legally sanctioned heterosexual marriage arrangement, our definition of a couple includes those individuals who self-define as involved in a committed partnership. This position expands our purview to work with lesbian, gay, bisexual, and transgendered couples, as well as those couples who self-identify as partnered with or without a signed legal contract.

Is it possible that the definition of a couple has broadened so far that it has lost all meaning and is overly inclusive? Would all individuals who self-define as couples automatically be accepted into couple therapy? Are there, in fact, individuals who self-identify as a couple who are inappropriate for a couple therapy modality? Two noteworthy examples come to mind. First, if the clinician ascertains that active physical violence is expressed between the couple, couple therapy is contraindicated. This topic is addressed more fully in a later section of this chapter. Second, if a clinician is asked and expected to maintain confidentiality for one or both partners about information not shared between the couple, couple therapy is inadvisable. In such a situation, the clinician colludes with the secrecy and betrayal of one or both partners, while losing effectiveness as a balanced, mediating influence.

JOHN AND MARIE, JOHN AND PAT, AND JOHN AND CHERISE ::
John, a thirty-four-year-old Caucasian male client of Eastern European descent, was employed as a National Park Service ranger, in charge of protecting wildlife. He telephoned me to inquire about couple therapy for himself
and his second wife of six years (referred to as partner 1, Marie). Both of them
were drinking heavily and using cocaine regularly, having slipped into a major relapse after a five-year period of collective abstinence and sobriety. John
also asked if I could meet in couple therapy with him and a girlfriend at work
with whom he was having an affair (partner 2, Pat). Finally, he wondered if I
could also meet with him and a third girlfriend, whom he had met within the
past few months (partner 3, Cherise). John experienced some level of commitment to each of the three women, and expressed major concerns about trying to coordinate these three relationships without each of the women finding out about the other. Only partner 2 (Pat) knew about his marriage, but
his legal wife (Marie) and partner 3 (Cherise) knew nothing about the other
partners, nor did partner 2 (Pat) know about partner 3 (Cherise). What initially sounded like a nexus of John's need-gratifying relationships, steeped in
exploitation and deception, shifted to a far more complex historical narrative.

After explaining to John on the telephone about the need for limited confidentiality in couple therapy, where the clinician holds no secrets with either
partner, he reluctantly agreed to meet for an individual psychotherapy consultation. Very soon, he spoke of a terrifying childhood during which an older
neighborhood adolescent boy had forced him to submit to fellatio and anal
sex, tyrannizing him from ages eight until eleven. When his family moved
from the area, John escaped from this tortuous sexual abuse, yet was plagued
in adulthood by disturbing memories. Throughout his adolescence and adulthood, John escaped by numbing his traumatic memories through substance
abuse and immersion in many sequential partnerships and affairs. He never
trusted anyone to provide basic love and support. During a nine-month
period of individual therapy, John addressed the legacies of his childhood
trauma including Phase I attention to self-care and renewed abstinence. Although a hiatus had been set around the marital issues for many months, I
then referred John with his wife to a couple therapist at this phase of the work,
as they both wanted to work out marital issues. In the interim, John had ended
partnership 3 with Cherise and had told both his wife, Marie, and partner 2,
Pat, about the other. He ultimately decided to suspend the affair with Pat
while he evaluated the future of his marriage.

Although the number of intimate partnerships added complexity to John's case, it was very important to avoid a common countertransference trap of victimizing him with punitive comments. In classroom discussions in response to this case presentation, an immediate collective countertransference response generated outrage and critical retaliation. However, the class participants then proceeded to discuss how such a morally charged judgmental response colludes with reenactment of the childhood abuse suffered by John. The class emerged as the victimizers! If enacted by the clinician, therapeutic change could well have been thwarted in this case. In the course of John's therapy, he had gained the courage to be more direct with his partners. The legacies of his life-threatening childhood abuse no longer terrorized and silenced him. He was able to be less exploitative toward his wife and girlfriends, as he relinquished his protective shield of deception.

In summary, this vignette intends to convey the importance of respecting the couple's self-definition of a partnership. However, a clinician should also maintain a strong clinical and ethical stance concerning the indications and contraindications of couple therapy as an optimally effective modality.

Another pivotal issue in couple therapy with survivors of childhood trauma is sexual orientation. Given the complexity of the topic, a thorough discussion is introduced in Chapter 13. As a general guideline, however, there is a compelling need to address the impact of heterosexism and homophobia, both external and internalized, on the lives of lesbian, gay, bisexual, and transgendered couples. In a similar vein, the influences of sociocultural context are central in all couple therapy, but are especially pronounced with intercultural, interracial, and interreligious couples. In these couples, attention to differences as well as commonalties may be guided by the principles of alpha and beta biases (Hare-Mustin, 1989). In approaching any issue of difference, it is important to be mindful of the unique experiences that are shaped by differences in race, sexual orientation, religion, ethnicity, and so forth, without slipping into polarized, stereotypical, alpha-biased thinking. On the other hand, the presumption of universality and commonality, in the spirit of promoting global unity, smacks of beta bias that trivializes important and salient differences. Hence, maintaining the balance of alpha- and beta-biased assumptions is critical throughout the course of couple therapy as differences and similarities are addressed.

The final topic involved in the composition of the couple relates to who has experienced childhood trauma. Has only one partner experienced childhood trauma, or have both partners? What was the nature of the earlier traumas? Have one or both partners participated in psychotherapy and other treatment approaches? If so, what have been the influences, in general and in particular, in relation to the legacies of childhood trauma? In general, the main differences between single- and dual-trauma couples relates to intensity (Balcolm, 1996). Many of the presenting issues are identical for all couples, yet, with single-trauma couples, there is usually more focus on the traumatized individual as the "identified client," accompanied by the supportive, ancillary spouse. However, this couple therapy practice model clarifies that, even with single-trauma couples, there is a process of mutual complementarity that sustains interactional patterns similar for dual-trauma couples.

When both partners have experienced childhood trauma, they often compete over who may have suffered more pain, voicing dissent about who is the more injured party! Some couples, with sound perspective and self-reflective abilities, have actually understood their competitive behavior as mirroring "Victimology Olympics"! For dual-trauma couples who lack secure attachments and the capacity for stable object relations, engagement in intractable, unrelenting struggles may aim to pronounce one the designated victim and the other one a designated victimizer in the battle. In this scenario, neither partner accepts the existence of a complex internalized "victim–victimizer–bystander" relationship template that includes elements of all roles. There may also be augmented emotional reactivity for dual-trauma couples, when both partners are intermittently triggered by childhood memories that might fuel misunderstanding and emotional eruptions. Finally, there may be a tendency to set particularly extreme boundaries between partners and family, friends, and community. Oftentimes, a family milieu distinguished by secrecy and isolation has been characteristic of abusive childhood homes. In a reenactment of this early relational trauma scenario, similar patterns may be replayed in adult life. The following vignette reveals this clinical dilemma in the case of a dual-trauma couple.

LARA AND VITOS :: Lara and Vitos are a middle-income heterosexual childless Roman Catholic couple reared as second-generation Slovak descendents. They have been married for twenty years and, throughout their time together, have both excelled in their sales and development jobs within the business world. In contrast, their home resembled a remote fortress. Only on very rare occasions did this couple choose to invite friends to their home, in part because they fought unrelentingly about how to plan collaboratively for a dinner gathering. Instead, they each projected onto the other a sense of shame and negative identity, emerging from the legacies of their respective childhood traumas. Each partner claimed that the other was hopelessly inadequate. Only when they recognized a possible benefit to opening their home ever so slightly were they willing to exert the enormous emotional energy to counter an entrenched, institutionalized reenactment of their relational trauma scenario. Quite tentatively, they expressed satisfaction and curiosity in broadening their social network. Then, within several months, their utter isolation from their social world eased, with each partner breathing a sigh of relief, albeit with anxiety about how they had changed. As each partner noted, sometimes a known enemy is far more comforting than an unknown possibility!

The Role of Violence

Many individuals who have been traumatized as children develop symptomatology of complex PTSD. One of the disturbing patterns that adult trauma survivors repeat is the reenactment of a traumatic relationship scenario reminiscent of the original relational abuse. This may involve emotional and/or physical abuse inflicted by one or both partners in a couple relationship. A cycle of violence can be understood in psychological terms with regard to escalating anger, culminating in out-of-control rage and the inflicting of violence, followed by the offender's wish for forgiveness, and ultimately, reconciliation initiated by the aggressor (Straus, Gelles, & Steinmetz, 1988; Walker, 1984). However, once a line is crossed into physical violence, we recommend addressing the problem as a criminal justice issue. Although we may identify interactional patterns of domestic violence, we must avoid "blaming a victim." Instead, an offender needs to be held accountable.

It is naive to think that only heterosexual couples engage in domestic violence. Gay, lesbian, bisexual, and transgendered couples have also been reared in patriarchal cultures that privilege the oppression of a subjugated group. As a result, many have internalized the abuse of power embedded in dysfunctional patriarchal structures. Another impediment to assessing domestic violence with gay, bisexual, lesbian, and transgendered couples is a pull for both the couple and the clinician to minimize domestic violence for fear of reinforcing negative stereotypes. Ironically, in an effort to protect these couples from the critical scrutiny of homophobia, a clinician's collusion to deny could render these individuals vulnerable to physical harm.

Until the past decade, domestic violence has not been widely acknowledged in the gay, lesbian, or transgendered community. Possible reasons for this oversight are homophobic and heterosexist attitudes leading to presumptions that gay males and lesbians are more sensitive and less violent than heterosexual couples (Elliott, 1996; Miller, Bobner, & Zarski, 2000). In the late 1980s and early 1990s, various studies documented that the type and frequency of domestic violence in gay and lesbian partnerships are similar to the incidence rates found in heterosexual samples (Elliott, 1996; Kelly & Warshafsky, 1987). Much of the current understanding of same-sex domestic violence comes from superimposing heterosexual templates onto lesbian and gay partnerships. For example, an inaccurate stereotype depicts a gay batterer as being more masculine and his victim being more feminine. In fact, researchers of same-sex relationships have not found masculine/feminine role-playing to be the norm (Miller, Bobner, & Zarski, 2000; Renzetti, 1992). Instead, the influence of patriarchal patterns, the role of alcohol and other substance abuse, and perceived powerlessness are more salient factors in understanding domestic violence in same-sex relationships. With these important influences in mind, careful attention must be paid to assess the potential for, and the actual reality of, violence for these couples, without creating alpha-biased stereotypical generalizations about the entire population.

For many years, supporters for the rights of victims of domestic violence have joined the professional community in encouraging an advocacy stance to be taken at the moment that a violent situation is determined. In a psychotherapeutic setting this translates into meeting the victim on an individual basis and helping her or him to locate an adequate safe shelter, emotional support, and legal representation. The violent offender is directed to a treatment program that usually includes group and/or individual psychotherapy modalities.

Numerous studies have substantiated the risks of meeting with a couple in therapy where there is active violence (Bograd & Mederos, 1999; Sprenkle, 1994). However, there remain many treatment programs, whose work is characterized by sensitivity to issues of power and gender inequity, that have been experimenting with couple therapy in domestic violence situations (Goldner, 1992; Goldner, Penn, Sheinberg, & Walker, 1990; Lipchik & Kubicki, 1996). Bograd and Mederos (1999) write a thoughtful review of the risks and liabilities of these approaches, in which clinicians may see couples together in a couple therapy modality if the offender assumes responsibility for his or her actions and if there is minimal abuse. Although a couple therapy session might unfold with reasonable restraint and civility, a violent offender may still retaliate toward the partner after the session in response to a perceived injury. Given the absence of adequate data to support the efficacy of treatment in cases where violence is active, it is safer and wiser to refer each partner to individual and/or group modalities. Typically, the time following a couple therapy session is most worrisome, when the couple reverberates with intense feelings that have been stirred in the meeting. Based on these significant risks, we iterate clearly our strong conviction that meeting with a couple is contraindicated where there is active physical violence.

This stance raises an obvious question. At what point in time is a couple eligible to enter couple therapy after they have completed their individual courses of treatment? Typically, literature in the domestic violence field points to at least a year of active treatment that has dealt with anger management before couple therapy is initiated (Bograd & Mederos, 1999). There are, of course, many clients in couple and family therapy who have histories of physical violence who have met the treatment criteria for completion of psychotherapeutic treatment. Yet any one of these individuals could relapse at any time. What are the safest ways to engage such a couple? Goldner et al. (1990) discuss at length the benefit in treating couples with histories of violence, as long as the clinician can assume a "both/and" position of understanding the interactional cycle of violence while holding the violent offender accountable for any violent behavior.

A difficult clinical situation involves an episode of physical violence by a partner in couple therapy after a lengthy period of violence-free recovery. Should the couple therapy be terminated immediately? Or, rather than an immediate termination, should a careful reevaluation be completed? What was the degree of violence? Were there physical injuries? Was the violence directed toward the person, or was there destruction of property? In cases in which the degree of violence involved physical injury and/or a fear of the partner, the couple therapy should be suspended immediately, with a recommendation for each partner to return to his or her respective individual and group work. The victimized partner should seek safety and legal advocacy, while the violent offender should be reported to the police or other authorities, if indicated, and advised to pursue treatment. However, if the violence was directed toward property and/or failed to inflict physical injury to a person, then the couple should be assessed as to their capacity to contract for safety. If the clinician ascertains that the couple is unwilling to, and/or incapable of, contracting for safety, then couple therapy should be suspended. Once again, the clinician should secure a safe place and therapeutic support for the victimized partner, including providing advocacy for legal and housing protections. The violent partner should be directed to individual and/or group therapy. However, if the couple is willing and able to contract for safety, plans are initiated to focus on relapse prevention. The following questions are posed: What efforts had the couple typically used to avert violent outbursts? What methods were used to regulate anger or rage? In summary, couple therapy may continue only if a safety contract is negotiated with the couple and relapse-prevention plans are put into place.

Parenting Issues

Survivors of childhood trauma often are fearful that they will impose traumatic legacies on their children. Anxious to break patterns of intergenerational trauma, many survivors consciously choose not to have children, feeling that is the only responsible and safe decision available to them. Often, others question the couple's decision not to have children. Family members or friends may label the couple as selfish and may induce patterns of guilt and shame for what many survivors feel is a responsible decision.

Survivors of childhood trauma often do verbalize their apprehensions about parenting. The theme emerges in the clinical process and many actively struggle with their abilities to parent effectively. Fears about the repetition of family of origin patterns abound (Banyard, 1997; Gelinas, 1983; Herman, 1981). Although many survivors of childhood trauma actively question their strengths as parents, many others are resilient and find ways to parent effectively and with sensitivity. Indeed, Kaufman and Zigler (1987) invite professionals to change the formulation of the question: "Do abused children become abusive parents?" to a question that asks: "Under what conditions is the transmission of abuse most likely to occur?" (p. 191). Certain factors contribute to resilience for parents. Levendosky and Graham-Bermann (2000) note that women who have low levels of depression and good social support systems are effective parents, regardless of the presence of trauma symptoms. Alexander, Teti, and Anderson (2000) and Buist (1998) note that the quality of the couple relationship influences a survivor's transition to parenthood and that supportive partnerships contribute to effective parenting. Banyard (1997) notes some differences in self-reports of traumatized women who described their views about parenting. African-American mothers expressed more optimism about future parenting, worried less about their children, experienced more satisfaction with their parenting style, and reported less use of harsh discipline than did other survivors of childhood sexual abuse (p. 1101). Likewise, women with higher levels of education expressed fewer worries about their children and were more optimistic about parenting in the future (p. 1101).

Hence, although it is clear that many survivors of childhood trauma are readily able to parent effectively, some are more compromised in their ability to parent. It is important for clinicians to be aware of certain risk factors and to listen for key themes during the therapy process. Although issues of parenting may emerge at any time during treatment, parenting themes often emerge as part of Phase I couple therapy work involving safety, stabilization, and establishing the context for change. In fact, concerns with parenting are often a very useful focus at the onset of couple therapy. Not only does the couple experience beginning successes with co-parenting and renewed optimism with problem-solving, but they also report building a therapeutic alliance with the clinician. However, survivors often have been told that they are vulnerable parents who might repeat a cycle of abuse. There is a danger of living out self-fulfilling prophecies around parenting issues or, even when a trauma survivor has broken the intergenerational cycle, she may feel like she is a walking time bomb in relation to her children (Kaufman & Zigler, 1987). Allen (2001) helps parents gain awareness of their past trauma histories as a way of breaking the cycle of intergenerational abuse (p. 64). Allen says, "By virtue of their capacity to reflect, parents can be receptive to their infant's attachment behavior despite their own trauma history" (p. 67). The capacity of the parents to reflect on their own mental states and those of their children yields a protective effect to children.

Certain contextual factors may compromise one's ability to parent. For example, partners who experience domestic violence, or the threat of domestic violence, often have difficulty parenting. Levendosky and Graham-Bermann (2000) note that vulnerable women may "have parenting that oscillates between periods of being disengaged or withdrawn, angry, or warm and loving, as they attempt to respond to the violence, to their internal traumatized state, and to the external demands of parenting" (p. 32). Poverty imposes many environmental stressors that create obstacles to obtaining financial, educational, and childcare resources. Clearly, the corrosive impact of heterosexism and homophobia burden lesbian, gay, bisexual, and transgendered parents with additional stressors while racism and prejudice impose additional pressures as well to parents from diverse cultural and racial backgrounds.

Benjamin and Benjamin (1994) discuss the challenges of parenting when a survivor utilizes dissociation or dissociative identity disorder as an adaptation to past trauma. These authors strongly encourage clinicians to focus on parenting issues with dissociative clients, and they say that "It holds the potential to interrupt the intergenerational cycle of abuse or neglect" (p. 239). They also note that "switching" behaviors, or the emergence of alter personalities, can contribute to confusing and contradictory messages to children. Switching may leave a parent affectively labile with a series of "inappropriate emotions" (p. 251). Likewise, alter personalities may frighten children or even attempt to harm them.

Burkett (1991) notes that survivors of childhood trauma may be more self-focused and less child-focused than other parents. She also notes that survivors may look to their children for emotional companionship, creating a blurring of boundaries that could be problematic for children. In a similar vein, Liotti (1992) thinks that an unresolved trauma history may cause a parent to turn to the children for emotional comfort when either or both parents experience attachment-related anxieties. Noting that the construct of role reversal is a complex phenomenon, Alexander, Teti, and Anderson (2000) observe that parents who have unresolved issues related to loss or abuse may rely on their children to provide comfort and help in regulating emotions (p. 835). These authors also assert that an unhappy couple relationship may contribute to the likelihood of some types of role reversal between parents and children (p. 836).

Maker and Buttenheim (2000) report that mothers who have been sexually abused may try to maintain an illusion of control in their own parenting by expecting self-reliance, passivity, and obedience from their children. Cole and Woolger (1989) note that mothers who have not had positive models for loving parental control may experience anxiety in some child-rearing situations. They noted that some survivors who continue to carry negative perceptions of their own mothers may prematurely foster autonomy in their children. However, Marcenko, Kemp, and Larson (2000) speculate that

"The trauma of sexual abuse creates greater empathy with children and a clearer demarcation between the role of child and parent" (p. 323).

This brief review reflects different components of parenting that, at times, are influenced by the legacies of the parents' childhood trauma history. In the clinical setting, we observe the insecurity of some parents when they assess their parenting skills. We also observe resilience with many individuals who have developed good parenting skills, regardless of their trauma histories. To assess the parenting capacities possessed by each parent, we have found the following open-ended questions useful: (1) How have cultural and religious beliefs shaped attitudes about parenting? (2) What are the strengths in their parenting? What are the strengths in their co-parenting? (3) What methods of discipline are used currently? What methods of discipline were used in the family of origin? (4) Have the parents prematurely fostered independence or autonomy in their children? (5) Is any role reversal noted between parent and child? (6) Do the parents experience a sense of empathy for their children? (7) Have the parents identified with the aggressive parts of their offender? (8) In what ways have parents been able to counterbalance maladaptive parenting patterns? (9) How do the parents manage frustration concerning their children's behavior? (10) In what ways do parents have the capacity to regulate affect that is stimulated in their childrearing experiences?

As both the research literature and clinical wisdom inform us that a harmonious couple relationship enhances parenting skills, problem-solving around parenting dilemmas in Phase I couple therapy can promote stabilization in the family as well as enhanced effectiveness in parenting.

Issues Related to Sexuality and Intimacy

Survivors of childhood trauma, especially survivors of childhood sexual abuse, often experience some difficulties related to the expression of sexuality in their intimate partnerships (Barnes, 1995; Maltz, 1988, 1994; McCarthy, 1990; Miehls, 1997; Munro, 2001; Talmidge & Wallace, 1991; Wilson & James, 1992). By contrast, many survivors of childhood trauma are able to enjoy the intimacy and sexuality of their partnership. However, we find that during the course of couple therapy, couples often eventually disclose some difficulty in sexual adjustment, or a lack of sexual pleasure. During the assessment phase, couples often deny any particular difficulties in their sexual lives. Only later, when the clinician has forged a strong treatment alliance with the couple, will the couple disclose some difficulties in the area of sexuality. Exploration and modification of the couple's sexual functioning most often occurs in Phase II and Phase III work.

Not surprisingly, some survivors of childhood sexual abuse develop attitudes about sexuality that are tainted as a result of past traumatic incidents. Survivors of childhood sexual abuse often feel responsible for past abuse; they may feel sexually damaged, and often have a poor sense of themselves as sexual beings. In addition, survivors of childhood sexual abuse may experience flashbacks or other dissociative experiences when they engage in sexual activity. Some individuals have unpleasant automatic physiological responses to sexual touch, responses that exacerbate dissociative experiences. Many survivors are vulnerable to further abusive sexual relationships, and some develop compulsive sexual behaviors that are destructive to themselves and to their partnerships.

We propose some cautionary notes when beginning to explore and offer interventions around sexuality with survivors of childhood trauma. First, it is important to keep a relational focus in mind when working with issues of sexuality. At times, clinicians unwittingly position a survivor of childhood trauma as the "identified patient" and his or her partner as the "benevolent helper" in the treatment of sexual difficulties (Bolen, 1993; Chauncey, 1994; Maltas & Shay, 1995). Miehls (1997) encourages clinicians to recognize the projective identification patterns in couple systems so as to ensure that the survivor of childhood sexual abuse is not unduly cast in the role of the identified patient in the couple system. He notes that partners of childhood survivors of sexual abuse may mask their own sexual dysfunctions when they focus on the "symptoms" of the survivor.

There is some agreement in the literature that certain preconditions should exist in the couple system before the clinician begins to do specific sexual therapy in the couple therapy. Of course, each partner should express willingness to explore fully his or her sexual relationship. A detailed sexual history of each partner will reveal areas of adaptation and areas of difficulty. McCarthy (1990) notes that it is important to take a detailed individual sexual history. He says, "In obtaining a chronological history, incidents that elicited guilt, confusion, negative feelings, and/or trauma need to be uncovered and discussed" (p. 142). It is useful to gain an understanding of avoidance patterns between the couple, in terms of their sexual interaction. It is also important to track the history and development of the sexual partnership. Since couples often experience an erosion of sexual intimacy over the course of the relationship, patterns of sexual approach/avoidance need to be made transparent and understood by each partner. Many survivors of childhood sexual trauma become frightened when sexually aroused. Of course, it is imperative that each partner understands that neither partner was responsible for sexual feelings during the childhood traumatic experiences. Rather, a full appreciation of the perpetrator's responsibility for the childhood abuse needs to be recognized at the outset of the treatment of the sexual dysfunction.

Follette (1991) speaks to the contraindications of couple work if there is any threat of physical violence between the couple. Maltz (1988) says that couple therapy for sexual dysfunctions, for survivors of childhood sexual abuse, is indicated only if the couple has a strong commitment to each other, has a general lifestyle compatibility, a mutual desire for change, and a shared comfort with nonsexual touch. She continues to comment: "Considering their sexual histories, touch problems, and responses to counseling, I quickly realized that traditional sex therapy was horribly missing the mark for survivors" (Maltz, 1994, p. 2). It is important to determine whether or not the partner of the survivor of childhood sexual abuse is coercing her or his partner into sexual therapy treatment (Barnes, 1995, p. 357).

When a couple agrees that they would like to assess and alter certain aspects of their sexual interaction, it is important to reassure them that they will be in control of the pace of the exploration and treatment. This fundamental reassurance sets the tone for the interaction.

Maltz (1994) argues that clients need to appreciate that all sexual dysfunctions are not "bad." Rather, she notes, "The sexual dysfunctions of some survivors are, in fact, both functional and important. Their sexual problems help them avoid feelings and memories associated with past sexual abuse" (p. 2). The following clinical vignette captures this dilemma.

SUSAN AND BARRY :: After Susan and Barry had successfully completed six months of Phase I tasks in couple therapy, Susan, a survivor of type II childhood sexual abuse, noted with dismay that she felt increasingly less interested sexually in Barry. The couple was confused about this development, as they reported that their therapy had assisted them to feel more connected in most areas of their relationship. In fact, the couple had avoided mentioning this "change," as they felt a great deal of shame about this new "symptom." We explored the issue over a number of sessions. As the couple reconstructed their sexual relationship history, each acknowledged that their earlier sexual experiences were "more physical and less emotional." We came to understand that their increased intimacy in other parts of their relationship had caused a shift in their sexual relationship. After discovering that the previous sexual responsiveness was devoid of a true emotional connection to Barry, Susan acknowledged that she felt undeserving of a caring relationship. Her enhanced connection with Barry had restimulated her view of herself as "damaged goods." With this shared insight, Susan and Barry were able to discover more tender ways of relating to each other sexually.

Since some survivors of childhood trauma experience dissociative episodes as a way of modulating their emotions when sexually aroused, it is useful to work with the survivor to find ways to modulate their emotions when engaged in sexual activity. Recognizing triggers and developing awareness of one's emotional responses is useful. For example, a survivor might learn to integrate techniques that promote relaxation and feelings of some safety during sexual contact with a loved partner. To stay connected with a loving partner during sexual activity, and to keep separated from memories and experiences of traumatic encounters, Munro (2001) suggests that "ways to separate include self-talk, reminding yourself where you are and who you are with, letting yourself know that you are safe, asking for a safe hug, and doing whatever you need to do to feel present again" (p. 7).

Survivors of childhood sexual abuse often experience intense negative emotions when touched sexually. Some survivors experience feelings of fear, dread, guilt, and shame, as well as physiological reactions, such as nausea or physical pain when touched in certain vulnerable areas of their bodies. In fact, some survivors report somatic memories, or physical symptoms that directly mirror the physical or sexual abuse inflicted during childhood. Given the power of these body memories, it is crucial for the survivor of childhood sexual abuse to experience control over receiving the partner's touch. Learning how to self-soothe is an important challenge for many trauma survivors. Both relaxation and breathing exercises can aid in developing a sense of control and calmness. An entire range of cognitive–behavioral techniques, based on patterns of gradual assimilation of new behaviors, often provides useful adjunctive interventions (Barnes, 1995).

As with other aspects of treatment, specific sex therapy may need to be temporarily halted when one or both partners become overwhelmed with affect. Then, Phase I couple therapy interventions should be reintroduced to restore homeostasis and safety to the couple system. While survivors of other forms of childhood trauma may also experience some sexual adaptation difficulties, a tempered but thorough sexual assessment of survivors of childhood abuse will often yield further areas of intervention for these couple systems. As in other areas, the goal of improving the sexual relationships involves an ongoing, gradual integration of ego-syntonic sexual functioning that is satisfying for each partner. Uncovering of childhood trauma memories is unnecessary to accomplish these gains.

Affairs and Infidelity

The disclosure or the discovery of an affair by one or both partners in a traumatized couple often activates a rupture in the relationship that is experienced as a crisis. It may become the proverbial straw that breaks the (relationship's) camel's back. For this discussion, we define an affair as a concealed relationship characterized by emotional closeness and/or sexual intimacy that represents a threat to the primary couple dyad. An affair involves a rupture and betrayal of an agreement, vow, or promise. We experience the rage responses of the aggrieved partner and the hostility and/or guilt of the enacting partner as mirroring a reenactment of the "victim–victimizer–bystander" dynamic. Heightened affective responses that oscillate between contempt, rage, shame, humiliation, fear, and guilt characterize the emotional tone of sessions. Clearly, the clinician needs to delicately balance empathic support to both partners. Either or both partners may be experiencing difficulty in identifying, managing, and articulating these intense emotions.

We approach couple therapy differentially when a dual- or single-trauma couple introduces the reality of an affair into their therapy. Guided by our phase-oriented approach, the treatment plan varies, depending on the degree of regression experienced by each partner at the time that the affair is discovered. The personal resources and resilience demonstrated by both partners in coping with the crisis also influence the direction of therapy. Focusing on the connections between a trauma scenario and the impact of an affair distinguishes our treatment strategies from other couple therapy models.

While some couples may try to understand the meaning of the affair imme-diately, such an effort is typically discouraged. Instead, most of the initial clinical interventions aim to stabilize the crisis with Phase I tasks that are ori-ented toward safety, homeostasis, and creating the context for change.

Clinician Response to Infidelity

In addressing the effects of an affair on a couple, clinicians need to be aware of their own values with regard to infidelity. Attitudes toward af-fairs are shaped not only by religious, ethnic, and familial influences, but also by societally imposed professional responses. Extramarital affairs are often flaunted in the media as evidence of the alleged immorality, or lack of fit-ness, of politicians and other world leaders. Attacking a person's moral char-acter as a result of an affair has become a collective national sport in the U.S. media. A challenge to this ethnocentric view points to attitudes expressed in many societies where affairs are normalized. However, given the current socio-political climate in the United States, we might expect that either partner entering couple therapy might assess the clinician's attitudes with acute sen-sitivity. Indeed, the popularized or socially constructed meanings of affairs in contemporary Western society may cloud the clinician's professional response. The aggrieved partner may scrutinize the clinician in a way that will validate her or his sense of victimization. Likewise, the partner who has had an affair will seek validation and empathy from the clinician, free of judgment or con-demnation. Clinicians are also influenced by practice wisdom and profes-sional literature that have often directly or indirectly imposed strict guide-lines for working with these couples in crisis.

A Brief Review of the Clinical Literature

Although most authors agree that there is no single etiology of infidelity in the couple and family therapy literature, it is clear that views about clinical interventions are evolving in the field. In the 1980s and early 1990s, authors and practitioners alike agreed that couple therapy could not proceed until the affair had stopped (Hoffman, 1981; Scharff & Scharff, 1991; Woods & Hollis, 1990). This approach clearly underscores the belief that in-fidelity is always damaging to the individual and to the couple relationship. However, contemporary writers such as Weil (2003) describe affairs as be-havioral manifestations of attempts to correct derailed development. She cautions clinicians against mandating the end of an affair as she says, "These relationships can be better thought of as efforts to revisit the traumatic experiences that have created the organizing patterns that have limited a patient's self-development" (p. 61). She proposes that a client, in the course of individual therapy, can develop understanding about the affair and thereby progress in his or her psychological development. The clinician is expected to maintain a professional stance that values the search for meaning of one's behavior without imposing moral judgments. Even if this model facilitates meaning-making about the affair for either partner within an individual psychotherapy framework, it fails to attend to the relational issues influencing the couple, including the intense hurt and narcissistic injury sustained by the aggrieved partner. The absence of parameters around the affair also interferes with contracting and maintaining a therapeutic alliance for both members of the couple.

Consensus among clinicians supports the idea that infidelity is motivated by a number of individual (intrapsychic) and interpersonal factors. Solomon (1989) conceptualizes affairs as expressions of individual narcissistic issues that mask fears of intimacy. Affairs may represent the need for admiration, love, and mirroring. Goldberg (1999) suggests that affairs are manifestations of a person's split and divided internal self. Wilson and Mitchell (1998) support this idea, framing infidelity as an attempt to reintegrate a previously disavowed aspect of one's self. As noted, Weil (2003) suggests that affairs may offer a context for reparative psychological work that manifests as a result of earlier developmental ruptures. Woods and Hollis (1990) suggest that an affair may be a defensive posture for individuals who fear engulfment or excessive dependency needs toward the partner.

Scharff and Scharff (1991) offer a complex differential assessment with several different possibilities. They suggest that partners with oral-based dependent yearnings for need gratification seek an affair partner to provide these emotional supplies. Partners who struggle with anal-phase psychosexual themes of control and mastery seek an affair to demonstrate domination and control over the other partner. Partners who yearn for narcissistic enhancement seek an affair partner to function as "phallic-ornamentation." Lastly, partners who wrestle with oedipal-level conflicts seek an affair partner to demonstrate superiority as the "winner," prevailing over all other competitors (Person, 1988). Miehls (1997), Scarf (1987), and Sharpe (2000), who also conceptualize affairs within an object relations framework, recognize that couples utilize triangular relationships to reduce interpersonal tensions.

Whether or not the triangular relationship reflects oedipal developmental strivings, it is clear that the inclusion of an outside person in a troubled relationship often helps to temporarily ease interpersonal tensions between the dyad while directing energy to a new relationship. From a family systems view, Bowen (1978) views triangles as reducing anxiety and modulating the ongoing tensions between the developmental push toward self-differentiation and away from fusion. Brown (1985) suggests that the triangular function of an affair might serve to avoid conflict, avoid intimacy, or provide a bereft, depressed couple with the chance to fill up on emotional supplies. Some couples react to aging and decline of sexuality at midlife with pursuit of an affair partner. In summary, most clinicians and theoreticians conceptualize an affair as a reflection of couple dissatisfaction or conflict that may or may not be related to a developmental issue such as midlife or aging (Spring, 1997; Woods & Hollis, 1990).

Infidelity as Trauma Reenactment

Although we agree that there are many factors that contribute to infidelity, we observe that survivors of childhood trauma often experience an affair as a crisis that restimulates earlier traumatic experiences. The "victim–victimizer–bystander" dynamic comes alive in the creation of an affair triangle. In fact, the infidelity may express a reenactment of a partner's childhood abuse history. Or, this pattern of betrayal might mirror intergenerational patterns of abuse passed along to subsequent offspring. If a partner experiences the affair as a betrayal of great magnitude, she may fail to contain affect, even erupting into rage storms. While feeling victimized, the aggrieved partner may view the therapist in a passive-bystander role, as condoning the partner's behavior. Or she may feel suspicion that the therapist had known about the affair. Survivors of childhood trauma are understandably vulnerable to these relational betrayals. They often recall potential helpers in childhood who stood by as helpless, inept bystanders while they suffered abuse. The narcissistic injury of an affair stirs strong emotions, especially for sexual abuse survivors. They may feel confusion about who should be trusted, doubt about sexual adequacy, or envy of the sexual satisfaction enjoyed by the partner.

At the start of couple therapy, it is crucial to assess the ability of each partner to manage the tumultuous feelings that often arise when one or both partners engage in an affair. In these instances, a focus on establishing safety and stabilization are primary goals that are central tasks in Phase I of this couple therapy model. As one or both partners may have trouble managing their emotions, the clinician must contain and "hold" the range of intense of emotions. The comforting structure of a flexible holding environment conveys to the couple the clinician's capacity to hold difficult emotions as well as stabilize the crisis. A range of cognitive–behavioral interventions is most useful here to promote affect regulation in the context of this steady holding environment. The following vignette illustrates the complexity of these issues following the early disclosure of an affair.

MARGARET AND TOM ∷ The couple was thrown into a crisis when Margaret's neighbor informed her that Tom had been having an affair for several months. The couple had originally entered therapy looking for help with their sexual relationship. For a few years, Tom had shown only sporadic sexual interest in Margaret. At the beginning of couple therapy, they were sexually inactive. Margaret had suffered sexual abuse perpetrated by her father, brothers, and cousins while Tom suffered childhood physical abuse. While working with this couple on Phase I tasks of safety and stabilization, they disclosed the affair. Plunging into immediate crisis, Margaret expressed rage storms and threats about leaving the marriage, while Tom retreated into passivity.

During an emergency session, Margaret raged toward Tom, appearing unable to control her affect. Tom was mute, with the exception of a quiet "I'm sorry" apology. When Margaret hurled a tissue box at Tom, I quickly intervened by asking them to turn away from each other. Margaret promptly became enraged with me, assuming that I was colluding with Tom. Although the "victim–victimizer–bystander" dynamic vividly consumed this couple, any attempt at talking about this dynamic, or clarifying this pattern, was contraindicated. It was evident that each partner's childhood trauma histories had been reactivated.

To help this couple manage their emotions, I initiated a path of directive, cognitive–behavioral clinical interventions. I stated the following directives to promote containment: "I do not want you to do further emotional damage to each other. I think you need a cooling-off period. You need to be temporarily apart so that each of you can calm your feelings. I am worried about the impact on your children." The effects on the children galvanized this couple as we spent the remainder of the session discussing structural issues re-garding childcare and sleeping arrangements during the next two days until the next therapy session. Each partner was urged to contact their respective individual therapists and support systems, while I planned to collaborate with the other helping professionals. The sessions ended with my recommendation that they not discuss the affair until it was safe to do so. As the couple expe-rienced a strong therapeutic alliance with me, they complied with these safety recommendations.

As this clinical vignette conveys, it is important to focus on containment and affect regulation during the early phases following disclosure of the affair. When the initiating partner decides to continue the affair, couple therapy as a modality is not especially useful. Without an intent to detriangulate the af-fair partner from the partnership, work on stabilization or healing from the impact of the affair is virtually impossible. However, for those traumatized couples who decide to move beyond the affair, it is especially helpful to at-tend to boundary issues. Glass (2003) discusses how "walls" and "windows" must be created in relation to the affair. The walls need to be constructed to assure both partners that the affair has ended. Plans to ensure that there is no contact with the affair partner in person, via telephone, or email comes first. Then, another way to rebuild trust is to structure times throughout the day when both partners check in with each other to maximize accessibility. The window approach relates to a titrated opening up of discussion about the se-cret affair. For example, a suggestion might be offered for each partner to write a list of particular questions or reactions to the affair. Each thought is recorded on a separate piece of paper and placed in a small box. At designated times throughout the week, the aggrieved partner chooses one issue at a time for discussion. These discussion times start out in couple therapy sessions for brief time periods (e.g., thirty minutes), and gradually increase to sixty or ninety minutes. Marathon discussions that last for hours on end are discouraged be-cause these endless talks usually escalate into chaotic, blaming sessions dom-inated by emotional reactivity in which neither partner listens. However, as the couple gains greater capacity to talk with each other in a titrated manner about the aftermath of the affair, trust may gradually be restored.

Another cognitive–behavioral intervention involves "neutralizing" or "detoxifying" particular sites associated with the affair. For example, Alice, a female partner in a dual-trauma heterosexual couple, regularly engaged in sexual activity with her affair partner in the bedroom of her family home while her husband, Sam, was away at work during the daytime. When her husband felt disgusted and outraged every time he entered the bedroom, he realized that early memories of the sexual abuse that he had suffered were rekindled. As a way to neutralize this physical space, this couple refurbished the bedroom with fresh paint and changed the furniture. They converted another room in their house into their new bedroom. Even with less space, the couple was pleased with their brightly colored sanctuary and newly acquired bed. Although the room was barely furnished, both partners felt a sense of renewal with this symbolic change.

Since this early phase of healing from the aftermath of an affair is so intensely emotional, couples often need help with specific methods to promote affect regulation. The techniques of neural relaxation explicated in Chapter 5 on trauma theories are used regularly in these circumstances. Other methods to promote self-soothing include meditation, guided imagery, and yoga. In some circumstances, when certain discrete affair-related imagery approximates a PTSD obsessional flashback, EMDR methods may be helpful. Until the couple has restabilized, clinicians should avoid any discussion of the meaning of the infidelity. Instead, our primary task is to ensure safety both within and outside of the couple therapy, so as to avoid further destruction and to strengthen the couple's highest level of functioning.

Only when a couple achieves a modicum of stability and completes Phase I tasks (safety, stabilization, and the establishment of a context for change) should the work focus on understanding the meaning of the infidelity. When couples enter Phase II work, they reflect on their trauma histories through the lens of the "victim–victimizer–bystander" dynamic. In the aftermath of an affair, many traumatized couples discover intergenerational patterns of abuse and betrayal that have influenced not only their generation, but also, frequently, previous and subsequent generations within the family. We refer to the "historical ghosts" as tenacious forces directing the lives of traumatized couples.

In summary, the experiences of betrayal, secrecy, and violation of boundaries associated with affairs contribute layers of complexity to the responses of partners who have suffered childhood trauma. Not only are these partners reacting to the here-and-now disillusionment, but in addition, their intense emotions are augmented by the powerful legacies of earlier betrayals in childhood.

:: COEXISTING TRAUMA-RELATED DISORDERS

The legacies of childhood trauma surface in a wide range of psychiatric disorders, substance abuse and addictive disorders, and physical illnesses. As van der Kolk (1996) expressed vividly in an early paper on the neurophysiology of trauma, the body clearly keeps score of earlier assaults. This section focuses on the role of substance/abuse and addictions, as well as other coexisting trauma-related psychiatric and physical illnesses, in the lives of trauma survivors.

Substance Abuse/Addiction

Since there is such a strong association between complex PTSD-related phenomena and substance abuse/addictions, let us now review the demographics and clinical issues that highlight differential assessment between substance abuse and dependence. We also discuss the use of medications, the paradox of powerlessness, the role of spirituality, and the usefulness of integrative models. We then review the most pressing coexisting mental health and physical illnesses.

Demographics

The association between PTSD and substance abuse/addictions has been established for many years based on studies of male combat veterans, especially those treated in Veterans Administration (VA) settings (Keane & Wolfe, 1990). Within the past ten years, mixed-gender studies with more diverse samples have revealed estimated rates of PTSD from 12% to 34% (Grice et al., 1995). More stunning findings have been revealed for women. For example, studies of women in the general population, without considering substance abuse, estimate lifetime trauma rates of 36% to 51% (Najavits, Weiss, & Shaw, 1997). Women in substance abuse treatment programs also show higher trauma rates than women in the general population, with rates ranging from 55% (Grice et al., 1995), to 85% (Najavits, Weiss, Shaw, & Muenz, 1998), to 99% (Fullilove et al., 1993). Without doubt, the syndromes of PTSD, complex PTSD, and substance abuse are strongly associated. Studies indicate that not only do substance abusers have a higher likelihood of subsequent traumatic events than nonusers (Laewig & Anderson, 1992), but also even a family history of substance abuse problems poses a significant risk factor for exposure to traumatic events (Breslau et al., 1991). Conversely, the presence of trauma has been associated with the emergence of substance abuse, supporting the "traumatogenic," or self-medication, theory of substance abuse disorders (O'Donohue & Elliot, 1992).

A major finding is that women are at much higher risk than men for developing PTSD. However, there are many contradictory studies that suggest these differences are due to methodological weaknesses and underreporting by men (Dansky et al., 1996). Because typical patterns of childhood sexual abuse of boys involve extrafamilial abuse in which the offender is more frequently a male, pernicious effects of homophobia inhibit reporting from many male trauma survivors. This silence has been broken in the past two years with the emergence of many male trauma survivors who have reported childhood abuses inflicted by members of the clergy, most notably priests (Benyei, 1998). Since the types of reported trauma are different for men and women, women report higher rates of physical and sexual assault than men. Men reported significantly higher rates of crime victimization, general disaster, or combat exposure (Najavits et al., 1997). Often the fears expressed by male combat veterans are different from the self-blame, suicide attempts, sexual dysfunction, and revictimization reported by women. Overall, there is a lack of attunement to gender issues demonstrated in research studies of the effects of trauma and coexisting disorders.

Clinical Issues

Several clinical issues arise regularly in couple therapy with trauma survivors when there is a question about, or admission of, substance abuse. They include: (1) substance abuse versus dependence, (2) labeling as therapeutic tool or stigmatized identity, (3) the use of medications, (4) the paradox of powerlessness, (5) the role of spirituality, and (6) integrative approaches to trauma-related disorders.

Substance Abuse versus Dependence   Continuing conflicts between clinicians in the mental health and chemical dependency fields have existed for decades. Many traditional psychodynamic approaches have maintained a consistent bias supporting the self-medication/abuse stance in evaluating substance use (Levin & Weiss, 1994). This traumatogenic approach to substance abuse suggests that if the trauma-related issues remit, there will be less need for self-medication with addictive substances. However, current approaches to dual diagnosis are supported by the disease model of addictions, drawing careful distinctions between substance use, abuse, and dependence (DSM-IV-TR, 2002).

To avoid a black-or-white perspective on this issue that would mirror the dichotomized cognition induced by addictive drug use, we presume that any unprescribed chemical use by trauma survivors has the potential to become a problem. This conclusion raises the question as to how these concerns should be dealt with in mental health treatment (i.e., couple or individual therapy). Should there be sequential treatment with an immediate referral for a substance abuse program? Or, rather than immediately referring a couple to substance abuse treatment, should the clinician engage the couple in decision-making around the effects of the substance abuse? Although parents claim that such an approach reinforces denial, an alternative view suggests that the couple might raise their collective consciousness about the depth of the substance-abuse problem. Prochaska, DiClemente, and Norcross (1992) describe a process, in their developmental model, that starts with a precontemplative stage. Partners recognize a beginning awareness of the substance abuse before any decision or action is taken. Along similar lines, a motivational interviewing approach also enables the partners to discuss and evaluate the nature, use, and function of their substance use (Miller & Rollnick, 1991). In addition, some sharing of psychoeducational information about the comorbidity of addictions with PTSD or complex PTSD is in order at this time as well. Indeed, both of these decision-making and psychoeducational approaches resonate with Phase I tasks that focus primarily on safety, stabilization, and self-care.

Labeling as Therapeutic Tool or Stigmatized Identity   Many addiction recovery programs encourage clients to self-identify as an "addict" or an "alcoholic" as a way to challenge denial. This labeling is intended to help participants acknowledge their drug dependence and promote connectedness within the community. Along similar lines, some recovery programs for trauma survivors have embraced the term "survivor" as a way to admit the reality of abuse while empowering them to serve as allies and role models for other trauma survivors. Critics of such labeling claim that a survivor's identity may be reified as a stigmatized role. If a person is limited to only one self-definition as a "victim" or "survivor," the philosophy of victimology is reinforced. Such a static, linear view robs the partner of a changeable, more complex self-identification. We recommend affirming the client's experience of victimization, yet also educating her about the "victim–victimizer–bystander" scenario. In this way, we hope to acknowledge the enormity of the abuse suffered, while also allowing for the client's self-determination to decide on her own self-identification. In fact, most clients in the course of couple therapy shift their self-definitions from "victim," to "survivor," "fighter," "thriver," or "overcomer." Many partners embrace some or all of these self-definitions concurrently, or at different phases in the couple therapy work, a stance that promotes acceptance of complex, multiple self-views.

Use of Medications   Historically, many traditional drug and alcohol counseling programs have maintained a strong bias against use of any psychotropic medications. Practice guidelines have shifted considerably in the fields of mental health, chemical dependency, and twelve-step programs during the past decade. Many substance abuse practitioners, mental health clinicians, and twelve-step groups now support the selective use of psychotropic medication when necessary (Evans & Sullivan, 1995). For example, an addicted trauma survivor who suffers panic attacks or psychotic-like aspects of acute dissociative states might need medication to reduce anxiety and promote coherent thinking. Endogenous depression and bipolar states may also require appropriate use of prescribed, nonaddictive medications to regulate moods, after careful and thorough evaluation.

Paradox of Powerlessness   One of the major empowerment goals in psychotherapy with survivors of childhood trauma is to facilitate enhanced control and mastery over their lives. When helplessness and absence of control are core experiences for trauma survivors, how can we address the loss of control over a drug that directs their lives? Paradoxically, if an empowerment focus neglects to acknowledge the destructive force of a disempowering physiological addiction, therapy colludes with denial. However, facing a state of powerlessness is complicated because so many women have felt disempowered in their lives. Therefore, they are wary about entering treatment that emphasizes their powerlessness. An alternative approach is a feminist reinterpretation of the twelve steps, in which the first step, which supports an admission of powerlessness over alcohol and the unmanageability of their lives, is amended. With an inclusion of the many ways in which an addict can, in fact, exert control over her life, a survivor is better able to accept total powerlessness, quite specifically in relation to the drug (Barrett & Trepper, 1991; Berenson, 1991).

Role of Spirituality   Many psychotherapy models for trauma survivors explore the importance of each client's spiritual or religious beliefs and resources (Northcut, 2000). When one or both partners have coexisting addictive disorders, it is important to explore their experiences of, and relationships to, God or a higher power. If a partner expresses strong agnostic or atheistic views, then it is important to make available, through referral, secular twelve-step recovery programs. For example, Women for Sobriety and Rational Recovery has established programs that report successful treatment outcomes (Ketcham & Asbury, 2000). Once again, it is important to avoid a cookie-cutter approach to treatment that assumes "one size fits all" couples.

Integrative Therapy Models   Although most models treat complex PTSD and substance abuse separately, there is a strong move toward integrative models that pay attention to the PTSD-related symptomatology and substance abuse simultaneously (Evans & Sullivan, 1995; Fullilove et al., 1993; Miller & Guidry, 2001; Najavits et al., 1997). Regrettably, some research studies have reported a lack of positive outcome for women with a dual diagnosis because of strong negative countertransference reactions from therapists who had difficulty handling multiple crises (Nace, Davis, & Gaspari, 1991). However, the integrative practice models focus more effectively on relational and interactional themes with traumatized addicts (Miller & Guidry, 2001), and hence we support this kind of practice.

Coexisting Mental Health Disorders and Physical Illnesses

Very often, survivors of childhood trauma who abuse or are dependent on chemical substances present symptoms that mimic a range of psychiatric conditions, including major depression, generalized anxiety, substance abuse psychoses, somatic complaints, or cognitive confusion. These symptoms may be directly caused by the substance abuse, or they may be evidence of an underlying psychiatric or medical disorder. Because so many substance abuse related symptoms are identical to trauma-related symptomatology, it is commonplace for a clinician to overlook a careful differential diagnosis. The risk involved in such oversight leads to an incorrect treatment plan with accompanying negative consequences.

Similarly, because many trauma-related symptoms and addiction-related symptoms mimic underlying physical conditions, a thorough physical examination is indicated at the onset of any couple therapy treatment. For example, one partner in a dual-trauma couple continually attributed her rage storms to the legacies of trauma. After I recommended three times in the period of one month that she pursue a medical examination, her endocrinologist ultimately diagnosed a severe thyroid condition that explained some of the emotional lability. As eating disorders and other compulsive disorders are frequently associated as trauma-related conditions, the clinician must recommend the appropriate assessment and treatment protocols for these conditions. The effects of chemotherapy in treating various cancers may mimic the effects of trauma-related disorders. As a result, a careful assessment of functioning prior to the onset of illness is essential as well.

In summary, given the sobering reality of the range of potential coexisting psychiatric disorders and physical illnesses, all clients must be thoroughly assessed, in collaboration with the appropriate professionals, to determine if there is a coexisting disorder.

Dissociation

Dissociation, as an adaptive defensive phenomenon, has been observed frequently in clients who have suffered traumatic experiences either in childhood or during their adult years. Considerable attention in the field of traumatology, focused primarily on individual clients, has been paid to understanding the function of dissociation as well as the clinical interventions that serve to minimize reliance on this defense (Allen & Smith, 1995; Cohen, Berzoff, & Elin, 1995; Courtois, 1999; Kluft, 1993, 1995; Putnam, 1989). We accept the notion that dissociation involves two key features of detachment and compartmentalization, operating on a continuum from mild to severe processes. Clients who may have suffered especially brutal childhood abuses often demonstrate the most extreme dissociative responses, resulting in dissociative identity disorders (DIDs). Acknowledging the ongoing controversies related to the validity of delayed memories and the cultural relativity of this diagnosis, we would like to demonstrate how complex-PTSD-related dissociation of differing degrees can be addressed in couple therapy with single- or dual-trauma couples. We will discuss how to approach the following issues: (1) memory lapses, (2) psychoeducation without reification of the "identified victim/client," and (3) fragmentation or integration.

Memory Lapses

Lapses in memory lasting several seconds to several hours may occur with dissociation. Dual- or single-trauma couples need to understand that memory lapses may well be related to dissociation. A psychoeducational approach helps clients understand that during an acute traumatic episode, a victim may automatically detach her emotions from the horrific frightening event as a natural protection from feeling completely overwhelmed. Providing an example of a common occurrence may help. For example, I often question a couple about whether they have ever witnessed an accident or injury. I ask them if they were aware, at the time, of the full range of their feelings; if they noticed that they may have felt numb; and if they shifted into action mode in order to attend to the crisis. Most frequently, clients can identify with and empathize with such a situation. Both partners generally report a state of shock, of numbness. I then encourage them to increase the intensity of the fear and horror associated with the event, and that they envision the extent to which the numbness and detachment intensifies.

Another current example that couples relate to easily is empathizing with soldiers or civilians engaged in combat, where the threat of death is imminent. To survive, the person who is threatened detaches from the associated emotions while acting in a protective, defensive manner. In one couple therapy session with Johnnie and Jeannie, a dual-trauma military couple, Jeannie blurted out that she felt herself rise from the room and hover over the ceiling watching her stepfather abuse her. Johnnie recalled feeling nothing at all when he flew his helicopter missions in Vietnam. Soldiers in combat are encouraged to detach emotionally and to focus on their work on a cognitive level. For example, the air force bombers in Iraq recently referred to launching their lethal weapons as "delivering their goods" and called their targets "destinations." In this case, abstract language, devoid of any human connection, aims to promote dissociation in combat. Typically, encouraging each partner to understand the protective function of dissociation promotes understanding and empathy. In the case of Johnnie and Jeannie, each partner ironically relied on dissociation regularly, yet lambasted the other for "lousy memory," "zoning out," and "lack of caring." After several sessions focused on this discussion, this couple relaxed their attacking modes toward each other.

Psychoeducation without Reification of the Identified Client

Dissociation is a common coping measure for trauma survivors, and thus it is important in most cases to define and normalize the process. Dissociation is defined as a protective process that exists along a continuum from mild withdrawal, to moderate disengagement, to more extreme detachment with compartmentalization. When partners have difficulty empathizing with this experience, I encourage them to recall times when they have been driving for several hours. Can they recollect all emotional and cognitive aspects of the trip? Have they ever arrived at their destination and wondered what the road looked like for the past half-hour? Usually the driver has paid adequate attention to the task, while also disengaging from both the emotional and pragmatic content of the specific events. This "forgetting" might not be defined as dissociation per se. Yet, it functions as a mild form of tuning out a whole range of information. Again, as part of the psychoeducational method, couples learn that some forgetting is related to PTSD.

When dissociation is most extreme, such as for clients diagnosed with dissociative identity disorders (DIDs), the lapses in memory may be more pronounced. Education is crucial for these individuals and their partners as well. In addition, the partner with DID might learn to record important information in an appointment book, electronic calendar, or journal as a way to independently keep track of her activities. At times, it may be helpful for the partner with DID to be reminded in a nonjudgmental tone by the other partner of what events transpired, as long as both partners have agreed to this plan. A few couple therapy models have focused on how the non-DID partner becomes a treatment ally (Karpel, 1995). Although the approach is useful in terms of educating both partners about the complexity of DID, there is minimal focus on the couple's interactions.

It is important to demystify the diagnosis of DID by talking about the ordinary nature of dissociation and the connections with the relationship. For example, in an early session with one DID couple, I stressed that although the partner diagnosed with DID reported seven fairly distinct parts that often operated conflictually, her partner also showed many different aspects of himself, in terms of mood, thoughts, and behavior. This dereification of the dissociative process helps to depathologize the partner with DID, as well as helps the couple to address their relationship issues. A common error with DID couples is to treat the alters as separate, distinct personalities. Although the client experiences each alter as distinct and separate, it is not useful to anthropomorphize the personalities. Rather than addressing each alter by the name assigned, I have found it helpful to refer to them as distinct entities as well as self-parts (or part-objects). For example, I might ask, "Is this the perspective from the infant part of you? Or the bullying persecutor part of you?" Although this intervention may prompt anger or, at times, a ruptured therapeutic alliance, partners are generally relieved to witness the clinician "holding" the notion of a unified entity with various parts trying to cohabitate and work together. This stance provides role modeling for both partners to think of the alters and parts as entities within the whole.

Fragmentation or Integration

As couples try to negotiate decision-making around financial planning, retirement, children, or the more day-to-day scheduling of activities and division of labor, the process becomes far more complicated when one or both partners are diagnosed with DID. Rather than working exclusively with the host alter of the DID partner(s), it is important to check in with all parts before a major decision is reached. Even with a single-trauma couple, I encourage both partners to check in with all parts (alters or aspects) of oneself, so as to improve the likelihood of a sound decision being reached. On a more intimate level, each partner (i.e., all parts, alters, and aspects) needs to express agreement or disagreement with sexual activities, especially during the early stages of couple therapy when parameters need to be defined, in order to assure both partners a right to participate voluntarily.

Overall, dissociation deserves considerable respect as a reliable protection against the painful legacies of childhood trauma. By depositioning the client diagnosed with a severe dissociative disorder, providing psychoeducational support about dissociative phenomena, and strengthening the coordination of "parts" perspectives, couples are better able to find more effective modes of coping with hurt.

In summary, this chapter has reviewed the basic principles underlying this couple therapy practice model for survivors of childhood trauma. Since the framework is case specific, each treatment plan varies according to the unique biopsychosocial profile developed for each couple. Once the assessment guides a decision-making process regarding a course of therapy, specific goals are established. Each phase of couple therapy is then described in detail to explicate the various tasks and challenges facing the couple. In all aspects of this course of couple therapy, rationales are offered to explain the synthesis of various social and psychological theory lenses to ground our understanding of the emerging phenomena. They also serve to direct the choices of useful clinical interventions that are aimed to address the designated presenting issues. All of the themes that are relevant for traumatized couples engaged in couple therapy have been highlighted. These include the composition of the "couple," the role of violence, parenting issues, sexuality, affairs, multiple/dual diagnoses of trauma-related disorders, and dissociation.

Clinician Responses: Working with Traumatized Couples

This chapter explores the myriad responses that a clinician may experience while working with traumatized couples. Social and political attitudes, as well as policies concerning trauma and violence, undoubtedly interact with the clinician and her or his responses (Gelinas, 1995; Herman, 1992; Merskey, 1995; Saakvitne, 1995). Although many clinicians examine and monitor their own belief systems concerning trauma, it is virtually impossible to escape the influence of societal attitudes about trauma and survivors of trauma.

It has been well documented that working with individual trauma survivors precipitates many potential countertransference responses within the clinician (Briere, 1996; Chu, 1988; Davies & Frawley, 1992, 1994; Mennen, 1990; Pearlman & Saakvitne, 1995). In fact, certain transference–countertransference schemas are unavoidable, and understanding these intersubjective dynamics is essential to successful therapeutic work with trauma survivors (Bowles, 1999; Brandell, 1999; Francis, 1997; Nadelson & Polonsky, 1991; Solomon, 1997; Wall, 2001; Wilson & Lindy, 1999). In working with dyads, the clinician responds to transference messages from each partner. Moreover, the triangular nature of therapeutic relationships with dyads often precipitates transference and countertransference themes that reflect the "victim–victimizer–bystander" dynamic (Herman, 1992; Miller, 1994, Staub, 2003). In instances in which each partner has encountered one or multiple traumatic experiences, reenactments of the "victim–victimizer–bystander" occur frequently. The conscious and unconscious processes among all three members of the exchange (each partner and the clinician) produce a fluid exchange of roles ("victim–victimizer–bystander") in which any given interaction represents multiple meanings for the couple and the clinician. In fact, this is a central dynamic that underscores many of the transference–countertransference themes illustrated in this chapter.

Developmental themes also emerge in transference–countertransference interactions. Within the psychodynamic frame, a traumatized individual who craves primary oral gratification may compete with his or her partner for the clinician's "emotional" stores. A partner struggling with anal psychosexual themes may attempt to fight over issues of power and control with both the therapist and the other partner. Triangular themes related to oedipal issues of identification, competition, and phallic exhibitionism may also influence transference–countertransference dynamics (Basham & Miehls, 1998a; Sharpe, 1997). Developmental themes become manifest through complex patterns of projective identification that impact the various dyads in the treatment relationship. The countertransference response of the couple therapist becomes an important assessment and treatment tool in the ongoing work with the couple (Sharpe 1997).

Clinicians also may experience vicarious traumatization when working with traumatized couples. Increasingly, authors demonstrate the residual effects on clinicians who work with individual trauma survivors (Charney & Pearlman, 1998; Cunningham, 1999; Dane, 2000; Figley, 1995; Maltz, 1992; McCann & Pearlman, 1990; Pearlman & Saakvitne, 1995). Because couple therapists also are subject to the impact of vicarious traumatization, it is imperative that they find ways to ameliorate the subtle but powerful changes that potentially can occur in their views of themselves, others, and the world (Janoff-Bulman, 1992; Pearlman & Saakvitne, 1995). It is an unfortunate reality that the traumatic events of September 11, 2001, have heightened the vulnerability of many individuals, including clinicians. Not only must clinicians find ways to balance the stressors associated with working with trauma survivors, but they must also find some way to make meaning of worldwide events that directly impact them, their families, and their friends.

This chapter, then, examines how the "person" of the clinician influences the work with traumatized couples. We discuss the personal characteristics therapists need to effectively manage the tensions that develop from using multitheoretical lenses in therapeutic work. We examine institutional factors as they relate to the clinician and discuss how these factors influence the treatment process. We articulate how countertransference and vicarious traumatization are related processes. To illustrate the differences between these two processes, we offer clinical vignettes that demonstrate the complexity of transference–countertransference paradigms in work with traumatized couples. The central triangular dynamic of "victim–victimizer–bystander" (Herman, 1992; Miller, 1994, Staub, 2003) also is reflected in the clinical vignettes. Finally, we discuss strategies to counteract the impact of vicarious traumatization on the clinician.

:: PERSONAL CHARACTERISTICS OF CLINICIANS

Implementation of a multitheoretical assessment and treatment model poses many challenges for the clinician. Utilizing discrepant theoretical models that articulate contradictory principles requires flexibility on the part of the therapist. Rather than adhering to the ideology of one theory, the model requires that the therapist fluidly move among theories. The clinical material presented by the couple will guide the clinician to the theory that is most helpful at each particular moment of assessment and intervention.

The clinician needs to have a sound capacity for abstract thinking and be able to tolerate uncertainty during the process of evaluation and assessment. In addition, it is important for the therapist to hold an open frame as to which theory is particularly relevant at any given time. Privileging one theory over another may negatively impact the therapeutic process. The therapist who is able to practice from a reflexive stance (Miehls & Moffatt, 2000) will be open to the potential influence that each couple system has on her or him. The clinician's own family of origin experiences, racial and ethnic identity development, sexual identity development, age, religion, and socioeconomic class status are among the factors that influence the therapeutic work. In addition, the therapist's attitudes about couples are undoubtedly influenced by his or her own relationship history and current intimate relationships. Certainly, the trauma history of the therapist influences the work (Canfield, 2002; Pearlman & Saakvitne, 1995; Wall, 2001).

:: INSTITUTIONAL/SOCIOCULTURAL FACTORS

As noted in the historical review in Chapter 2 of this book, conscious and unconscious attitudes that shape the cultural response to trauma wield strong influences on psychotherapy practice. Herman (1992) has postulated that the study of trauma has been legitimized only as a result of the incidence of posttraumatic stress disorder (PTSD) diagnoses observed in Vietnam war veterans. Essentially, she notes that the study of familial or domestic violence has been less privileged in the mental health field. Minimization or denial of interpersonal violence, characterized by physical, sexual, and emotional abuse, persists in the context of the dominant discourse of patriarchy, a worldview held by many individuals and communities. For a more detailed description of controversies related to privileging certain lines of enquiry in the trauma field, the reader is encouraged to refer to the chapter on history in this text.

It is important for the clinician to discern how she has been influenced by the political discourse concerning trauma. How do one's personal and professional values and ethics shape a clinical stance when working with survivors of childhood trauma? Is the clinician aware of the current incidence and prevalence of trauma in his or her culture? At the assessment level, does the clinician over- or underemphasize the impact of trauma on the couple's presentation? Does the clinician inquire about childhood sexual abuse with male clients, or is there a gender-biased stance that presupposes that only women are survivors? When trauma is disclosed, does the therapist pathologize the survivor, or are the interactional patterns also explored? Does the therapist deny or minimize the trauma? Are certain racial or cultural groups presumed to have high levels of violence? Is the clinician aware of high-risk populations? Does the therapist recognize the particular resilience and adaptation demonstrated by the couple?

Has the clinician been able to separate his or her own opinions and attitudes from the often verbalized discourse about survivors of domestic violence and/or childhood trauma having precipitated their own abuse? This "blaming-the-victim" mentality needs to be systematically challenged so that the clinician does not fall prey to the internalization of negative stereotypes of trauma survivors. If only one partner in the dyad discloses a trauma history, does the clinician assume that the survivor is the "identified patient" of the system?

On a macro level, has the clinician formulated a thoughtful position about public funding issues for domestic violence programs in which policies are often organized around feminist or radical feminist ideology? On a practice level, does the clinician utilize this sort of community resource? Or does the clinician tend to minimize the potentially dangerous aspects of working with traumatized couples that have histories of ongoing violence? Is the therapist complicit in ignoring the range of domestic violence presentations? For example, does the clinician assess gay, lesbian, bisexual, and transgendered couples for domestic violence? Does the clinician assess whether the ethnicities or cultural backgrounds of couples influence their reporting and acceptance of domestic violence? Does the clinician consciously or unconsciously retain attitudes of patriarchy or sexism that privilege male partners in heterosexual couples? How do these attitudes influence the clinician's response to the use of forceful or threatening tactics by males?

In terms of practice dilemmas, does the clinician understand the complexity of the professional debate concerning false memories (Loftus, 1993; McFarlane & van der Kolk, 1996)? Has he internalized attitudes that influence his stance toward clients who are uncertain of their traumatic histories? Or does the clinician prematurely or inappropriately push clients to retrieve and describe traumatic memories? Does the clinician devalue clinical work with trauma survivors if the individuals are not uncovering repressed memories? Is the clinician aware of her tendency to experience vicarious, voyeuristic pleasure in hearing about sexual abuse or the couple's sexual relationship? Does the clinician repress or act out any of his own sexual feelings in the clinical experience?

With regard to parenting practices, several questions arise for the clinician. What are the clinician's views about appropriate disciplinary measures for children? Does he or she legitimize spanking and other physical discipline as acceptable forms of childhood discipline? How does the public discourse about discipline impact the clinician? How does the clinician's own parenting style influence his or her thinking about "normative" parenting? In terms of child discipline, how are cultural differences understood and integrated by the clinician? What are the views of the clinician in terms of the efficacy of child protective services? Does the clinician try to avoid issues of mandated reporting of abuse? Does the clinician work cooperatively with other social service agencies? Does the agency or setting of the clinician legitimize work with couples who are trauma survivors?

Within this framework of the institutional and sociocultural factors that impact the clinician, let us now turn to the concept of countertransference. A review of countertransference in individual psychotherapy is followed by the elucidation of countertransference phenomena when working with single- or dual-trauma couples.

:: COUNTERTRANSFERENCE

Evolution of the Concept

The psychotherapy literature contains many understandings of countertransference. Both Hanna (1993) and Siegel (1997) trace the evolution of countertransference. Hanna notes that "The classical view of counter-transference posits unconscious conflict in the therapist, activated in reaction to the patient's transference" (p. 27). In the classical view, countertransference responses are considered impediments to the maintenance of therapeutic neutrality (Jacobs, 1983; Siegel, 1997) and, as such, are viewed as counterproductive to the successful therapy of the individual or couple.

In the 1950s, a number of authors (Heimann, 1950; Spitz, 1956; Tower, 1956; Winnicott, 1975) argued that the therapist's responses or reactions to clients should not be viewed as antithetical to successful treatment. Rather, they argued that the responses of the clinician, both conscious and unconscious, are useful pieces of information that can help the clinician understand the client's experiences. This view, termed the totalist perspective, argues that while the therapist indeed becomes the object of the client's projections, the reactions of the therapist take shape as a result of the specific dynamic constellations of the client. Racker (1968) described how therapists will be induced to express certain responses as a result of either concordant or complementary identifications or countertransference. In a concordant identification, the therapist temporarily experiences the client's internal world. In this identification, the therapist's empathic connection to the client's internal world is stimulated. In a complementary identification, the therapist is induced to play a part in the client's internal world and to enact a projected part of the internal conflict. This identification, when recognized, can be used to understand further and potentially to interpret the origin of the interpersonal style of the client. The clinician often feels unsettled when she or he feels compelled to enact a response that feels punitive or sadistic toward the client. However, this process often reflects the playing out of the "victim–victimizer–bystander" dynamic (Herman, 1992; Miller, 1994). For example, aggressive or punitive feelings are often aligned with the projected victimizer role. Siegel (1997) argues that the concepts of totalist countertransference can be utilized in couple therapy. Citing Scharff (1989) and Siegel (1992), she comments, "In the same way that the spouse is provoked to accept and respond in ways that bring to life a previously internalized conflict, the therapist is similarly stimulated to experience aspects of both partners' internalized conflicts" (p. 11).

Contemporary views of countertransference postulate that client–therapist interactions are intersubjective in nature (Benjamin, 1998; McMahon, 1997; Miehls, 1999; Noonan, 1998; Trop, 1997). Drawing from postmodernism, these authors recognize that therapist neutrality is a myth, and that, indeed, all participants in the therapeutic process bring their "subjectivity" into the room (Hanna, 1993; Noonan, 1998; Rustin, 1997). In this conceptualization, the clinician is not privileged as an objective or neutral person who has the authority or power to determine the definition of normalcy. Rather, intersubjective theorists presume that the therapeutic process is co-created by the client's and the therapist's subjectivities.

Siegel (1997) says that the culture and personal belief systems of the therapist, if not understood by the therapist, can prevent genuine authenticity in the therapeutic interaction. Hanna (1993) states that clients' affective responses are always stimulated by some real, interpersonal, communication of the therapist. This implies that there is no such thing as "pure" transference. Rather, any interaction in the relationship needs to be conceptualized as a transference–countertransference intersubjective experience. In couple therapy, it is important to realize that the therapist's relationship history, current relationship patterns, values, and beliefs all influence the intersubjective relationship and interactions between the couple and the therapist (Siegel, 1997; Trop, 1997).

Definition of Countertransference in This Text

Our view of countertransference is closely aligned with the views of intersubjective theorists (Aron, 1996a, 1996b; Benjamin, 1998; Bowles, 1999; McMahon, 1997; Mitchell, 1988; Noonan, 1998; Trop, 1997). We agree that both therapist and client bring their subjectivity to the treatment relationship. Given this, we define countertransference in a broad manner. We understand countertransference to be comprised of the conscious aspects of feelings, ideas, and physical sensations that are stimulated within the therapist as a result of the therapist's interaction with the real person of the client, including the client's transference material and the reenactments that the therapist is likely to experience as an aspect of projective identification.

We agree with Pearlman and Saakvitne (1995) when they argue that countertransference is also manifest in unconscious defense mechanisms that are activated within the therapist. These defenses are instituted to counterbalance the feelings or the responses to the stimuli mentioned in the preceding. The therapist's own personal history interacts with the unique characteristics of clients.

It is useful to make a distinction between objective, personal, and cultural countertransference phenomena. We consider objective countertransference to be those clinician responses that are stimulated within the therapist, regardless of her history. Objective countertransference is manifest in the projective identification patterns that the client enacts with the therapist (Catherall, 1992; Miehls, 1997; Ogden, 1982; Siegel, 1991). However, personal countertransference is directly related to the clinician's history and unconscious world. In this type of reaction, clinicians respond differentially to client material based on the lived experience of the clinician. Personal countertransference can either help or hinder the therapeutic work. Last, the clinician may experience cultural countertransference that results from cultural similarity or dissimilarity between the clients and clinician, as well as worldviews related to cultural themes.

In regard to cultural countertransference, it is important for the clinician to be aware of his or her responses to the multiple factors that shape the client's identity. The client's social, cultural, racial, religious, and socioeconomic class characteristics may have a particular impact on the clinician's countertransference (Chediak, 1979). Schoenewolf (1993) comments that the clinician's multiple identities can lead to a cultural counterresistance, and this needs to be monitored to prevent a countertransference enactment that positions the client in a compromised or misunderstood position. Pérez-Foster (1998) speaks to this issue when she says, "The recognition of the contributing role of the therapist's own subjectivity in psychodynamically oriented practice cannot be more vital than in the treatment of patients whose culture, race, or class markedly differs from that of the therapist" (p. 255). In sum, we view countertransference as a process that is fundamentally shaped in the complex interactions between client and therapist. Embedded within the multiple identities of both client and therapist, the interpersonal therapeutic relationship becomes the site of conscious injunctions and unconscious reenactments of internal dynamics that fundamentally influence the person of the therapist in complex ways.

Countertransference Themes with Trauma Survivors: Individual Therapy

Briere (1996), Chu (1988), Dalenberg (2000), Davies and Frawley (1992), and Pearlman and Saakvitne (1995) all recognize the potential for transference–countertransference themes when working with survivors of childhood trauma in individual therapy. Lindy (1996) says that individuals with trauma backgrounds have a propensity to repeat the trauma in the therapeutic relationship. Chu claims that trauma survivors are often difficult clients to treat, and suggests that there are predictable impasses or "traps" that occur in the treatment of trauma survivors. He recognizes that client and therapist each contribute to the development of the impasses, and that client and therapist each attempt to guard themselves from overwhelming anxiety and extreme affective pain (p. 192).

Briere (1996) comments that the clinician's own history of trauma influences the therapeutic process. While the therapist may have increased empathic connection with trauma survivors, he or she may be particularly susceptible to being overwhelmed by the intensity of affect generated in psychotherapy with such clients. The reawakening of suppressed or repressed thoughts, feelings, or memories related to the therapist's trauma history can be frightening or overwhelming owing to the intrusive and often unexpected nature of such processes (Canfield, 2002; Pearlman & Saakvitne, 1995). Previously held defensive postures become challenged and intersect with the client's transference reactions. There may be a reenactment experience that draws its origin from the intersubjective interaction of the trauma histories of client and clinician. Particular "victim–victimizer–bystander" dynamics activate arousal for all participants in the therapeutic dyad. Pearlman and Saakvitne suggest that shame-filled therapists may have difficulty setting appropriate boundaries in therapy and may unwittingly allow clients to be abusive toward them. Davies and Frawley (1994) note that therapists who uncover painful repressed material while conducting therapy may have strong countertransference responses toward their clients for precipitating such uncomfortable feelings. It is difficult for therapists to hear clients' histories of trauma that closely resemble their own. Ongoing supervision/consultation and psychotherapy assist the therapist/survivor to conduct good clinical work. Regardless of the trauma history of the therapist, the establishment and maintenance of firm boundaries are essential to the formation of a healthy psychotherapeutic treatment alliance.

Pearlman and Saakvitne (1995) suggest that countertransference is present in every therapeutic relationship and that the countertransference "provides information about the unique aspects of the therapist and the client in the therapeutic relationship" (p. 33). They note that many trauma survivors precipitate a reaction within the therapist that appears protective and parental. This is often in response to the client's fear of abandonment. It is important for the therapist to have an accurate assessment of the client's attachment and developmental history. A thorough assessment of the client will assist the therapist in understanding and utilizing the reenactment dynamics of the client. While transference–countertransference themes manifest in varied issues, we find it helpful to contextualize process-related themes continually in the powerful reenactment of the internal conflict template of "victim–victimizer–bystander" (Herman, 1992; Miller, 1994; Staub, 2003). Often, one or more parts of this triangular dynamic are present in transference–countertransference interactions.

At times, therapists need to accept the idealization of the trauma survivor (Chu, 1988). Turner, McFarlane, and van der Kolk (1996) note that the client needs to "idealize them in order to replace the sources of security that were destroyed by the trauma" (p. 553). Here, the clinician often is positioned as the bystander, who will rescue the client. This temporary idealization may be necessary in order that the trauma survivor can internalize the safety of the therapeutic relationship. When some internalization of the benign, caring therapist has occurred, the client then can begin to enact unconscious affects associated with the rage, sadism, disappointment, and devaluation of his or her internal world. Client themes that precipitate countertransference responses often are related to feelings of being further exploited, abused, or traumatized. If clinicians are not able to allow the perpetrator transference to unfold, they may miss an opportunity in the therapeutic relationship to examine fully the complexity of the reenactment.

Trauma survivors often position the therapist as a parent figure who is perceived as a collusive bystander-partner to the perpetrator of the childhood abuse (Davies & Frawley, 1994; Herman, 1992; Pearlman & Saakvitne, 1995). This central dynamic often pulls the therapist into the countertransference trap of being unhelpful, forgetful of specific details of the client, or minimizing of the client experience. Initially, the client may protect the therapist from this dynamic by adopting a false-self compliance to the perceived wishes of the therapist. Then, when the therapist does not "see" or recognize the survivor's pain or emotional fragility, the client will become enraged.

Survivors of childhood trauma frequently identify with the sadistic aspects of their perpetrators. In the role of victimizer, they may enact sadistic internalized aspects of self, and the therapist needs to guard against being positioned, countertransferentially, as the helpless victim who is powerless to counteract the client's aggression. Survivor/therapists are especially vulnerable to being immobilized by a client's aggression. The therapist may respond with anger and retaliatory fantasies, and may feel a sense of shame when he or she becomes aware of the wish to retaliate against the client. Clients may enact their sadism by becoming intrusive and disrespectful of the clinician's personal boundaries. While the "unconscious identification with and enactment of her abuser's lack of boundaries offers some sense of power and inviolability . . . the therapist being intruded upon on by the patient may experience great discomfort at and anticipatory anxiety about being exposed and penetrated" (Davies & Frawley, 1994, p. 172). Internalized identification with the sadism of the perpetrator may also cause the client to sexualize the treatment relationship (Pearlman & Saakvitne, 1995). Here, the therapist may feel shame if there is a recognition of any sexual excitement within him- or herself. Often, therapists deny or intellectualize their own sexual feelings, and this may lead to a treatment impasse. Self-destructive acting-out behavior by the client may be another manifestation of aggressive victimizer behavior toward the therapist.

Clinicians who are solicitous of a client's requests for special attention (extra sessions, phone calls, lengthened sessions) in fact may be yielding to countertransference rescuer pulls. As such, they are setting the stage for another transference–countertransference enactment. Trauma survivors may become exploitative of the clinician's willingness to be available. The clinician may think, initially, that this behavior might strengthen the treatment alliance. For example, Davies and Frawley (1992) comment that as the clinician attempts to rescue the abused child, he or she may unwittingly reinforce the idea that it is indeed possible to offer compensation for the past injuries. However, as noted, it is important to stay within the therapeutic frame or boundaries, as many trauma survivors develop a wish to have all of their needs met by the therapist. Indeed, they may escalate their demands to a level that the therapist cannot meet, thereby leaving the therapist feeling incompetent.

At times, the clinician will experience feelings of helplessness. Often reduced to the stance of trying to appease the client at any cost, "the therapist experiences himself as concerned and available, determined to rescue, while to the patient he is cruelly withholding or dangerously seductive" (p. 29).

Although it is clear that transference patterns manifested by trauma survivors may precipitate countertransferential responses in the clinician, it is important to state that our descriptions of transference paradigms are not being offered so as to pathologize survivors of trauma. Rather, we recognize the trauma survivor's internal world as having been damaged in specific ways that undoubtedly will be reenacted in individual therapy. The unconscious reenactments are viewed as attempts to engage the clinician in a process that, ultimately, will be therapeutic for the trauma survivor. The ability of the clinician to utilize countertransference responses in an adaptive, nondefensive manner will aid the survivor to become free of her or his internal conflicts. In fact, Davies and Frawley (1994) suggest that it "is the enactment and interpretation of transference–countertransference phenomena combined that facilitate integration and healing" (p. 168).

Countertransference Themes with Trauma Survivors: Couple Therapy

Careful examination of the therapist's personal experience in the presence of the couple is a central responsibility of the clinician. The clinician needs to be aware of what is motivating him to feel and/or behave in certain ways with any particular couple. If the clinician is operating in a way that is discrepant from his usual frame, it is useful to consider whether he has fallen into a countertransference trap (Chu, 1988). Solomon (1997) speaks to the benefits of remaining attuned to one's fluctuating reactions. She suggests that the therapist consider such questions as: "Who am I to them? Whom does she/he represent to me? Are my reactions unique to this couple? Do I feel differently in this particular session than I generally feel with this couple?" (p. 27). As noted in the preceding, it is important that clinicians continuously monitor the interplay of their own multiple identity statuses with those of their clients. In this vein, survivor/therapists who find themselves being reminded of their own trauma histories may intellectualize or deny the trauma material that the couple brings to therapy (Canfield, 2002; Pearlman & Saakvitne, 1995).

It is useful to consider that the clinician's countertransference is comprised of multiple levels of interaction with the couple. The clinician responds to the two individuals in the room, but more importantly responds to the couple unit and the characteristics, projective identification patterns, and the couple's "shared" transference to the clinician. Scharff and Scharff (1991) describe that each couple system develops both individual and shared transference responses to the clinician. We also experience the couple as holding certain aspects of the interactional process that is enacted with the clinician. This is particularly relevant in the "victim–victimizer–bystander" dynamic. In those transference–countertransference phenomena, the couple often develops a shared dynamic that is projected to the clinician. Clinicians need to be aware of the fluidity of the "victim–victimizer–bystander" roles in the dynamic, and should be prepared to acknowledge the presence of each of these roles within the couple and the therapist. If the couple wrestles with their shared "victim–victimizer–bystander" dynamic, the internal conflict may be projected outward. The vignettes in this chapter demonstrate how clinicians then enact one of the projected roles as an externalization of this couple's shared internal drama of the "victim–victimizer–bystander" scenario (Herman, 1992; Miller, 1994; Staub, 2003).

The vignettes highlight seven common countertransference themes that are often enacted in couple therapy: (1) aggression, (2) passive indifference, (3) detachment, (4) boundary violations, (5) eroticized feelings, (6) helplessness, and (7) reaction formation. (Refer to Figure 8.1.)

Countertransference Aggression

In my work with Dave and Janet, I eventually became aware of my rage toward Dave when he would complain about Janet's lack of emotional availability.

DAVE AND JANET :: Janet had a history of severe trauma, characterized by ongoing sadistic sexual abuse at the hands of her father and her older brother. Also, during her late adolescence, she was raped by two strangers. She had undergone extensive inpatient treatment to ameliorate her dissociative identity disorder. At the time of my contact with the couple, Janet was being seen twice weekly for outpatient psychotherapy and was attending a survivor group in a local mental health center. At that point, her tendency to dissociate was minimal, although when pressed for increased attachment and intimacy from her husband, she sometimes would retreat into a dissociated state. The couple had been referred to me by Janet's therapist, who speculated that Dave's insistence on closeness was negatively influencing Janet's progress in her individual treatment.

Dave was a highly intelligent chemistry professor. Graduate students clamored to become part of his research team, as his work was internationally respected. He seemed to have an intellectual understanding of the impact of PTSD and, at times, was empathic to Janet's adaptations to her traumatic history. While I was aware of my tendency to adopt an all-protective, nurturing stance toward Janet, I was less aware, initially, of my rage toward Dave. Generally, I was able to assist him to understand, intellectually, the impact of his behavior on Janet. At times, he understood that he needed to modulate his expectations of intimacy. He recognized that Janet was making progress and that, in time, she might become more emotionally engaged with him.

Other times, Dave expected intimacy from Janet and, then, I was conscious of feeling impatient with him. However, while I was aware of my irritation, it became clear that I was repressing my rage. In one session, he turned his demanding, childlike stance toward me. In a frantic, high-pitched voice, he accused me of taking Janet's side. He demanded that I make her more responsive to him. He demanded that I understand his needs. He said he would not leave my office unless I convinced Janet to accompany him to a conference. He accused me of wrecking the couple's marriage, saying that he thought I was legitimizing Janet's withdrawal from him. In this session, my defensive posture was challenged. I began to have fantasies of going across the room and slapping him across the side of the head. In the fantasy, I took great delight in seeing that I had given him a bloody nose with the blow, and I became aware of my sadistic pleasure in imagining him reduced to a teary, whiny, helpless child.

When I became consciously reengaged in the content of the interview, Dave was expectantly looking at me. He asked me again what I was going to do to make Janet attend the conference with him. I impulsively replied that I wasn't sure what I was going to do, but I knew what I wanted to do to him in the moment. My sadism was obvious, and he readily experienced my aggression. Clearly, this frightened him. He started to retreat from me, physically pushing his chair away from me and adopting a look that I perceived as being terrified. He said that he would be quiet. I could see that my comment had shaken him.

As I was aware immediately of my countertransference enactment, I told Dave, calmly, that I could see I had frightened him and that I was not going to hurt him. I began to speak soothingly about how upset I could see he was and about how I wanted to be able to understand better what his needs were in the moment. He began to cry quietly and seemed unable to manage a verbal response. Janet also was shaken, but she was about to tell me some of Dave's history. I already knew that Dave's mother had died of breast cancer when he was seven years old. His father had been described as preoccupied and emotionally unavailable. Dave had said that his father was kind but had protracted grief. Dave had retreated to books, school, and teachers in an effort to find a way to deal with his own grief. His relationship with his maternal grandparents provided him with some solace and security.

Janet explained that Dave had not been completely honest with me about his history. She revealed that Dave's father had been physically abusive toward him whenever he would show sadness about his mother's illness. Dave then said that he had often wished his father could have "made his mother better" so that she was available to him. I understood that it was quite likely that Dave's expression of sadness because of his mother's illness and death may have prompted his father's sadistic response. I wondered if Dave's father had projected his own unresolved grief onto his son and if his abuse toward Dave might have been his attempt to rid himself of his own unconscious fears and longings.

I recognized that Dave was not yet ready to attach a great deal of insight to the complex dynamic that was made up of the abuse he suffered and the way his nuclear family had handled his mother's illness and death. I did see that there were a number of enactments present in this scenario. I had previously understood Dave's wish for closeness to Janet to be a repetition of his wish to be close to his deceased mother. I now better understood that Dave had a wish also to be attached to his father and to be protected from further hurt by his father. He was envious of my protective nature toward Janet. He wanted me to protect him also. In addition, I had enacted the complementary projective identification pattern of becoming the sadistic, abusive father toward Dave. Had I examined my initial irritability toward Dave, I might have understood better his injunction to me. However, with this new information, and with the recognition of my sadistic feelings toward Dave, I could better help him begin to work through his trauma history.

I directly apologized to Dave for my aggressive comment. I said that I thought there would be a great deal for us to understand further about these dynamics. I said also that I could understand his wish that I facilitate Janet being closer to him. Janet told Dave that she would accompany him to the conference, if he would agree that she could determine the nature of their sexual closeness. Previously, we had discussed the couple's management of sexual closeness, and so the rest of that session was spent revisiting some of those ground rules. Again, I empathized with Dave, saying that his wish for closeness was understandable and that we would continue to find ways to have his emotional needs met in the partnership.

In this vignette, it is clear that I engaged in at least two reenactments with this couple. I had adopted a rescuer enactment with Janet; in so doing, I had made a primary identification with Janet. In addition, I had become the victimizer in the exchange with Dave. While I had initially repressed my anger toward Dave, the aggression that eventually broke through was a reenactment of Dave's positioning me in a complementary projective identification. I later became aware that my attitudes toward Dave were fueled, very likely, by my own gender bias—that men should be more independent. My own dependency needs may have been projected onto Dave, and my sadistic response, so like his father's, may have been an attempt to rid myself of my own unconscious ambivalence about dependency. In addition, the couple had projected their shared conflict about "victim–victimizer–bystander" roles within their dyad, and I had enacted their shared conflict in my aggression toward Dave.

Passive Indifference Countertransference

A common countertransference enactment when working with traumatized couples is the development of a passivity or indifference to volatile interactions between the couple. Likewise, the therapist may be dispassionate in hearing the horrendous details of trauma in either partner. This is often a repetition of the "victim–victimizer–bystander" dynamic (Herman, 1992) so often experienced by survivors of childhood trauma. Often, I am aware of this countertransference response when I am listening to the de-

tail of horrific trauma and find myself feeling somehow bored or emotionally neutral. My work with Bob and Linda underscores this dynamic.

BOB AND LINDA :: Bob's mother had brutalized him as a child. His partner, Linda, had knowledge of some of the abuse, but she did not know the details of the many physical assaults that Bob experienced. I had worked with
this couple for many months and was clearly doing Phase II work (reflection
on the trauma narrative) with the couple. However, in one interview, Bob
started to disclose the specific details of his mother's abuse toward him. In
graphic detail, he reported that, with some regularity, his mother would rip
his toenails out, using pliers. He reported that she would not extract his
fingernails, as the effects of this would be obvious to other adults. I was aware
of my own nausea as he described that his mother's pleasure increased if he
cried or showed any emotional response to the brutalizing behavior. I became
aware that Linda was increasingly agitated in the interview. I could see that
she was flushing and tearful as Bob described vivid details of blood, ripped
skin, and excruciating pain.

In this instance, the "victim–victimizer–bystander" dynamic was clearly enacted. Bob (the victimizer) was verbally brutalizing the victim (Linda), while
I (the bystander) protected myself from my horror by being a silent observer.
In retrospect, I became aware that my detachment further fueled the intensity of the language that Bob utilized in his descriptions of the past abuse.

Detachment Responses

Similar to the previous example, a countertransference response
of detachment or dissociation from affect is often enacted. An adult survivor
of childhood trauma has experienced a range of responses from bystanders,
both in childhood and adult life. Some have responded effectively and proactively, some have launched themselves into overly zealous rescuing, and
some have ignored the abuses. Through the process of projective identification, a clinician may enact any or all of these bystander roles. The clinician's
detachment is illustrated in the following vignette.

MARIA AND RAMON :: In couple therapy with a middle-aged couple of
Central American cultural heritage, I found that their presenting issues of
power conflicts regarding parenting styles concealed relationship templates es-

tablished early on in their respective childhoods, which were riddled with horrific trauma. Maria recalled assaults from guerrilla insurgents who held her family hostage during a period of acute political violence. While her parents and siblings were tortured physically, she was raped and shot in the intestines, an attack that required multiple surgeries. Ramon reported similar experiences of torture as his family was seized by political terrorists. During their adolescence, both Maria and Ramon escaped with their families to Mexico, where they ultimately met and fell in love. Although traumatic bonding initiated this couple's early connection, they went on to establish a strong marriage, forged during their flight to the United States. As refugees from a war-torn nation, they wrestled with multiple stressors involving emigration, acculturation, and adaptation to many losses.

While hearing their reflections on their experiences of childhood torture, I found myself feeling very sleepy, distracted, and anxious to end the session. On reflection, I recognized that my detachment mirrored their collective dissociation of their early trauma experiences. Once I recognized my countertransferential detachment, I was able to be more emotionally available to this couple's narratives. Interestingly, as they reported their memories, they recalled that both their families and their cultural values discouraged the emotional expression of any childhood difficulties. Thus, cultural prohibition to express any affect related to traumatic experiences allowed me to continue on with a certain degree of emotional detachment while respecting cultural sensitivity. However, it was essential to tease out how much of my detachment was related to personal countertransference and how much was ultimately proactively designed as a clinical intervention.

Boundary Violations

Clearly survivors of childhood traumatic events often experienced violations of boundaries that compromised their physical and psychological space. Dual-trauma couples are particularly vulnerable to enacting boundary violations enactments between each other and jointly in their interactions with their therapist. The tendency to enact symbiotic-like patterns that cloud parameters is illustrated in the following vignette.

JIM AND CATHY ∷ Jim and Cathy started couple therapy with the explicit goal that the therapy would assist them to solidify their beginning sobriety from alcohol and drug usage. Each had long-term addiction difficulties. They had decided to tackle their addictions before their young children would be negatively impacted by their daily habits of drinking and marijuana usage. Jim and Cathy were engaging individuals and easily won my approval and support for their sobriety. The couple attended twelve-step programs and used their couple therapy to strengthen further their support network and connections. The couple was engaged in Phase I therapy work (establishment of safety and stabilization) when the enactment occurred.

The couple asked me if I would object if they smoked cigarettes during their sessions. They reported that though they would try to kick their nicotine habit in the future, in the interim, they believed that nicotine and caffeine were relatively harmless addictions. They felt that they needed cigarettes to help quell their anxiety and cravings for alcohol and marijuana. I clearly did not encourage cigarette smoking in my office or waiting room area, and this policy had been formulated some years prior to Jim and Cathy's therapy. Although I initially said that I would not permit smoking during the session, the couple began consistently to voice their concern about relapse with drugs and alcohol. I became increasingly worried about their relapse and eventually said that I would permit smoking during their session. In addition, I did not question the couple's habit of coming to sessions with coffee and doughnuts. In fact, the couple began to bring me a coffee as well, and I welcomed their thoughtfulness.

The boundary violations were so pronounced that other clients began to complain of the smell of smoke in the office area. Other clients began to ask if they could smoke during their sessions. It was clear that I had fallen into an enactment of the couple's shared transference. They each positioned me as holding the key to their sobriety. They had convinced me that my limits around smoking were unreasonable and punitive. Not only had I fallen into a reaction formation response, I blurred my usual boundaries in this instance. I had become the victim to the couple's victimizing behavior (smoking) and also stood by as a bystander, helpless to protect myself or my other clients. The couple were relieved when I reinstituted my "no smoking" policy and admitted that they had wished that I had protected them from their own smoking. Each acknowledged that their parents had not protected them from family members who had abused them as children. In addition, neither had been given appropriate limits as teenagers, and thus each had developed drinking and drug addictions. In my attempt to help them solidify their recent sobriety, I had inadvertently contributed to their anxiety concerning the safety in the holding therapy environment.

Eroticized Clinician Responses

In other instances, erotic transference–countertransference responses may become activated. In my work with Joanne and Jill, I became aware of an eroticized transference–countertransference enactment.

JOANNE AND JILL :: Joanne, a mental health worker, was familiar with my work with trauma survivors and referred herself and her partner for couple therapy. Although I told Joanne that I considered myself a gay-affirmative therapist, I wondered why they, as a lesbian couple, would choose to work with a male therapist. She responded by saying that I had been highly recommended to her and that both she and Jill were comfortable working with a male therapist.

When I completed the assessment, I heard that Joanne was a survivor of childhood sexual abuse. Her stepfather had sexually abused her for a two-year period when she was a young adolescent. She reported that she had ambivalent feelings about her stepfather, as she had viewed him initially as someone who was warm, attentive, and loving toward her. Her mother, who had chronic mental health problems, was described as emotionally unavailable to Joanne. Joanne's birth father committed suicide when Joanne was sixteen. Joanne married her high school sweetheart when she was seventeen. She was pregnant and felt that the marriage would provide an opportunity for her to escape from the family home. Her husband abused substances and physically beat her. She managed to flee the marriage when her daughter was two years old, moving to her older sister's home, and was supported by government social assistance.

Jill had been raised in a very liberal family. She reported that her parents were "hippies" and that she was raised in a community of families living a simple life tied to the environmental/conservation movement. The members of her rural community were free spirits, and marijuana was readily available to any community member. Jill commented that the adults of the community were sexually promiscuous and that she often observed groups of people involved in sexual activities. She did not have any memories of "direct" childhood sexual abuse, but she acknowledged that she had adopted a somewhat puritanical response to sexuality. She had engaged in one lesbian relationship before meeting Joanne, and she identified as lesbian.

The initial sessions with the couple were productive. They were co-parenting Joanne's twelve-year-old daughter, and had examined their roles as parents. Each wanted to find more adaptive ways of dealing with their angry feelings. As well, they identified that they wanted to be able to communicate more directly and wanted to improve their sexual relationship. We agreed that we would work on communication patterns and parenting issues at the out-set, as part of Phase I couple therapy. They agreed that they would work on the sexual relationship following the completion of this Phase I focus on safety and stabilization. I was struck by my fondness for Joanne, finding her to be quite engaging. She had a good sense of humor and seemed to have an inter-personal manner that was both entertaining and substantive. She had ego strength, and her resilience impressed me. She seemed to have a capacity to verbalize her feelings. I had more difficulty engaging with Jill. She seemed self-righteous and complained that therapy had focused more on Joanne's con-cerns than on hers. She had difficulties expressing her feelings, and I often found myself thinking that she was boring. I made efforts to empathize with Jill, but was aware that I felt more connected to Joanne.

As the sessions progressed, I became aware that Joanne was indeed taking up more of the "air time" in the interviews. I also became aware that I was feeling increasingly sexually attracted to Joanne. While I noted my reaction, I did not feel that I was enacting my feelings in any observable way. I was less aware of Joanne's increasingly flirtatious behavior toward me. During one in-terview, I had thought that she was being sexually provocative with me, but I remember dismissing the idea (somewhat naively), reassuring myself that she identified as lesbian.

The transference–countertransference reenactment became clear during one session in which Joanne came to the session without Jill. She reported that the couple had agreed previously to meet at the office for the session. I in-formed Joanne that we would start the session when Jill arrived, and I en-couraged her to come to the inner consulting office when they were ready to start. After approximately ten minutes, Joanne came into the office and said that we might as well use the time as, clearly, Jill was not arriving. As usual, she appeared playful, using sarcastic humor to imagine the scenario in which Jill was being detained. I was about to interrupt her when Jill came into the office and simply assumed her usual chair. Jill apologized for being late, but said she knew that I wouldn't mind having Joanne all to myself.

I was uncomfortable and imagine that I flushed. I was immobilized by my very apparent discomfort and blurted out to Jill that we had just started the interview a moment before she arrived. Joanne said that she had pushed herself on me, but that I had seemed to enjoy the joke that she made about Jill. Jill watched this exchange without showing any sign of discomfort. I denied Joanne's allegation, but she insisted that I had been enjoying myself before Jill arrived at the meeting. Jill quietly said that it was no big deal, that she had seen the two of us flirting during many of the sessions.

Jill's sense of resignation finally registered with me, and I commented that I could see she was deflated and lonely in the room. I was empathically attuned to Jill, perhaps for the first time. I commented that she had waited a long time for me to truly see her. She again said that she saw Joanne was having fun playing with me and that she didn't want to stand in the way. Once again, I said that it must have been painful for her to watch these interactions. In the interim, Joanne seemed to become more reserved. She made the historical connection between this exchange and her own family. She acknowledged that her mother would often sit in silence while Joanne and her stepfather enjoyed playful banter. She had not been aware that we had re-created that dynamic in the couple therapy.

This enactment took place on multiple levels. My relationship with Joanne had an erotic quality, and Joanne was unconsciously testing the safety of the relationship. I was dismissing my sexual pleasure in our exchanges by rationalizing, naively, that, since Joanne identified as lesbian, she and I were safe from sexualized feelings. Jill was reenacting her history of being an observer to the sexually promiscuous behavior of her parents and their community. She became the onlooker in the internalized "victim–victimizer–bystander" dynamic that was being enacted. While she was aware of the flirtatious behavior between Joanne and myself, she felt helpless to alter the dynamic. With this couple, each partner had sufficient ego strength to understand these issues through the facilitation of reflection and insight. They went on to engage in long-term couple therapy that was productive for the relationship. In retrospect, the turning point of the treatment happened during this difficult, yet powerful, enactment.

Helplessness in the Countertransference

Another common transference–countertransference paradigm that becomes operative with traumatized couples is the positioning of the therapist as a helpless victim. Often, trauma survivors have internalized the sadistic aspects of their perpetrators, and they can be relentless in pursuing the therapist and trying to position him or her in the victim role. The therapist is well advised to understand fully his or her own tendencies toward staying in a one-down, masochistic position. Recognition of this dynamic will assist the therapist in discerning any sadistic behavior in clients. Through the process of projective identification, a couple may project the internalized conflict related to the "victim–victimizer–bystander" dynamic. Consequently, the clinician is vulnerable to experiencing any of these roles, alternately or concurrently, during enactments, when the projected externalized drama is reflecting the client's inner world. The following clinical vignette highlights an example of countertransferential victimization/helplessness.

JACOB AND SARAH :: After six months of couple therapy with Jacob, a forty-one-year-old graphic artist and his wife Sarah, a thirty-nine-year-old teacher and second-generation survivor of the Holocaust, the focus shifted from their power struggles around parenting two adolescent children to issues related to their own intimate partnership. Although both partners practiced reformed Judaism with steadfast devotion, Sarah proceeded to attack Jacob during one session for "not being serious enough about his Judaism and betraying his people." As I ventured to ask questions about the source of Sarah's disappointment in Jacob, she lashed out at me, claiming that I had lost neutrality. "You're just like everyone else. You minimize my pain. I don't care if you are Jewish or non-Jewish. You are not listening, just like Jacob, and you are just like him."

I immediately fell silent, experiencing helplessness, guilt, and anxiety. I thought that Sarah might be expressing not only her own personal distrust of both Jacob and me, but also the couple's collective distrust of me. My response was surprise and indignation. I was preoccupied with thoughts such as: Why don't they know who I am? It's too bad that they do not know that I have been committed to research efforts focused on the intergenerational effects of the Holocaust, and that I have participated in several research projects in this area. I wanted to defend myself. Of course, they did not know this, as, mindful of the boundaries of the clinical setting, I had not shared the information with them. However, I wished for them to understand me for who I was. So, feeling unjustly accused, my anger and hurt were compounded by my already existing anxiety, guilt, and inertia grounded in utter helplessness. My experience of victimization became complete as I started to pity myself about my clinical work and, in a more global sense, about my career.

Fortunately, my cognitive monitor rallied as I began reflecting on my reactions. I sorted through both personal and objective countertransference responses and recognized my slippage into the victim countertransference enactment. I was able to explore with this couple the ways in which both of them—not only Sarah—might be experiencing my minimization of the seriousness of their emotional realities of victimization. Gradually, both Sarah and Jacob expressed their fears, bitter regrets, and sadness about hurtful experiences in which they felt misunderstood and ignored. They reowned the pattern of victimization that was projected during the session. In time, they came to recognize the cyclic "victim–victimizer–bystander" dynamic in their marriage and in other venues of their lives, including therapy, family, and friendships.

Reaction Formation Countertransference

In the following vignette, I enacted the couple's shared projection that was manifest in their desire to be perfect parents. Deconstructing my countertransference response facilitated the couple's awareness that they had unconsciously shared a wish to never enact any harshness (victimizing behavior) toward the couple's daughter, Grace.

CLIFF AND SONYA :: The couple therapy of Cliff and Sonya had been interrupted for three weeks when Sonya delivered the couple's first child, a long-awaited and highly cherished daughter. Cliff and Sonya each had been raised in volatile, physically abusive homes, and they were vigilant about their parenting skills. They were anxious to provide their baby, Grace, with a different childhood experience than either one of them had experienced. When the couple resumed treatment, they brought Grace to their sessions. They were proud parents, and I was responsive and congratulatory about their daughter's beauty and engaging demeanor. I was aware that I felt somewhat irritated by the child's presence in the room. However, seeing the parents' engagement with their daughter, I dismissed my irritation with the process. The couple said that they wanted to continue couple treatment. However, they started to arrive late for sessions, citing Grace's schedule and needs, and also were preoccupied during the sessions, tending exquisitely to Grace's every need and action. I became more solicitous, often extending sessions, engaging in dialogue about Grace's latest developmental accomplishments, and eliciting proud parent stories.

I was unaware of my irritation with Grace's presence until I found myself actively supporting Cliff's assertions that Sonya focused obsessively on Grace at the expense of everyone and everything else in their interactions. He had grown tired of taking the back seat to Grace. He noted that Grace was four months old and that she could be left at home with a babysitter, for short periods. Sonya was dismayed when I joined Cliff's refrain that Grace did interfere with the process of the sessions. I became aware that I had suppressed my frustration with the couple's preoccupation, and that I had overcompensated by forgoing my usual boundaries concerning time, content, and focus of the sessions. In deconstructing the process, the couple regained some equilibrium in their own interaction. Each ultimately acknowledged that taking some private individual time and/or couple time did not mean that Grace would be cast as a neglected child. Rather, my acknowledgment of my reaction formation to the child's interruptions during sessions facilitated my ability to open up the discussion with the couple. Each had been feeling somewhat victimized by the demands of their daughter, and each was reluctant to express this for fear of appearing like a victimizer who did not take their daughter's needs into account.

We move now to a discussion of vicarious trauma. As noted previously, countertransference and vicarious traumatization are related, though discrete phenomena. Table 10.1 highlights the similarities and differences between the two concepts. Aspects of vicarious traumatization are detailed next.

:: VICARIOUS TRAUMATIZATION

Vicarious traumatization, a well-developed concept, speaks to the insidious impact on the therapist working with traumatized individuals. Sometimes termed compassion fatigue (Figley, 1995), or secondary traumatic stress (Stamm, 1999), vicarious traumatization is defined as "the transforma-

enced her view that any couple could learn adaptive and effective problem-solving skills. As we discussed the impact of vicarious traumatization on her, she was able to become more engaged with her clients and less pessimistic about the future of their relationships. Fortunately, some of her couples demonstrated beginning change, and she became more heartened with the work.

Antidotes to Vicarious Traumatization

Clinicians attempt to manage the impact of vicarious traumatization through a variety of methods. Although the following are not necessarily prescriptive, Pearlmann and Saakvitne (1995) suggest a range of methods that clinicians find useful.

Institutional Methods/Factors

It is important to understand that vicarious traumatization is a *natural and expected* outcome of working with trauma survivors. The therapist who is alert to the vicissitudes of vicarious traumatization will be open to a variety of methods to counterbalance the process.

Catherall (1995), Pearlman and Saakvitne (1995), and Rosenbloom, Pratt, and Pearlman (1999) recognize that the attitudes at the agency or institution in which one works may either contribute to, or inoculate against, vicarious traumatization. Although it is clear that clinical supervision is a useful tool for helping therapists deal with the effects of vicarious traumatization (Elsass, 1997; Pearlman & Saakvitne, 1995), the agency as a whole can help as well (Catherall, 1995; Munroe et al., 1995; Pearlman & Saakvitne, 1995). Institutions that recognize the impact of vicarious traumatization may sponsor supportive team groups in the setting. These teams should allow enough time for each clinician to process how listening to trauma narratives impacts his or her clinical work. Separate from supervision, these forums allow an opportunity to reflect on the multiple meanings of being a trauma therapist. Catherall comments that a supportive team can provide many functions for trauma therapists, including listening, empathy, reframing of the meaning of trauma, and suggestions for resources in dealing with trauma survivors. Munroe et al. note the importance of the social support system for the therapist. Such systems are well positioned to help therapists disentangle themselves from countertransference enactments and/or from the effects of vicarious traumatization.

Balancing one's workday is also a useful antidote to the effects of vicarious traumatization. Agencies need to help therapists in diversifying their caseloads and/or their other therapeutic activities. For example, agencies that offer flexible hours, so as to meet the different needs of staff members, foster an organizational climate that shows respect for the workers. Many agencies offer professional and continuing education for their workers. Although individual workers can mediate their own tendencies toward vicarious traumatization, it is clear that the organizational attitudes also are important in counterbalancing the impact of vicarious traumatization.

Individual Factors

Pearlman and Saakvitne (1995) report that "The most important recommendation we make to our colleagues about their personal lives is to have one" (p. 393). Here, they underscore that losing one's own interests or relationships negatively impacts the resilience and adaptation of the psychotherapist. Self-care practices are also important. Because these activities will vary from person to person, it is important for the therapist to know which activities help her feel replenished and to maintain those activities with some regularity.

Yassen (1995) notes the relevance of physical self-care for trauma therapists. She suggests that exercise, adequate sleep, and adequate nutrition are important to self-care. Other physical activities, such as yoga, dance, drumming, and gardening, can be useful tools in maintaining a physically balanced perspective. Williams and Sommer (1995) suggest that the therapist find activities that will help her "to find adrenaline highs" (p. 243).

Because vicarious traumatization alters one's sense of hope and optimism, Pearlman and Saakvitne (1995) and Yassen (1995) note the importance of spirituality to counterbalance the potential negativity of a pessimistic worldview. Knowing and practicing one's spiritual beliefs and being able to make meaning of one's work can be powerful antidotes to the horror that undermine the therapist's sense of well-being. Therapists need to feel that the clinical work is useful, meaningful, and contributive to individual growth. A supportive community can assist the therapist to stay grounded in fundamental belief systems that offer a context for healing.

Self-awareness is vital. As noted in the preceding, self-awareness helps the clinician to set limits in the therapy and to understand that reenactments are inevitable and necessary when working with trauma survivors. A self-attuned therapist will recognize the change in her or his moods, attitudes, and feelings in any given clinical situation. Likewise, the ability to stand back and assess the cumulative effects of working with trauma survivors might be assisted by the therapist undergoing his or her own therapy (Pearlman & Saakvitne, 1995; Williams & Sommer, 1995). Yassen (1995) encourages therapists to recognize the complexity of working with trauma survivors. She argues that therapists need to set realistic goals for working with individuals affected by violence. She notes that, unfortunately, no amount of self-sacrifice on the therapist's part will eradicate interpersonal or traumatic violence in the world. However, we can function as activists to promote peace.

Training Programs

We have mentioned the value of supervision, consultation, and supportive teams in addressing vicarious traumatization. Another important site for intervention would be graduate clinical programs. Bennet-Baker (1999) describes the benefits and complexities of teaching about trauma in the classroom. Some students need assistance in finding resources to handle the individual feelings that are stimulated when traumatic narratives are discussed in the classroom. It is our opinion that graduate social work curricula need to integrate regular course content on the issues raised in this chapter.

:: SUMMARY

In summary, we have discussed how the "person" of the clinician influences the therapeutic process. We summarized the personal characteristics of the clinician that promote successful implementation of a multi-theoretical couple therapy model, and examined how institutional factors influence the therapy process. After summarizing countertransference literature and highlighting the intersubjective nature of countertransference, we offered a number of clinical vignettes that demonstrate reenactments of the "victim–victimizer–bystander" scenario (Herman, 1992; Miller, 1994; Staub, 2003). We also discussed vicarious traumatization and, finally, described ways to counterbalance the effects of vicarious traumatization. The next chapter features a detailed case example that illustrates the use of our couple therapy practice model.

Clinical Case Illustration

We have now considered the factors necessary to complete a thorough biopsychosocial assessment and relevant treatment processes embedded in this couple therapy practice model. This chapter offers a clinical case illustration that demonstrates the applicability of the full range of social and psychological theories in the assessment, decision-making, and treatment processes.

The following discussion introduces the reader to the presenting issues facing this couple, a review of their developmental histories in their social context, and the detailed biopsychosocial assessment that follows the assessment guideline (see Table 8.2). Finally, a review of the decision tree processes demonstrates how the ongoing assessment guides the direction of therapy during the initial contact, the assessment phase, and subsequent Phases I, II, and III of treatment with traumatized couples.

Although a range of social and psychological theoretical models are available in the knowledge base of the clinician at any given moment, data forthcoming from the couple's presenting issues determine which set of theoretical lenses advance to the foreground. Certain models are used directly from the onset of treatment. For example, in a relationship-based practice model, it is essential to understand relationship patterns through the lenses of object relations, attachment, and relational theories. In addition, social constructionist, feminist, and racial identity development theoretical models are useful in any given case to explore the couple's social context. As the couple reveals their shared and individual narratives, the presenting issues then signal which theoretical perspective may be especially relevant. For example, symptoms of clinical depression signal the need for trauma, biological, and cognitive–behavioral theoretical lenses to explore possible physical illness, affect regulation, and cognitive distortions. Stated concerns about relationships call forth the use of an historical intergenerational family perspective to explore family patterns that influence the couple. A narrative family theoretical perspective may also illuminate the unique meaning of issues presented.

Although an assessment of each partner's trauma history is necessary in all cases, trauma may not be central to the assessment. However, in situations in which there has been evidence of childhood or adult trauma for one or both partners, trauma theory remains one of the central lenses situated in the foreground throughout the therapy. In the following case, we demonstrate how all of the stated social and psychological theoretical lenses are present from the onset and throughout the therapy. However, one or more theoretical lenses may advance to the foreground at times in the therapy, when that perspective may be relevant to a particular presenting issue.

:: THE COUPLE

The course of couple therapy with Yolanda and Rod Smith spanned a period of seven months. We met a total of twenty times, approximately every ten days, with each session lasting ninety minutes. Rod Smith, a forty-three-year-old African American, and his marital partner of sixteen years, Yolanda Smith, a forty-two-year-old African American, both work full time outside the home. For the past twenty years, Rod has worked as a skilled laborer and manager with the same printing company, where he has earned the respect of his colleagues and supervisors. Yolanda currently works in an administrative job in a health care facility, a responsible position that involves mediation and conflict resolution with staff. The Smiths recently adopted a fifteen-month-old baby girl, Mary, the offspring of an extended family relative. During the past seven years, the couple suffered major disappointment and grief following the painful losses of a stillborn baby girl and two miscarriages. The stillbirth occurred three years prior to the adoption of baby Mary.

Rod was reared as the third of four children in a poor rural Southern community. He struggled to complete his high school degree while also working full time from the age of thirteen. At the urging of many family members, he sought prosperity by venturing north. There he met and married Yolanda.

Reared in a middle-income, urban, African-American community that highly valued education and professional success, Yolanda completed high school and an AA college degree in human resources. Both Rod and Yolanda were reared in Christian faith–based communities, yet neither partner was a practicing member of any formal religious group at the time of intake. In spite of differences in education and socioeconomic status, a shared world-view that valued family and work achievement fortified this couple's marital bond.

Presenting Issues

Based on the recommendation of a friend who, with her husband, had met with me in couple therapy, Yolanda telephoned me requesting help to "successfully tackle tough marital issues." Yolanda complained about Rod's "lack of involvement," "constant mean and vicious fighting," "the threat of divorce," and what she referred to as "her depression." Loss of energy, intermittent tearfulness, insomnia, damaged self-esteem, and di-minished enthusiasm plagued Yolanda daily. She expressed unhappiness about perceived inequities in household and childcare responsibilities, wor-rying that Rod absented himself to "hang with friends." Rod saw Yolanda as "cold," "mean and critical," and "always rejecting me sexually." A sense of helplessness subsumed both partners. Although both partners reported acute distress during the past five months, they also reported increasing estrange-ment from each other during the past two years.

Developmental and Family Histories

Developmental and family histories revealed that Yolanda, as the oldest of six children, had been recruited early on to help care for her five younger siblings. This caretaking role became a source of pride and accom-plishment (see Figure 11.1). When Yolanda was five years old, her father's drinking worsened. He passed out regularly at home. In rageful outbursts, he screamed loudly and regularly beat her and her siblings with hangers or belts. Yolanda remembered trying not to cry, but wincing when she saw her bloody scars afterward. While learning to appease her father by working as hard as she could, she suffered sexual abuse inflicted by a maternal uncle on several occasions, which involved fondling and forced fellatio. In spite of the burdensome effects of this molestation, Yolanda managed to excel in her ac-ademic work. At school, her endearing personality earned accolades from

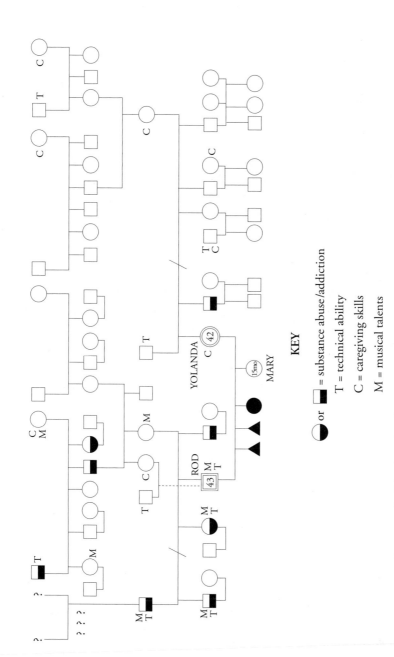

KEY

◐ or ◧ = substance abuse/addiction

T = technical ability

C = caregiving skills

M = musical talents

FIGURE 11.1 :: Genogram for Yolanda and Rod.

teachers as well as the esteem of her peers. Growing up in a middle-income, urban community, where at least 50% of the population report African-American heritage, Yolanda was shielded from continuous, overt racist insults. However, she experienced more indirect, covert expressions of racism from schoolmates.

Rod, as the third of four children reared by his parents in the rural South, struggled with poverty and violence inflicted by an alcoholic father. Rod described his father as embittered and destructive, often greeting his children with yelling and cursing as they arrived home from school. He often erupted with violent outbursts, beating Rod and his brothers with his hands or a large stick. On many an occasion, he literally threw Rod outside into the backyard and forbade him to return until he apologized. None of Rod's family members tried to intervene, with the exception of his mother, who unsuccessfully tried to mediate the conflicts. Typically, her efforts placed her in the direct line of violent assaults herself.

From age twelve to fourteen, Rod was invited to live with a paternal aunt and uncle. This respite provided Rod with safety from harm, allowing him to earn passing grades at school and to immerse himself in a part-time laborer job. With great regret, Rod was sent home again at the age of fourteen to resume high school in his childhood community. Physical beatings continued until, one day, Rod struck back, knocking his father to the ground. At the young age of seventeen, Rod was banished from his home by his enraged father. Hoping to leave his family far behind, both geographically and psychologically, Rod ventured north. He was full of enthusiasm for starting his new life, but stunned that harsh racial insults, similar to those hurled at him in the South, were inflicted in the North as well. Nevertheless, within two years he completed his high school equivalency exam while also working full time. At the age of nineteen, Rod met Yolanda at a party given by a mutual friend. At the onset of couple therapy, Rod remained estranged from his family of origin.

Although both partners were reared in complicated family homes, undermined by the corrosive effects of physical, sexual, and racialized abuses, their marriage was a blessing and a relief for both of them. Their sixteen-year bond was far from perfect, but Rod and Yolanda shared mutual respect and commonality in values related to steady work, religious convictions, and the priority of family. Thus, these various strengths helped to fortify the strong foundation underlying their marriage throughout the years.

:: BIOPSYCHOSOCIAL ASSESSMENT

What follows are some of the institutional, interactional, and intrapersonal factors that contributed to both the vulnerabilities and strengths of this couple. The biopsychosocial assessment guideline introduced in Chapter 8 on assessment (see Table 8.2) is used to complete the biopsychosocial assessment of Rod and Yolanda (see Table 11.1).

Institutional Factors

The assessment of institutional factors focuses on the surrounding social context that influenced this couple. First, it is important to query how the current political environment, previous mental health service experiences, social policies, and service delivery affect the couple. Second, the role of each partner's extended family and community needs to be explored as well. Third, it is important to assess how diversity themes shape the structure and essence of this couple's relationship. Such themes include race, ethnicity, gender, sexual orientation, disability, age, and religion. Finally, we wonder how the clinician's attitudes and responses affect the work. For example, what countertransference traps are apparent? What assumptions and cultural biases does each individual bring to the work? How does the clinician's racial-identity development form and influence attitudes and clinical interventions? What are the working definitions of trauma? How does vicarious traumatization influence the work? In considering these questions, our understanding of the social context is informed by social constructionist, feminist, and racial-identity developmental theories, while our understanding of the clinician's responses and the clinical work in general is informed primarily by psychodynamic and trauma theories.

Social Context

Sociocultural factors influence any therapy endeavor; however, this cross-cultural therapy involving a middle-income African-American couple and a white, middle-income female clinical social worker at an urban community mental health center deserves special attention. Yolanda approached this couple therapy with hope, as three years earlier, after the stillbirth of her daughter, she had completed an effective period of brief (four-month) therapy with a clinical social worker. In that therapy, she had been

TABLE 11.1 :: Phase-Oriented Couple Therapy:
Biopsychosocial Assessment of Yolanda and Rod

I. INSTITUTIONAL (grounded in social constructionist, feminist, and racial identity development theories)

Strengths	Stressors
• Shared worldview related to family, religious convictions, education, and children • Responsible wage-earners • Financial stability • Strong family support from maternal family of origin • Culturally responsive accessible mental health services • Openness to racial and cultural diversity	• Estrangement from faith-based community • Aversion to counseling • Cross-cultural therapy • Threat of separation/divorce • Rigid gender roles • Conflicts about co-parenting • "Overly zealous" caregiving to disabled mother • Clinician's response including vicarious traumatization, racial-identity development, and countertransference

---

II. INTERACTIONAL (grounded in intergenerational and narrative family theories)

Strengths	Stressors
• Capacity to trust • Work through conflict without physical violence • Generally effective problem-solving capacities around division of labor • Support from Yolanda's family of origin • Previously satisfying sexual relationship	• Intergenerational pattern of victim–victimizer–bystander • Destructive arguments • Thwarted problem-solving • Different constructions of intimacy • Strained sexual relationship • Unresolved grieving of deceased children • Absence of healing ritual to memorialize the deceased children • Absence of a transition ritual to welcome adopted daughter

---

III. INTRAPERSONAL

A. Individual, cognitive, affective, and behavioral functioning (grounded in trauma theories)

Strengths	Stressors
• Rod: Exercises reasonable self-care, including monitoring of alcohol use and sound physical health; resilience • Yolanda: Exercises sound self-care related to healthcare; good work and family relationships; resilience	• Rod: Affect dysregulation; startle response; low self-esteem; lowered stimulus barrier; poor nutrition; and lack of exercise • Yolanda: Affect dysregulation; startle response; clinical depression; low self-esteem; somatization; lowered stimulus barrier; inhibited sexual desire; weight gain; hypertension

---

B. Intrapsychic (grounded in object relations and attachment theories)

Strengths	Stressors
• Rod: Capacity for trust; beginning capacity for ambivalence • Yolanda: Capacity for trust; beginning capacity for ambivalence	• Rod: Insecure, ambivalent attachment; internal victim–victimizer–bystander dynamic; internal saboteur; extensive projective identification processes • Yolanda: Insecure, ambivalent attachment; internal victim-victimizer-bystander dynamic; internal saboteur; extensive projective identification processes

able to address some of the legacies of her childhood trauma of physical and sexual abuse and to recognize her predisposition to depression. Rod, on the other hand, had no interest in therapy because "it is for crazy people." He also asserted that he "didn't like white people a whole lot." Although the couple was estranged from Rod's family of origin, they were provided with strong validating support from Yolanda's family, their respective work communities, and their friends.

With all clinical cases, it is important to ascertain any barriers to availability of services. The community mental health center received reasonable funding and offered distinct cultural diversity among staff as well as clients. A small waiting list allowed for rapid access to treatment. As a result, some potential initial barriers around financial support, availability of services, and cultural sensitivity were minimized. However, although this agency authorized the engagement of some long-term therapy contracts, it strongly urged all clinicians to start with a brief time frame (i.e., six to twenty-four sessions). Hence, the agency policy influenced the time frame for the work from the first contact onward.

Diversity Themes

In terms of social variables (e.g., race, ethnicity, gender, sexual orientation, age, religion, and disability), certain factors advanced more distinctly to the foreground as this couple discussed their presenting concerns. Although all diversity themes are relevant for all clients, it is important to assess each dimension and then recognize which themes assume greatest centrality. The diversity themes that regularly assumed central positions for Rod and Yolanda, both alternately and concurrently, were race, gender, religion, and disability.

Race   As noted earlier, previous experiences involving racialized incidents, the complexities of cross-racial therapy, and internalized racism all played significant roles through this course of therapy. Both partners expressed a racial-identity status reflective of Emersion (i.e., recognizing achievements and solidarity within one's own racial group) (Helms & Cook, 1999), as well as some evidence of Internalization, in which people of color integrate complex information and analyses of race. Rod and Yolanda expressed deep feelings of pride related to the struggles and successes experienced by their respective families and communities. During the early years of their marriage, both Rod and Yolanda enjoyed a more extensive friendship and community base, within a primarily African-American community. This enriching network was absent as they embarked on couple therapy.

In this couple therapy, the issue of race arose with Rod's initial expression of distrust of white people. Could Rod's concern be a sign of reluctance shared by Yolanda as well? Was this an expression of "culturally congruent paranoia" that emerges as understandable distrust and wariness from a client who has suffered marginalization (Grier & Cobbs, 1968)? Or was the couple choosing a white clinician based on positive transference? Were they choosing this white clinician based on her clinical expertise? As a manifestation of internalized racism, could one or both partners be repudiating their own cultural backgrounds? All of these questions held some validity for Rod and Yolanda as they approached couple therapy with both anticipation and trepidation. Finally, how did the clinician's racial-identity development influence and inform her understanding of the couple, her own countertransference responses and enactments, and her treatment recommendations?

To sift through the complexity of these possibilities, in our first telephone conversation, I decided to engage Yolanda in a discussion about the meaning of cross-racial therapy after she mentioned that Rod "disliked white people." Below are segments of this exchange.

> Y: I really want to be in some type of therapy because I think that our marriage might be ready to explode and I am crying all of the time. But I can't imagine Rod coming in to see anyone in therapy. He thinks of therapy as something for crazy people. When I met with Ms. Jones, a social worker, several years ago, she kept saying, "I know you have gotten help from her, but why should you need something like this, when we can talk about this stuff at home?"
>
> KB: So, you are expressing some strong feelings about the need to address the threats to your marriage and your frequent crying, but I hear a lot of concern that Rod might not be interested in starting any therapy.
>
> Y: Oh, absolutely, he's opposed.
>
> KB: What conversations have you had so far about addressing your unhappiness and worries about your marriage?
>
> Y: Oh, we talk a little, and then it turns into a nasty argument.

KB: Are you willing to describe what those arguments look like?

Y: Well, I get frustrated and start yelling, then Rod yells back calling me a cold b—h! Before we know it we are screaming nasty things at each other back and forth. Then Rod goes off to the garage, and I don't see him for hours.

KB: Do these arguments ever involve throwing things or physically touching each other?

Y: No. We don't do that. Both of us were brought up with being beat on when tempers got out of control. But I guess we do get out of control with our yelling.

KB: And so, is that an issue that you want to deal with?

R: Yes, especially since Mary (baby) hears this. I hate to look at her face when she looks so frightened.

KB: And, what is Rod's response to Mary at those times?

Y: I don't know. I never bothered to look.

KB: I gather that you do not know Rod's feelings about these arguments around Mary. Do you think he would be interested in talking with you and me here about what it is like to be parenting Mary with these pressures?

Y: He says that he wants to fight less and wants to stay together. I'm the one who threatens to leave the marriage. But he will never come in.

KB: Would you like him to come in with you?

Y: Oh, yes, but it sounds so impossible.

KB: What might be helpful in inviting Rod in?

Y: Well, I told him I was calling, and he said, well do whatever you want, but I don't want to call that woman, so why don't you go ahead.

KB: Very often in setting an initial consultation meeting, I have found it helpful to talk briefly with both partners on the phone, so that I can explain the purpose of such a meeting and to get some sense of where each of your are with your issues. It also gives each partner a chance to talk directly with me before my meeting.

Y: Well, since Rod said that he would not call anyway, I don't care if you call him, even though it will probably be a waste of time.

KB: I hear from you that both of you are concerned about wanting to parent Mary as well as possible. I hear your strong love and commitment to her. And so, are you OK with my calling Rod?

Y: Well, we both do care a lot about her. She is really a blessing.

Before calling Rod, I was aware that Yolanda was experiencing positive transferential feelings toward me, as I had treated her close friend and husband in couple therapy some months before. So, on the surface, the cross-racial work did not represent a barrier. Yet I wondered if her depiction of her husband's wariness also reflected her own ambivalence. Was a process of projective identification occurring where Rod became the primary repository for expressed wariness? Yolanda's concern for her marriage, her mental health, and her new baby came through loudly, as did Rod's concern for his child. As this was an obvious strength, I was mindful of focusing on this theme in my ensuing phone conversation.

Following my telephone conversation with Yolanda, I called Rod to explain that I was particularly interested in understanding his perspective on their family situation, rather than trying to understand his point of view through Yolanda's comments. I stressed my awareness that he and Yolanda hoped to act in Mary's best interest. Rod proceeded to tell me about his family's rule never to talk about family business outside the home, and about his belief, based on many real disappointments, that white people should not be trusted. I asked if he would be more comfortable meeting with an African-American clinician. After several minutes of hesitation, he said, "No, not really. I would feel really embarrassed to admit these problems with my people. I think it would be bad either way."

Since empowerment and cultural responsiveness are basic values embedded in this practice model, I made it clear to Rod that I would facilitate a referral to an African-American clinician if he and Yolanda chose that path. Or, they could meet with me for one consultation session. This would give them an opportunity to discuss their issues to the extent that they chose, and I would be in a better position to share with them my reflections and recommendations. They would then have an opportunity to make their decision about the next steps. At this point, Rod said, "Well, since Mary seems to be caught in the middle of this, maybe we could have one meeting and talk about it." With Yolanda on the other telephone extension, we set up a scheduled consultation meeting. I also assured both partners that, if they had particular questions about my professional qualifications and experience, or if they experienced any hesitations, they were welcome to discuss them, if they chose to do so. Language that attempted to preserve the locus of control with the client, in this case the couple, framed the initial conversations.

In summary, therapy starts with the initial encounter. It was clear that my first phone conversation with Yolanda, and then Rod, represented an exploration of presenting issues along with multiple resistances. Preserving the locus of control with both partners was essential. From the onset, open disclosure between partners was encouraged, as has been an exploration of their concerns about race and cross-cultural practice. While mindful of Yolanda's and Rod's relational capacities, I drew on object relations and attachment theories to ascertain each partner's capacity for trust (albeit tentative), as well as each of their beginning capacities for ambivalence. In addition, racial-identity theory helped me with exploring not only the client's attitudes toward race, but also my own. Further discussion of this process may be found later in the section that reviews clinicians' responses. Here, we will continue reviewing diversity themes in the biopsychosocial assessment, moving now to issues of gender, religion, and disability.

Gender   Since Yolanda and Rod learned about gender roles from their families of origin, both intergenerational and narrative family theories help to provide direction to clarify meaning in this arena. Rather than challenging their family-of-origin paradigms, Yolanda and Rod maintained many stereotypically gendered patterns. For example, they had divided chores along traditional gender lines. Yolanda cooked, shopped, and completed most housekeeping chores. Rod cared for the cars, emptied the garbage, and repaired technical problems. Generally, this division of labor worked well until the adoption of baby Mary. When the additional childcare responsibilities fell to, and were ultimately assumed by Yolanda, the balance of distribution of work responsibilities tipped and conflicts erupted.

As both partners worked full time outside the home (a work pattern that differed from their respective families of origin), they had created new roles for sharing their financial management. However, in other respects, both partners reflected societally imposed stereotypic roles around race and gender. Yolanda described Rod as "lazy, carefree, and irresponsible," matching an all too frequently held negative stereotype of African-American men. Rod believed that Yolanda was "so strong as a caretaker" that she should "tough it out" and "endure her pressures." Such an archetypal, matriarchal stereotype of a caretaker is often unfairly ascribed to many African-American women. Rod and Yolanda had negotiated the societal imposition of these stereotypes, but unfortunately, each had internalized some of the negative stereotypes as well. A question that resounded throughout the couple therapy was: In what ways are Rod and Yolanda content with their identifications and commonalities with their respective families of origin, and in what ways have they moved toward enhanced self-differentiation vis-à-vis ascribed gender roles, family patterns, and community expectations?

Religion   Religion had been vitally important to both partners in imbuing a basic sense of values relating to family, marital responsibility, and the primacy of childrearing. However, their estrangement from their faith-based communities was problematic, fueling a state of alienation and hopelessness.

Disability   The theme of disability loomed large for this couple, especially in recent years. Although skillful as a caregiver, both professionally and within her family, Yolanda was often pulled into an "overly zealous caregiver" role, leaving little time for herself. After eight years of frustrating and disappointing infertility treatments, Yolanda turned her attentions to caring for her mother, whose diabetes had worsened, requiring her to use a wheelchair. Rod bitterly resented the attention that Yolanda paid to her mother, which he hoped would be saved for him.

In summary, the biopsychosocial assessment revealed that the Smiths expressed relative satisfaction with their work lives and their current financial stability. Except for the past two years, they had experienced their heterosexual marriage as essentially positive, especially in the first seven years of their relationship, when shared enjoyment and sexuality were rewarding. Overall, the diversity themes that assume prominence are race, gender, religion, and disability, representing areas of strength as well as sources of stress and vulnerability.

Clinician Responses

Now that an assessment of the influence of diversity themes has been outlined, it is important to return to the effects of the clinician's responses. These include the therapist's level of racial-identity development, vicarious traumatization, and countertransference responses.

Racial-Identity Development   As evidenced in the previous discussion, race was a powerful influence in Rod and Yolanda's lives. The reality of cross-cultural practice necessitated further exploration of the clinician's as well as the client's racial-identity development. Only then could the complexity of the intersubjective field be understood more clearly.

I met Rod and Yolanda after eighteen years of working as a clinical social worker in multicultural environments where I had been challenged to explore my own sense of racial/cultural identity and the influence that had on my clinical work with clients. My cultural responsiveness had slowly developed over the years while my humility deepened as I met face to face the profound pain suffered by clients in response to racist behavior imposed by others. Throughout these years, I shifted back and forth from the more familiar statuses of Immersion (recognizing and altering previous distortions about race) and Emersion (involving identification with other white individuals who are actively working on their racial-identity status). I was continually aiming toward the status of Autonomy, in which Helms and Cook (1999) suggest that white individuals flexibly analyze responses to racial situations. Similar to other stage models, evidence of fluctuation and circular movements between different statuses typically characterized movement and progress. Although I have frequently encountered wariness or distrust from clients who identify with racial backgrounds that are different from mine, I have come to recognize this stance as adaptive. Even with this awareness, it is still difficult at times to function as the container for intense negative feelings. As I entered the couple therapy with Rod and Yolanda, I hoped to remain cognizant of my reactions and biases.

Vicarious Traumatization   Because many of my clients wrestle with the legacies of childhood trauma, I entered this case prepared to monitor my own potential vicarious traumatization. Keenly evident was the pain of hearing about physical, sexual, and racialized abuses, as well as profoundly sad traumatic losses of the three "lost babies." The tragedies followed me home. Mindful of the potential strain of vicarious traumatization, I steadfastly met each week with an esteemed colleague who provided invaluable collegial support.

Countertransference Traps   Many potential countertransference traps are possible in couple therapy with trauma survivors. Countertransference is understood in a broad sense to include those thoughts, feelings, and enactments experienced by the clinician in response to intrapsychic conflicts, value stances, cultural beliefs, and engagement in projective identification exchanges. We assume that enactments on the part of the clinician are inevitable. However, it is essential for the clinician to understand these enactments and to be able to interpret their meaning. Enactments may be understood as a part of the assessment as well as events that may strengthen an empathic connection with the couple. Efforts are also made to minimize the occurrence of these unconscious enactments; but when they occur, self-scrutiny is essential.

In this particular case, the "victim–victimizer–bystander" template was evident. Projective identification processes help to explain the various countertransference enactments. One countertransference trap involved my assuming a rescuer role, an expression of the helpful bystander. Given the perceived successes of my previous couple therapy with Rod and Yolanda's friends, I was predisposed to assume a position of comfortable confidence. However, to keep my own potential grandiosity (as the rescuer) in check, I explored not only their positive transference, but also the complexity of other multiple transferences. From my position as a member of the dominant culture, I also needed to be mindful of the limits of my full understanding of each partner's experience. Certainly any criticism or dismissal of either partner could be understood as a countertransference enactment of the victimizer role. Although it is impossible to ensure the absence of all cultural bias, efforts were made to minimize my personal cultural and racial biases as best as possible. Certainly any criticism or lack of attunement on my part toward this couple could be understood as a countertransference enactment in the victimizer role.

Throughout the course of my work with Rod and Yolanda, I found myself alternating between enactments and potential enactments of the "victim–victimizer–bystander" roles. This beginning journey into the realm of intersubjectivity revealed the interface of Rod and Yolanda's personal, family, and racial-identity development with my own personal, racial identity, and professional development. I regularly found myself restraining myself or enacting the passive bystander; the overly zealous rescuer; the aggressive, harsh victimizer; or the helpless victim, wondering at times why I took on such a complicated case. The continuing pull that I experienced to enact a victimizer, victim, or bystander role may be understood as a part of the projective identification process associated with the couple's internal struggles with this same "victim–victimizer–bystander" dynamic. Within this intersubjective context, my self-doubting stance was regularly counterbalanced by curiosity, heartened respect for this couple's resilience, and a commitment to provide optimally useful clinical services.

In summary, the assessment of institutional factors revealed a number of strengths and stressors. The areas of strength expressed by Rod and Yolanda included their shared worldviews related to valuing family, religious convictions, and educational successes. Both partners had sustained responsible jobs throughout the years, while earning substantial income to provide basic support as well as recreational comforts. Although Rod expressed some tentativeness about therapy, both he and Yolanda revealed motivation and openness to improve their co-parenting. Each partner was also well liked and respected among colleagues and friends and strong family support was regularly extended by Yolanda's family of origin. Instrumental barriers to service delivery were minimal as the Smiths had adequate financial resources and insurance reimbursement, and their local community mental health agency provided culturally responsive services. Stressors related to Rod's aversion to therapy and the tensions regarding cross-racial therapy. Estrangement from their faith-based community and conflicts with respective families of origin contributed to a paucity of emotional support for this couple. Since the arrival of their baby daughter, their gender roles had rigidified, contributing to major conflicts around co-parenting. The "victim–victimizer–bystander" dynamic was apparent with Yolanda's overly zealous caretaking of her disabled mother and the vicious combative arguments between Yolanda and Rod. Finally, a remaining institutional factor that strongly influenced the course of therapy relates to the clinician's response including vicarious traumatization, racial-identity development, and the complexity of countertransference phenomena.

Interactional Factors

The interactional factors, often salient for trauma survivors, are related to the interplay of the "victim–victimizer–bystander" dynamic, intimacy, trust, power and control, boundaries, communication, and sexuality. Each partner attaches unique meaning to the recollections and reflections of his or her childhood traumatic experiences, which often remain obscure or misunderstood between partners. All of these themes may surface in intergenerational patterns that perpetuate the existence of both constructive and troublesome ways of relating. When parents who have abused their children violate the basic integrity of ethical parenting, they typically fail to honor family life cycle events through appropriate transition rituals. Both inter-generational and narrative family theoretical lenses provided direction and guidance in choosing questions for this couple for exploring these various interactional patterns. The following discussion addresses how Rod and Yolanda negotiated these various interactional themes.

"Victim–Victimizer–Bystander" Pattern

Between Yolanda and Rod there was a fragile level of trust, allow-ing them to sustain some fledgling hope. Even so, the "victim–victimizer–bystander" scenario was pronounced in their ways of relating. Polarizations in thought, affect, and behavior surfaced regularly. For example, Rod and Yolanda continually battled about who was in control. Yolanda presented herself as emotionally responsive, while Rod prided himself on containing his emotions. Yolanda viewed herself as overly responsible and her husband as not responsible enough. Rod, on the other hand, perceived himself as relaxed, rather than irresponsible, yet burdened by his wife's railings. Rod often felt persecuted and victimized by Yolanda, complaining that she failed to understand him or express affection. Instead, she criticized. Yolanda re-jected the notion that she was verbally abusive, even though this was con-firmed by many friends and relatives. Yolanda felt victimized by what she viewed as Rod's cavalier attitude, abandoning her to all childcare and house-hold responsibilities.

A rhythmic "victim–victimizer–bystander" dynamic thereby unfolded, with Rod and Yolanda taking alternating roles. Each partner had the capac-ity to hold on to some ambivalence in discussing the other partner, although they easily shifted into polarized harangues toward the other. This alternat-ing yearning for connection, mixed with a fear of loss of affection, fueled a destructive pattern that set the stage for abusive communication. Typically, each partner leaped forward with an aggressive or defensive response, while neither offered empathic understanding toward the other. Although verbal exchanges were often brutally nasty, they never escalated to a physical level. In fact, neither partner reported experiences of physical eruptions or physi-cal abuse throughout the years. This strength is noteworthy, given the repet-itive patterns of physical abuse suffered by both Rod and Yolanda in their families of origin. Here, Yolanda and Rod interrupted the intergenerational pattern of physical abuse toward children and adults.

Boundaries

Boundaries between this couple were usually too rigid and distant, or, at the other extreme, were experienced as intrusive. Rod's expectation of intimacy involved "puttering in the garage" while Yolanda worked somewhere else in the home, to be followed by physical affection and sexual intimacy. However, Yolanda experienced Rod's physical overtures as "overly dominating and intrusive," especially when there had been limited communication preceding his affectionate overture.

Meaning of the Trauma Narrative

As Rod and Yolanda talked about their early family years, each characterized a history of abuse in a unique manner. Yolanda recognized her strength in outwitting her aggressors through various ways of coping. Intermittently, she resorted to overwork, solicitous caregiving, and subjugation of her wishes. Even so, Yolanda often felt victimized and rendered helpless to assert her needs. Rod claimed that his childhood history of physical and emotional abuse had no effect on him since he left home. As a firm believer in a cure made possible by geographic distance, he initially minimized the existence and impact of his brutal beatings during childhood. However, in couple therapy, Rod started to recognize some of the pernicious legacies of his childhood physical abuse.

The Role of Ritual

Since healing and transition rituals usually ease the pain of change and loss for families, questions were raised with Rod and Yolanda as to how the losses of the stillborn baby girl and the two miscarried infants were dealt with. There had been no funerals or memorial services. In fact, neither parent was even allowed to see the deceased infant after the birth. As a result, Rod and Yolanda were left bereft without any opportunity to memorialize their "lost babies." In summary, the interactional strengths for this couple include their capacities to (1) trust, (2) deal with conflict without resorting to physical violence, (3) problem solve around the division of labor, (4) engage support from Yolanda's family of origin, and (5) work toward the recovery of their earlier sexual intimacy. Areas of stress included (1) the intergenerational legacy of the "victim–victimizer–bystander" pattern, (2) destructive abusive arguments, (3) thwarted problem-solving related to parenting, (4) different constructions of intimacy and meaning of childhood trauma, (5) strained sexual relationship, (6) unresolved grieving of children lost through miscarriages and stillbirth, (7) absence of a healing ritual to memorialize the deceased children, and (8) absence of a transition ritual to welcome their adopted daughter.

Intrapersonal Factors

Intrapersonal factors that affected this couple include the cognitive, affective, and behavioral functioning and intrapsychic worlds of each partner. Certain neurophysiological effects of childhood trauma often lead to aftereffects in the individual in adulthood, while intrapsychic factors shape each partner's inner world. Each partner's capacity for relationship included attachment patterns and object relations, especially with regard to the role of projective identification. Trauma, object relations, and attachment theories approached the foreground as useful tools for understanding these two individuals.

Individual Cognitive, Affective, Biological, and Behavioral Functioning

First, the neurophysiological symptomatology of complex post-traumatic stress disorder (PTSD) influenced this couple. Although Rod reported neither somatic complaints nor physical illnesses, he had not met with a physician during the past ten years. He was physically fit in terms of weight, but ate "junk food." Physical exertion at his job allowed him the benefit of serendipitous exercise. Yolanda reported that Rod liked to hang out with his friends several nights per week, during which he reported drinking two to three beers. He did not drink at home, in part because Yolanda regularly complained about his drinking. Rod's periodic moderate drinking of alcohol reflected some efforts to modulate his affect by numbing the hyperarousal pendulum. He also responded abruptly to touch, demonstrating a lowered stimulus barrier that affected intimacy. For example, when Yolanda approached him affectionately by touching his neck and shoulders, he often bristled and yelled. Rod described himself as often feeling "low," "tired," and "numb." In addition to Rod's neurophysiological symptoms, the primary legacy of his childhood emotional and physical trauma, compounded by harsh racial assaults, revealed itself in serious damage to his self-esteem. His self-soothing strategies consisted of woodworking, puttering in his garage to maintain his car, and "hanging out" with his friends. Similar to Yolanda, Rod had renounced his religious connections when he stopped attending church.

Yolanda described symptoms of clinical depression (i.e., emotional lability, tearfulness, lethargy, irritability, and a fifty-pound weight gain in the past two years). These symptoms started several months after the stillbirth of their baby daughter. Yolanda was perimenopausal, with uncomfortable symptoms of hot flashes, emotional instability, and insomnia. She reported headaches several times weekly and battles with borderline hypertension. Yolanda did not drink alcohol or use any other drugs, except for drinking caffeinated soda continually. Her sexual desire had been inhibited for the past three years. Although Yolanda made some effort to eat nutritious foods, she did not exercise. She also suffered a startle response, disliked surprises, and experienced touch as physically painful at times. Persistent undermining assaults to self-esteem were also apparent. Because Yolanda had abandoned all spiritual supports, she was functioning without a spiritual or community connection, proper nutrition, adequate exercise, or self-soothing exercises. In fact, she reported no methods of soothing herself except for compulsive eating.

Intrapsychic Factors

In exploring the inner worlds of Yolanda and Rod, it must be noted that, in spite of persistent and intrusive physical abuse during childhood years, each partner had been able to benefit from some "good-enough" nurturing relationships as children. They had established a sixteen-year partnership characterized by mutual love, respect, and loyalty; shared work responsibility; and a dream to rear children together. Each partner had the capacity for ambivalence in talking with and referring to the other partner, although they easily shifted into polarized descriptions of the other. Neither partner experienced annihilation anxiety in the face of disappointment. While relying on projective identification regularly, there was some evidence of splitting.

In exploring their inner worlds, the processes of projective identification unfolded vividly. When this occurred, each partner repressed, split off, and projected onto the other partner his or her disavowed feelings, conflicts, and internal states. What surfaced were the conflicts that neither partner had been able to address internally. Thus, core issues emerged as polarizations of attributes, as examples of overresponsible versus underresponsible, expressive versus restrained, and emotional versus logical. By maintaining rigid views of each other, each partner began to recognize the disavowed parts of her- and himself that had been projected onto the other. In fact, Rod and Yolanda experienced only minimal awareness of their projective identification processes. For example, Yolanda projected her conflict around spontaneity and a balance of emotion/logic onto Rod; Rod projected his conflicts around responsibility and expressiveness onto Yolanda. The result was that Yolanda alternated between admiring Rod and bitterly resenting and envying him for these qualities. Yolanda regularly picked fights with Rod about this. Rod also projected his conflicts surrounding a wish for affirmation, countered by experiences of punishing abuse, leading to Yolanda's enactment of a victimizer role. Yolanda disowned her own internal conflicts surrounding her dependency needs. For example, she yearned for a loving connection, yet anticipated abandonment. Ultimately, she criticized and condemned Rod's behavior precipitating his enactment of a passive bystander role through withdrawal.

Each partner's efforts to dominate or alienate the other could be understood then as the interplay of Fairbairn's (1952a, 1952b) "internal saboteurs." For example, Rod initially disowned any distress related to his childhood physical abuse. Instead, he had internalized the "saboteur" that operated to sustain his view of Yolanda as the "critical, rejecting, yet omnipotent" victimizer; while he held on to a self-view based on self-doubt, tentativeness, and suppressed initiative. For Yolanda and Rod, this forceful influence of the "internal saboteur" undermined efforts toward resolving the "good–bad" splits in the relationship. However, Rod, in particular, held on to an idealized notion of his oppressive father.

According to American object relations theorists, Rod and Yolanda revealed rapprochement themes in their continuous dance of pursuit and distancing. In other words, each partner sought self-differentiation. However, when anxiety related to the distancing or separation took hold, each partner then sought solace in the relationship, only to be followed by another push toward distanced autonomy (Bader & Pearson, 1988; Horner, 1984; Mahler, 1968; Sharpe, 2000). Rod and Yolanda struggle with sustaining object constancy in that most of the time they are able to hold on to the capacity for ambivalence in the relationship, even when disappointed. However, they often slipped into polarized, dichotomized positions in which each partner experienced an insecure and ambivalent attachment.

In summary, the intrapersonal assessment factors include both individual neurophysiological responses as well as intrapsychic phenomena, that is, object relations and attachment styles. Both strengths and stressors exist within these intrapersonal and individual realms. For example, in the individual arena, the neurophysiological legacies of childhood trauma surfaced in Rod's startle response, inadequate nutrition, porous stimulus barrier, unbalanced affect regulation, and diminished self-esteem. Yolanda experienced somatization, fear of touch, inhibited sexual desire, affect dysregulation, weight gain, startle response, clinical depression, and diminished self-esteem. Strengths included partial maintenance by both partners of their physical and psychological health. Neither partner abused substances. Yolanda never drank, and Rod drank one to three beers on a twice-weekly basis with his buddies. In the intrapersonal realm, relational abilities included each partner's capacity for trust, love, respect, and intermittent capacity for ambivalence. However, their insecure–ambivalent attachment patterns and regular engagement in preconscious projective identification processes remained areas of vulnerability.

In conclusion, a full biopsychosocial assessment revealed a resilient couple who had overcome considerable adversity during their respective childhoods, yet who faced major stressors in the institutional, interactional, and intrapersonal realms. To design an effective treatment plan, it was important to document a comprehensive biopsychosocial assessment, including the legacies of childhood trauma, that establishes a focus for treatment and a useful phase-oriented treatment plan.

:: PHASE-ORIENTED COUPLE THERAPY

This section reviews the various phases of couple therapy with Yolanda and Rod including the following areas: (1) how the decision-making process, grounded in the biopsychosocial assessment, informs and guides the development of a couple therapy treatment plan; (2) the establishment of therapy goals; and (3) the tasks, challenges, and interventions of different therapy phases (see Table 11.2). The realm of intersubjectivity (including transference–countertransference phenomena) is considered throughout this case summary.

Decision-Making: Biopsychosocial Assessment as Compass and Anchor

After completing a thorough biopsychosocial assessment, the following question inevitably arises: How does an assessment inform and direct the development of a couple therapy treatment plan? Clearly, a review of the strengths and stressors expressed by the couple is essential. As mentioned previously, all social and psychological theoretical lenses are available to the clinician at the onset of therapy. How then does a clinician decide which theoretical lenses are most useful in crafting a treatment plan? The theoretical models that are immediately useful at the onset of couple treatment are object relations and attachment theories, as they inform an understanding of the couple's capacities to engage with the clinician, as well as the capacity for attachment in their relationship. Because any couple therapy must be contextualized within a sociopolitical frame, social constructivist, feminist, and racial-identity development theory models are especially useful from the start. At the point of the initial encounter, on the telephone or in person, these theoretical models then proceed to the foreground. As the clinician engages the couple in describing their presenting issues, strengths, and wishes for a future outcome, a focus for the initial phase of couple therapy emerges. In keeping with the metaphor of couple therapy as a journey, this biopsychosocial assessment serves as a compass, by guiding the choice of questions. Furthermore, it functions as an anchor, providing coherence and balance to the treatment plan.

Balance of Strengths and Presenting Issues

Yolanda and Rod Smith presented with uncertainty about the direction of their marriage, concerns about persistent "mean" fighting, Yolanda's "depression," and Rod's "lack of involvement with parenting." These issues became the immediate focus of attention. All strengths that each partner brought to the marital relationship needed to be acknowledged, as they fortified the couple's capacities to confront difficult issues. The Smiths clearly demonstrated the following considerable strengths: (1) a shared worldview related to the centrality of family, strong religious convictions, and education; (2) financial security; (3) responsible wage-earning; (4) conflict resolution without physical violence; (5) generally effective problem-solving around division of labor; and (6) support from the maternal family

PHASE I (six weeks)	PHASES II and III (fourteen weeks)	
Institutional Factors	Interactional Factors	Intrapersonal Factors
• Aversion to counseling • Sociocultural influences • Fear of change • Cross-cultural therapy • Threat of separation/divorce • Estrangement from family and religion	• Misunderstandings and harsh communication • Daily "mean" arguments • Unresolved grieving of lost children through stillbirth and miscarriages • Absence of healing rituals • Intergenerational legacy of victim–victimizer–bystander pattern	• Preponderance of projective identification patterns (e.g., Rod projects his conflict surrounding a wish for affirmation countered by experiences of punishment, leading to Yolanda's persecution of Rod. Yolanda disowns her internal conflict surrounding her dependency needs. She yearns for a loving connection yet anticipates abandonment, and ultimately, behaves in ways that precipitate Rod's withdrawal.) • Polarizations of attributes assumed by each partner (e.g., emotional vs. logical, responsible vs. carefree, expressive vs. contained)
Goals	Goals	Goals
• Explore sociocultural attitudes and biases • Reduce depression for symptomatic partner • Clarify decision re: directions for the family (i.e., stasis, active working, or separation) • Reduce arguments • Enhance self-care • Strengthen co-parenting	• Develop more effective ways to express thoughts and feelings • Explore meaning of intimacy for each partner • Facilitate grieving and creation of healing rituals • Minimize victim–victimizer–bystander dynamic • Strengthen co-parenting	• Enhance self-differentiation • Promote self-care • Develop sexual intimacy • Expand family and community connections
Interventions	Interventions	Interventions
• Establish alliance through respectful listening and exploration • Affirm sound coping skills and resilience • Clarify presenting issues • Discuss attitudes regarding cross-racial therapy • Assess strengths and vulnerabilities within the couple relationship throughout the history of the relationship • Discuss the role of power, religion, class, race, disability, and gender roles within the family • Provide referrals and psycho-educational resources re: depression and complex PTSD	• Build communication skills • Explore different meanings and constructions of intimacy • Explore affect related to the multiple losses • Question modes of healing within their spiritual context • Plan a healing ritual to commemorate the lost children and celebrate the arrival of their adopted toddler	• Explore, question, and clarity victim–victimizer–bystander family of origin pattern • Question polarizations of roles • Clarify projective identification patterns • Share survivorship tales with shifts in roles from victim to survivor to pioneer

of origin. Individual strengths include both Yolanda's and Rod's capacities for some rudimentary self-care skills in terms of health care and avoidance of substance abuse; a strong work ethic; generosity; and the capacity for a trusting, albeit ambivalent, attachment.

Therapy Goals

The immediacy of the relationship crisis and Yolanda's symptoms of depression advanced to the foreground as pressing concerns. Crisis intervention and trauma theory informed a treatment plan that involved the resolution of the immediate crisis, stabilization and the establishment of safety, and the context for change. As a result, the initial therapy goals included the following: (1) reduce symptoms of depression for Yolanda; (2) explore sociocultural attitudes and biases; (3) reduce arguments; (4) clarify a decision regarding the direction for the marriage (i.e., stasis, active working on issues, or separation/divorce); (5) develop understanding of PTSD and complex PTSD syndrome and promote remediation of PTSD-related symptoms; (6) enhance self-care for each partner; and (7) strengthen family, community, and faith-based support systems. Knowledge about the neurobiology of depression as well as the sequelae of childhood trauma would also provide clarity in understanding the symptoms of clinical depression. In all cases, clinicians must be aware of the indicators that warrant a referral for a psychiatric or medical consultation. Finally, the need to learn constructive, nonviolent problem-solving techniques calls for cognitive–behavioral interventions. Although the clinician needs to be aware of family patterns and the meaning ascribed to the childhood trauma narratives, intergenerational and narrative family theoretical lenses remain in the background for the time being, until the presenting crisis has stabilized. Again, the absence of stability regarding the future of the relationship and the presence of acute symptomatology signaled the need for resolution of these issues first, before the treatment could proceed to Phase II tasks, including reflection on each partner's trauma narratives.

Although each partner possessed the attachment and object relational capacities for reasonably solid object constancy and the developing capacities for an ambivalently held attachment, an insight-oriented therapy approach was considered inappropriate at the time, owing to the urgency of the relational crisis. The range of therapy goals shifted during this seven-month time period, and the diverse therapy goals are summarized in Table 11.2. Phase I therapy tasks are the focus of treatment in the first eight sessions. After these goals have been met and stabilization established, new Phase II goals then emerge. At that point, Rod and Yolanda renegotiated a treatment plan to continue on in couple therapy for another twelve weeks with a focus on Phase II and IIII tasks. Phase II goals included the following: (1) explore the meaning of their childhood traumatic experiences; (2) minimize the intergenerational "victim–victimizer–bystander" pattern; (3) strengthen empathic attunement; (4) develop more effective ways to express thoughts and feelings; (5) facilitate grieving and the creation of healing rituals; (6) explore the meaning of sexual and emotional intimacy; and (7) strengthen co-parenting. While Yolanda and Rod reflected not only on the course of their sixteen-year marriage, but also on their experiences with their families of origin, the impact of the legacies of trauma became more pronounced. Therefore, during the last month of therapy, a number of Phase III goals were addressed. They included (1) strengthen co-parenting; (2) expand family, community, and faith-based community ettort; (3) strengthen self-care and self-differentiation; and (4) shift identity from survivor to thriver.

Phases of Couple Therapy

Phase I: Safety, Stabilization, and Establishment of Context for Change

Because this couple therapy model is case specific and phase oriented, it is important to start with Phase I tasks, which involve the establishment of safety, stabilization, and a context for change. The presenting issues expressed by these clients narrowed the therapy focus to specific goals as noted earlier. In brief, they included: (1) establishing safety; (2) relief from symptoms of clinical depression (Yolanda) and PTSD-related symptomatology (Rod and Yolanda); (3) clarification of decision regarding status of the marriage; (4) reduction of arguments; (5) enhancement of self-care; and (6) strengthening family and community connections. Because Rod and Yolanda expressed considerable ambivalence about therapy, sociocultural attitudes and biases required attention at the onset so that a workable therapeutic alliance could be established and, to a lesser extent, throughout the therapy.

Safety   The beginning of any couple therapy starts with the exploration and establishment of safety (i.e., the assurance of adequate food, shelter, medical care, and an absence of violence). The establishment of safety and stabilization is a twofold process: (1) exploration of the current safety for the couple and family and (2) establishment of a stable, predictable "holding environment" that facilitates movement in the ongoing therapy (Winnicott, 1954). Not only is it important to provide a safe, predictable couple therapy framework with regard to structure, but it is also imperative that the clinician be prepared to function as an "emotional container" who holds the positive and negative emotions and conflicts.

First, it was important to determine the relative safety for this couple as well as for each partner and baby Mary. Because Yolanda expressed some suicidal ideation and vegetative signs of depression (e.g., emotional lability, tearfulness, insomnia, and weight gain), her emotional stability was tenuous. During the first meeting, I introduced the idea of Yolanda seeking a psychiatric consultation, so as to be evaluated for antidepressant medications. Although this suggestion was met with fierce resistance and feelings of deep shame, I urged her to consider this option as just one path to possibly fortify her resilience. After agreeing to meet for a medication evaluation, Yolanda started a trial of Selective Serotonin Reuptake Inhibitors (SSRIs). Within three weeks, she reported an increase in energy, better sleeping, the absence of suicidal ideation, and a beginning hopefulness. Rod denied any suicidal ideation, parasuicidal behavior, or aggressive outbursts. A noteworthy reality was that this couple never resorted to physical outbursts or violent behavior, although both were reared in families where this was the modus operandi for discipline. Instead, they engaged in loud, angry fighting over parenting responsibilities, which was disturbing to both partners as well as to Mary, who began to cry as soon as she heard these exchanges. Although the emotional safety was unclear in this home, it was clear that Rod and Yolanda lived in a comfortable home in a middle-income community and earned substantial incomes that enabled them to provide more than adequately for their shelter, food, basic needs, and recreation.

Second, certain specific therapeutic interventions aimed to create a "safe-enough holding environment" including (1) clarity of structure, (2) agreements, (3) permission to interrupt negative exchanges, and (4) psychoeducational approaches regarding the purpose and objectives of the couple therapy. As mentioned earlier, therapeutic exchanges occurred at the time of the first contact. In terms of structure for the couple therapy sessions, I had already conveyed to both Rod and Yolanda on the telephone that we might meet initially for a consultation session of one and one-half hours for me to have the opportunity to hear, in depth, the nature of their concerns and to offer specific recommendations. It would also provide them with the opportunity to meet me and make their decision about how they might like to proceed. This intervention was deliberately aimed toward maintaining the locus of control and decision-making with the couple. Such an empowerment intervention can be useful in all couple therapy, yet is especially important for trauma survivors who have been disempowered by their abusive offenders. By encouraging commitment to only one consultation meeting, rather than an expectation of an open-ended therapy, distrust is acknowledged and emotional intensity is titrated. Attempts were made to convey my concerned interest, curiosity, and respect for their strengths as well as for the complexity of their situation.

Since Rod's perception of psychotherapy was quite negative, demystifying the process engaged both Rod and Yolanda in talking about their families' views about seeking help. What emerged was an outcry from Rod that only "crazy" people sought treatment, and that the "family was betrayed" by any discussion with people outside the family. Yolanda commented that she was the only family member who accepted therapy, although she covertly shared their assumptions that therapy should be relegated to the "weak" and "indulged." However, Yolanda had challenged her mother's and sisters' views about therapy, as she had already benefited from individual therapy several years before. As mentioned earlier, the experience of cross-cultural therapy was explored with each partner. After talking about his many hurtful racist encounters with white people throughout the years, and his wariness about revealing his vulnerabilities, Rod finally decided to meet for several sessions. However, for the first six sessions, Rod and Yolanda agreed to commit to each therapy session, one session at a time. I encouraged both partners to evaluate this decision-making/stabilization phase during the course of these six meetings. Early on in the work, Yolanda denied any difficulty with my "whiteness," asserting that she trusted her friend's judgment and my professional training. Knowing that there were collective racialized undercurrents as well as a stated wariness about the cross-racial alliance, we tentatively moved forward.

For trauma survivors, experiences with rules are often laden with memories of betrayal and insidious quid pro quo deals in which submission to abuse was exchanged for favors or privileges. As a result, using the language of "guidelines," "agreements," or "parameters" rather than "rules" can provide a neutral, flexible frame as well as a greater sense of stabilization and safety for the couple and the clinician.

Parameters for the couple therapy frame included: (1) length and frequency of sessions, (2) fee and payment, (3) nature of involvement with insurance companies and adjunctive therapies, (4) privacy, and (5) limited confidentiality. It is especially important to ask partners for permission to interrupt any abusive verbal exchanges. With prior permission in place, the clinician can then ensure a baseline of safety during sessions, without risking the imposition of an unwanted interruption at any given moment. An agreement that allows the clinician to intervene when partners speak or behave abusively is also necessary to ensure the physical and emotional safety of the couple and the clinician.

Based on familiarity with pastoral counseling in their church, Yolanda and Rod wondered if I would be "telling them how to redirect their lives." At this phase of the work, an exclusively nondirective reflective stance might have been experienced as unresponsive and culturally insensitive. Instead, at this point in the therapy, a psychoeducational approach regarding the purpose and processes of couple therapy helped. As most clients can identify with metaphors related to traveling, I suggested that they should determine the goal and destination for the couple therapy. If they could envision sharing the driving of their car, my role would be serving as a navigator, who detects obstacles along the way and points out the most unencumbered path toward the designated destination.

Self-Care   In the effort to facilitate improved self-care, it was important to explore how each partner cared for his or her basic physical, psychological, and spiritual needs. Although Yolanda had learned in her previous individual psychotherapy to use a journal for recording her moods and thoughts, she stopped using it two years ago, even though it provided relief and perspective. In fact, Yolanda had abandoned all spiritual supports and other self-soothing strategies. In an effort to normalize a focus on self-care, I regularly mention to clients that it is important to explore fully how their physiological, psychological, spiritual, and social selves work together. Such a frame allows me to explore with both partners the full range of their health and mental health status, nutrition, exercise, drug consumption (including prescription and nonprescription drugs), and prior experiences of any type I, II, or III trauma. As Yolanda started to talk about her self-care, she noted a major decline in her mood and physical health in the past three years. What became evident was that Yolanda's unresolved grief following the loss of her stillborn baby and two earlier miscarriages fueled a state of clinical depression, accompanied by helplessness, inhibited sexual desire, and poor self-care. Her historical feelings of self-blame and unworthiness, related to her childhood sexual abuse, were reinforced by her self-blame regarding her infertility. The adoption of baby Mary, although a source of joy, also reminded Yolanda of her earlier losses and self-hatred.

Since depression and somatization are often related to complex PTSD, the related symptoms should be discussed with clients in this light. Self-care can actually be strengthened through psychoeducational support about PTSD and complex PTSD symptomatology. Before a connection was drawn between these physical symptoms and PTSD, Yolanda's physical complaints signaled the need for a referral to her internist for a general physical examination. After some reluctance, Yolanda made an appointment with her internist, and discovered that she was suffering from borderline hypertension. Her physician advised her to exercise more regularly; reduce intake of dietary fat, carbohydrates, and soda; and start a weight-loss plan. These measures were aimed to remediate her hypertension and possibly deter the onset of type 2 diabetes. Because Yolanda was determined to regulate her hypertension, we discussed avenues for stress reduction including yoga, relaxation exercises, and meditation. Following up with her request for resources, we discussed a range of options and ways to access these supports.

The biopsychosocial assessment was discussed with both partners in terms of their relationship as well as their individual functioning. The criteria for the DSM-IV-TR (2000) classification of PTSD and some educational literature regarding complex PTSD were actually shared with this couple, as they responded well to detailed information. Yolanda's symptoms of clinical depression and somatization were linked to her unresolved grief surrounding their "lost babies" and the "plague of infertility," as well as the legacy from her childhood trauma. Information about this connection felt liberating to Yolanda as she began to further challenge her self-perception of unworthiness. She also understood that her "edginess" and "uptightness" were common aftereffects of childhood trauma. They were associated with a startle response and affect dysregulation, rather than her self-view suggesting "alleged evidence of weakness or meanness."

While the content of this discussion related to individual issues, it was important to encourage each partner to listen as attentively as possible, so as to strengthen an empathic understanding of the other partner. In fact, when we discussed the "startle response" associated with PTSD and complex PTSD symptomatology, Rod accepted that his "bristliness" when touched on the neck might have something to do with being beaten by his father. Although Rod exercised some control over his drinking, his family history of alcoholism placed him at high risk for a substance abuse problem. Rod continued to minimize the influence of childhood trauma, but he successfully experimented with limiting his drinking to no more than two beers on weekends. As we talked about the sequelae of childhood trauma, Rod recognized that his pattern of hyperarousal, withdrawal, battles with low self-esteem, and "numbness" all could be understood as physiological and psychological legacies of his childhood trauma. To minimize the intrusiveness of the startle response experienced by both partners, Rod's self-care plan included finding new ways to self-soothe. When he discussed the power of music in calming him, he recalled earlier memories of retreating from his family into the world of jazz. When both partners understood how the PTSD-related neurophysiological legacy of trauma explained a startle response, both partners agreed to call out to the partner rather than risking surprise.

An important concept discussed at this phase was how the pattern of "victim–victimizer–bystander," internalized during childhood, plays out in adult relationships as a formidable legacy of childhood trauma. Both partners could recognize feeling victimized and helpless when attacked or ignored by the other. With some reluctance, Yolanda saw that her berating comments might appear to be "aggressive" to Rod. Rod had more difficulty seeing how his failure to follow through on agreed on tasks and his withdrawing from Yolanda might relate to the passive bystander or the silent victimizer roles. When he actively engaged in verbal fights with his wife, he saw his victimizing behavior more vividly. Although such understanding began on a strictly cognitive level, it introduced the examination of a dynamic pattern that was fueled by both partners. In summary, through the process of exploring and strengthening each partner's self-care, including medical and psychiatric consultations, a full range of psychoeducational, cognitive–behavioral, and body–mind interventions were made available.

Family, Religious, and Community Supports   To facilitate the strengthening of this couple's family, religious, and community supports, questions were asked to elicit discussion about individuals and supports that were available. As the couple discussed the changes in their support networks, it became apparent that Yolanda's family of origin remained a source of nurturance and affirmation. However, the change of events over the past year positioned Yolanda in the new role of caretaker for her mother. The dramatic emotional cutoff that Rod described vis-à-vis his family of origin was presented as a fait accompli; however, the emotional baggage left from these relationships surfaced in ghost-like ways in Rod and Yolanda's own family. The need to recognize the importance of this situation was noted, as was the apparent dearth of support from their faith-based community.

Although Yolanda was deeply attached to her mother, sisters, and extended family, she felt burdened by having to assume sole responsibility for helping her mother. As the couple talked about ways they might enlist one sister to help out in the effort and another sister to help with baby Mary, both partners expressed some relief. The drastic emotional cutoff from Rod's family of origin was more daunting at this early phase of the couple therapy, but the pressure imposed by the alienation was noted.

The absence of spiritual support was noted as a stressor in the first session. What emerged was Rod and Yolanda's shared belief that God had abandoned them by allowing all three of their potential children to die. In response to these painful losses, both partners experienced a spiritual crisis characterized by alienation, hopelessness, and pessimism. Neither partner regularly utilized methods of self-soothing, other than detachment for Rod and overeating for Yolanda. In Phase II of the work, this issue was dealt with intensively.

Communication   Communication difficulties plagued this couple. These involved faulty attributions associated with emotionally abusive communication patterns and mutual projective identification processes characterized by rigid, polarized thinking and affect. Although Rod and Yolanda were capable of some self-reflection regarding these patterns, there were several contraindications for insight-oriented work at this early phase. First, the couple was experiencing a crisis of possible separation or divorce. Second, Rod, in particular, was wary about psychotherapy. Third, both partners presented rigid, polarized depictions of the other that immobilized discussions.

To provide stabilization in the crisis and relief from the destructive exchanges of polarized thoughts and feelings, specific cognitive–behavioral interventions were selected (Basham, 1999b; Gottman, 1999). To address fixed polarizations, the couple was taught to identify uncomfortable, disturbing emotions by acknowledging their feelings as well as the automatic thoughts that entered their minds. A written automatic thought record might have been useful in self-monitoring emotional reactions. Rod and Yolanda discussed the possibilities for cognitive distortions, including polarized thinking, overgeneralizations, and mind reading. Again, they were introduced to tools that helped them to challenge their own thinking. To slow down the escalating course of arguments, each partner asked him- or herself: What information supports or challenges my interpretation? Is there logic that supports my perception of what I have assigned to him or her? Could there be any other explanation for this behavior? While challenging these nonproductive cognitive and affective distortions (or faulty attributions), Yolanda was able to recognize that her perception of Rod as lazy and incompetent did not hold up given Rod's lengthy history of reliability on the job. Rod also saw that Yolanda was, in fact, very caring, but tired and yearning to depend on him for support. Over the course of the first eight sessions, Rod and Yolanda challenged their projective identifications on a cognitive level. Although each partner reported some easing in the inflexibility and nastiness of their exchanges, it was unclear that any insight had actually been attained. However, the change in behavior provided enormous relief.

Because Yolanda and Rod generally spoke to each other in blaming and condemning tones, they needed to learn more constructive modes of communicating. By the sixth session, Rod and Yolanda were willing to experiment with communication skills–building exercises (Guerney, 1987). Each partner was expected to listen for a period of three minutes to the partner, with the task of "putting oneself in the emotional shoes of the other." The next step was to reflect to the speaker the content and affect that was heard and observed. The speaker then affirmed what was correct, and added any additional information. Then, the roles were reversed. Both Rod and Yolanda became vividly aware that each was waiting impatiently for his or her turn to defend a position, rather then listening empathically. Over time, the skills of reflective listening, empathy building, and constructive communication were slowly acquired.

Decision-Making on the Status of the Partnership   During the first six sessions, Yolanda and Rod agreed to commit to a primary goal of evaluating the "state of the relationship." A review of all strengths and vulnerabilities during these early meetings provided them with a balanced account of many commonalities in values and in a worldview, countered by problems in intimacy, problem-solving, and communication. Following a structured discussion of the strengths and problem areas in the marriage, Rod and Yolanda ultimately agreed to contract for a three-month period of couple therapy sessions. They both acknowledged improvement during the past month in the following areas: (1) improved self-care, (2) increased understanding of legacies of PTSD and complex PTSD, (3) expansion of family supports, (4) improved communication with reduced arguments, (5) strengthened co-parenting; (6) clarity regarding a renewed commitment to work on their marital difficulties, and (7) a rekindling of hope in their sixteen-year relationship built on shared values and dreams. As the resolution of this decision marks relative closure on Phase I tasks, Rod, Yolanda, and I embarked on Phase II tasks in the therapy—reflection on the trauma narratives.

Phase II: Reflection on the Trauma Narratives

The focus for this phase of couple therapy with Yolanda and Rod involved the following identified goals: (1) to explore the meaning of their childhood traumatic experiences; (2) to reflect on the intergenerational legacies of childhood trauma by questioning and clarifying the "victim–victimizer–bystander" dynamic; (3) to strengthen empathy in response to each partner's trauma narrative, embracing resilience and survivorship; (4) to develop more effective ways to express thoughts and feelings; (5) to grieve the losses of the "lost babies" and plan a healing ritual to memorialize their lives; (6) to strengthen emotional and sexual intimacy; and (7) to strengthen co-parenting skills. Because Rod and Yolanda possessed the object relational capacities and cultural compatibility to benefit from an insight-oriented psychotherapeutic approach, efforts were made to clarify the ongoing interplay of mutual projective identification processes. During this phase of work, object relations, attachment, and trauma theories remained in the foreground. When intergenerational family patterns and unique meanings of the trauma narratives were also explored, both intergenerational and narrative family theories entered the foreground to guide clinical interventions.

Intergenerational Legacy of the "Victim–Victimizer–Bystander" Pattern
Since a major complaint from Yolanda early on was feeling overburdened by the care of Mary and resentment over Rod's disappearances, the issue of co-

parenting was front and center. As a way to neutralize the intractable, venomous exchanges, therapeutic efforts were aimed at expanding and deepening the dialogue about their families of origin. To ascertain their prevailing views on parenting and discipline, the following questions were raised: What did you learn about parenting in your families of origin? Who had power in decision-making? How were conflicts handled? How was anger dealt with? How were different opinions dealt with? What was considered unacceptable behavior? How was discipline handled? What aspects of this parenting style do you identify with? What aspects of this parenting do you reject? What values are important to you in terms of parenting? How has your culture and religion influenced your ideas about parenting?

Yolanda approached these questions with great eagerness, noting the frightening and unpredictable violent outbursts expressed by her father, countered by the benign, nurturing, consistent parenting offered by her mother, aunts, and an uncle. She proudly described the ways that she tried to outwit her alcoholic father by appeasing his demands. Offhandedly, she mentioned that her uncle had abused her sexually, causing serious aftereffects, but "That had nothing to do with parenting." In listening attentively to Yolanda's narrative, Rod asked her why she was not angry at her parents for failing to protect her or to intervene to stop the sexual abuse. She yelled back to him that he had no right to talk because he was "completely useless and uninvolved himself with parenting." This exchange captured the tenacious grip that the "victim–victimizer–bystander" dynamic had on the interactions between Rod and Yolanda. Rather than responding with gratitude for his understanding, Yolanda attacked Rod in a victimizing manner, hurling insults that degraded him. Rod felt victimized. I was the only bystander at the moment, and I commented, "It is noteworthy that when you questioned why Yolanda lacked feelings about the absence of protection, she criticized you for failing to be involved with Mary, rather than talking about her lack of protection in her childhood home." Although initially bristly and defensive, Yolanda settled into a quiet calm, responding that she would think about this.

With great reluctance, Rod talked about "learning nothing about parenting" except the worst ways to look after children. He recalled escaping to school and to friends' homes to avoid the wrath of his father, who yelled at Rod and his brothers the minute they unlocked the front door. He was angry and frightened of agitating his father, knowing that it was just a matter of time before his father grabbed the belt and struck him with it. He felt very sorry for his mother, who was also beaten by his dad, but wondered why she did not run away. When Rod stated that he rejected everything that his parents did as parents, Yolanda wondered if he felt any sympathy for his mother because she had no financial or family support to ease her burdens. Rod screamed at Yolanda that she, just like they, was more concerned about other people's feelings than about his. Once again, as the bystander, I commented that Rod seemed very angry, as Yolanda was not reflecting what she heard about his needs or pain. Instead of telling her that he felt misunderstood, he lashed out in a victimizing way to silence her. Rod responded, "Well, it is better to be the one on the offensive than the one who is ignored." In this way, Rod and Yolanda recognized that her incomplete empathy led to Rod's feeling of victimization, followed by his victimizing stance toward Yolanda.

An important step in identifying projective identification processes is to recognize strong polarities in thought or behavior. In this case, Rod and Yolanda continually battled about who was in control, or who was in charge. Polarizations prevailed! Yolanda presented herself as emotionally reactive, while Rod prided himself as being emotionally contained. Yolanda viewed herself as burdened and Rod as underresponsible; Rod perceived himself as more relaxed, yet productive. He saw himself as burdened by his wife's railings. While Yolanda complained continually about Rod's withdrawal from her and baby Mary, Rod described himself as "laid-back" and "relaxed," yet persecuted by his wife.

Gradually, the processes of projective identification unfolded vividly. When this occurs, each partner represses, splits off, and projects onto the partner the side of the internal dispute that is disowned. What is fought out are the problems that neither partner has been able to address internally. Thus, core issues emerge as polarizations of attributes, such as "overresponsible/underresponsible," "expressive/contained," and "carefree/constricted." By maintaining a rigid view of these differences, each partner was unable to recognize the disavowed parts of self that had been projected onto the partner.

In fact, at the beginning of therapy, Yolanda and Rod had only minimal awareness of their projective identification processes. For example, Yolanda projected her logical, carefree, and cheerful attributes onto Rod, and ended up alternating between admiring and envying these qualities, which Rod embodied. Rod projected his responsible and expressive side onto Yolanda, projecting his internal conflicts outward, thus inviting her to victimize him through criticism. With great righteousness, Rod complained that Yolanda victimized him.

Another important projective identification pattern involving the "victim–victimizer–bystander" dynamic emerged in relation to the cross-racial therapy. Although the couple's initial resistances were understood as culturally congruent wariness, various racialized themes surfaced periodically during the work. When Yolanda complained at one point that I sounded insensitive and critical of her for challenging a slanderous, blaming remark, she was able to recognize the projection of her own inner conflicts around internalized oppression onto me. Had she viewed me in the moment as the oppressive victimizer rather than recognizing her own internalized negative views? Before arriving at any conclusion, the guiding mantra "to explore countertransference" should be addressed thoroughly. Questions needed to be asked. Was Yolanda's experience of me as oppressive, controlling, and critical related solely to projective identification? Or was there a reality-based racialized countertransference that required attention? Was I behaving in too "color-blind" a way, assuming that Yolanda would not be affected by my interrupting her critical harangue and encouraging her to explore her empathic response to her husband, when, in fact, she experienced this as a lack of understanding on my part? There was no way that I could feel the full depth of Yolanda's pain, which had been etched deeply during her many episodes with painful racist insults. When I acknowledged my empathic failure and apologized for my insensitivity to her feelings, Yolanda thanked me in a quiet voice. This encounter reminded me of the complexity of the "victim–victimizer–bystander" dynamic that is passed along intergenerationally and reinforced by racist attitudes in society as well as within the micro-interactions of our couple therapy alliance.

As both partners spoke about their childhood experiences of abusive treatment at the hands of their parents as well as their racist neighbors, they saw the mirroring of the "victim–victimizer–bystander" dynamic as not only associated with the aftereffects of childhood abuses but also as reflecting societal racist attitudes. When Yolanda recognized that her devaluation of Rod's competence and her regular harangues of his alleged "laziness" and "uselessness" reflected a pejorative racial stereotype, she was horrified. Only then did she begin to talk about her own vulnerabilities related to internalized oppressions. This startling insight ultimately enabled Yolanda to apologize to

Rod for many unjustified verbal attacks. Rod, in response, was able to understand the enactments and to forgive Yolanda for her hurtful remarks.

Healing Rituals   During the discussions about parenting baby Mary, questions were raised about Rod and Yolanda's experience with eight years of infertility treatment and about the impact on them of the "lost babies." Yolanda talked about her feelings of failure in trying to bring a baby to full term, sadly recounting how strong her desire had been to give birth to her own biological children. Rod focused on the joy he felt in adopting Mary, asserting that it was "morbid to talk about death." In spite of his reticence, Rod shared his disappointment in the loss of a miscarried boy infant. He had always dreamed of teaching his son mechanics and of watching him grow up. He also expressed shock and regret that he and Yolanda were unable to see their stillborn baby girl, delivered three years ago. In several heart-wrenching meetings, both at home and during the couple therapy sessions, Yolanda and Rod grieved their lost babies, freeing themselves to move on in their emotional lives. As their religious beliefs confirmed the importance of funeral rites, Rod and Yolanda planned a grieving ritual officiated by the minister of their church and attended by several family members and two of Rod's work buddies. At that time, they gave names to the lost babies, naming the boy infant after Rod's benevolent uncle, who had rescued him from the family chaos. Now, less burdened by the sadness of unresolved grief, Yolanda could see Rod as a playful yet responsible and caring parent. At the same time, Rod could appreciate Yolanda's emotional expressiveness as a sign of caring rather than solely as a weapon of oppression. As each partner expressed the capacity to love ambivalently, they relaxed some of their fiercely entrenched polarized projections. In fact, Yolanda experienced herself as more emotionally balanced and playful, while Rod enjoyed the responsibilities of parenting Mary. With a renewed sense of hope, the couple then planned a celebratory adoption party to welcome baby Mary into their home and family.

Emotional and Sexual Intimacy   As Rod and Yolanda discussed their notions of intimacy, significant differences emerged. Rod felt closest to Yolanda when he was off in the garage, quietly working away at one of his projects, at the same time sensing her presence in the home. Often, his sexual interest brought him into the house seeking lovemaking with Yolanda. Rod's overtures were usually met with angry indignation because for Yolanda, experiencing intimacy involved talking about feelings and thoughts and feeling understood. She felt victimized and controlled by Rod's "urges." Rod retreated back to the yard or garage, or went away from home, feeling wounded, disempowered, victimized, and controlled by Yolanda's rebuff. Yolanda worried about her loss of sexual interest; she wondered if that would drive Rod away from her. The impact of her depression related to unresolved grief, the side effects of the SSRI medication, and the effects of perimenopausal hormonal changes were discussed openly. Following the sharing of their expectations, wishes, and disappointments, Rod and Yolanda were able to talk about finding some middle ground instead of facing off against each other on their usual battleground for control. They agreed to set aside about twenty minutes each day to check in with each other about events of the day and their feelings. Yolanda also agreed to experiment with initiating giving Rod a hug or a kiss, rather than sitting back passively. Such strategies were aimed at disrupting the power balance and the retraumatizing experience of intrusive overtures. Instead, as mutual projections were reowned, Rod and Yolanda experienced more affection and attraction toward each other, in a more equitable manner, without fear of domination or subjugation. In time, they reported, with some gleeful embarrassment, that they had made love after putting Mary to bed, and then heading to bed themselves at 8 P.M., an uncharacteristically early turning-in time.

In summary, after the first two months of clinical work, the Smiths had established reasonable safety, improved self-care, and an expanded support network. This overall stabilization enabled them to move onward to Phase II tasks that involve reflecting on the trauma narratives. As Rod and Yolanda talked about the intergenerational legacies of the "victim–victimizer–bystander" dynamic perpetuated by the effects of their childhood abuses and racial insults, they recognized with alarm how they had been treating each other in similarly abusive ways. New, more positive ways of talking about difficult feelings enabled them to focus not only on their arguments, but also on their vulnerabilities. Feelings of profound sadness and unresolved grief related to their lost babies emerged with force. In the process of unraveling the intricate web of mutual projective identifications, Rod and Yolanda expressed an entire range of feelings that previously had been suppressed or dissociated. Many tears were shed as they grieved their lost babies and the losses of their beleaguered childhoods. Ultimately, with the reowning of mutual projections, Yolanda and Rod were able to shift from an entrenched "victim–victimizer–bystander" pattern to relating to each other more equitably.

Phase III: Consolidation of New Perspective,
Attitudes, and Behaviors

With significant remediation of presenting issues and strengthened capacities for self-differentiation, Rod and Yolanda were ready to consolidate their more collaborative, equitable ways of relating. Phase III goals included: (1) strengthen co-parenting; (2) expand family, community, and faith-based community effort; (3) strengthen self-care and self-differentiation; and (4) shift self-identity from survivor to thriver. These efforts involved problem-solving around parenting responsibilities as well as greater mutuality in their friendship and sexual relationship. As they discussed the ways in which they most hoped to parent Mary, Yolanda and Rod borrowed some qualities from their respective families of origin while rejecting other qualities. Both Rod and Yolanda agreed that any physical punishment was unacceptable, and this challenged them to find ways to set limits with a curious, willful toddler. They decided to join a parenting group at their church, which ushered in reconciliation with their faith-based community. Here, they were able to discuss, with other parents, alternative approaches to parenting that allowed for greater flexibility along with benevolent limit setting. While reflecting on their narratives of childhood trauma, each partner was able to affirm the resilient behaviors that distinguished them as survivors rather than victims. As each partner shared his or her recollections in the presence of the other, a strong empathic connection was forged.

As they planned the ending of their sessions, both Rod and Yolanda felt saddened to say goodbye to me. I felt saddened to say farewell as well. Yet, we could all celebrate the important, restorative work that they had accomplished in strengthening their marriage and family. They also reported relief from the insidious burden of internalized oppression, which rendered them helpless to their internalized bigotry about race and gender. At the beginning of therapy, Rod and Yolanda operated from different statuses in terms of their respective racial-identity development. Rod had regressed back to an Immersion schema (Helms & Cook, 1999), with denigration and distrust of the "white world," while Yolanda had retreated into an avoidance of thinking about issues of race, although on the surface she identified with her family and cultural heritage (reflected in Emersion status). Although I was regularly tempted to avoid discussions of race because of my own discomfort, I pressed ahead to explore the meaning of racial events for this couple in an effort to address directly the profound impact of these experiences. At the last session, Rod and Yolanda talked about how they had risked taking chances so as to learn and to thrive. At this phase, neither partner embraced an identity as victim or survivor. Instead, they were moving ahead, both individually and as a couple, with a strong pioneering commitment to navigate rewarding life paths together.

As Rod and Yolanda progressed in the course of their therapy, I needed continually to respond to the multilayered complexity of their lives and their inner worlds with a range of theoretical lenses. Only a synthesis of social and psychological theories could do justice to their nuanced presenting issues and the crafting of an effective treatment plan. The metaphor of renovating an historic home comes to mind. Even though an original architectural design guides the direction of the project, changes occur in the process and plans shift. Old materials are restored and reintegrated into the home while new windows allow for greater openness. Although new structures aim to buttress the original foundation, they do not completely replace the original historically sound base. Along similar lines, Rod and Yolanda negotiated difficult relational territory, learning new ways to relate while challenging repetitive and destructive intergenerational patterns of victimization. During their work in couple therapy, they held on to the positive legacies from their cultural and family heritages, as they created a more positive relationship. The supports of the original relationship scaffolding were clearly strengthened while buffered by new perspectives and skills.

SECTION IV

SPECIFIC CLINICAL ISSUES

This final section of the text introduces three particular client populations in which specific issues emerge in couple therapy practice. Although the couple therapy practice model may be useful in working with these traumatized couples and families, specific characteristics of the populations warrant a focused examination.

In Chapter 12, Military Couples and Families, we summarize issues related to working with traumatized couples who are connected with the armed services, including active duty soldiers, reservists, veterans, civilians in the military, and their families.

In Chapter 13, Gay/Lesbian/Bisexual/Transgendered Couples and Families, we discuss how homophobia and heterosexism permeate society, thus affecting clinical practice with gay, lesbian, bisexual, and transgendered couples and their families. Connections between the legacies of childhood trauma and issues of sexuality, parenting, fertility, and pregnancy are illustrated in clinical case vignettes.

In the final chapter of the book, Immigrant and Refugee Couples and Families, we discuss the specific experiences of individuals who have emigrated to the United States and Canada. We demonstrate how issues of loss permeate the immigrant and refugee population. In addition, we note the importance of challenging Eurocentric views of mental health in efforts to practice in a culturally sensitive manner. Clinical case examples illustrate the application of the couple therapy practice model.

Military Couples and Families

The lives of military couples are shaped not only by the values and responsibilities integral to a military role but also, in specific ways, by the impact of active combat and exposure to armed conflict. As mentioned earlier in the historical review in Chapter 2, interest in traumatology burgeoned in the aftermath of World War I, spurred by the emergence of "shell shock" (Young, 1995). In the years after World War II, clinicians were better prepared to assist war veterans in dealing with their combat reactions, offering a combination of pharmacological and supportive methods. In 1980, with thousands of veterans returning from the Vietnam war, a definable diagnosis of posttraumatic stress disorder (PTSD) emerged to describe combat-related phenomena. In the decades from the 1980s onward increased attention has been directed to the mental health and health needs, not only of the active military member, but also of the partners and families affected by the veteran's mental health status. As a result, a variety of psychoeducational methods have been introduced to assist couples and families in coping with combat-related phenomena (Compton & Follett, 1998; Hogencamp & Figley, 1983; Johnson, Feldman, & Lubin, 1995; Nelson & Wright, 1996; Rabin & Nardi, 1991; Riggs, Byrne, Weathers, & Litz, 1998; Solomon, 1988).

It has become increasingly evident that partners and families were deeply affected, as were the active-duty servicemen and -women directly involved in or exposed to combat. Veterans of the Gulf War and their families faced the additional burden of having to respond to threats of biological and chemical weapons (Yerkes & Holloway, 1996). As this was one of the first wars to be televised via "live simultaneous footage" (Norwood & Ursano, 1996), family members were bombarded with immediate exposure to these wartime events. More recently, the wars in Afghanistan and Iraq have rapidly transformed soldiers into veterans. Many are currently returning to their families affected by their experiences of hand-to-hand combat, participation in (or seeing) the decimation of women and children, and exposure to the destruction of their valued property. Once again, the threats of chemical, biological, and nuclear weapons of mass destruction loom large, a frightening specter of potential, impending terror in the Iraqi war zone. In addition, threats of guerrilla warfare leave military personnel vulnerable to danger and death. This chapter explores, first, the culture of the military, the legacies of childhood trauma, and the impact of armed conflict and combat on military couples and their partners. Second, unique features that are specific to these military couples are reviewed in the context of a thorough biopsychosocial assessment. Third, the assessment is shown to guide the selection of useful clinical interventions in couple or family therapy with military couples.

:: CULTURE OF THE MILITARY

Life in the military involves adherence to and respect for a hierarchical structure within which there are clear expectations for behavior and role conformity. Loyalty, patriotism, and obedience are requisite values that enable an active military member to function optimally. For some survivors of childhood trauma, the structure of the military provides a benign, external scaffolding for their lives, guiding them to master earlier trauma-related experiences of powerlessness. In contrast, other survivors of childhood trauma might experience this rigidly delineated structure as a traumatic reenactment of their childhood victimization. When some survivors of childhood trauma enter active combat, they may be more susceptible to develop PTSD following the active combat period. On the other hand, some research data suggest that other survivors of childhood trauma (those who typically have resolved the distressing aftereffects) enter combat with resilience and in a state of preparedness to deal with dangerous situations. In their lives, they have transformed the legacies of their childhood traumatic experiences into enhanced capacities to deal directly and effectively with combat and violence.

During peacetime, the lives of military families are affected by predictable transitions, often a move for a two-year tour of duty to a different location within the country or overseas. These frequent moves require couples to flexibly negotiate many farewells and garner the initiative to set up their lives with brand new circumstances, often facing a different language and cultural environment. Paradoxically, although military couples often travel extensively and live in many different regions of the world, they often discover homogeneity in the military community (i.e., the base or compound). The military provides many benefits for families in terms of basic security needs, including financial compensation; housing; free medical and mental health care; and reduced costs of prescription drugs, food, and other purchases at the commissary. In spite of these provisions, many active duty military struggle to survive economically, given limited salaries. Yet, there still remains the assurance of clear sources of income, shelter, care, and, ultimately, education and retirement benefits.

Along similar lines, military couples are often cushioned during their transitions to a new base and buffered by orientations to insulated communities that provide their own schools, interfaith chapels, and recreational activities. Many couples who have lived at international military bases seldom enter local towns or interact with local citizens. In fact, many couples have left their assignments without having learned the local language or customs. In some situations, the interface between military couples and their host communities occurs infrequently, setting the stage for a transportable xenophobia. Other military couples seek learning and connection with citizens in their region, reporting a wonderful enrichment of their lives.

While these active military couples negotiate many changes, their parents and extended family also experience the impact of continuous separations and reunions. All military families are taxed to deal with decisions made by a commanding officer that affect where in the country or world their beloved relatives will be sent. Learning to deal with uncertainty, the inability to make major life decisions autonomously, and the pain of separations often create anxiety. In contrast, enormous pride expressed by some parents and extended family members often provides a buffering salve that tempers worries and fears.

Paradoxically, cultural and racial diversity exists in all branches of the armed forces. However, the protections offered by the military provide greatest security to those members reared within families of origin from the dominant culture. In contrast, the many reports of pervasive institutional racism and homophobia in the military point to limited opportunities for members of marginalized communities. In fact, enlistees of color from poorer socioeconomic backgrounds often encounter obstacles to their advancement. Yet, these same recruits are drawn to the educational opportunities and promise of retirement benefits that are largely unavailable to them in their civilian lives.

An interesting study addressing racial differences with regard to combat stress in the Vietnam war concluded that "Blacks, if showing more symptoms in the present, are doing so primarily because the stressors that they experienced in combat were more extreme than those experienced by whites in combat" (Green, Grace, Lindy, & Leonard, 1990, p. 392). A sample of 181 enlisted men revealed comparable age, education, and marital status variables between black and white soldiers. The only noteworthy demographic difference was that blacks reported significantly more childhood trauma prior to age eight than did their white cohorts.

Subjects were measured on their military history and experiences, childhood trauma, current symptomatology, and general psychopathology. Findings revealed that rates for both lifetime and current incidence of PTSD were higher for blacks (47%) than for whites (30%). These data were higher than national survey rates, in part because one-third of the sample was derived from a clinical population. The prevalence in the nonclinical portions of the sample (16% whites and 37% blacks) come closer to the national figures of 14% for whites and 21% for blacks (Kulka et al., 1988). Interestingly, when social class factors were controlled, the differences between black and white veterans' symptom ratings disappeared. In addition, when preservice variables were controlled, there were still differences in combat-related phenomena, with higher levels of war stress for blacks than for whites.

This study confirms poignant accounts of the black experience in Vietnam (Parson, 1984, 1985), revealing their uniquely painful experiences. For example, although racism in combat was less pronounced, many blacks found racism at base camps quite apparent, with displays of rebel flags, higher incidence of disciplinary reprimands, disparities in promotion (9% of the white respondents were officers, whereas there were no black officers), and differential assignments to more dangerous jobs. Important differences existed during wartime, with blacks reporting higher levels of injury, exposure to grotesque deaths, and general levels of combat exposure. On their return home, racism continued. Blacks were more likely to be unemployed and, when employed, to earn less than their white counterparts (Boulanger, 1981). The only diagnostic difference reported is a higher rate of lifetime prevalence of simple phobia for blacks as compared with whites, evidenced by higher avoidance rates on the Impact of Event Scale (Green, Grace, Lindy,

& Leonard, 1990; Horowitz et al., 1989). Critics who might surmise that the diagnostic differences are due to differences in reporting assume possible overreporting by blacks. The increased tendency among blacks to minimize and "remove their experiences from memory" actually support the validity of the reported data. The sociocultural critique embedded in this report is impressive, in that the outcome easily could be misinterpreted to mean that blacks suffer greater PTSD related to earlier childhood trauma-related vulnerabilities or intrinsic weaknesses, which might support a racist view. However, these groundbreaking researchers conclude that the differences noted in reports of PTSD clearly relate more closely to the higher levels of stresses borne by blacks during their wartime experiences (Green, Grace, Lindy, & Leonard, 1990; Terry, 1984).

Based on these troubling events during the Vietnam war, all branches of the armed services have since exerted efforts to open opportunities for enlisted servicemen and -women to gain promotion to higher-ranking positions. Because the current war in Iraq involves a disproportionate number of servicemen and -women of color, it will be important to review the impact of institutional racism on their adaptation to active combat and their reentry on return home. Moreover, the fact that 8% of active duty military recruits are citizens of other countries with "green card" immigrant status in the United States raises another question about potential differential treatment based on race, ethnicity, and nationality. In fact, as of August 2003, almost 40,000 non-U.S. citizens served in the U.S. armed forces in Iraq, with 7% of those killed thus far being "green card" immigrants (Contreras, 2003).

:: UNIQUE THEMES RELEVANT TO
TRAUMA-RELATED EFFECTS

Value Base: Loyalty, Patriotism, and Stoicism

Once again, to avoid a presumption of psychopathology, we need to be reminded that many men and women subjected to armed combat demonstrate unique resilience in coping with terrifying life-threatening circumstances (O'Connell & Higgins, 1994). Extensive literature on survivors of torture reveals extraordinary tales of courage and adaptation, as captives coped with extreme adversity (Marsella, Friedman, Gerrity, & Scurfield, 1996). Likewise, many survivors of armed conflicts return to their lives and report positive adjustments to family and work without PTSD symptomatology (King, King, Keane, Fairbank, & Adams, 1998). Although emphasizing resilience ensures the recognition of the strengths possessed by the veteran and his or her family members, we must be careful about idealizing heroism at the expense of ignoring suffering. Survivors of combat are usually expected to cope stoically and to conceal their combat-related fears. Success in the armed forces is predicated on the values of loyalty, obedience to hierarchical authority, and stoicism in the face of danger. Machismo, as the prevailing ethos, promotes fighting aggressively while eschewing fear. This steeled, purposive stance is highly rewarded in a war zone. However, this same value base can foster humiliation in a veteran who feels helpless or vulnerable when recalling violent events.

CHARLES AND BARBARA :: Charles, a twenty-nine-year-old enlisted Air Force helicopter pilot, returned to reenter his work world in Washington, D.C., after having been promoted to officer rank as a result of his bravery during combat in Vietnam. Several years later, Charles and his fiancée, Barbara, on the verge of separation, sought counseling at a community mental health center. Barbara complained that Charles was detached and isolated from everyone. What emerged was Charles's vivid story of trying to suppress terrifying dreams and flashbacks during the previous six months. Loud whirring noises from a construction site, a lawn mower, or an air conditioner could trigger a full-blown flashback in which Charles visualized himself dropping napalm on villages only a few hundred feet beneath his helicopter. He was unable to see the maiming and killing of the women, men, and children struck by the bombs. However, on his return to the States, Charles read newspaper clippings and watched live footage of these mutilated victims. He was haunted constantly by these violent images and tried desperately to defend himself from them. Ultimately, he told Barbara that he felt the enemy (the Viet Cong) was tracking him at home and following him to work. His PTSD-related terrors had shifted into a psychotic defensive structure through projection. Charles submitted that he would "have preferred to die in Vietnam than face his weakness and childishness."

The powerful impact of gender and cultural influences had socialized Charles to suppress his emotional vulnerability! Paradoxically, his steadfast resolve actually rendered him more vulnerable emotionally as he grappled with psychotic delusions. Ultimately, Charles agreed to accept the recommendation for psychotropic medications and supportive counseling. Sadly, this step came too late for his partner, Barbara, who could no longer bear the emotional roller coaster of Charles's emotional world and ended the relationship.

Postwar PTSD Aftereffects

The full range of PTSD symptomatology affects not only the veteran but also his or her partner and family. As discussed in Chapter 5 on trauma theories, the full range of symptoms of secondary stress disorder includes affective instability, nightmares, startle responses, pendulums of hyperarousal to numbness, flashbacks, depersonalization, somatization, and a disturbed stimulus barrier (Figley, 1995). Violence, social isolation, rigid rules, gun collections and bunkers in the basement, chaotic employment patterns, and a generally negative home environment are not uncommon features. Couples may try to maintain a closed system, and often become isolated from their families and community. The veteran may have difficulty carrying out parenting responsibilities. He may be impatient and may sometimes worry about hurting his children. He may have little tolerance for children's playing, crying, or fighting, and may expect orderliness and perfection (Johnson, Feldman, & Lubin, 1995).

Several studies suggest that those PTSD symptoms directly affect partners and family members through the process of secondary trauma (Figley, 1985, 1989, 1995; Maloney; 1987; Mikulincer, Florian, & Weller, 1993; Nelson & Wright, 1996). The development of indirect traumatization, or secondary trauma, typically surfaces when "a family discovers that one member, who is not in contact with the family has experienced a trauma or . . . a chasmal effect, when the traumatic stress appears to infect the entire family after making contact with the victimized family member" (Figley, 1985, p. 410). In these situations, partners might develop a full range of PTSD symptomatology as well. Other reports point to the impact of PTSD symptoms on relationships (Brende & Goldsmith, 1991; Nelson & Wright, 1996; Solomon, 1988). Many partners express concerns about distancing and numbness, which affect emotional and sexual intimacy. Without an understanding of the origin of this detachment, partners often interpret this behavior as lack of love and support. In more extreme situations, the partner may feel totally abandoned.

Another major symptom is affect dysregulation, which might manifest in self-medication through substance use. Turning to alcohol, marijuana, barbiturates, tranquilizers, or stimulants serves to regulate a poorly balanced physiological state of emotions, often leading to patterns of abuse or addiction. Clearly, direct clinical intervention is needed to deal with the substance abuse and to interrupt the risk of a slide down the slippery slope to addiction. Treatment interventions that directly address the substance abuse or focus on pretreatment decision-making should be the priority before any other issues are addressed.

SAM AND ANNA :: A naval couple, consisting of Sam, age forty-seven, a second-generation Armenian American, and Anna, forty-five, a second-generation Turkish American, entered therapy following Sam's return from a tour of duty on an aircraft carrier during the Gulf War. Sam and Anna talked about how their respective Turkish and Armenian families had emigrated to the United States, accompanied by a history of ancestral ethnic battles with each other. Both families had opposed Sam and Anna's marriage from the onset, and they clashed regularly over ideological and political beliefs. During therapy, the question arose about whether Sam and Anna were carrying out an intergenerational imperative to fight unrelentingly.

As a navy captain, Sam was in charge of overseeing the schedule for deployment of fighter jets from the aircraft carrier. This assignment would be his last one prior to an anticipated retirement from the navy after twenty-five years of service. On his return home, Anna expressed frustration, turning to outrage, about what she perceived as his "complete lack of connection." She complained, "I feel as if I am living with an automaton." This couple had weathered the aftermath of Sam's return from Vietnam several decades earlier, but in Vietnam, Sam had experienced a sense of fulfillment in helping the South Vietnamese return their lives to some order at the end of the war. Although Sam had not been exposed to direct combat at the time, he had witnessed the devastation of homes and villages, as well as the severe injuries and disfigurements suffered by many local citizens. Sam did not report any symptoms of PTSD.

In his more recent assignment, Sam experienced himself as a "detached participant" in the destruction of specific targets, presumably weapons warehouses. On his return from the Gulf War, he was met with congratulatory applause for his "heroic" contributions. His wife, family, and friends expected that he would now look forward to a well-earned and desired retirement with high honors. Instead, Sam was plagued with insomnia, nightmares, and feelings of "deadness" throughout the day. Often unresponsive to Anna's complaints, he retreated into drinking one or two mixed drinks at the end of the day. Undoubtedly, his detachment needed to be understood in terms of his immediate and cumulative responses to his wartime experiences, as well as the intergenerational transmission of trauma-related combat.

Gender Roles: Power, Powerlessness, and Dependency

The third and final theme relevant to trauma effects among many military couples regards gender roles and the ways in which those roles may shift over the course of the family's military career. Historically, the structure of the U.S. armed forces, including the army, navy, air force, and marines, has reinforced patriarchal family patterns. In contrast, over the past decade, there has been more equity in the military, with a considerable increase in servicewomen, servicemen, and couples, both heterosexual and homosexual, who endorse more egalitarian relationships. However, for those couples who embrace more conventional stereotypic gender roles, entry into the military generally conforms with their family expectations. In spite of the apparent congruence of family and military values, military couples are often jarred into adjusting their role expectations. For example, when an active serviceman is transferred to a new location or called up for active duty, his wife is expected to assume all family responsibilities, including those formerly designated to the husband. Many couples negotiate these changes effectively, with the military wife assuming primary care for the home, children, finances, and general day-to-day functioning. In the case of an active duty servicewoman, the male partner might similarly assume primary responsibilities. On the other hand, many active duty lesbian and gay couples experience a sharp prohibition against openness that forces both partners to address issues in secrecy.

However, when the active duty serviceman returns home, he may expect to resume his earlier role of authority in certain areas. At times, the wife might experience gratitude and relief to share family responsibilities, once again. At other times, the wife might resent what feels like an intrusion into her smoothly running "ship." If the active serviceman experiences a loss of role, and consequently a loss of valued purpose on homecoming, tensions may develop. Often the veteran experiences a sense of powerlessness while reestablishing a place for himself in the family. If the couple's relationship cannot flexibly adapt to these changes, the husband's anger might increase in response to intensifying powerlessness. If PTSD symptomatology induces the veteran to detach, then his partner may feel negated or further alienated.

Many partners of veterans wrestling with PTSD assume a caretaking role. They may attend closely to their partner's cues that precede triggers of flashbacks or substance abuse (Nelson & Wright, 1996). If one partner's caretaking role robs the other partner of a sense of agency, then a couple might shift into an alternating pattern of an underfunction/overfunction dynamic. This dynamic sets the stage for struggles over power and powerlessness, ultimately leading to enactments of the "victim–victimizer–bystander" scenario. Such patterns may surface not only with active duty heterosexual couples, but with active duty gay and lesbian couples as well.

:: AGGRESSION AND VIOLENCE

During wartime, soldiers are encouraged to fight aggressively, when necessary, to accomplish their mission to protect their country or the citizens of another country. Fighting aggressively becomes a way of life, not only on an ideological (political) level, but also on psychological and physiological levels as well. If a soldier upholds the political belief that his acts of violence are justified, based on an ethical position regarding the protection of human rights, then combat remains syntonic with his beliefs, and social justice themes prevail. However, if a soldier begins to doubt the ethical justification for violent actions, he is likely to experience internal dissonance with regard to his own violent actions or those he witnesses being enacted by other people.

Typically, a psychological rationale for violence is based on the understanding that certain problems and conflicts are justifiably solved through aggressive action. Notions of self-protection and the protection of one's nation provide justification for aggressive action. Many soldiers facing combat discover that physical aggression is antithetical to their basic religious and ethical beliefs. A level of internal dissonance then sets the stage for augmented guilt and/or shame, as well as a complicated postcombat adaptation. An example of this occurred when African-American soldiers in Vietnam reported some identification with, first, the oppressed citizens of South Vietnam, and later, some of the Viet Cong, who had started to garner sympathy toward the end of the war. A shared experience of oppression and marginalization made active duty combat and killing far more difficult for these black soldiers than for some of the white soldiers, who reported a detachment from the victims, experiencing them simply as "other" (Green, Grace, Lindy, & Leonard, 1990). Current reports of high suicide rates among active-duty servicemen and -women returning from Iraq are also alarming.

Finally, we must be mindful of the physiological responses related to aggression that become activated in all violent situations. As discussed in Chapter 5 on trauma theories, individuals engaged in combat must mobilize their "fight/flight" responses in order to act. Because their sympathetic and parasympathetic autonomic systems fire simultaneously, a freeze effect occurs. To interrupt this immobilization, a soldier needs to mobilize his fight tendencies, fueled by an adrenergic surge. Although many wartime soldiers return home believing that it is wrong to deal with all conflicts through violence, their bodies and minds have been trained to respond violently. Not surprisingly, many veterans and their partners report high incidences of domestic violence (Dutton & Holtzworth-Munroe, 1997; Langhinrischen-Rohling, Neideg, & Thorn, 1995). In fact, following the Vietnam war, 25% of the female partners of veterans reported that their male partners had physically abused them (Nelson & Wright, 1996). Research findings suggest that both male- and female-initiated violence is more prevalent among couples in which one partner is a PTSD-diagnosed veteran than among unaffected couples (Jordan et al., 1992). Although either partner may initiate violence, it should be clarified that male-initiated violence leads to more severe outcomes than does female-initiated violence (Holtzworth-Munroe, Beatty, & Anglin, 1995). Let us return to the vignette of Sam and Anna to demonstrate the interactional buildup of relational violence.

SAM AND ANNA (continued) :: After experiencing months of intensifying powerlessness following his return home, Sam tried to assert some influence in the management of the family finances, only to be met with resentment from Anna. She complained that Sam was "completely emotionally absent" and "useless." With the buildup of tensions, Sam detached himself further into drinking, further enraging Anna, who pursued him unrelentingly. One morning, when Anna asked Sam to help their youngest son with his homework, Sam failed to reply. Anna started yelling at Sam in a victimizing voice that he was "inept" and "passive–aggressive." Sam's feeling of guilt and remorse triggered a sudden flashback. He reexperienced himself as a "passive, benevolent-yet-useless bystander" during his tours of duty in Vietnam and the Persian Gulf.

He recalled a memory of staring, helplessly, as a wounded Vietnamese woman buried her tiny child. This memory then slipped into another, from decades later, of standing still and staring blankly as jets launched methodically from the floating tarmac of the aircraft carrier. Sam then burst into rage, yelling that Anna did not understand him. He screamed that Anna was vicious, since all she did was criticize and emasculate him. His sense of powerlessness fueled a surge of adrenaline-based "fight" response, and he pushed Anna up against the wall. She braced herself, while falling to the ground.

Sam stopped immediately, but not soon enough. His anger had crossed the line into dangerous violent behavior, though he could not understand the intensity of his response. Sam's action prompted Anna to seek help from the domestic violence unit at their local military hospital, where staff recommended that Sam receive treatment for PTSD, including medications and anger management. After a six-month period of treatment, the couple was referred to a community provider for couple and family therapy.

In summary, this review of pertinent themes associated with combat-related effects, illustrated through clinical vignettes, highlights the importance of personal and political values and their effects on couples. Other important factors include the omnipresence of racism and homophobia in social structures of the military, shifting gender roles, the effects of exposure to or direct involvement with combat, and the negative impact of PTSD symptomatology on both individual well-being and relationship satisfaction.

:: CLINICAL INTERVENTIONS IN
COUPLE/FAMILY THERAPY

Most clinical approaches in practice with military couples have focused on the provision of psychoeducational interventions in group, couple, or family modalities. In more recent years, other contemporary practice approaches have addressed the dynamic interactional processes related to PTSD, the meaning of the trauma narratives, and relational changes. The next section of this chapter addresses these diverse approaches.

Psychoeducational Methods

As attention focused on the impact of PTSD on family members as well as veterans, early intervention efforts focused on the veteran as the designated identified client. Treatment goals typically were based on the views of the partner and family members affected by, or reacting to, the veteran's PTSD symptomatology. As a result of secondary stress disorder, most families suffer PTSD symptomatology as well.

Psychoeducational methods are very useful in helping family members understand often inexplicable phenomena (Nelson & Wright, 1996; Rabin & Nardi, 1991). They are very important clinical interventions that promote self-care and feature prominently in Phase I of the couple therapy model, which focuses on safety, stabilization, and establishing a context for change. Because symptomatology is often confusing or misinterpreted, the sharing of knowledge helps couples to clarify misinformation or distortions. Psychoeducational methods involve the full range of education about PTSD, including symptomatology, the pendulum of hyperarousal versus numbness, the physiology of trauma ("fight/flight" and rage responses), effects on relationship dynamics and sexuality, the "victim–victimizer–bystander" trauma scenario, vulnerability to substance abuse and addictions, psychopharmacology, and approaches to self-care. In addition to PTSD-related content, many veterans have suffered the aftereffects of physical injury or illness, resulting in long-term disability. For example, many Gulf War veterans experienced undiagnosed physical ailments that affected their neurological and immunological systems. The long-term effects of exposure to chemical and/or neurological weapons may well explain the profound debilitating conditions suffered by many of these veterans. Research directed at understanding these difficult conditions is imperative to counteract the overwhelming traumatic nature of a devastating, undiagnosed condition. All of these topics can be shared in a group context that facilitates dialogue and mutual support among group members, or directly in couple, individual, or family therapy. The following clinical vignette illuminates the utility of this method.

JOHNNIE AND JEANNIE :: Johnny, a forty-two-year-old retired Marine veteran of the Vietnam war, and Jeannie, a thrice-married beautician, are a dual-trauma couple. Each partner struggled with severe trauma in childhood and chronic, repetitive trauma in adulthood. Early months of couple therapy focused primarily on self-care, physical safety, reduction in self-mutilation behavior for Jeannie (who had recently attempted suicide), relapse prevention, and strengthening of social networks. The "victim–victimizer–bystander" relationship template was introduced as a concept to consider that influences people who have been traumatized as children or adults. The couple's repetitive emotional abuse and fantasized territorial ownership of the other lessened as their interactions were explicated through this frame.

For example, Johnny frequently referred to Jeannie as an "airhead" or a "dumb floozy," because of her gaps in memory. We discussed the meaning of dissociation and how that may have led to Jeannie's memory gaps. Not only did Johnny's understanding improve, but his awareness of his emotionally abusive language was also heightened. Similarly, Jeannie felt enraged by Johnny's physical recoiling any time she approached to hug him. As Johnny described how the surprise factor elicited in him a state of alarm, the discussion of the PTSD-related startle response helped Jeannie to feel less rejected. Further, Johnny's desire to control all of Jeannie's comings and goings enraged her. The discussion about this issue initiated their talking about Johnny's need to rescue, based on his early, valiant efforts to protect his mother and siblings from his father's alcoholic railings, and his failed rescue efforts as a soldier. As Johnny recalled his failure to spare women and children from being killed, he also remembered the bitter criticism hurled at him by fellow Americans after he came home. Since that time, Johnny had felt compelled to expiate his guilt through demonstrating his competence at helping others.

In fact, Jeannie and Johnny met in the emergency room of a local hospital, while they were waiting to receive treatment for their respective ailments. At that moment, Johnny quickly launched into rescuing Jeannie from her self-harming wrist-cutting behavior. This form of "traumatic bonding" is very common among trauma survivors. With an understanding of the recurrent "victim–victimizer–bystander" dynamic in place, Jeannie became less emotionally reactive toward Johnny's domination whenever he tried to control her. Instead, she asserted her right to make her own decisions about her clothing and food, while reassuring Johnny that he possessed many competencies that could be channeled into projects other than her self-improvement. Throughout the couple therapy, as Johnny and Jeannie learned more about PTSD-related phenomena, each partner developed stronger capacities for empathic understanding.

This clinical vignette demonstrates the usefulness of psychoeducational methods to promote increased knowledge and understanding while fostering empathic connections between the partners. However, the model lacks attention to the range of interactional processes between the partners that either augment or sustain destructive relational problems. Relational models focus more directly on the relational patterns associated with PTSD-related phenomena.

Relational Models

Prevailing clinical practice wisdom now suggests that couple or family therapy is very important for veterans suffering from PTSD, especially given the high rates of domestic violence. A reduction in dysfunction not only helps the veteran, but also may reduce the negative trauma-related effects on the spouse and children. Figley (1989) provided an interesting overview of family therapy with traumatized families that involves a five-phase approach. These include: (1) building commitment, (2) framing the problem, (3) reframing the problem, (4) development of a healing theory, and (5) closure. Grounded in structural, systemic, and narrative therapies, this approach provides education, increases capacities for mutual support, develops relationship and communication skills, and makes peace of the traumatic events. However, full abreaction of traumatic memories is not encouraged nor mentioned. In fact, at a recent presentation at the Annual Psychotherapy Networker Conference in Washington, D.C., Figley (2003) stated that, based on current research findings, earlier methods that promoted full retrieval of traumatic memories are generally contraindicated.

Johnson, Feldman, and Lubin (1995) described a relationship-based approach. They identify "critical interaction" as a "repetitive conflict . . . that is covertly associated with the traumatic memory of the veteran" (p. 404). Interpersonal conflict between the partners evokes a traumatic memory in the veteran without any overt conscious recognition of the parallels between past and current events. The authors conceptualize a process by which the veteran and his or her partner are triangulated with a shadow (i.e., the traumatic memory). Here, the therapy goal is to integrate the family reality with the disturbing, often unconscious, historical event. Clinicians typically follow this sequence: (1) identification of the conflict, (2) evocation of the distressing emotion of shame or anger, (3) guiding the veteran's attention to the earlier wartime event, (4) retelling of the story to his partner and a grieving in his or her presence, (5) linking of the memory to the relationship conflict, (6) expressing comfort by the veteran to the spouse, (7) reviewing the sequence of the interactions, (8) assignment of homework to facilitate conflict resolution at home, and (9) rehearsal of these behaviors in the session.

A strength of this method is the development of mutual empathic understanding. However, steps three and four of the model are challenged because the use of abreaction, along with uncovering of traumatic memories, has been questioned, as this process has facilitated decompensation for some couples. We question the utility of such an approach until all criteria for Phase I tasks have beeen met. The capacity for sound object relations, the ability to withstand intense affect, and cultural congruence are also relevant criteria for methods that involve affective reexperiencing.

An alternative to the "critical interaction" approach is our couple therapy practice model, which starts with the full review of Phase I tasks of safety, stabilization, and the establishment of a context for change. Following the completion of these Phase I tasks, a couple may present a traumatic reenactment. First, each partner is asked to establish his or her own emotional balance, relying on affect regulation and body–mind techniques. Partners might then reflect on past traumatic experiences that are linked to the here-and-now traumatic reenactments. Cognitive reflections on the traumatic memory, as they relate to the here-and-now, do not involve abreaction. The couple continues to speak openly about their perspectives without regression or decompensation. Connections may also be drawn between the current manifestations of the "victim–victimizer–bystander" scenario in day-to-day life and the historical intergenerational transmission of this relational dynamic.

This clinical approach is generally compatible with Figley's (1989, 2003) focus on the titration of emotional intensity while the clinician reflects on links between the trauma narrative and the currrent traumatic reenactment. We now return to the clinical vignette featuring Sam and Anna to demonstrate Phase II couple therapy interventions.

SAM AND ANNA (continued) :: After Sam had completed individual and group therapy to deal with acute PTSD symptomatology, substance abuse, and rage reactions, he was prepared to address relationship issues with Barbara. On one occasion, the couple reported an incident in which Sam was absorbed in working at his computer and did not hear Anna calling to him to help her check out a problematic light fixture. When Sam failed to respond, she stormed into his room and screamed, "How could you be so deaf! All I wanted was for you to come help me with the ladder in the dining room." Sam felt his blood rushing to his face and his hands trembling. Rage started to overwhelm him. Suddenly, he yelled a string of profanities at Anna, who called a time-out as she retreated into another room until both of them calmed their tempers.

In the couple therapy session, I asked if each partner was able to talk about the situation calmly. They concurred and proceeded to talk about what had been triggered in Sam at that moment. I asked, "What historical ghost has affected you?" Sam thought for a few minutes and recalled that he hated being called deaf! He remembered standing on the deck of the aircraft carrier. Unable to hear anything above the roar of the fighter planes, he failed to hear a command from his supervising officer. Consequently, he gave an incorrect directive, which resulted in the crash landing of a jet returning to the sanctuary of the vessel. The pilot broke his left arm and leg, but otherwise recovered full capacity. Sam was assured that such accidents occur and that alleged "friendly fire" events should be taken in stride. Nevertheless, he was struck with shame and immobilizing guilt that he had not heard his supervisor's command.

As the couple recognized the connections between their here-and-now rage responses and the "victim–victimizer–bystander" scenario, they were able to make sense of what had seemed an inexplicable rage reaction. Sam expressed having felt victimized by Anna's railings, yet he retaliated with an aggressive victimizing stance. A sense of powerlessness had driven Anna to assert her need for help, and her frustration at being ignored had stirred anger and a denigrating victimizing stance. This couple not only drew "victim–victimizer–bystander" links from their past histories to their day-to-day dynamics, but also traced intergenerational patterns of the scenario as well. Interestingly, they wondered if they were also enacting a historical, intergenerational legacy of trauma and warfare, considering the centuries of interethnic conflict between Turks and Armenians. Anna and Sam served as living memorials, paying tribute to those irreconcilable ideological, ethnic conflicts.

In summary, this vignette captures the tasks of Phase II couple therapy. Goals were to reflect on the trauma narrative in an effort to increase empathic understanding of the pervasive "victim–victimizer–bystander" scenario, while at the same time reducing the ferocity of its presence. Our additional reflection on the intergenerational interethnic conflict provides a socio-cultural context to the couple's "domestic war zone."

As we anticipate the return of thousands of servicemen and -women from the current war in Iraq, clinicians should be alert to the pressing need for additional psychotherapeutic and psychoeducational services. Ironically, as I complete this chapter about military couples, voices in the background from a CNN special are reporting the experiences of an unnamed photojournalist. He is describing the aftermath of a suicide bombing in a neighborhood of Baghdad. A mentor had advised him that he should never look into the eyes of a dead person while photographing the body, as the face would then haunt him for life. Once, in a desperate effort to avoid the eyes of a corpse, the photojournalist was struck instead by the tragedy of seeing a dead baby in the road. He imagined who had been holding the baby just hours before. He then proceeded to wonder about the corpse of a young man. Whose son was he? Who was searching for him at that moment? In spite of wise counsel from his colleague, this photojournalist may well join the ranks of veterans who desperately need assistance in transforming their visceral wartime experiences into palatable memories that do not burden him, his family, or successive generations to come.

Gay/Lesbian/Bisexual/Transgendered Couples and Families

This chapter complements and elaborates theory and practice issues related to dual- or single-trauma clients who identify as gay, lesbian, bisexual, or transgendered briefly mentioned in previous chapters. As noted in Chapters 8–10 on assessment and treatment, GLBT couples face a range of institutional and societal factors that impede a smooth passage to coupling. We use the term GLBT to encompass gay, lesbian, bisexual, transgendered, and transsexual clients. Reference to specific "subpopulations" of the larger group will be noted, as appropriate. This chapter addresses the heterosexist attitudes, homophobic responses, gender socialization, internalization of shame, fear of and exposure to interpersonal violence, and social policy legislation that influence the partnering process for these couples. In addition, we demonstrate the interface of childhood trauma histories with the coupling process. Further discussion addresses the clinical implications in dealing with issues of domestic violence, sexuality, and parenting issues, including fertility and impregnation.

It is important for us as clinicians to recognize potential biases in clinical practice with GLBT couples. Basham (1998) discusses the utility of Hare-Mustin's (1989) conceptualization of alpha–beta bias when working with lesbian couples. She says that exaggerating differences between homosexuals and heterosexuals, an alpha bias, may lead clinicians to view GLBT individuals as pathological. Supported by this biased stance, benign but misguided clinicians valorize difference only to perpetuate stereotypes and myths. Alternatively, a beta bias in which a clinician ignores differences between heterosexuals and homosexuals, or differences within the GLBT community, may lead to an unfortunate generic understanding of issues that fails to reflect the unique experiences of individuals. For example, the lesbian client who is a survivor of childhood sexual abuse should not categorically be viewed as traumatized. Rather, the specific resilience of the survivor, the particular characteristics of her family of origin, and the unique features of her inner world need to be examined fully and understood. An interesting quantitative research project explored the psychological adaptation for 115 women differing in sexual abuse history and sexual orientation. Findings that challenged usually stereotypic notions revealed that heterosexual women with abuse histories had higher levels of depression than did lesbians with abuse histories as determined using the same measure (Griffith, Myers, Cusick, & Tankersley, 1997). The authors speculated that the lesbian participants had engaged in more active self-reflection and psychotherapy to address identity issues, which perhaps provides an explanation for their less dysphoric adaptations.

Historically, biases and stereotypes about GLBT individuals have existed previously in the mental health profession. However, within the past several decades, mental health professionals have evolved their understanding of GLBT individuals. Once considered a psychiatric disorder, the American Psychiatric Association declassified homosexuality as a mental disorder in 1973. The organization, however, replaced the original classification with a category termed ego dystonic homosexuality. This label also engendered a great deal of controversy within the mental health field (Krajeski, 1996, p. 25). Advocacy efforts from gay and lesbian psychiatrists and other allied mental health professionals prompted the eventual removal of homosexuality from the Third Revised Edition of the *Diagnostic and Statistical Manual of the American Psychiatric Association* (1987). Although the mental health field has made some changes, a great deal of negative societal influences still affect GLBT couples. In spite of harsh societal attitudes, Green, Bettinger, and Zacks (1996) found, in a study comparing self-reported levels of satisfaction among heterosexual, lesbian, and gay couples, that "Lesbian couples are exceptionally close and more satisfied with their relationships than gay male and heterosexual couples" (p. 204). Similarly, these authors found that gay male couples are more cohesive than heterosexual couples. This finding underscores the strengths and resilience of many GLBT couples. For others, however, a sense of personal shame is internalized and exacerbated by pejorative societal attitudes concerning sexual orientation. We now turn to a discussion of these institutional/societal factors.

:: INSTITUTIONAL/SOCIETAL FACTORS

Heterosexism/Homophobia

Heterosexism is viewed as the belief system that presumes that intimate relationships between men and women are the norm. This system denigrates, denies, and stigmatizes any nonheterosexual behavior, identity, relationship, or community (Davies, 1996; Drescher, 2001; Glazer, 2001; Herek, 1990, 1996; Kitzinger & Coyle, 2002). For example, heterosexism reinforces the myth that "normal" sexual activity is genital in nature and, more specifically, is "second-best" if the sexual activity is devoid of a phallus (Burch, 1997). Basham (1998) warns that theoretical models often contain heterosexist biases. As a result, we contend that it is imperative for clinicians to deconstruct theoretical and practice models critically to clarify the negative influences of heterosexist values.

Homophobia, the hatred or fear of GLBT individuals, couples, families, or communities, arises from heterosexist attitudes. Embedded in cultural practices that privilege men in families and society, homophobia is present within individuals and institutions. While patriarchal values imbue men with power, any personal or social practice that challenges the dominance of "traditional" (read heterosexual) family structure is feared and loathed (Laird, 1993; Luepnitz, 1988). Any couple, then, that challenges the dominant discourse may be scorned and stigmatized. Gay men are often the subjects of disdain as heterosexists perceive that gay men "opt out" of patriarchy and abdicate the privilege and power ascribed to men (Davies, 1996). All GLBT individuals are subject to the impact of homophobia and few escape the script that contributes to internalized homophobia as well (Burch, 1997; Davies, 1996; Herek, 1996; O'Dell, 2000). We argue that GLBT individuals are subject to ongoing incidences that are experienced as a form of type III trauma. Here, we borrow from Pouissant and Alexander's (2000) concept, which explains how ongoing—perhaps daily—assaults of marginalization and oppression may be experienced as traumatic. The intersection between the legacies of childhood trauma and the impact of heterosexism and homophobia stirs intense conflict, as the following vignette demonstrates.

KIRK AND WAYNE :: Kirk grew up in a liberal middle-class family in which he and his siblings were encouraged to be true to their interests and personalities. While Kirk's parents expressed some disappointment when he disclosed that he was gay (at age seventeen), Kirk reported that his family was quite accepting of him and had been supportive of his long-term relationship with Wayne. Wayne came from a troubled family in which he was brutally abused by his father. He grew up in a small town in eastern Canada, where his working-class family lived in impoverished circumstances. Wayne left the small town at his first opportunity and followed a beloved older sister to Toronto who helped him find employment. Kirk and Wayne met while each was working in Toronto. They moved to London, Ontario, so that Wayne could pursue a part-time college program in child and youth work.

The couple had become embroiled in a power struggle related to Kirk's insistence that Wayne disclose his sexual orientation to his family of origin. Wayne was unable to convince Kirk that he did not see any particular need to make this disclosure, especially not to his father. Wayne had made a decision to separate himself emotionally and geographically from his family. He was comfortable with his own sexual orientation, in spite of not being out to his family. Kirk was determined to persuade Wayne to come out to his family. Ultimately, he accused him of being disloyal to himself and to the couple relationship. Kirk escalated his demands and insisted that Wayne comply with his wish. He threatened that he could not live in a partnership with someone who was not out to everyone in his family.

Although Kirk had presented his coming-out process as a relatively easy transition, I had previously detected some ambivalence pointing to a somewhat troubled process, punctuated by a number of painful experiences with his own father. It became clear that Kirk's insistence that Wayne "out" himself to his family was Kirk's projection of his own coming-out process. He had not healed from his father's negative reaction to his sexual orientation. Even so, Kirk continued to idealize the manner in which he and his family had dealt with the process. During the therapy, Kirk was able to see that his projection to Wayne of his own wish to reach resolution with his father as a manifestation of his own internalized homophobia. He was still fearful of experiencing possible hurt from his father's reaction, as Kirk and his father had settled into a collusive, polite but superficial relationship. As Kirk was able to process issues with his father, discussing their respective homophobic feelings, he became less demanding toward Wayne. It appeared that Wayne's decision to avoid his still abusive family remained an adaptive decision for him.

Impact of Social Policies

GLBT individuals meet discrimination in numerous public arenas in which their sexual orientation intersects with legal systems, government agency systems, and the military, to name a few. A brief overview of these pertinent issues is offered so as to contextualize couple therapy practices with this population. Sodomy laws, for example, were often instituted to prevent any nonmarital or nonprocreative sexual activity (Purcell & Hicks, 1996). To this day, laws concerning sodomy vary and for the most part, the disguised intent is often to criminalize homosexual sodomy practices, as opposed to heterosexual sodomy activity (Rivera, 1991). However, many GLBT activists welcomed the recent U.S. Supreme Court ruling, with a count of six to three (*Lawrence and Garner vs. the State of Texas*), declaring sodomy laws as unconstitutional throughout the United States (June 26, 2003) (www.sodomylaws.org/lawrence/lawrence.htm).

The legal recognition of same-sex relationships varies greatly within the United States. The insistence of some GLBT couples to have their partnerships formally recognized by the larger society has instigated controversy and debate among church officials and public representatives. In a landmark ruling in November 2003, the Massachusetts Supreme Judicial Court ruled that the ban on gay marriage was unconstitutional. The Massachusetts state legislature was given six months to rewrite the state's marriage laws for the benefit of gay couples. Although highly celebrated by GLBT individuals and activists as a step that paves the way for lesbian and gay couples in Massachusetts to marry, there has been criticism and immediate efforts to overturn the ruling by other legislators and politicians across the United States (www.cnn.com/2003/LAW/11/18/samesex.marriage.ruling). Other regions of the world are more accepting of same-sex marriage; since the early 1990s, the countries of Scandinavia have expanded their definitions of marriage to include same-sex couples (Purcell & Hicks, 1996), and in 2003 the Canadian Parliament formally legalized same-sex marriages in Canada (www.globeandmail.com/servlet/story/RTGAM.20030612). Contemporary legal decisions related to adoption, family visitation rights, surrogacy, and alternative insemination are also of great interest to GLBT couples (Buell, 2001).

Although policies within the military and military-related organizations have ostensibly created opportunities for GLBT individuals to advance and succeed, contemporary practices are replete with reports of harassment, discrimination, and discharges of gay and lesbian personnel (Gallagher, 1994). As U.S. soldiers return from the war in Iraq, partners and families of gay and lesbian soldiers have reported discrimination in their access to medical decision-making as well as visiting their loved ones in medical facilities. Sadly, many gay and lesbian partners of active-duty soldiers killed in combat have been denied the usual ceremonial honors granted to their heterosexual colleagues.

The compelling directive "Don't ask–Don't tell," promoted by the commander-in-chief of the armed services, persuades many gay and lesbian military to stifle openness or self-disclosure that could potentially threaten one's job. For example, in the couple therapy with a lesbian couple, Paula and Colette, previously introduced in Chapter 4 on family theories, Paula continually expressed fear about losing her maximum-security clearance if her sexual orientation was revealed. She lived every day under the mantle of institutional homophobia and heterosexism, rendering her totally silent about her relationship life in her workplace. As this adaptation of secrecy and concealment crept into her personal life, both she and Colette started isolating themselves from family and friends as well. Regrettably, this self-imposed sequestered life called forth the earlier "historical ghosts" from Colette's traumatic childhood, when her sexually abusive stepfather insisted that she and her siblings remain isolated at home.

Immigration and naturalization policies in the United States also discriminate against GLBT couples, as illustrated in the following vignette.

STEPHEN AND MICHAEL :: Stephen and Michael contacted me when the couple had reached a stalemate pertaining to indecision about the viability of reinstituting a long-distance living arrangement. Each was accomplished in his profession and upwardly mobile in terms of a career path. At the time of the referral, the couple lived in Ontario and Michael had been offered an excellent position in Chicago, Illinois, after an American headhunter had pursued him to ascertain his interest in moving to a larger American firm. Because the couple had previously agreed that they would not live separately again, this offer confounded their decision. While Michael was considering the position, he inquired as to what Stephen's immigration status would be in the United States. He was disappointed to learn that Stephen would need to emigrate to the United States, as a single individual. As a gay man, he would not be considered Michael's partner, and thus his immigration status could not be facilitated by Michael's move. In addition to the couple struggling with the symbolic meaning of this potential move, each was aware of the discriminatory immigration policy that precluded an easier transition for them, as a gay couple, to the United States.

Within the framework of these institutional factors, the remainder of the chapter examines the clinical implications with traumatized GLBT couples in the areas of interpersonal violence, sexuality, and fertility/parenting issues.

:: INTERFACE OF TRAUMA AND GLBT COUPLES:
CLINICAL IMPLICATIONS

Interpersonal Violence

Many GLBT individuals are subject to hate crimes arising primarily from homophobic responses, a harsh reality that has been documented in reports of continuing violence and discrimination practices against gay and lesbian youth in U.S. schools (Human Rights Watch, 2001). As enactments of legacies of childhood trauma are witnessed in couple therapy regularly, it is important for the couple therapist to assess directly a couple's potential for domestic violence. Misguided stereotypes that preclude full assessment contribute to the silencing of partners who are being abused in their partnerships (Descamps, Rothblum, Bradford, & Ryan, 2000; Klinger & Stein, 1996; Morrow & Hawxhurst, 1989; Tully, 2001; Walsh, 1996). Therefore, the clinician and the couple need to challenge stereotypes that suggest that women are not violent, that gay men do not "fight," or that both partners in a GLBT couple have equal power in their relationship (Tully, 2001, p. 93).

Lesbian couples, in particular, may not report issues of violence, as the threat of dissolution of the relationship has major implications for each partner's continued contact with support systems. As many lesbian couples have limited social support systems, an admission of violence in the relationship may indeed have a ripple effect in the social support network of the couple. Issues of safety dominate in these instances and couple therapy is actually contraindicated for physically volatile couples (Klinger & Stein, 1996; Walsh, 1996). Instead, advocacy efforts involving individual and/or group interventions are often indicated for the battered partner; while individual or group psychotherapy interventions are indicated for the perpetrator.

If the active violence has dissipated and the couple is willing and safe to engage in couple treatment, Phase I couple therapy tasks become central to the treatment process. Criteria for engagement in a couple therapy format include the full recognition of safety, structure, and certainty that each partner has achieved an effective level of affect regulation. Trauma-related symptoms that intersect with previous interpersonal violence experiences need to be understood cognitively as manifestations of complex posttraumatic stress adaptations.

The following vignette demonstrates the interface of past trauma with current adaptations.

JANE AND CARLITA :: Jane, a thirty-seven-year-old Irish-American teacher, and Carlita, a thirty-four-year-old Latina occupational therapist, sought couple therapy to discuss their different opinions about parenting their three-year-old adoptive twin girls. In their twelve-year partnership, both partners had expressed strong desires to have children yet rarely discussed how each woman might actually parent in real life. Since the adoption of their Guatemalan twins, at the age of four months, Jane and Carlita have argued regularly about what constitutes "good-enough parenting." Jane complained bitterly that Carlita "zoned out," failing to respond to the toddlers' cries. As Jane lambasted Carlita in a harsh, victimizing voice, Carlita retreated further, quietly disappearing into distant recesses of the house. As both partners reflected on their immediate crisis, Carlita reflected on her own childhood and how she learned about parenting from her sexually abusive father and kind but tentative mother. As a child, Carlita's usual mode of coping was physical retreat from the house and dissociation. As she recognized that her "historical ghosts" inhabited her current family home, Carlita realized that Jane's shrieking activated, or triggered, these early traumatic memories and her subsequent protective coping. Only when Jane and Carlita agreed to a "no-violence" contract, that is, no aggressive physical touching, destruction of property, or intimidation, could they move along to productively address their models of nonabusive co-parenting.

Issues of Sexuality

Sexual practices of GLBT couples have often been critiqued through theory and practice models that are formulated with heterosexist assumptions (Burch, 1997). Frye (1990) acknowledges that the predominant view of sexual activity is genital/phallic in nature, and thus sexual practices among GLBT couples, from a heterosexist viewpoint, are "second-best" or pathological. This context influences the sexual adaptation of survivors of childhood trauma who identify as gay, lesbian, bisexual, or transgendered. As these couples present in therapy, they have often internalized the popular misconception that childhood sexual abuse leads to a homosexual sexual identity (Cvetkovich, 2003). A thorough discussion that explores how childhood sexual abuse experiences interface with the clients' perceptions of their sexual orientation is indicated at the outset of couple therapy. Here, Phase I couple therapy interventions that focus on safety and stabilization might include psychoeducation about these myths. As discussed in the chapters focused on treatment issues, survivors of childhood trauma experience a range of responses to sexuality, including physiological and psychological repercussions of traumatic events. For many lesbian couples, traumatic experiences in which they were sexually or physically violated may inhibit a full range of sexual expression between the partners. As noted earlier in this text, the body may keep a corporal record of the person's trauma history.

SALLY AND DEIRDRE :: Sally, a thirty-five-year-old artist often reported to her lesbian partner of ten years, Deirdre, age thirty-six, that whenever she was touched sensually on her arms or near her groin area, she felt "electrical sensation running along the surface of her skin." She described feeling "tingling, painful sensations that would crawl up and down my skin," and she would say, "I had no control over my body!" As Sally reflected on her history of severe sexual abuse inflicted by her stepfather from ages five to ten, she remembered the many times that he pinned her arms down on the bed and penetrated her with vaginal intercourse. Most sexual overtures from her partner, Deirdre, rekindled these "historical ghosts" of her stepfather's violation. Sally's instantaneous physiological response signaled danger, a state of alert, and a physical boundary. In couple therapy, Sally and Deirdre discussed ways that they could neutralize these highly sensitive areas of Sally's body. First, they decided to enjoy bathing together where they could use healing oils to massage Sally's skin, especially on her arms and her groin area. The soothing effects of the warm water and oils provided a sensorimotor calming for Sally before any sexual activity was initiated. They also decided to redecorate their bedroom with brighter lights and vivid colors, to differentiate the environment from Sally's historical memories of a dark, dreary, and frightening child-hood bedroom.

Survivors of childhood trauma may have difficulty in initiating any sexual activity that they perceive as aggressive and dominant. The complementarity of dominant and submissive roles in sexual activity may contribute to a reenactment of an internalized "victim–victimizer–bystander" dynamic fueled by feelings of aggression or passive helplessness. Kerewsky and Miller (1996) recognize the tendency for survivors to project feelings that characterize their partners as "dangerous, violating, or repulsive" (p. 302). To ward off these negative feelings, many trauma survivors dissociate as a way to protect themselves from facing such horror. Such detachment and numbing often interfere with sexual arousal and sexual responsiveness. Once again, couples need to discuss ways to address dissociation in the context of their sexuality. Methods for "staying present" during sexual activity must be agreed on. For example, Sally and Deirdre found that talking during lovemaking tempered Sally's dissociation, as she was able to experience herself as an active, engaged, and *willing* participant.

The intersection of trauma with the sexual practices of gay male couples also needs to be explored during assessment. It is important to determine if either one or both partners have a damaged sense of sexual self, which may contribute to a presumption of ineffectiveness as a satisfying long-term sexual partner. Coleman and Simon Rosser (1996), Greenan and Tunnell (2003), and Johnson and Keren (1996) assert that gay male couples often make decisions to be nonmonogamous in terms of their sexual behavior. Most couples expect emotional fidelity but find "rules" that determine the practice of recreational or cruising sexual activity with other men, while maintaining their partnership. Although controversial, we wonder if, at times, the choice to be nonmonogamous in the sexual relationship may be a reenactment of previous trauma history and/or a defensive posture warding off anxiety or depressive symptoms.

Issues of Fertility/Parenting

The decision to parent, as a GLBT couple, can be a difficult and joyful decision. These couples often need to combat internalized heterosexist attitudes suggesting that children should ideally be reared in a heterosexual, nuclear family comprised of a biological mother and a biological father. Long-held biases about the supremacy of such family systems are difficult to resist for the lesbian couple or gay male couple (Crespi, 2001). When GLBT couples decide to parent, they face difficult decisions about how they will become parents. They also encounter many institutional obstacles and homophobic attitudes along the path in dealing with adoption, medical, and/or legal services. Although adoption used to be one of the only available options for GLBT couples, changes in reproductive medicine now afford other options (Buell, 2001).

For survivors of childhood sexual or physical abuse, the decision to attempt impregnation through alternative insemination may force the woman into a psychologically and physically compromised position. Survivors of childhood trauma may have internalized a sense of bodily self in which they feel they are "damaged goods." Invasive medical procedures that are necessary to assess the viability and maintenance of conception may indeed be unconsciously experienced as a further assault on the prospective mother's bodily integrity. Often, the absence of control over the medicalized procedures can trigger feelings of helplessness and powerlessness associated with childhood abuses.

In addition, the disappointment and frustration experienced if a pregnancy does not occur further contributes to the questioning of the survivor's ability to be proactive or procreative in her world. The loss of potential mothering also frequently rekindles the losses of childhood associated with childhood trauma. As the prospective co-mothers grieve the many losses associated with their hoped for child and parenting, they also actively grieve the losses of their innocence in childhood. The following clinical vignette illuminates these struggles.

EMILY AND HOLLY :: Emily, age thirty-nine, and Holly, age forty-four, are a professional lesbian couple who, during the past three years of their fourteen-year partnership, decided to plan a family. After much deliberation about alternative insemination versus adoption, they decided that Emily would try to get pregnant, primarily as she was the younger partner, and presumably more likely to get pregnant. After three miscarriages, Emily and Holly entered couple therapy to address their profound sense of loss and helplessness. What emerged in talking about their wishes and dreams regarding parenting were the models they learned about parenting. As Emily talked about the destructive effects of the sexual abuse suffered from her stepfather, she insisted that she would never repeat this in her adult life. What emerged were her fantasies that pregnancy, and impregnation in particular, was associated with a symbolic representation of the presence of an unwanted intruder—her stepfather. She wondered if her needs to eject these memories may have influenced her difficulties with getting pregnant and holding her pregnancies. Whether this causality existed or not, Emily went on to conceive a baby girl delivered eight months later. This newborn was welcomed heartily into the family as special in her own right without unwanted tainted associations with her abusive step-grandfather.

In summary, the issues involving parenting and fertility are strongly influenced by the toxic effects of homophobia and heterosexism. To offset these insidious undermining influences, GLBT couples that have experienced childhood trauma have to work additionally hard to create supportive family environments and develop new nonabusive parenting approaches. For those lesbian couples who face the physical and psychological difficulties involved in alternative insemination, the joy of conception and birth may often be accompanied by difficult events leading up to the birth. However, many couples report that their successes in navigating these obstacles provided fortification and a sense of unity in approaching their co-parenting.

:: SUMMARY

In conclusion, the resilience and steadfast determination of many lesbian, gay, bisexual, and transgendered couples who have suffered childhood trauma must be acknowledged clearly. Whether these couples now cope with symptomatology of complex posttraumatic syndrome or have managed to adapt to their childhood abuses in alternate ways, they all face the additional burdens of societally imposed discrimination and bigotry. The unrelenting, continuous nature of these daily assaults challenges a basic sense of meaning and place in the world that must be negotiated regularly. Given the destructive effects of these persistently traumatic psychological injuries, the triumphs demonstrated by the couples featured in this chapter are all the more impressive. Clearly, these couples rely on their noteworthy fortitude and perseverance to create more fulfilling lives, frequently with the sustaining support of their extended community networks.

Immigrant and Refugee Couples and Families

This chapter summarizes the experiences of refugee and immigrant families who seek assistance from health care providers as they adapt to living circumstances in a new environment. Clearly, refugees who have experienced some form of torture or observed war atrocities in their homelands will have different needs from those families who have voluntarily emigrated to a new country. However, some similarities between these two groups do exist. This chapter briefly addresses issues that immigrants face in their relocation. The bulk of the chapter discusses the couple and family treatment of refugees who have experienced trauma. Of course, there are many cultural differences among immigrant and refugee populations, and a culturally responsive clinical social worker will discern these differences and will practice accordingly. In addition, although some generalizations may be made, the reader is advised to question those theories that espouse a universal understanding of the experiences of immigrants or refugees.

This chapter starts with a brief description of the immigration experience, including the specific aspects of that experience that may precipitate the need for mental health services. Second, aspects of refugee experiences are described, including the impact of torture on survivors and the impact of immigrant and refugee status on an individual's identity. Third, clinical implications for couples and families are discussed. Fourth, as the clinical needs of these couples and families demonstrate the efficacy of our phase-oriented model of intervention, clinical examples illustrate the theoretical aspects of the treatment model. The chapter concludes with a discussion of specific clinician responses in working with these client groups.

However, before proceeding, the reader should refer to Tables 14.1 and 14.2 to gain some perspective of the demographic features of immigrant and refugee populations in Canada and the United States.

Tables 14.3 and 14.4 show current statistics for refugees. The 1951 convention relating to the status of refugees defines a refugee as a person who, "owing to a well-founded fear of being persecuted for reasons of race, religion, nationality, membership of a particular social group, or political opinion, is outside the country of his nationality, and is unable to or, owing to such fear, is unwilling to avail himself of the protection of that country" (www .unhcr.ch/cgi-bin/texis/vtx/basics). The United Nations High Commissioner for Refugees reports 19,783,100 individuals worldwide who fit this description. Clearly, the global refugee population is a multiracial, multicultural group of individuals, couples, and families.

TABLE 14.1 :: Immigration by Source Area to Canada (1999–2001)

Region	1999	2000	2001
Africa and Middle East	33,490	40,815	48,078
Asia and Pacific	96,437	120,539	132,711
South and Central America	15,221	16,944	20,219
United States	5,528	5,814	5,894
Europe and the United Kingdom	38,390	42,885	43,204
Not stated	316	316	330
Total immigrants	189,922	227,313	250,346

SOURCE: Facts and Figures 2001, Immigration Overview, Citizenship and Immigration Canada. Retrieved May 1, 2003, from http://www.cic.gc.ca.

TABLE 14.2 :: Immigration by Source Area to the United States (1999–2001)

Region	1999	2000	2001
Africa	36,700	44,731	53,948
Asia	199,411	265,4000	349,776
Central America	43,216	66,443	75,914
South America	41,585	56,074	68,888
North America (includes Mexico)	271,365	344,805	407,888
Europe	92,672	132,480	175,371
Unknown or unstated	1,159	1,181	2,334
Total immigration	646,568	849,807	1,064,318

SOURCE: The United States Bureau of Citizen and Immigration Services. Retrieved March 10, 2003, from www.immigration .gov/graphics/aboutus/statistics.

TABLE 14.3 ∷ Refugees by Source Area Now Living in Canada

Region	1999	2000	2001
Africa/Middle East	8,487	10,288	9,585
Asia/Pacific	7,250	9,297	9,845
South/Central America	1,408	2,218	2,644
Europe/United Kingdom	7,181	8,110	5,658
Unknown/unstated	67	159	167
Total	24,393	30,072	27,899

SOURCE: Facts and Figures 2001, Immigration Overview, Citizenship and Immigration Canada. Retrieved May 1, 2003, from http://www.cic.gc.ca.

TABLE 14.4 ∷ Refugees by Source Area Now Living in the United States

Region	1999	2000	2001
East Asia	10,204	4,561	3,725
Near East	4,076	10,079	12,086
Europe/USSR	55,576	37,093	30,664
Africa	13,088	17,549	18,979
Latin America	2,110	3,233	2,972
Total	95,006	72,515	69,426

SOURCE: United States Committee for Refugees. Retrieved May 1, 2003, from www.refugees.org/world/articles/nationality_rro1_12.cf.

∷ THE IMMIGRANT EXPERIENCE

The central issue for immigrants is loss, which really means a range of losses, and the family's adaptation to the experience of loss (Akhtar, 1999; Alvarez, 1995; Falicov, 2003; Lee, 1997; Mirkin, 1998; Mock, 1998). Most individuals experience ambivalent feelings about leaving their homeland. Although the migration holds some promise for a new beginning, it also holds difficulty in leaving behind of family and friends, language, familiar customs, and other components of the cultural heritage. Indeed, many leave behind their professional or occupational status, and retraining is often necessary in the new country. Falicov says, "Although beloved people and places are left behind, they remain keenly present in the psyche of the immigrant; at the same time, homesickness and the multiple stresses of adaptation may leave some family members emotionally unavailable to support and encourage others" (p. 283).

Although some immigrants will have a relative or two living in the adopted country, many must face losing the support of their extended families. Lee (1997) notes that the "new isolated family unit is, for the first time, responsible for making and maintaining its own set of rules and adjusting to a new environment with its strange demands" (p. 18). For many Asian-American families, the loss of extended families challenges the central cultural belief that family involvement is a central factor in identity development, personal security, and agency. Further stressors may be felt as family roles become confused. For example, English-speaking children of immigrant families often become the cultural brokers for their family systems. This upsets the power dynamic of the family, eroding some of the importance of the elderly who, traditionally, have the most influence in the family system (Falicov, 2003; Lee, 1997; McGoldrick, 1982). Power related to gender may also shift as immigrant women often experience an increased status in the host country while men's power is diminished or challenged in Western culture (Agger & Jensen, 1989). Family members may differ as to the need for acculturation in the new country, while intergenerational conflicts may destabilize the family unit (Falicov, 2003; Lee, 1997; Mirkin, 1998).

Immigrant families oscillate continually between maintaining loyalty to past experiences in their homeland and bowing to the necessity to integrate into their new chosen homes. The dual vision of continuity/change is difficult to hold (Falicov, 2003), and families need to develop some internal patterns that honor their old traditions while integrating traditions from the new country. It is an unfortunate reality that many immigrants experience forms of racism and discrimination in their new environment (Falicov, 2003; Mirkin, 1998). Again, family members rely on each other to weather the ongoing assaults that are experienced in the postmigration phase of adaptation.

:: THE REFUGEE EXPERIENCE

Refugee couples and families also experience the factors noted in the immigrant experience. However, there is a fundamental difference between the two populations. Usually, immigrants have chosen consciously to leave their homelands; refugees have more often been pushed out of their homelands and they leave to escape some form of oppression or persecution (Akhtar, 1999; Mock, 1998). Mock says, "Refugee families are involuntarily displaced, often fleeing under conditions over which they have minimal or no control, and often moving from one country to another" (p. 348). Daniel and Knudsen (1995) note that the sociopolitical circumstances that necessitate fleeing from one's homeland threaten one's way of being in the world as well as cause one to see the world differently.

As clinicians, we must face the unfortunate reality that many refugees have experienced some form of torture or have witnessed torture in their country of origin. Kira (2002) notes, "Torture is a multilateral cumulative type III trauma that can traumatize the body, the autonomy and identity of the individual, his/her self-actualization enterprises, and his sense of safety and survival" (p. 23). (While Kira refers to this trauma as type III, we use type III trauma to denote ongoing assaults to marginalized populations as described by Pouissant and Alexander [2000].) In addition, surviving torture influences one's beliefs and systems of meaning, attachment patterns, and sense of connection. Elsass (1997) and Turner (1993) identify four common themes that are often observed as the psychological sequelae of the experience. Highlighting the abnormality of the torture rather than pathologizing the individual, the survivor of torture experiences: (1) incomplete emotional processing (akin to posttraumatic stress disorder [PTSD]), (2) somatic symptoms, (3) depressive reactions, and (4) the existential dilemma. Kanninen, Punamaki, and Qouta (2002) make some distinctions between the symptoms of torture survivors and survivors of other forms of trauma. They note, "Torture and ill-treatment formed a risk for intrusive, and acute trauma for avoidance symptoms" (p. 251).

:: CLINICAL IMPLICATIONS FOR COUPLES
AND FAMILIES

At the outset, some cautionary notes are indicated when working with immigrant/refugee populations. When clients from these populations request mental health services, many clinicians precipitously assess that the presenting symptom(s) result from the immigrant/refugee status of the client. While this should be considered part of the assessment, it is important to look for specific and unique factors in each instance. The presenting concerns may be related to other factors, such as biological or interpersonal factors, in addition to the trauma-related histories (Papadopoulos, 2001).

Clinicians and agencies need to be mindful that traditional psycho-therapy may not be desired by or indicated for refugees (Sveaass & Reichelt, 2001). Especially at the outset, many are not able to work on psychological issues unless there is some attention paid to daily stressors. Issues of resources, options, employment, and the establishment of social networks are often the vital work of the clinician/helper (Sveaass & Reichelt, 2001). Kira (2002) suggests that cultural differences may determine the most effective interventions. Citing Morris and Silove (1992) and Gonsalves (1990), Kira says, "Examples of this include South Americans patients who were receptive to psycho-therapeutic approaches that focus on detailed recollection of past trauma, while Indochinese patients responded to a broader-base rehabilitation approach that could include psychotropic medication, supportive psychotherapy and assistance in meeting practical needs" (p. 27).

It is important to underscore that the trust level of refugees toward social service or mental health agencies may be minimal, if it exists at all. If caseworkers present highly systematized, rule-bound methods of assessment and intervention, refugees might further experience a social order filled with conditions that are confining and rigid. Discussing the issue of trust in social orders, Daniel and Knudsen (1995) note, "Refugees imagine, either independently or in reaction to the ones presented by caseworkers, social orders of their past in equally frozen and unreal terms" (p. 4). They also say, "A refugee must be free to choose to provide information and must feel assured that the information provided will not be given a meaning that could be used against him or her" (p. 4).

Reichelt and Sveaass (1994) note that some individuals may value authority and advice from the clinician while others may value self-reflection as a means to healing past violations. Zur (1996) notes clearly that "Real, meaningful understanding of the effects of trauma needs to include a person's own interpretations of the layers of context involved" (p. 305). Using the term experience-near to describe culturally specific and sensitive responses to trauma, Zur notes that many Western mental health professionals have tended to look for universalistic (experience-distant) responses to trauma so as to provide adequate treatment for increasing numbers of refugees who leave war-torn countries.

While the process of reconstructing meaning systems after traumatic experiences is highly culturally determined, Boehnlein and Kinzie (1996) suggest that the search for meaning itself and dealing with some form of grief are universal experiences for all groups of people who have experienced trauma. That said, a full disclosure of details of the trauma or an uncovering of memories is often contraindicated. Kira (2002) notes, "Premature disclosure may lead to serious and possibly uncontrollable distress" (p. 27). Indeed, with the refugee who has been tortured, there is a clear potential of a reenactment of the "victim–victimizer–bystander" dynamic (Herman, 1992; Miller, 1994). In these instances, the three different roles are enacted by the victim/survivor, the military/torturer, and the therapist/human rights activist. The therapist, as bystander–observer, has a responsibility to ensure appropriate treatment without retraumatizing the refugee. For example, if the clinician pushes for a retelling of the torture experience, the survivor may experience this as an injunction that must be followed. Thus, the survivor is, once again, robbed of his or her sense of agency. Elsass (1997) comments, "The torture survivor may experience that this more or less unspoken requirement—to live through his trauma story and its sufferings—is similar to the situation in which he was forced by the torturer to undergo the worst humiliation and devastation" (p. 21). Reenactments of the trauma scenario are likely in cases in which the torture survivor numbs himself when he is exposed to circumstances provoking anger or physical aggression. A brief clinical vignette illuminates this triggered rage-response in an encounter in couple therapy with an intercultural couple.

CHARIHN AND JOHN :: Charihn, a twenty-eight-year-old immigrant from Iran, and John, her husband of five years, a second-generation Czech American, sought couple therapy when both expressed animosities and sexual dissatisfaction. Charihn had also reneged on a previously agreed-on plan to begin a family. She had lived in the United States for eight years, arriving from her war-torn country at age twenty with work skills as an interpreter.

Because this single-trauma couple needed to meet during an evening hour, and because the building where my office was located was locked after hours to ensure physical safety, I typically met them at the front door of the building shortly before the time of the appointment, and then escorted them to my third-floor office. On one occasion, when I arrived in the lobby to greet this couple five minutes before our appointed meeting time, Charihn expressed frustration about waiting, and wondered why I worked in such an "unsafe" building. After providing explanations about the ordinariness of this procedure in the midst of a relatively safe commercial urban environment, she proceeded to talk about how unsafe it felt living in the United States, compared to her homeland.

At the next session, once again, I arrived in the lobby five minutes before our designated starting time. When I unlocked the door to welcome this couple, Charihn yelled at me that she had never been treated so badly before. "Don't you know how enraging it is to have to wait even a few minutes?" she railed. "Why can't you find an office that is more convenient for John and me?" Within seconds, Charihn escalated into a full-blown rage storm, with reddened face and frustrated rantings. Charihn and John then proceeded to my office, and I asked if she would be willing, after she felt more balanced, to talk about the meaning of what had just happened. Charihn took several deep breaths, sighed, and then burst into tears. Her husband stood by silently, a passive stance that further enraged her.

Charihn proceeded to blurt out that she "*Hates, hates, hates and thoroughly despises waiting.*" After asking her about previous experiences with waiting, she proceeded to recall a period of one and one-half years when she, her parents, and sisters sought refuge in the home of a sympathetic Iranian rescuer. Because Charihn's father was viewed as a political dissident, the military police actively pursued him. Charihn recalled many hours, when she was sixteen, that she spent huddled in a basement room with her sisters, quietly hiding out. She recalled many occasions where she was expected to wait for many hours on end.

As she retold this trauma narrative, Charihn drew the connection between her fears related to a lack of safety and the terror involved in waiting for danger to pass. During this flashback, Charihn clearly experienced me as a protective yet coercive helper in her traumatic reenactment of the "victim–victimizer–bystander" scenario. During the process of reflecting on the connections of this traumatic event and her current reenactment, Charihn gained a greater sense of mastery and agency through the recognition of her impressive fortitude. These interventions involved a Phase II cognitive reflection on the trauma narrative.

It is useful to glean an impression from the refugee and his or her family about whether or not one or all of them resisted any of the political terror that prompted their departure from their country of origin. Does the client perceive that he was a helpless bystander while others were being victimized? Individuals will have different meanings for events, based on their internalization, at different points in their personal experience, of different aspects of the "victim–victimizer–bystander" dynamic.

:: CLINICAL PRACTICE ISSUES:
SPECIFIC INTERVENTIONS

Again, the clinician needs to be culturally attuned in order to intervene with the most beneficial techniques (Gorman, 2001). For example, Ying (2001) notes that Southeast Asian refugees are most likely to be diagnosed with PTSD and major depression (p. 68). She says that of Southeast Asian refugees, Cambodians and Hmong are most susceptible to psychological distress, as they were least familiar with American society and culture before their immigration to the United States. She notes that many Southeast Asian refugee clients view their issues as primarily somatic, and thus they often expect to be treated with some form of medication. Some refugees develop psychotic thinking that has paranoid aspects. This is usually short lived when appropriately treated with support and antipsychotic medication (Woodcock, 2001).

As in the case of other clients who have experienced trauma, an explanation of symptoms from a culturally sensitive psychoeducational approach is often indicated. Taking into account the meaning of symptoms for diverse groups, many individuals do find some symptomatic relief when they understand that their symptoms are expected and understood as "normative" in response to their immigrant/refugee experience. This cognitive approach encourages a collaborative attitude so that the client may view him- or herself as a self-reflective individual who can benefit from receiving some of the professional's knowledge about the aftereffects of trauma.

When appropriate, many clinicians advocate the use of testimony in the therapeutic process (Agger & Jensen, 1990; Elsass, 1997). This was the primary intervention used in Chile after their political coup in 1973. Chilean psychologists collected testimonials from political prisoners in an attempt to document the impact of the repressive regime. These psychologists also utilized testimony as a treatment method. The telling, reprinting, and reading through of the description of the trauma several times provided many benefits. In addition to creating a historic, public document of the repressive regime, participants also recaptured their political consciousness and, to a larger extent, their own meaning system (Elsass, 1997, p. 128).

Daniel and Knudsen (1995) support the use of testimony for refugee torture survivors. They propose that the ability to tell one's story of horror, without overwhelming the listener, can serve as an important function in the reclamation of one's identity. If the survivor experiences guilt or shame for having witnessed the brutality of others, or for having disclosed information while being tortured, the testimony method provides the space to understand that "The inevitability of personal action in such circumstances becomes a reason for anger at the perpetrators of violence rather than a cause for self-condemnation" (p. 68).

Kira (2002) recommends the use of wraparound services for these families. This holistic, comprehensive, flexible, and multilayered delivery of social services often readily assists the refugee through the relocation experience. He recognizes the benefits of stabilization factors in the recovery process and understands that "The goal is to switch the client from the survival mode to a transformation, growth, and self-actualization mode" (p. 31).

Couple/Family Issues

Citing Figley (1988), Kira (2002) suggests that torture experiences contribute to different forms of family disruptions and difficulties. Kira notes that "Children of tortured parents reveal more psychosomatic symptoms, headaches, depression, learning difficulties and aggressive behavior. They manifest more severe ADHD, eneuresis, and trauma related psychotic symptoms" (p. 24). Becker, Weine, and Vojvoda (1999) note that the adolescent refugees most at risk of developing posttraumatic stress symptoms are the children whose parents are having difficulty in their own adjustments. Often, trust becomes a crucial issue in the couple or family dynamic. Woodcock (2001) notes that "Secrecy has an enormous impact on people who have been living in repressive regimes where in order to survive it had been imperative to keep quiet about beliefs, values and activities that were against the ruling regime" (p. 138). He goes on to say that secrecy about either innocuous or dangerous events may become part of the family's interactional process, contributing to the erosion of trust within the couple system. Partners of imprisoned or political dissidents may have a difficult time understanding how the survivor can valorize that time period of his history. Many survivors may "equate those times as the period when life really had meaning whereas life after may feel like an anticlimax" (p. 139).

Although there is a paucity of literature that specifically explicates couple therapy with refugee and immigrant systems, some generalizations and extrapolations can be made from the existing literature and from contemporary practice experiences. As with other populations, it is essential that Phase I therapeutic work be thoroughly integrated in the clinical process with these couple and family systems. Offering a therapeutic relationship that provides security and support is essential. It is imperative to provide culturally sensitive psychoeducation about trauma experiences (Boehnlein & Kinzie, 1995; Cherepanov & Bui, 2003, personal communication) and to ensure the appropriate use of pharmacology to reduce intrusive symptoms (Boehnlein & Kinzie, 1995; Ying, 2001). Attending to concrete physical symptoms can certainly strengthen the therapeutic relationship. Mock (1998) notes that "Cultural empathy without cultural stereotyping is essential to creating therapeutic rapport" (p. 340). Acknowledging the resilience and strengths of refugee families will help them to maintain some semblance of control. Richman (1998) echoes the appropriate nature of integrating culturally sensitive supportive forms of treatment. He emphasizes the value of addressing the practical needs of the refugee, including needs for recreation and community activities. For example, Vicary, Searle, and Andrews (2000) reported that Kosovar refugees benefited from services geared toward education, parenting information, recreation, and support. Likewise, Akhtar (1999) notes the value of helping the refugee to access language training, job training, and medical services.

Cherepanov and Bui (2003, personal communication) state that immigrant/refugee populations are often closed communities. As such, traditional group therapy that encourages disclosure of personal information is not a helpful form of treatment. Rather, psychoeducational groups that provide assistance with parenting skills, discussion of symptoms, and information about social service systems (e.g., Department of Social Services, Department of Mental Health) are often sought by their clients. In her personal communication, Ms. Bui reported that it is highly unusual for Vietnamese couples to readily disclose personal details related to authority, power, or sexuality. Her credibility in the Vietnamese community has been established by word of mouth because she understands that certain subjects are not considered appropriate to discuss with a counselor. Ms. Bui notes that talking indirectly about sensitive issues, for example by teasing or laughing, helps the family to become somewhat more at ease. In addition, she regularly conducts home visits in which she pays attention to the hierarchy within the family. For example, the elders of the system clearly need to give approval to the counselor's involvement in the family.

While many of Ms. Bui's clients experience symptoms of complex PTSD, she does not prematurely push the clients to talk about their history of traumatic events. Rather, when the family has achieved some stability in external circumstances (e.g., financial resources, schools, physical health), families may begin to talk about past traumatic experiences. Even then, secrets often cannot be explicitly asked about, as they may cause the individual to feel shame. Ms. Bui shared a poignant story of a Vietnamese woman who could not discuss the reason why one of her children had different physical attributes and a different name from her other children. She had conceived this child when a Thai man raped her. Although others knew of the parentage of the child, the open discussion of this trauma would inflict further shame on the mother and the child.

Thus, it is clear that couple work with immigrant/refugee systems will largely focus on the achievement of Phase I tasks of safety, stabilization, and symptom reduction. Kira's (2002) wraparound model of service delivery is consistent with this type of intervention. As well, Gorman (2003, personal communication) notes that his work with torture survivors often enlists the support of family members to help moderate the acute symptoms of the survivor. Once stabilization has occurred, the couple or family system may benefit from some Phase II and Phase III work. For example, H. Abdulkhaleq reported to Kira (2003, personal communication) that he successfully worked with a Romanian-American man and his Romanian-American partner. Mr. Abdulkhaleq described that Mr. X had been tortured in his home country, after he had converted to a Pentecostal religion from his more traditional Orthodox background. Once Mr. X had experienced some relief from PTSD symptoms (through Phase I interventions), the therapist engaged both Mr. and Mrs. X in cognitive–behavioral treatment to address the interactional issues of the couple. In this instance, the partner complained of Mr. X's coldness toward her and his complaints toward her. In addition, Mr. X. was domineering in the couple's interactions, a pattern reminiscent of the "victim–victimizer–bystander" dynamic. Working with Phase II interventions that promoted enhanced understanding of interpersonal issues, the therapist used cognitive–behavioral techniques that challenged the working assumptions and automatic thoughts of Mr. and Mrs. X. This couple, then, was able to find new adaptive patterns of interaction.

We would agree that some retelling of trauma narratives might be indicated after successful completion of Phase I tasks. Woodcock (2001) recounts treating a couple in which an Iranian women was relieved of her symptoms of depression and weakness/paralysis in her arm when she remembered the details of her brother's violent death at the hands of revolutionary guards. When she became conscious that her brother's body had acted as a shield for the right side of her body, the symptomatic weakness/paralysis of her right arm began to dissipate and eventually was healed (p. 142). However, in many instances, active pursuit of trauma memories is contraindicated, especially if ill timed, because it may exacerbate symptoms. Last, many immigrant/refugee couples can create new connections, a Phase III task, as they take leadership positions in their community through which they may offer assistance to other new immigrant/refugee families (van der Veer, 2000).

A specific clinical vignette, involving a Salvadoran couple who immigrated to the United States, highlights the movement between Phases I, II, and III in couple therapy. Both families of origin had initially sought refuge in Mexico after having fled the political strife in their homeland of El Salvador.

MARIA AND PAOLO :: Paolo, age forty-five, was reared as the eldest son, with five siblings, by parents described as "bourgeois-elite." Both parents worked as professionals, providing loyal support to the dominant political regime. When insurrectionist forces challenged the status quo and ultimately overthrew this oppressive regime, Paulo's family became the enemy and they were pursued. After several months of hiding within the country, the family escaped to Mexico City when Paulo was twelve years old. Along a parallel path, Maria was reared as the second of two girls to parents who worked for the Department of Public Resources. During a period of political upheaval, the entire family was arrested and sequestered. The father was sent off to a penitentiary, while the mother and the girls were incarcerated in a detention camp. While living for six months at this camp, Maria recalls being regularly brutalized by physical beatings and rape. She assumes that her mother and sister were subjected to similar treatment. One evening, a coalition liberated this camp, and at age eleven, Maria fled with her mother and sister to Mexico City. Her father was murdered in jail.

These two families grew to know each other well as they adapted to their new homes in Mexico. Paulo and Maria attended the same Catholic high school. Following graduation from high school, they decided to marry and immigrate to the United States. So, at the ages of twenty-five and twenty-six, Paulo and Maria moved to the United States, where they both worked in the health care field. Almost two decades later, they sought help to deal with their family conflicts regarding their older adoptive daughter's unplanned out-of-wedlock pregnancy. Seventeen-year-old Lisa chose to continue with her pregnancy in spite of her ambivalence toward the baby's father and the shame and disapproval expressed by her parents. A younger brother, Juan, named after Maria's deceased father, faltered in school and had serious problems of fighting other children.

Because the basis for the treatment related to Lisa's pregnancy and Juan's aggression, I knew virtually nothing at the time about the parents' respective trauma histories. When I met the couple, and then the entire family, I learned that both children were adopted from bicultural Anglo-Saxon and Latino families. Although completely fluent in both English and Spanish, both children boldly renounced their Spanish language skills. Similarly, they rejected their El Salvadoran cultural heritage.

After ensuring that this family had adequate supports in terms of basic safety and self-care issues (i.e., completing Phase I tasks of safety, stabilization, and establishing a context for change), the couple and I moved into Phase II themes related to reflections on their trauma narrative. When I posed the question to each parent about how they had been parented during their adolescence, Maria revealed a harrowing contradictory description of a joyful adjustment to high school in Mexico, intermittently shrouded in childhood memories of torture while growing up in El Salvador. As she expressed her anxiety about her daughter's pregnancy, Maria shared that she became infertile after the prison guards had raped her so aggressively that her uterus and ovaries were irreparably damaged. Sadness and fear based on this history and on the anticipated worries for her daughter enabled Maria to reflect on how the "victim–victimizer–bystander" scenario repeated itself. In this process, connections were formed between the legacies of her childhood trauma and her relationship patterns in adult life without abreaction.

In this immediate crisis, as Maria watched her daughter make what she viewed as risky choices, she experienced herself as alternating between being a helpless victim and a passive bystander. She and her husband projected this victimizing historical ghost onto her daughter and her daughter's developing baby. As a result, they feared that the daughter and her boyfriend would mistreat the baby. Because Paulo had similarly learned to suppress emotion related to his childhood horrors, neither partner had talked much about their respective experiences. Because there is a cultural prohibition against sharing such personal details with intense affect, Maria and Paulo felt comfortable with reflecting on these experiences only in terms of how their trauma legacies affected their daily lives.

To what extent is this emotional restraint neurophysiologically determined with the pendulum of numbness and dissociation? To what extent did their parents' shared denial and minimization of the emotional effects lead to an intergenerational transmission of unresolved trauma-related grief and loss? In this vein, were the children, Lisa and Juan, displaying the unexpressed and unresolved feelings related to grief and loss passed along from previous generations? A question surfaced about how much of the restraint of independence was culturally determined and how much was trauma related. The answer involved both perspectives. In reaction to overly cautious parental protectiveness, self-doubt, tentativeness, and a lack of self-differentiation were encouraged in the children. However, both Lisa and Juan rebelled against what they experienced as oppressive victimization.

As both Maria and Paulo recognized the complexity of this pervasive "victim–victimizer–bystander" pattern, they were able to respond more compassionately to their children and, ultimately, to their new infant granddaughter. In these ways, the Phase III tasks of consolidation of new perspectives and behaviors occurred when Maria and Paulo's grandparenting desires and skills strengthened. In addition, this couple shifted into a dynamic pattern that was far more balanced and mutually reciprocal. Within the context of these positive changes, Maria and John were able to talk more openly about the complexity of their cultural backgrounds. Rather than responding exclusively with a negative outlook toward their cultural identities, Lisa and Juan mirrored the developing complexity of their social identities. Only when their horrific experiences were acknowledged within the family were they able to reclaim a more positive connection to their Salvadoran heritage. This Phase III couple therapy task allowed for the emergence of valued complex, social identities that had previously been devalued and marginalized.

:: CLINICIAN RESPONSES

Clinicians and other refugee workers conduct their work in the broader societal context. It is quite likely that clinicians will have been exposed to media coverage or other information about the country of origin of the immigrant/refugee. Thus, in addition to the psychological responses of people who are fleeing their countries of origin, a myriad of other factors may impact the clinical situation as well. Papadopoulos (2001) notes that the clinician may be influenced by the host country's attitudes about any particular group of immigrants/refugees seeking asylum. At times, Western governments and agencies may have been implicated in the political turmoil of the refugee's country of origin (Woodcock, 2001). In these instances, the refugee may perceive the clinician as a potential victimizer who holds imperialistic or colonizing values.

Professionals are influenced when they work with immigrant/refugee populations (Comas-Diaz & Padilla, 1990; Gorman, 2001; Woodcock, 2001). Hearing narratives of torture or other forms of trauma often shakes the clinician's worldview (van der Veer, 2000). Feelings of powerlessness, within the worker, are also difficult to integrate into one's professional sense of self (van der Veer, 2000). Ying (2001) notes that "Treating refugees indeed involves suffering on the part of the clinician. After all, compassion means 'to suffer with'" (p. 76). Some clinicians may inadvertently sabotage the development of trust in the treatment relationship; this unconscious behavior saves the worker from hearing the narrative of trauma of the survivor (Woodcock, 2001). It is useful to have trusted colleagues with whom we may process our own responses (Pearlman & Saakvitne, 1995).

:: SUMMARY

In summary, this chapter specifies clinical practice interventions with both immigrant and refugee populations. Although each group experiences myriad losses, the traumatic experiences of both need to be understood specifically so as to maximize benefits for the couples engaged in therapy.

REFERENCES

Adams, J. (2000). Individual and group psychotherapy with African American women: Understanding the identity and context of the therapist and patient. In L. Jackson & B. Greene (Eds.), *Psychotherapy with African American women: Innovations in psychodynamic perspectives and practice* (pp. 33–61). New York: Guilford Press.

Agger, I., & Jensen, S. (1989). Couples in exile: Political consciousness as an element in the psychosexual dynamics of a Latin American refugee couple. *Sexual and Marital Therapy, 4*(1), 101–108.

Agger, I., & Jensen, S. (1990). Testimony as ritual and evidence in psychotherapy for political refugees. *Journal of Traumatic Stress, 3*(1), 115–131.

Ainsworth, M. (1973). The development of infant–mother attachment. In B. Caldwell & N. Ricciuti (Eds.), *Review of child development research* (Vol. 3, pp. 1–94). Chicago: University of Chicago Press.

Ainsworth, M. (1982). Attachment: Retrospect and prospect. In C. Parkes & J. Stevenson-Hinde (Eds.), *The place of attachment in human behavior* (pp. 3–30). New York: Basic Books.

Ainsworth, M., Blehar, M., Waters, E., & Wall, W. (1978). *Patterns of attachment: A psychological study of the strange situation.* Hillsdale, NJ: Lawrence Erlbaum.

Akamatsu, N. (1998). The talking oppression blues: Including the experience of power/powerlessness in the teaching of "cultural sensitivity." In M. McGoldrick (Ed.), *Revisioning family therapy: Race, culture and gender in clinical practice* (pp. 129–143). New York: Guilford Press.

Akhtar, S. (1999). *Immigration and identity: Turmoil, treatment, and transformation.* Northvale, NJ: Jason Aronson.

Alexander, P.C. (1985). A systems theory conceptualization of incest. *Family Process, 24,* 79–88.

Alexander, P.C. (1992). Application of attachment theory to the study of sexual abuse. *Journal of Consulting and Clinical Psychology, 60*(?), 185–195.

Alexander, P.C., Anderson, C.L., Brand, B., Schaeffer, C.M., Grelling, B.Z., & Kretz, L. (1998). Adult attachment and the long-term effects in survivors of incest. *Child Abuse and Neglect, 22*(1), 45–61.

Alexander, P.C., Teti, L., & Anderson, C.L. (2000). Childhood sexual abuse history and role reversal in parenting. *Child Abuse and Neglect, 24*(6), 829–833.

Allen, I.A. (1998). PTSD among African Americans. In A. Marsella, M. Friedman, E. Gerrity, & R. Scurfield (Eds.), *Ethnocultural aspects of posttraumatic stress disorder: Issues, research and clinical implications* (pp. 209–238). Washington, DC: American Psychological Association.

Allen, J.G. (2001). *Traumatic relationships and serious mental disorders.* New York: John Wiley.

Allen, J.G., & Smith, W.H. (1995). *Diagnosis and treatment of dissociative disorders.* Northvale, NJ: Jason Aronson.

Alvarez, M. (1995). *The experience of migration: A relational approach in therapy.* (Work in Progress, No. 71). Wellesley, MA: The Stone Center, Wellesley College.

American Psychiatric Association. (1980). *Diagnostic and statistical manual* (3rd ed.). Washington, DC: Author.

American Psychiatric Association. (1987). *Diagnostic and statistical manual of mental disorders* (3rd ed., rev.). Washington, DC: Author.

American Psychiatric Association. (2000). *Diagnostic and statistical manual of mental disorders* (4th ed., text rev.). Washington DC: Author.

American Psychological Association (2001). *Publication manual* (5th ed.). Washington, DC: Author.

Ancharoff, M.R., Munroe, I.F., & Fisher, L. (1998). The legacy of combat trauma: Clinical implications of intergenerational transmission. In Y. Danieli (Ed.), *International handbook of multigenerational legacies of trauma.* New York: Plenum Press.

Anderson, C.M., & Stewart, S. (1983). *Mastering resistance: A practical guide to family therapy.* New York: Guilford Press.

Andolfi, M., Angelo, C., & Nichilo, M. (1989). *The myth of Atlas: Families and the therapeutic story.* New York: Brunner/Mazel.

Applegate, J. (1996). The good-enough social worker: Winnicott applied. In J. Edward & J. Sanville (Eds.), *Fostering healing and growth* (pp. 77–96). Northvale, NJ: Jason Aronson.

Aron, L. (1996a). *A meeting of the minds: Mutuality in psychoanalysis.* Hillsdale, NJ: Analytic Press.

Aron, L. (1996b). Symposium on the meaning and practice of intersubjectivity in psychoanalysis: Introduction. *Psychoanalytic Dialogues, 6*(5), 591–597.

Atkinson, B. (1999). The emotional imperative. *Family Therapy Networker, 23,* 22–33.

Atkinson, B. (2002). Brain to brain. *Psychotherapy Networker, 26,* 38–45.

Bader, E., & Pearson, P. (1988). *In quest of the mythical mate: A developmental approach to diagnosis and treatment in couples therapy.* New York: Brunner/Mazel.

Balcolm, D. (1996). The interpersonal dynamics and treatment of dual trauma couples. *Journal of Marital and Family Therapy, 22*(4), 431–442.

Balcolm, D., Lee, R., & Tager, J. (1995). The systemic treatment of shame in couples. *Journal of Marital and Family Therapy, 21*(1), 55–65.

Banyard, V.L. (1997). The impact of childhood sexual abuse and family functioning on four dimensions of women's later parenting. *Child Abuse and Neglect, 21*(11), 1095–1107.

Barnes, M.F. (1995). Sex therapy in the couple's context: Therapy issues of victims of sexual trauma. *American Journal of Family Therapy, 23*(4), 351–360.

Bar-On, D. (1998). Multigenerational perspectives on coping with the Holocaust experience: An attachment perspective for understanding the developmental sequelae of trauma across generations. *International Journal of Behavioral Development, 22*(2), 315–338.

Barrett, M.J., & Stone-Fish, L. (1991). *Marital therapy with the survivors of childhood sexual abuse.* Paper presented at the annual symposium of the Family Therapy Networker Conference, Washington, DC.

Barrett, M.J., & Trepper, T.S. (1991). Treating women drug abusers who were victims of childhood sexual abuse. In C. Bepko (Ed.), *Feminism and addiction* (pp. 127–146). Binghamton, NY: Haworth Press.

Bartholomew, K., & Horowitz, L.M. (1991). Attachment styles among young adults: A test of a four-category model. *Journal of Personality and Social Psychology, 61,* 226–244.

Basham, K. (1999a). Therapy with a lesbian couple: The art of balancing lenses. In J. Laird (Ed.), *Lesbians and lesbian families: Reflections on theory and practice.* New York: Columbia University Press.

Basham, K. (1999b). A synthesis of theory in couple therapy: No longer an unlikely coupling. In T. Northcut & N. Heller (Eds.), *Enhancing psychodynamic therapy with cognitive behavioral techniques* (pp. 135–157). Northvale, NJ: Jason Aronson.

Basham, K., & Miehls, D. (1998a). Integration of object relations theory and trauma theory in couples therapy with survivors of childhood trauma: Part I, Theoretical foundations. *Journal of Analytic Social Work, 5*(3), 51–63.

Basham, K., & Miehls, D. (1998b). Integration of object relations theory and trauma theory in couples therapy with survivors of childhood trauma: Part II, Clinical illustrations. *Journal of Analytic Social Work, 5*(3), 65–78.

Basham, K., & Miehls, D. (2002). Transforming the legacies of childhood trauma in couple therapy: The biopsychosocial assessment as compass and anchor. *Smith College Studies in Social Work, 72*(2), 253–277.

Bass, E., & Davis, L. (1988). *The courage to heal: A guide for women survivors of child sexual abuse.* New York: Harper & Row.

Baucom, D.H., & Epstein, N. (1990). *Cognitive–behavioral marital therapy.* Prospect Heights, IL: Waveland.

Beavers, W.R., & Hampson, R.B. (2003). Measuring family competence: The Beavers systems model. In F. Walsh, *Normal family processes: Growing diversity and complexity* (3rd ed., pp. 549–580). New York: Guilford Press.

Becker, D., Weine, S., & Vojvoda, D. (1999). Case series: PTSD symptoms in adolescent survivors of "ethnic cleansing." Results from a one-year follow up study. *Adolescent Psychiatry, 38*(6), 775–781.

Beebe, B. (2000). Co-constructing mother–infant distress: The microsynchrony of maternal impingement and infant avoidance in the face-to-face encounter. *Psychoanalytic Inquiry, 20,* 412–440.

Beebe, B., & Lachman, F. (1988). The contribution of mother–infant mutual influence to the origins of self and object representations. *Psychoanalytic Psychology, 5,* 305–337.

Benjamin, J. (1992). Recognition and destruction: An outline of intersubjectivity. In N. Skolnick & S. Warshaw (Eds.), *Relational perspectives in psychoanalysis* (pp. 43–60). Hillsdale, NJ: Analytic Press.

Benjamin, J. (1998a). *The bonds of love: Psychoanalysis, feminism, and the problem of domination.* New York: Pantheon Books.

Benjamin, J. (1998b). *The shadow of the other: Intersubjectivity and gender in psychoanalysis.* New York: Routledge Press.

Benjamin, L.R., & Benjamin, R. (1994). Utilizing parenting as a clinical focus in the treatment of dissociative disorders. *Dissociation, 7*(4), 239–245.

Bennet-Baker, A.A. (1999). The resilient psychotherapist: An heuristic inquiry into vicarious traumatization. *Dissertation Abstracts International, 60,* 1B, p. 357 (UMI No. AAM 9916976).

Benyei, C.R. (1998). *Understanding clergy misconduct in religious systems: Scapegoating, family secrets, and the abuse of power.* New York: Haworth Press.

Berenson, D. (1991). Powerlessness—liberating or enslaving? Responding to the feminist critique of the twelve steps. In C. Bepko (Ed.), *Feminism and addiction* (pp. 67–84). New York: Haworth Press.

Bergart, A.M. (1986). Isolation to intimacy: Incest survivors in group therapy. *Social Casework, 67,* 266–275.

Berman, W.H., Marcus, L., & Berman, E.R. (1994). Attachment in marital relationships. In M.B. Sperling & W.H. Berman (Eds.), *Attachment in adults: Clinical and developmental perspectives* (pp. 204–231). New York: Guilford Press.

Bernstein, M.M. (1998). Conflicts in adjustment, WWII prisoners of war and their families. In Y. Danieli (Ed.), *International handbook of multigenerational legacies of trauma.* New York: Plenum Press.

Boehnlein, J.K., & Kinzie, J.D. (1996). Refugee trauma. *Transcultural Psychiatric Research Review, 32,* 223–252.

Bograd, M., & Mederos, F. (1999). Battering and couples therapy: Universal screening and selection of treatment modality. *Journal of Marital and Family Therapy, 25*(3), 291–312.

Bolen, J. (1993). Sexuality-focused treatment with survivors and their partners. In P. Paddison (Ed.), *Treatment of adult survivors of incest.* Washington, DC: American Psychiatric Publishing.

Boulanger, G. (1981). Conditions affecting the appearance and maintenance of traumatic stress reactions among Vietnam veterans (Doctoral dissertation, Columbia University, 1981). *Dissertation Abstracts International 42,* 2516B.

Bowen, M.C. (1974). Toward the differentiation of self in one's family of origin. In F. Anders & J. Lorro (Eds.), *Georgetown Faculty Symposium Papers, I* (p. 77). Washington, DC: Georgetown University Press.

Bowen, M. (1978). *Family therapy in clinical practice.* New York: Jason Aronson.

Bowlby, J. (1958). The nature of the child's tie to his mother. *International Journal of Psychoanalysis, 33,* 350–373.

Bowlby, J. (1969). *Attachment and loss* (Vol. I): *Attachment.* New York: Basic Books.

Bowlby, J. (1973). *Attachment and loss* (Vol. II): *Separation.* New York: Basic Books.

Bowlby, J. (1980). *Attachment and loss* (Vol. III): *Loss, sadness, and depression.* New York: Basic Books.

Bowlby, J. (1982). *Attachment and loss* (Vol. I): *Attachment* (Rev.). New York: Basic Books.

Bowlby, J. (1988). *A secure base: Parent–child attachment and healthy human development.* New York: Basic Books.

Bowles, D.B. (1999). Intersubjectivity: Expanding our understanding of the worker–client relationship. *Smith College Studies in Social Work, 69*(2), 359–371.

Bozmormenyi-Nagy, I., & Spark, G.L. (1973). *Invisible loyalties: Reciprocity in intergenerational family therapy.* New York: Harper & Row.

Bracken, J. (1998). Hidden agendas: Deconstructing post traumatic stress disorder. In P. Bracken & C. Petty (Eds.), *Rethinking the trauma of war.* New York: Free Association Press.

Brandell, J. (1997). Psychoanalytic theory. In J. Brandell (Ed.), *Theory and practice in clinical social work.* New York: Free Press.

Brandell, J. (1999). Countertransference as communication: Intersubjectivity in the treatment of a traumatized adolescent patient. *Smith College Studies in Social Work, 69*(2), 405–429.

Brandon, J.Y. (2000). Working models of self and other in adult attachment and vicarious traumatization. *Dissertation Abstracts International, 60,* 10-B, p. 5219 (UMI No. AAI9949082).

Braun, B.G. (1988). The BASK model of dissociation. *Dissociation, 1*(1), 4–23.

Bremner, J.D. (2002). *Does stress damage the brain? Understanding trauma-related disorders from a mind–body perspective.* New York: W.W. Norton.

Bremner, J.D., Innis, R.B., Ng, C.K., Staib, L.H., Salomon, R.M., Bronen, R.A., et al. (1997). Positron emission tomography measurement of cerebral metabolic correlates of yohimbe administration in combat-related posttraumatic stress disorder. *Archives of General Psychiatry, 54,* 246–254.

Brende, J. (1994). A twelve-theme psychoeducational program for victims and survivors. In M.B. Williams & J.F. Sommer (Eds.), *Handbook of post-traumatic therapy.* Westport, CT: Greenwood Press.

Brende, J., & Goldsmith, R. (1991). Post-traumatic stress disorder in families. *Journal of Contemporary Psychotherapy 21,* 115–124.

Brenner, I. (2001). *Dissociation of trauma: Theory, phenomenology, and technique.* Madison, CT: International Universities Press.

Breslau, N., David, G.C., Andreski, P., & Peterson, E. (1991). Traumatic events and posttraumatic stress disorder in an urban population of young adults. *Archive General Psychiatry, 48,* 216–222.

Bretherton, I. (1985). Attachment theory: Retrospect and prospect. In I. Bretherton & E. Waters (Eds.), *Growing points of attachment theory and research* (Monographs of the

Society for Research in Child Development, Serial 209, Vol. 50, No. 1–2, pp. 3–35). Ann Arbor, MI: University of Michigan.

Briere, J. (1996). *Therapy for adults molested as children: Beyond survival* (rev. ed.). New York: Springer.

Brown, D. (1990). The variable long-term effects of incest: Hypnoanalystic and adjunctive hypnotherapeutic treatment. In M. Fass & D. Brown (Eds.), *Creative mastery in hypnosis and hypnoanalysis.* Hillsdale, NJ: Lawrence Erlbaum.

Brown, E. (1991). Patterns of infidelity and the treatment process. New York: Brunner/Mazel.

Brown, S. (1985). *Treating the alcoholic: A developmental model of recovery.* New York: John Wiley.

Buell, E. (2001). Legal issues affecting alternative families: A therapist's primer. *Journal of Gay and Lesbian Psychotherapy, 4*(3/4), 75–90.

Buist, A. (1998). Childhood abuse, postpartum depression, and parenting difficulties: A literature review of associations. *Australian and New Zealand Journal of Psychiatry, 32,* 370–378.

Burch, B. (1997). *Other women: Lesbian/bisexual experience and psychoanalytic views of women.* New York: Columbia University Press.

Burkett, L.D. (1991). Parenting behaviors of women who were sexually abused as children in their families of origin. *Family Process, 30,* 421–434.

Burkitt, I. (1994). The shifting concept of the self. *History of the Human Sciences, 7*(2), 7–28.

Busby, D., Steggel, G., Genn, E., & Adamson, D. (1993). Treatment issues for survivors of physical and sexual abuse. *Journal of Marital and Family Therapy, 19*(4), 377–392.

Canfield, J. (2002). *An exploratory study of secondary traumatic stress and vicarious traumatization among child psychotherapists.* Unpublished doctoral dissertation, Smith College School for Social Work, Northampton, MA.

Carter, R. (1995). *The influence of race and racial identity in psychotherapy: Toward a racially inclusive model.* New York: John Wiley.

Cashdan, S. (1988). *Object relations therapy: Using the relationship.* New York: W.W. Norton.

Cashin, J. (2000). Trauma and multigenerational trauma caused by genocide and oppression: A comparison of western and Native American healing methods. *Dissertation Abstracts International, 61,* 12B.

Catherall, D. (1992). Working with projective identification in couples. *Family Process, 31,* 355–367.

Catherall, D. (1995). Preventing institutional secondary traumatic stress disorder. In C. Figley (Ed.), *Compassion fatigue: Coping with secondary traumatic stress disorder in those who treat the traumatized* (pp. 232–247). New York: Brunner/Mazel.

Chambon, A. (1999). A Foucauldian approach: Making the familiar visible. In A. Chambon, A. Irving, & L. Epstein (Eds.), *Reading Foucault for social work* (pp. 51–81). New York: Columbia University Press.

Charney, A.E., & Pearlman, L.A. (1998). The ecstasy and the agony: The impact of disaster and trauma work on the self of the clinician. In P. Kleespies (Ed.), *Emergency psycho-*

logical services: The evaluation and management of life-threatening behavior. New York: Guilford Press.

Chauncey, S. (1994). Emotional concerns and treatment of male partners of female sexual abuse survivors. *Social Work, 39,* 669–676.

Chediak, C. (1979). Counter-reactions and countertransference. *Journal of Psycho-Analysis, 60,* 117–129.

Christopher, J. (2001). Culture and psychotherapy: Toward a hermeneutic approach. *Psychotherapy, 38*(2), 115–128.

Chu, J. (1988). Ten traps for therapists in the treatment of trauma survivors. *Dissociation, 1*(4), 24–32.

Chu, J. (1998). *Rebuilding shattered lives.* New York: John Wiley.

Citizenship and Immigration Canada. (2001). *Facts and figures: immigration overview.* Retrieved May 1, 2003, from *www.cic.gc.ca.*

Cohen, L., Berzoff, J., & Elin, M. (Eds.). (1995). *Dissociative identity disorder.* Northvale, NJ: Jason Aronson.

Cohen, M. (1998). *Culture of intolerance: Chauvinism, class, and racism in the United States.* New Haven: Yale University Press.

Cohen, P. (1995). Motherhood among incest survivors. *Child Abuse and Neglect, 19,* 1423–1429.

Cole, P., & Woolger, C. (1989). Incest survivors: The relation of their perceptions of their parents and their own parenting attitudes. *Child Abuse and Neglect, 13,* 409–416.

Coleman, E., & Simon Rosser, B. (1996). Gay and bisexual male sexuality. In R. Cabaj & T. Stein (Eds.), *Textbook of homosexuality and mental health* (pp. 707–721). Washington, DC: American Psychiatric Publishing.

Collins, N.L., & Feeney, B.C. (2000). A safe haven: An attachment theory perspective on support seeking and caregiving in intimate relationships. *Journal of Personality and Social Psychology, 78*(6), 1053–1073.

Comas-Diaz, L., & Padilla, A. (1990). Countertransference in working with victims of political repression. *American Journal of Orthopsychiatry, 60*(1), 125–134.

Compton, J., & Follette, V. (1998). Couples surviving trauma: Issues and interventions. In V. Follette, J. Ruzek, & F. Abueg (Eds.), *Cognitive–behavioral therapies for trauma* (pp. 321–352). New York: Guilford Press.

Contreras, R.L. (2003). The ultimate sacrifice and US citizenship. Retrieved August 18, 2003, from *www.calnews.com/archives/contreras141.htm.*

Cornell, S., & Hartman, D. (1998). *Ethnicity & race: Making identities in a changing world.* Thousand Oaks, CA: Pine Forge Press.

Corrigan, F.M., Davidson, A., & Heard, H. (2000). The role of dysregulated amygdalic emotion in borderline personality disorder. *Medical Hypotheses, 54,* 574–579.

Courtois, C. (1988). *Healing the incest wound: Adult survivors in therapy.* New York: W.W. Norton.

Courtois, C. (1993). *Adult survivors of child sexual abuse.* Milwaukee, WI: Families International.

Courtois, C. (1997a). Treating the sexual concerns of adult incest survivors and their partners. *Journal of Aggression, Maltreatment and Trauma, 1*(1), 293–310.

Courtois, C. (1997b). Guidelines for the treatment of adults abused or possibly abused as children. *American Journal of Psychotherapy, 51*(4), 497–510.

Courtois, C. (1999). *Recollections of sexual abuse: Treatment principles and guidelines.* New York: W.W. Norton.

Crespi, L. (2001). And baby makes three: A dynamic look at development and conflict in lesbian families. *Journal of Gay and Lesbian Psychotherapy, 4*(3/4), 7–29.

Cross, W. (1991). *Shades of black.* Philadelphia: Temple University Press.

Cross, W. (1998). Black psychological functioning and the legacy of slavery. In Y. Danieli (Ed.), *International handbook of multigenerational legacies of trauma.* New York: Plenum Press.

Cunningham, M. (1999). The impact of sexual abuse treatment on the social work clinician. *Child & Adolescent Social Work Journal, 16*(4), 277–290.

Cvetkovich, A. (2003). *An archive of feelings: Trauma, sexuality, and lesbian public cultures.* Durham, NC: Duke University Press.

Dalenberg, C. (2000). *Countertransference and the treatment of trauma.* Washington, DC: American Psychological Association.

Danaher, G., Schiratz, T., & Webb, J. (2000). *Understanding Foucault.* Thousand Oaks, CA: Sage.

Dane, B. (2000). Child welfare workers: An innovative approach for interacting with secondary trauma. *Journal of Social Work Education, 36*(1), 27–38.

Daniel, E.V., & Knudsen, J.C. (1995). *Mistrusting refugees.* Berkeley: University of California Press.

Daniel, J. (1994). Exclusion and emphasis reframed as a matter of ethnic. *Ethics & Behavior, 4*(3), 229–235.

Daniel, J. (2000). The courage to hear: African American women's memories of racial trauma. In L. Jackson & B. Greene (Eds.), *Psychotherapy with African American women: Innovations in psychodynamic perspectives and practice* (pp. 126–144). New York: Guilford Press.

Danieli, Y. (Ed.). (1998). *International handbook of multigenerational legacies of trauma.* New York: Plenum Press.

Dansky, B.S. Brady, K.T., Saladin, M.E., Killeen, T., Becker, S., & Roitzsch, J. (1996). Victimization and PTSD in individuals with substance use disorders: Gender and racial differences. *American Journal of Drug and Alcohol Abuse, 22*(1), 75–93.

Davies, D. (1996). Homophobia and heterosexism. In D. Davies & C. Neal (Eds.), *Pink therapy: A guide for counselors and therapists working with lesbian, gay, and bisexual clients* (pp. 41–65). Buckingham: Open University Press.

Davies, J.M., & Frawley, M.G. (1992). Dissociative processes and transference–countertransference paradigms in the psychoanalytically oriented treatment of adult survivors of childhood sexual abuse. *Psychoanalytic Dialogues, 2*(1), 5–36.

Davies, J.M., & Frawley, M.G. (1994). *Treating the adult survivor of childhood sexual abuse: A psychoanalytic perspective.* New York: Basic Books.

Davis, L. (1991). *Allies in healing.* New York: Harper Perennial.

Deighton, J., & McPeek, P. (1985). Group treatment: Adult victims of childhood sexual abuse. *Social Casework, 66,* 403–410.

Descamps, M., Rothblum, E., Bradford, J., & Ryan, C. (2000). Mental health impact of child sexual abuse, rape, intimate partner violence, and hate crimes in the national lesbian health care survey. *Journal of Gay and Lesbian Social Services, 11*(1), 27–55.

Dicks, H. (1967). *Marital tensions: Clinical studies toward a psychological theory of interaction.* New York: Basic Books.

DiNicola, V. (1996). Ethnocultural aspects of PTSD and related disorders among children and adolescents. In A. Marsella, M. Friedman, E. Gerrity, & R. Scurfield (Eds.), *Ethnocultural aspects of posttraumatic stress disorder.* Washington, DC: American Psychological Association.

Drauker, C.D. (1992). *Counseling survivors of childhood sexual abuse.* Newbury Park, CA: Sage.

Drescher, J. (2001). The circle of liberation: A book review essay of Jesse Green's *The Velveteen Father: An Unexpected Journey to Parenthood.* In D. Glazer & J. Drescher (Eds.), *Gay and lesbian parenting* (pp. 119–131). New York: Haworth Press.

Driver, J., Tabares, A., Shapiro, A., Nahm, E., & Gottman, J.M. (2003). *Interactional patterns in marital success and failure: Gottman laboratory studies* (pp. 493–513). New York: Guilford Press.

Dutton, D.G., & Holtzworth-Munroe, A. (1997). The role of early trauma in males who assault their lives. In D. Cicchetti & S.L. Toth (Eds.), *Developmental perspectives on trauma: Theory, research, and intervention* (pp. 379–401). Rochester, NY: University of Rochester Press.

Dutton, D.G., Saunders, K., Starzomski, A., & Bartholomew, K. (1994). Intimacy–anger and insecure attachment as precursors of abuse in intimate relationships. *Journal of Applied Social Psychology, 24*(15), 1367–1386.

Dyche, L., & Zayas, L. (1995). The value of curiosity and naiveté for the cross-cultural psychotherapist. *Family Process, 34,* 389–399.

Dyche, L., & Zayas, L. (2001). Cross-cultural empathy and training the contemporary psychotherapist. *Clinical Social Work Journal, 29*(3), 245–258.

Ehrenreich, B. (2001). The silenced majority: Why the average working person has disappeared from American media and culture. In M. Andersen & P.H. Collins (Eds.), *Race, class, and gender: An anthology* (4th ed., pp. 143–145). Belmont, CA: Wadsworth Press.

Elliott, P. (1996). Shattering illusions: Same-sex domestic violence. In C.M. Renzetti & C.H. Miley (Eds.), *Violence in gay and lesbian domestic partnerships* (pp. 1–8). New York: Haworth Press.

Elsass, P. (1997). *Treating victims of torture and violence: Theoretical, cross-cultural, and clinical implications* (J. Andersen & H. Fuglsang, Trans.). New York: New York University Press.

Eron, J.B., & Lund, T.W. (1999). Narrative solutions in brief couple therapy. In J.M. Donovan (Ed.), *Short-term couple therapy* (pp. 291–324). New York: Guilford Press.

Espy, K.A., Kaufman, P.M., & Glisky, M.L. (1999). Neuropsychological function in toddlers exposed to cocaine in utero: A preliminary study. *Developmental Neuropsychology, 15,* 447–460.

Evans, K., & Sullivan, J.M. (1995). *Treating addicted survivors of trauma.* New York: Guilford Press.

Ewing, J.A. (1984). Detecting alcoholism: The CAGE questionnaire. *Journal of the American Medical Association, 252,* 1905–1907.

Fairbairn, W.R.D. (1952a). *An object relations view of the personality.* New York: Basic Books.

Fairbairn, W.R.D. (1952b). *Psychoanalytic studies of the personality.* London: Routledge & Kegal Paul.

Fairbairn, W.R.D. (1963). Synopsis of an object-relations theory of the personality. *International Journal of Psychoanalysis, 44,* 224–225.

Falicov, C. (1998). The cultural meaning of family triangles. In M. McGoldrick (Ed.), *Re-visioning family therapy: Race, culture and gender in clinical practice* (pp. 37–49). New York: Guilford Press.

Falicov, C.J. (2003). Immigrant family processes. In F. Walsh (Ed.), *Normal family processes: Growing diversity and complexity* (pp. 280–300). New York: Guilford Press.

Feeney, J. (1998). Adult attachment and relationship-centered anxiety: Responses to physical and emotional distancing. In J. Simpson & W. Rholes (Eds.), *Attachment theory and close relationships* (pp. 189–217). New York: Guilford Press.

Feinauer, L.L. (1989). Relationship of treatment to adjustment in women sexually abused as children. *American Journal of Family Therapy, 17,* 326–334.

Felsen, I. (1998). Transgenerational transmission of effects of the Holocaust. In Y. Danieli (Ed.), *International handbook of multigenerational legacies of trauma* (pp. 43–68). New York: Plenum Press.

Fergusson, D.M., Woodward, L., & Horwood, L.J. (1998). Maternal smoking during pregnancy and psychiatric adjustment in late adolescence. *Archives of General Psychiatry, 55,* 721–727.

Figley, C.R. (1985). *Trauma and its wake: The study and treatment of post-traumatic stress disorder.* New York: Brunner/Mazel.

Figley, C.R. (1988). A five–phase treatment of post–traumatic stress disorder in families. *Journal of Traumatic Stress, 1*(1), 127–141.

Figley, C.R. (1989). *Helping traumatized families.* San Francisco: Jossey-Bass.

Figley, C.R. (Ed.). (1995). *Compassion fatigue: Coping with secondary stress disorder in those who treat the traumatized.* New York: Brunner/Mazel.

Figley, C. (1998). A five-phase treatment of PTSD in families. *Journal of Traumatic Stress, 1,* 127–141.

Figley, C.R. (2003). *Current research in PTSD.* Paper presented at the Psychotherapy Networker Conference, Washington, DC, March.

Fine, M., & Asch, A. (2000). Disability beyond stigma: Social interaction, discrimination, and activism. In M. Adams, W. Blemenfeld, R. Castaneda, H. Hackman, M. Peters, & X. Zuniga (Eds.), *Readings for diversity and social justice* (pp. 330–339). New York: Routledge.

Fisher, J.V., & Crandell, L.E. (1997). Complex attachment: Patterns of relating in the couple. *Sexual and Marital Therapy, 12*(3), 211–233.

Follette, V.M. (1991). Marital therapy for sexual abuse survivors. In J. Briere (Ed.), *Treating victims of child sexual abuse.* San Francisco: Jossey-Bass.

Fonagy, P. (1998). An attachment theory approach to treatment of a difficult patient. *Bulletin of the Menninger Clinic, 62*(2), 147–169.

Fonagy, P. (1999). Male perpetrators of violence against women: An attachment theory perspective. *Journal of Applied Psychoanalytic Studies, 1*(1), 7–27.

Fonagy, P. (2001). *Attachment theory and psychoanalysis.* New York: Other Press.

Fonagy, P., Gergely, G., Jurist, E., & Target, M. (2002). *Affect regulation, mentalization, and the development of the self.* New York: Other Press.

Foucault, M. (1979). *Discipline and punish: The birth of a prison* (A. Sheridan, Trans.). New York: Vintage Books.

Foucault, M. (1980). Power and strategies. In C. Gordon (Ed.), *Power/knowledge: Selected interviews and other writings* (pp. 134–145). New York: Pantheon Books.

Fraenkel, P., Schoen, S., Perko, K., Mendelson, T., Kushner, S., & Islam, S. (1998). The family speaks: Family members' descriptions of therapy for sexual abuse. *Journal of Systemic Therapies, 17,* 39–60.

Francis, C. (1997). Countertransference with abusive couples. In M. Solomon & J. Siegel (Eds.), *Countertransference in couples therapy* (pp. 218–237). New York: W.W. Norton.

Freedman, J., & Combs, G. (1996). *Narrative therapy: The social construction of preferred realities.* New York: W.W. Norton.

Freud, S. (1959). The aetiology of hysteria (1896). In E. Jones (Ed.), *Sigmund Freud: Collected papers* (Vol. 1). New York: Basic Books.

Friedman, M., & Marsella, A. (1996). Posttraumatic stress disorder: An overview of the concept. In A. Marsella, M. Friedman, E. Gerrity, & R. Scurfield (Eds.), *Ethnocultural aspects of posttraumatic stress disorder: Issues, research, and clinical applications.* Washington, DC: American Psychological Association.

Frye, M. (1990). Lesbian sex. In J. Allen (Ed.), *Lesbian philosophies and cultures.* Albany, NY: SUNY Press.

Fullilove, M.T., Fullilove, R.E., & Smith, M. (1993). Violence, trauma, and posttraumatic stress disorder among women drug abusers. *Journal of Traumatic Stress, 6,* 533–543.

Gallagher, J. (1994). Some things never change. *The Advocate,* 46–47 (May 17).

Gelinas, D. (1983). The persisting negative effects of incest. *Psychiatry, 46,* 312–332.

Gelinas, D. (1995). Dissociative identity disorders and the trauma paradigm. In L. Cohen, J. Berzoff, & M. Elin (Eds.), *Dissociative identity disorder: Theoretical and treatment controversies* (pp. 175–222). Northvale, NJ: Jason Aronson.

Gergen, K. (1985). The social constructionist movement in modern psychology. *American Psychologist, 40*(3), 317–329.

Gergen, K. (1991). *The saturated self: Dilemmas of identity in contemporary life.* New York: Basic Books.

Gil, E. (1992). *Outgrowing the pain together: A book for spouses and partners of adults abused as children.* New York: W.W. Norton.

Glass, S.G. (2003). *Not just friends: Protect your relationship from infidelity and heal the trauma of betrayal.* New York: Free Press.

Glazer, D. (2001). Introduction. In D. Glazer & J. Drescher (Eds.), *Gay and lesbian parenting* (pp. 1–6). New York: Haworth Press.

Globe and Mail website (2003). *www.globeandmail.com/servlet/story/RTGAM.20030612.*

Goffman, E. (1963). *Stigma: Notes on the management of a spoiled identity.* Englewood Cliffs, NJ: Prentice-Hall.

Goldberg, A. (1999). *Being of two minds.* Hillsdale, NJ: Analytic Press.

Goldner, V. (1989). Generation and gender: Normative and covert hierarchies. In M. Mc-Goldrick, C. Anderson, & F. Walsh (Eds.), *Women and families: A framework for family therapy* (pp. 42–60). New York: W.W. Norton.

Goldner, V. (1992). Making room for both/and. *Family Therapy Networker, 16,* 54–62.

Goldner, V. (1993). Current trends in feminist thought and therapy. *Journal of Feminist Family Therapy, 4,* 73–83.

Goldner, V. (1999). Morality and multiplicity: Perspectives on the treatment of violence in intimate life. *Journal of Marital and Family Therapy, 25,* 325–336.

Goldner, V., Penn, P., Sheinberg, M., & Walker, G. (1990). Love and violence: Gender paradoxes in volatile attachments. *Family Process, 29,* 343–364.

Goldstein, E. (2001). *Object relations theory and self psychology in social work practice.* New York: Free Press.

Gonsalves, C. (1990). The psychological effects of political repression on Chilean exiles in the U.S. *American Journal of Orthopsychiatry, 60,* 143–153.

Goodwin, J. (1990). Applying to adult incest victims what we have learned from victimized children. In R. Kluft (Ed.), *Incest related syndromes of adult psychopathology* (pp. 55–74). Washington DC: American Psychiatric Publishing.

Gorman, W. (2001). Refugee survivors of torture. *Professional Psychology: Research and Practice, 32*(5), 443–451.

Gottman, J. (1999). *The marriage clinic: A scientifically based marital therapy.* New York: W.W. Norton.

Graber, K. (1991). *Ghosts in the bedroom: A guide for partners of incest survivors.* Deerfield Beach, FL: Health Communication.

Graves, K. (2004). Resilience and adaptation among Alaska Native men (Doctoral dissertation, Smith College School for Social Work, 2004).

Green, B.L., Grace, M.C., Lindy, J.D., & Leonard, A.C. (1990). Race differences in response to combat stress. *Journal of Traumatic Stress 3*(3), 379–393.

Green, R.J., Bettinger, M., & Zacks, E. (1996). Are lesbian couples fused and gay male couples disengaged? Questioning gender straightjackets. In J. Laird & R.J. Green (Eds.), *Lesbians and gays in couples and families: A handbook for therapists* (pp. 185–230). San Francisco: Jossey-Bass.

Greenacre, P. (1957). The childhood and the artist: Libidinal phase development and giftedness. *Psychoanalytic Study of the Child, 12*(2), 7–72.

Greenan, D., & Tunnell, G. (2003). *Couple therapy with gay men.* New York: Guilford Press.

Greenberg, J., & Mitchell, S. (1983). *Object relations in psychoanalytic theory.* Cambridge, MA: Harvard University Press.

Greenberg, L., & Johnson, S. (1988). *Emotionally focused therapy for couples.* New York: Guilford Press.

Greene, B. (2000). African American lesbian and bisexual women in feminist–psychodynamic psychotherapies: Surviving and thriving between a rock and a hard place. In L. Jackson & B. Greene (Eds.), *Psychotherapy with African American women: Innovations in psychodynamic perspectives and practice* (pp. 82–125). New York: Guilford Press.

Grice, D., Brady, K., & Dustan, L. (1995). Sexual and physical assault history and posttraumatic stress disorder in substance-dependent individuals. *American Journal of Addiction, 4,* 297–305

Grier, W.H., & Cobbs, P.M. (1968). *Black rage.* New York: Basic Books.

Griffith, P.L., Myers, R.W., Cusick, G.M., & Tankersley, M.J. (1997). MMPI–2 profiles of women differing in sexual abuse history and sexual orientation. *Journal of Clinical Psychology, 53*(8), 791–800.

Grinker, R., & Spiegel, J. (1945). *Men under stress.* Philadelphia: Blakiston Press.

Grolnick, S. (1990). *The work and play of Winnicott.* Northvale, NJ: Jason Aronson.

Guerney, B. (1987). *Relationship enhancement manual.* State College, PA: Ideals.

Hairi, A.R., Bookheimer, S.Y., & Mazziota, J.C. (2000). Modulating emotional responses: Effects of a neocortical network on the limbic system. *NeuroReport, 11,* 43–48.

Hanna, E. (1993). The implications of shifting perspectives in countertransference on the therapeutic action of clinical social work: Part 1, The classical and early-totalist position. *Journal of Analytic Social Work, 1,* 25–52.

Hardtmann, G. (1998). Children of the Nazis: A psychodynamic perspective. In J. Danieli (Ed.), *International handbook of multigenerational legacies of trauma* (pp. 85–95). New York: Plenum Press.

Hare-Mustin, R. (1989). The problem of gender in family therapy theory. In M. McGoldrick, C. Anderson, & F. Walsh (Eds.), *Women in families: A framework for family therapy* (pp. 61–77). New York: W.W. Norton.

Hare-Mustin, R., & Maracek, J. (1994). Feminism and post-modernism: Dilemmas and points of resistance. *Dulwich Centre Newsletter, 4,* 13–19.

Harris, M. (1998). *Trauma recovery and empowerment: A clinician's guide for working with women in groups: Maxine Harris and the community connections trauma work group.* New York: Free Press.

Hartmann, A. (1996). Social policy as a context for lesbian and gay families: The political is personal. In J. Laird & R.J. Green (Eds.), *Lesbians and gays in couples and families: A handbook for therapists* (pp. 69–85). San Francisco: Jossey-Bass.

Hartmann, H. (1939). *Ego psychology and the problem of adaptation.* New York: International Universities Press.

Hazan, C., & Shaver, P. (1987). Romantic love conceptualized as an attachment process. *Journal of Personality and Social Psychology, 52*(3), 511–524.

Heiman, J. (1986). Treating sexually distressed marital relationships. In N. Jacobson & A. Gurman (Eds.), *Clinical handbook of marital therapy.* New York: Guilford Press.

Heimann, P. (1950). On countertransference. *International Journal of Psycho-Analysis, 31,* 81–84.

Helms, J. (1995). An update of Helm's white and people of color racial identity models. In J. Ponterotto, J. Casas, L. Suzuki, & C. Alexander (Eds.), *Handbook of multicultural counseling.* Thousand Oaks, CA: Sage.

Helms, J., & Cook, D. (1999). Models of racial oppression and sociorace. In *Using race and culture in counseling and psychotherapy* (pp. 69–100). Boston: Allyn & Bacon.

Herek, G.M. (1990). The context of anti-gay violence: Notes on cultural and psychological heterosexism. *Journal of Interpersonal Violence, 5,* 316–330.

Herek, G.M. (1996). Heterosexism and homophobia. In R.P. Cabaj & T.S. Stein (Eds.), *Textbook of homosexuality and mental health* (pp. 101–113). Washington, DC: American Psychiatric Publishing.

Herman, J. (1981). *Father–daughter incest.* Cambridge, MA: Harvard University Press.

Herman, J. (1992). *Trauma and recovery.* New York: Basic Books.

Herman, J., & Hirschman, L. (1977). Father–daughter incest. *Signs: Journal of Women in Culture and Society, 2,* 735–756.

Herman, J., & Lawrence, L. (1994). Group therapy and self-help groups for adult survivors of childhood incest. In M.B. Williams & J.F. Sommer (Eds.), *Handbook of post-traumatic therapy.* Westport, CT: Greenwood Press.

Herman, J., Perry, J., & van der Kolk, B.A. (1989). Childhood trauma in borderline personality disorder. *American Journal of Psychiatry, 146,* 490–495.

Hesse, E., Main, M., Abrams, K., & Rifkin, A. (2003). Unresolved states regarding loss or abuse can have "second-generation" effects: Disorganization, role inversion, and frightening ideation in the offspring of traumatized, non-maltreating parents. In M. Solomon & D. Siegel (Eds.), *Healing trauma: Attachment, mind, body, and brain* (pp. 57–106). New York: W.W. Norton.

Higginbotham, E., & Weber, L. (2001). Moving up with kin and community: Upward mobility for black and white women. In M. Andersen & P.H. Collins (Eds.), *Race, class, and gender: An anthology* (4th ed., pp. 156–167). Belmont, CA: Wadsworth Press.

Higgins, G.O. (1994). *Resilient adults.* San Francisco: Jossey-Bass.

Hindy, C.G., & Schwarz, J.C. (1994). Anxious romantic attachment in adult relationships. In M.B. Sperling & W.H. Berman (Eds.), *Attachment in adults: Clinical and developmental perspectives* (pp. 179–203). New York: Guilford Press.

Hoffman, L. (1981). *Foundations of family therapy: A conceptual framework for systems change.* New York: Basic Books.

Hogancamp, V., & Figley, C. (1983). War: Bringing the battle home. In C. Figley & H. McCubbin (Eds.), *Stress and the family* (Vol. II). *Coping with catastrophe.* New York: Brunner/Mazel.

Holtzworth-Munroe, A., Beatty, S.B., & Anglin, K. (1995). The assessment and treatment of marital violence: An introduction for the marital therapist. In N.S. Jacobson & A.S. Gurman (Eds.), *Clinical handbook for couple therapy* (pp. 316–339). New York: Guilford Press.

Horner, A. (1984). *Object relations and the developing ego in therapy.* New York: Jason Aronson.

Horowitz, M.J. (Ed.). (1989). *Essential papers on posttraumatic stress disorder.* New York: New York University Press.

Horowitz, M.J. (1998). *Cognitive psychodynamics: From conflict to character.* New York: John Wiley.

Human Rights Watch. (2001). *Hatred in the hallways: Violence and discrimination against lesbian, gay, bisexual, and transgender students in U.S. schools.* New York: Author.

Imber-Black, E. (1989). Rituals of stabilization and change in women's lives. In M. McGoldrick, C.M. Anderson, & F. Walsh (Eds.), *Women in families: A framework for family therapy* (pp. 451–469). New York: W.W. Norton.

Imber-Black, E., Roberts, J., & Whiting, R. (Eds.). (1998). *Rituals in families and family therapy.* New York: W.W. Norton.

Jacobs, T.J. (1983). The analyst and the patient's object world: Notes on an aspect of countertransference. *Journal of the American Psychoanalytic Association, 31,* 619–642.

Janoff-Bulman, R. (1992). *Shattered assumptions: Towards a new psychology of trauma.* New York: Free Press.

Jehu, D. (1988). *Beyond sexual abuse: Therapy with women who were childhood victims.* New York: John Wiley.

Jenkins, J. (1996). Culture, emotion, and PTSD. In A. Marsella, M. Friedman, E. Gerrity, & R. Scurfield (Eds.), *Ethnocultural aspects of posttraumatic stress disorder.* Washington, DC: American Psychological Association.

Johnson, D., Feldman, S., & Lubin, H. (1995). Critical interaction therapy: Couples therapy in combat-related posttraumatic stress disorder. *Family Process, 34,* 401–412.

Johnson, S.M. (2002). *Emotionally focused couple therapy with trauma survivors: Strengthening attachment bonds.* New York: Guilford Press.

Johnson, S.M., & Greenberg, L.S. (Eds.). (1994). *The heart of the matter: Perspectives on emotion in marital therapy.* New York: Brunner/Mazel.

Johnson, S.M., Makinen, J.A., & Millikin, J.W. (2001). Attachment injuries in couple relationships: A new perspective on impasses in couples therapy. *Journal of Marital and Family Therapy, 27*(20), 145–155.

Johnson, S.M., & Williams-Keeler, L. (1998). Creating healing relationships for couples dealing with trauma: The use of emotionally focused marital therapy. *Journal of Marital and Family Therapy, 24*(1), 25–40.

Johnson, T., & Keren, M. (1996). Creating and maintaining boundaries in male couples. In J. Laird & R.J. Green (Eds.), *Lesbians and gays in couples and families* (pp. 231–250). San Francisco: Jossey-Bass.

Jordan, B.K., Marmar, C.R., Fairbank, J.A., Schlenger, W.E., Kulka, R.A., Hough, R.L., & Weiss, D.S. (1992). Problems in families of male Vietnam veterans with posttraumatic stress disorder. *Journal of Consulting and Clinical Psychology, 60*(6), 916–926.

Kanninen, K., Punamaki, R.L., & Qouta, S. (2002). The relation of appraisal, coping efforts, and acuteness of trauma to PTS symptoms among former political prisoners. *Journal of Traumatic Stress, 15*(3), 245–253.

Kaplan, H.S. (1974). *The new sex therapy: Active treatment of sexual dysfunctions.* New York: Times Books.

Kardiner, A. (1941). *The traumatic neuroses of war.* Washington, DC: National Research Council.

Karpel, M. (1995). The role of the client's partner in the treatment of multiple personality disorder. In L. Cohen, J. Berzoff, & M. Elin (Eds.), *Dissociative identity disorder* (pp. 509–542). Northvale, NJ: Jason Aronson.

Kaufman, J., & Zigler, E. (1987). Do abused children become abusive parents? *American Journal of Orthopsychiatry, 57*(2), 186–192.

Kaye/Kantrowitz, M. (2000). Jews in the US: The rising costs of whiteness. In M. Adams, W. Blumenfeld, R. Castaneda, H. Hackman, M. Peters, & X. Zuniga (Eds.), *Readings for diversity and social justice* (pp. 138–144). New York: Routledge.

Keane, T., Weathers, F., & Foa, E. (2000). Diagnosis and assessment. In E. Foa, T. Keane, & M. Friedman (Eds.), *Effective treatments for PTSD.* New York: Guilford Press.

Keane, T., & Wolfe, J. (1990). Co-morbidity in post-traumatic stress disorder: An analysis of community and clinical studies. *Journal of Applied Social Psychology, 20,* 1776–1788.

Kellerman, N. (2001). Perceived parental rearing behavior in children of Holocaust survivors. *Israel Journal of Psychiatry and Related Sciences, 38*(1), 36–48.

Kelly, C., & Warshafsky, L. (1987). *Partner abuse in gay male and lesbian relationships.* Paper presented at the Third National Family Violence Research Conference, Dunham, NH.

Kerewsky, S.D., & Miller, D. (1996). Lesbian couples and childhood trauma. In J. Laird & R.J. Green (Eds.), *Lesbians and gays in couples and families* (pp. 298–315). San Francisco: Jossey-Bass.

Kernberg, O. (1975). *Borderline conditions and pathological narcissism.* New York: Jason Aronson.

Kernberg, O. (1976). *Object relations theory and clinical psychoanalysis.* New York: Jason Aronson.

Kersky, S., & Miller, D. (1996). Lesbian couples and childhood trauma: Guidelines for therapists. In J. Laird & R. Green (Eds.), *Lesbians and gays in couples and families.* San Francisco: Jossey-Bass.

Ketcham, K., & Asbury, W.F. (2000). *Beyond the influence: Understanding and defeating alcoholism.* New York: Bantam Books.

Khan, M. (1992). Introduction. In D.W. Winnicott (Ed.), *Through paediatrics to psycho-analysis: Collected papers*. New York: Brunner/Mazel.

King Keenan, E. (2001). Using Foucault's "disciplinary power" and "resistance" in cross-cultural psychotherapy. *Clinical Social Work Journal, 29*(3), 211–228.

King, L.A., King, D.W., Keane, T., Fairbank, J.A., & Adams, G.A. (1998). Resilience–recovery factors in post-traumatic stress disorder among female and male Vietnam veterans: Hardiness, postwar social support, and additional stressful life events. *Journal of Personality and Social Psychology, 74*(2), 420–434.

Kira, I.A. (2002). Torture assessment and treatment: The wraparound approach. *Traumatology, 8*(1), 23–51.

Kitzinger, C., & Coyle, A. (2002). Introducing lesbian and gay psychology. In A. Coyle & C. Kitzinger (Eds.), *Lesbian and gay psychology: New perspectives* (pp. 1–29). London: B.P.S. Blackwell.

Klein, M. (1948). *Contributors to psychoanalysis: 1921–1945*. London: Hogarth.

Klein, M. (1975). *Envy and gratitude & other works, 1946–1963*. New York: Delacorte Press.

Klinger, R., & Stein, T. (1996). Impact of violence, childhood sexual abuse, and domestic violence and abuse on lesbians, bisexuals, and gay men. In R. Cabaj & T. Stein (Eds.), *Textbook of homosexuality and mental health* (pp. 801–818). Washington, DC: American Psychiatric Publishing.

Kluft, R.P. (1992). Discussion: A specialist's perspective on multiple personality disorder. *Psychoanalytic Inquiry, 12*, 139–171.

Kluft, R.P. (1993). The initial stages of psychotherapy in the treatment of multiple personality disorder patients. *Dissociation, 6*(2/3), 145–161.

Kluft, R.P. (1995). The confirmation and disconfirmation of memories of abuse in DID patients: A naturalistic clinical study. *Dissociation, 8*(4), 253–258.

Kobak, R.R., & Hazan, C. (1991). Attachment in marriage: Effects of security and accuracy of working models. *Journal of Personality and Social Psychology, 60*(6), 861–869.

Kobak, R.R., & Sceery, A. (1988). Attachment in late adolescence: Working models, affect regulation and representations of self and others. *Child Development, 59*, 135–146.

Kondrat, M.E. (1999). Who is the "self" in self-aware: Professional self-awareness from a critical theory perspective. *Social Service Review, 73*(4), 451–477.

Krajeski, J. (1996). Homosexuality and the mental health professions: A contemporary history. In R. Cabaj & T. Stein (Eds.), *Textbook of homosexuality and mental health* (pp. 17–31). Washington, DC: American Psychiatric Association Press.

Krystal, J., Kosten, T., Southwick, S., Mason, J., Perry, B., & Giller, E. (1996). Neurobiological aspects of PTSD: Review of clinical and preclinical studies. In A. Marsella, M. Friedman, E. Gerrity, & R. Scurfield (Eds.), *Ethnocultural aspects of posttraumatic stress disorder: Issues, research and clinical applications*. Washington, DC: American Psychological Association.

Kudler, H., Blank, A., & Krupnick, J. (2000). Psychodynamic therapy. In E. Foa, T. Keane, & M. Friedman (Eds.), *Effective treatments for PTSD* (pp. 176–198). New York: Guilford Press.

Kulka, R.A., Schlenger, W.E., Fairbank, J.A., Hough, R.L., Jordan, B.K., Marmar, C.R., & Weiss, D.S. (1988). *Report of findings from the national Vietnam veterans readjustment study.* Research Triangle Park, NC: Research Triangle Institute.

Lachkar, J. (1992). *The narcissistic/borderline couple.* New York: Brunner/Mazel.

Laewig, G.B., & Anderson, M.D. (1992). Substance abuse in women: Relationship between chemical dependency of women and past reports of physical and/or sexual abuse. In C.M. Simpselle (Ed.), *Violence against women.* New York: Hemisphere.

Laird, J. (1993). Lesbian and gay families. In F. Walsh (Ed.), *Normal family processes* (2nd ed., pp. 282–328). New York: Guilford Press.

Laird, J. (1998). Theorizing culture: Narrative ideas and practice principles. In M. McGoldrick (Ed.), *Re-visioning family therapy: Race, culture and gender in clinical practice* (pp. 20–36). New York: Guilford Press.

Laird, J., & Green, R.J. (1996). Introduction: Lesbians and gays in couples and families: Central issues. In J. Laird & R.J. Green (Eds.), *Lesbians and gays in couples and families: A handbook for therapists* (pp. 1–12). San Francisco: Jossey-Bass.

Langhinrischen-Rohling, J., Neidig, P., & Thorn, G. (1995). Violent marriages: Gender differences in levels of current violence and past abuse. *Journal of Family Violence, 10,* 159–176.

Langston, D. (2001). Tired of playing Monopoly? In M. Andersen & P.H. Collins (Eds.), *Race, class, and gender: An anthology* (4th ed., pp. 125–134). Belmont, CA: Wadsworth Press.

Lansky, M. (1986). Marital therapy for narcissistic disorders. In N. Jacobson & A. Gurman (Eds.), *Clinical handbook of marital therapy.* New York: Guilford Press.

Lansky, M. (1991). Shame and fragmentation in the marital dyad. *Contemporary Family Therapy, 13*(1), 17–31.

Lee, E. (1997). *Working with Asian Americans: A guide for clinicians.* New York: Guilford Press.

Levendosky, A.A., & Graham-Bermann, S.A. (2000). Trauma and parenting in battered women: An addition to an ecological model of parenting. *Journal of Aggression, Maltreatment & Trauma, 3*(1, No. 5), 25–35.

Levin, J., & Weiss, R. (1994). *The dynamics and treatment of alcoholism: Essential papers.* Northvale, NJ: Jason Aronson.

Lewis, M. (1998). Shame and stigma. In P. Gilbert & B. Andrews (Eds.), *Shame: Interpersonal behavior, psychopathology, and culture* (pp. 126–140). New York: Oxford University Press.

Lindy, J. (1996). Psychoanalytic psychotherapy of post-traumatic stress disorder. In B. van der Kolk, A. McFarlane, & L. Weisaeth (Eds.), *Traumatic stress: The effects of overwhelming experiences on mind, body and society* (pp. 525–536). New York: Guilford Press.

Linehan, M. (1993). *Cognitive behavioral treatment of borderline personality disorder.* New York: Guilford Press.

Linehan, M. (1995). *Understanding borderline personality disorder: The dialectical approach.* New York: Jason Aronson.

Liotti, G. (1992). Disorganized/disoriented attachment in the etiology of the dissociative disorders. *Dissociation, 5,* 196–204.

Lipchik, E., & Kubicki, A. (1996). Solution-focused domestic violence views: Bridges toward a new reality in couples therapy. In D.M. Scott, M. Hubbell, & B. Duncan (Eds.), *Handbook of solution-focused brief therapy* (pp. 65–98). San Francisco: Jossey-Bass.

Liu, P., & Chan, C. (1996). Lesbian, gay, and bisexual Asian Americans and their families. In J. Laird & R.J. Green (Eds.), *Lesbians and gays in couples and families: A handbook for therapists* (pp. 137–152). San Francisco: Jossey-Bass.

Loftus, E.F. (1993). The reality of repressed memories. *American Psychologist, 48*(5), 518–537.

Loftus, E.F., Polonsky, S., & Fullilove, M.T. (1994). Memories of childhood sexual abuse: Remembering and repressing. *Psychology of Women Quarterly, 18,* 67–84.

LoPiccolo, J., & LoPiccolo, L. (Eds.) (1978). *Handbook of sex therapy.* New York: Plenum Press.

Lorber, J. (2000). "Night to his day": The social construction of gender. In M. Adams, W. Blumenfeld, R. Castaneda, H. Hackman, M. Peters, & X. Zuniga (Eds.), *Readings for diversity and social justice* (pp. 203–213). New York: Routledge.

Luepnitz, D.A. (1988). *The family interpreted: Feminist theory in clinical practice.* New York: Basic Books.

Lyons-Ruth, K., Alpern, L., & Repoacholi, B. (1993). Disorganized infant attachment classification and maternal psychosocial problems as predictors of hostile–aggressive behavior in the preschool classroom. *Child Development, 64,* 572–585.

Lyons-Ruth, K., & Block, D. (1996). The disturbed caregiving system: Relations among childhood trauma, maternal caregiving, and infant affect and attachment. *Infant Mental Health Journal, 17*(3), 257–275.

Lyons-Ruth, K., & Jacobvitz, D. (1999). Attachment disorganization. Unresolved loss, relational violence, and lapses in behavioral and attentional strategies. In J. Cassidy & P.R. Shaver (Eds.), *Handbook of attachment: Theory, research and clinical applications* (pp. 520–554). New York: Guilford Press.

Mahler, M. (1968). *On human symbiosis and the vicissitudes of individuation.* New York: International Universities Press.

Mahler, M., Pine, F., & Bergman, A. (1975). *The psychological birth of the human infant: Symbiosis and individuation.* New York: Basic Books.

Main, M. (1995). Recent studies in attachment: Overview, with selected implications for clinical work. In S. Goldberg, R. Muir, & J. Kerr (Eds.), *Attachment theory: Social, developmental, and clinical perspectives* (pp. 407–474). Hillsdale, NJ: Analytic Press.

Main, M., & Goldwyn, R. (1984). Predicting rejection of her infant from mother's representation of her own experience: Implications for the abused–abusing intergenerational cycle. *Child Abuse and Neglect 8,* 203–217.

Main, M., Kaplan, N., & Cassidy, J. (1985). Security in infancy, childhood, and adulthood: A move to the level of representation. In I. Bretherton & E. Waters (Eds.), *Growing points of attachment theory and research* (Monographs of the Society for Research in

Child Development, Serial 209, Vol. 50, No. 1–2, pp. 66–104). Ann Arbor, MI: University of Michigan.

Main, M., & Solomon, J. (1986). Discovery of a new, insecure–disorganized/disoriented attachment pattern. In T. Brazelton & M.W. Yogman (Eds.), *Affective development in infancy* (pp. 95–124). Norwood, NJ: Ablex.

Main, M., & Solomon, J. (1990). Procedures for identifying infants as disorganized/disoriented during the Ainsworth strange situation. In M. Greenberg, D. Cicchetti, & E.M. Cummings (Eds.), *Attachment during the preschool years: Theory, research and intervention* (pp. 121–160). Chicago: University of Chicago Press.

Maker, A.H., & Buttenheim, M. (2000). Parenting difficulties in sexual-abuse survivors: A theoretical framework with dual psychodynamic and cognitive–behavioral strategies for intervention. *Psychotherapy, 37*(2), 159–170.

Maloney, L.J. (1987). Post-traumatic stresses on women partners of Vietnam veterans. *Smith College Studies in Social Work,* 122–143.

Maltas, C., & Shay, J. (1995). Trauma contagion in partners of survivors of childhood sexual abuse. *American Journal of Orthopsychiatry, 65*(4), 529–539.

Maltz, W. (1988). Identifying and treating the sexual repercussions of incest: A couples therapy approach. *Journal of Sex and Marital Therapy, 14,* 142–170.

Maltz, W. (1991). *The sexual healing journey: A guide for survivors of sexual abuse.* New York: HarperCollins.

Maltz, W. (1992). Caution: Treating sexual abuse can be hazardous to your love life. *Treating Abuse Today, 2*(2), 20–24.

Maltz, W. (1994). Sex therapy with survivors of sexual abuse. *Moving Forward, 3*(1). Retrieved from *http://movingforward.org.*

Manson, S. (1997). Cross-cultural and multiethnic assessment of trauma. In J.P. Wilson & T.M. Keane (Eds.), *Assessing psychological trauma and PTSD* (pp. 239–266). New York: Guilford Press.

Marcenko, M.O., Kemp, S.P., & Larson, N.C. (2000). Childhood experiences of abuse, later substance use, and parenting outcomes among low-income mothers. *American Journal of Orthopsychiatry, 70*(3), 316–326.

Marsella, A., Friedman, M., Gerrity, E., & Scurfield, R. (Eds.). (1996). *Ethnocultural aspects of posttraumatic stress disorder: Issues, research, and clinical applications.* Washington, DC: American Psychological Association.

Matsakis, A. (1994). Dual, triple and quadruple trauma couples: Dynamics and treatment issues. In M.B. Williams & J. F. Sommer (Eds.), *Handbook of posttraumatic therapy* (pp. 78–93). Westport, CT: Greenwood Press.

McCann, I.L, & Pearlman, L.A. (1990). Vicarious traumatization: A contextual model for understanding the effects of trauma on helpers. *Journal of Traumatic Stress, 3*(1), 131–149.

McCarthy, B.W. (1990). Treating sexual dysfunction associated with prior sexual trauma. *Journal of Sex and Marital Therapy, 16*(3), 142–146.

McCloskey, L.A., & Walker, M. (2000). Posttraumatic stress in children exposed to family violence and single-event trauma. *Journal of the American Academy of Child and Adolescent Psychiatry, 39*(1), 108–115.

McFarlane, A., & van der Kolk, B. (1996). Trauma and its challenge to society. In B. van der Kolk, A. McFarlane, & L. Weisaeth (Eds.), *Traumatic stress: The effects of overwhelming experience on mind, body, and society* (pp. 24–46). New York: Guilford Press.

McGoldrick, M. (1998). *Re-visioning family therapy: Race, culture and gender in clinical practice.* New York: Guilford Press.

McIntosh, P. (2001). White privilege and male privilege. In M. Andersen & P. Collins (Eds.), *Race, class, and gender: An anthology* (pp. 95–105). Belmont, CA: Wadsworth.

McMahon, M. (1997). Creating harmony out of dissonance: Applying theories of intersubjectivity to therapy with couples. *Journal of Analytic Social Work, 4*(3), 43–61.

McNay, L. (1992). *Foucault and feminism: Power, gender, and the self.* Boston: Northeastern University Press.

Melano Flanagan, L. (1996). Object relations theory. In J. Berzoff, L. Melano Flanagan, & P. Hertz (Eds.), *Inside out and outside in: Psychodynamic clinical theory and practice in contemporary multicultural contexts* (pp. 127–171). Northvale, NJ: Jason Aronson.

Mennen, F.E. (1990). Dilemmas and demands: Working with adult survivors of sexual abuse. *Affilia, 5*(4), 72–86.

Merscham, C. (2000). Restorying trauma with narrative therapy: Using the phantom family. *Family Journal: Counseling and Therapy for Couples and Families, 8*(3), 282–286.

Merskey, H. (1995). The manufacture of personalities: The production of multiple personality disorder. In L. Cohen, J. Berzoff, & M. Elin (Eds.), *Dissociative identity disorder* (pp. 3–32). Northvale, NJ: Jason Aronson.

Miehls, D. (1993). Conjoint treatment with narcissistic couples: Strategies to increase empathic interaction. *Smith College Studies in Social Work, 64*(1), 3–17.

Miehls, D. (1996). Somatic illness: An attempt to further intrapsychic growth in couple systems. *Smith College Studies in Social Work, 67*(1), 7–19.

Miehls, D. (1997). Projective identification in sexual abuse survivors and their partners: Couple treatment implications. *Journal of Analytic Social Work, 4*(2), 5–22.

Miehls, D. (1999). Couple therapy: An integration of object relations and intersubjective theory. *Smith College Studies in Social Work, 69*(2), 335–355.

Miehls, D. (2001). The interface of racial identity development with identity complexity in clinical social work student practitioners. *Clinical Social Work Journal, 29*(3), 229–244.

Miehls, D., & Moffatt, K. (2000). Constructing social work identity based on the reflexive self. *British Journal of Social Work, 30*, 339–348.

Mikulincer, M., Florian, V., & Weller, A. (1993). Attachment styles, coping strategies and posttraumatic psychological distress: The impact of the Gulf War in Israel. *Journal of Personality and Social Psychology, 64*(5), 817–826.

Miliora, M. (2000). Beyond empathic failures: Cultural racism as narcissistic trauma and the disenfranchisement of grandiosity. *Clinical Social Work Journal, 28*(1), 43–54.

Miller, D. (1994). *Women who hurt themselves: A book of hope and understanding.* New York: Basic Books.

Miller, D. (2003). The end of innocence. *Psychotherapy Networker,* 24–33 (July/August).

Miller, D., & Guidry, L. (2001). *Addictions and trauma recovery: Healing the body, mind and spirit.* New York: W.W. Norton.

Miller, R.J., Bobner, R.R., & Zarski, J.J. (2000). Sexual identity development: A base for work with same-sex couple partner abuse. *Contemporary Family Therapy, 22*(2), 189–200.

Miller, W.R., & Rollnick, S. (1991). *Motivational interviewing: Preparing people to change addictive behavior.* New York: Guilford Press.

Mirkin, M.P. (1998). The impact of multiple contexts on recent immigrant families. In M. McGoldrick (Ed.), *Re-visioning family therapy: Race, culture, and gender in clinical practice* (pp. 370–383). New York: Guilford Press.

Mitchell, S. (1988). *Relational concepts in psychoanalysis.* Cambridge: Harvard University Press.

Mitchell, S. (1993). *Hope and dread in psychoanalysis.* New York: Basic Books.

Mitchell, S., & Black, M. (1995). *Freud and beyond: A history of modern psychoanalytic thought.* New York: Basic Books.

Mock, M. (1998). Clinical reflections on refugee families. In M. McGoldrick (Ed.), *Re-visioning family therapy: Race, culture and gender in clinical practice* (pp. 347–359). New York: Guilford Press.

Modell, A. (1998). Windows opened and closed: Repetition and deficit in the negotiation of affect. In J. Teicholz & D. Kriegman (Eds.), *Trauma, repetition & affect regulation: The work of Paul Russell.* New York: Other Press.

Moffatt, K. (1999). Surveillance and government of the welfare recipient. In A. Chambon, A. Irving, & L. Epstein (Eds.), *Reading Foucault for social work* (pp. 219–245). New York: Columbia University Press.

Moffatt, K. (2001). *A poetics of social work: Personal agency and social transformation in Canada, 1920–1939.* Toronto: Toronto University Press.

Morris, P., & Silove, D. (1992). Cultural influences in psychotherapy with refugee survivors of torture and trauma. *Hospital and Community Psychiatry, 43*(8), 820–824.

Morrow, S., & Hawxhurst, D. (1989). Lesbian partner abuse: Implications for therapists. *Journal of Counseling and Development, 68,* 58–62.

Munro, K. (2001). Sexual abuse survivors and sex. *Healing Words Newsletter, 3.* Retrieved from *www.kalimunro.com/article_sexualabuse_and_sex.html.*

Munroe, J., Shay, J., Fisher, L., Makary, C., Rapperport, K., & Zimering, R. (1995). Preventing compassion fatigue: A team treatment model. In C. Figley (Ed.), *Compassion fatigue: Coping with secondary traumatic stress disorder in those who treat the traumatized* (pp. 209–231). New York: Brunner/Mazel.

Nace, E.P., Davis, C.W., & Gaspari, J.P. (1991). Axis II comorbidity in substance abusers. *American Journal of Psychiatry, 70*(1), 118–120.

Nadelson, C., & Polonsky, D. (1991). Childhood sexual abuse: The invisible ghost in couple therapy. *Psychiatric Annals, 21*(8), 479–484.

Nader, K., Dubrow, N., & Stamm, B.H. (1999). Foreword. In K. Nader, N. Dubrow, & B. Stamm (Eds.), *Honoring differences: Cultural issues in the treatment of trauma and loss.* Levittown, PA: Brunner/Mazel.

Nagata, D.K. (1998). Intergenerational effects of the Japanese American internment. In Y. Danieli (Ed.), *International handbook of multigenerational legacies of trauma.* New York: Plenum Press.

Najavits, L., Weiss, R., & Shaw, S. (1997). The link between substance abuse and post-traumatic stress disorder in women: A research review. *American Journal on Addictions, 6,* 273–282.

Najavits, L., Weiss, R., Shaw, S., & Muenz, L. (1998). "Seeking safety": Outcome of a new cognitive–behavioral psychotherapy for women with post-traumatic stress disorder and substance dependence. *Journal of Traumatic Stress, 11*(3), 437–456.

National Association of Social Workers. (2000). *NASW code of ethics.* Washington, DC: NASW Press.

National Clearinghouse on Child Abuse and Neglect. Retrieved March 22, 2004, from *www.nccanch.acf.hhs.gov/.*

Neal, J.H., Zimmerman, J.L., & Dickerson, V.C. (1999). Couples, culture and discourse: A narrative approach. In J. M. Donovan (Ed.), *Short-term couple therapy* (pp. 360–400). New York: Guilford Press.

Nelson, B., & Wright, D. (1996). Understanding and treating post-traumatic stress disorder symptoms in female partners of veterans with PTSD. *Journal of Marital and Family Therapy, 22*(4), 455–467.

Nijenhuis, E.R.S., Vanderlinden, J., & Spinhoven, P. (1998). Animal defensive reactions as a model for trauma-induced dissociative reactions. *Journal of Traumatic Stress, 11*(2), 243–260.

Noonan, M. (1998). Understanding the "difficult" patient from a dual person perspective. *Clinical Social Work Journal, 26*(2), 129–141.

Noonan, M. (1999). Difficult dyads: Understanding affective and relational components from an intersubjective perspective. *Smith College Studies in Social Work, 69*(2), 388–402.

Northcut, T. (1999). Integrating psychodynamic and cognitive–behavioral theory: A psycho-dynamic perspective. In T. Northcut & N. Heller (Eds.), *Enhancing psychodynamic therapy with cognitive–behavioral techniques* (pp. 17–51). Northvale, NJ: Jason Aronson.

Northcut, T. (2000). Constructing a place for religion and spirituality in psychodynamic practice. *Clinical Social Work Journal, 28*(2), 155–169.

Norwood, A., & Ursano, R. (1996). The Gulf War. In R. Ursano & A. Norwood (Eds.), *Emotional aftermath of the Persian Gulf War: Veterans, families, communities, and nations.* Washington, DC: American Psychiatric Press Association.

O'Connell-Higgins, G. (1994). *Resilient adults: Overcoming a cruel past.* San Francisco: Jossey-Bass.

O'Dell, S. (2000). Psychotherapy with gay and lesbian families: Opportunities for cultural inclusion and clinical challenge. *Clinical Social Work Journal, 28*(2), 171–182.

O'Donohue, W., & Elliot, A. (1992). The current status of posttraumatic stress disorder as a diagnostic category: Problems and proposals. *Journal of Traumatic Stress, 5*, 4221–4239.

Office of the United Nations High Commissioner for Refugees. *Statistics.* Retrieved March 10, 2003, from *www.unhcr.ch/cgi–bin/texis/vtx/basics.*

Ogden, P., & Minton, K. (2000). Sensorimotor psychotherapy: One method for processing traumatic memory. *Traumatology, 6*(3), 1–20.

Ogden, T.H. (1982). *Projective identification & psychotherapeutic technique.* New York: Jason Aronson.

Olson, D.H., & Gorrall, D.M. (2003). Circumplex model of marital and family systems. In F. Walsh (Ed.), *Normal family processes: Growing diversity and complexity* (3rd ed., pp. 514–548). New York: Guilford Press.

Olson, D.H., Russell, C.S., & Sprenkle, D.H. (1980). Circumplex model of marital and family systems, II: Empirical studies and clinical intervention. *Advances in Family Intervention, Assessment, and Theory, 1*, 129–179.

Ortner, S. (1996). *Making gender: The politics and erotics of culture.* Boston: Beacon Press.

Osofsky, J.D. (1988). Attachment theory and research and the psychoanalytic process. *Psychoanalytic Psychology, 5*(2), 159–177.

Paddison, P.L., Einbender, R.G., Maker, E., & Strain, J.J. (1993). Group treatment with incest survivors. In P.L. Paddison (Ed.), *Treatment of adult survivors of incest.* Washington, DC: American Psychiatric Publishing.

Papadopoulos, R.K. (2001). Refugee families: Issues of systemic supervision. *Journal of Family Therapy, 23*, 405–422.

Parson, E.R. (1985). The intercultural setting: Encountering black Vietnam veterans. In S.M. Sonnenberg, A.S. Blank, Jr., & J.A. Talbott (Eds.), *The trauma of war: Stress and recovery in Vietnam veterans* (pp. 359–387). Washington DC: American Psychiatric Publishing.

Pearlman, L., & Saakvitne, K. (1995). *Trauma and the therapist: Countertransference and vicarious traumatization in psychotherapy with incest survivors.* New York: W.W. Norton.

Pérez-Foster, R.M. (1998). The clinician's cultural countertransference: The psychodynamics of culturally competent practice. *Clinical Social Work Journal, 26*(3), 253–270.

Perry, B.D., Pollard, R., Blakely, T., Baker, W.L., & Vigilante, D. (1995). Childhood trauma, the neurobiology of adaptation and "use dependent" development of the brain: How "states" become "traits." *Infant Mental Health Journal, 16*(4), 271–291.

Perry, P. (1997). Incubated in terror: Neurodevelopmental factors in the "cycle of violence." In J. Osofsky (Ed.), *Children, youth and violence: The search for solutions.* New York: Guilford Press.

Persinger, M.A., & Makarec, M. (1991). Greater right hemisphericity is associated with lower self-esteem in adults. *Perceptual and Motor Skills, 73*, 1244–1246.

Person, E.S. (1988). *Dreams of love and fateful encounters.* New York: Bruner/Mazel.

Piastro, D. (1999). Coping with the transitions in our lives: From "afflicted" identity to personal empowerment and pride. *Reflections,* 42–46 (Fall).

Pinderhughes, E. (1998). Black genealogy revisited: Restorying an African-American family. In M. McGoldrick (Ed.), *Re-visioning family therapy: Race, culture and gender in clinical practice* (pp. 179–199). New York: Guilford Press.

Piper, A. (1994). Multiple personality disorder. *British Journal of Psychiatry, 164,* 600–612.

Piper, A. (1995). A skeptical look at multiple personality disorder. In L. Cohen, J. Berzoff, & M. Elin (Eds.), *Dissociative identity disorder.* Northvale, NJ: Jason Aronson.

Pistorello, J., & Follette, V. (1998). Childhood sexual abuse and couples' relationships: Female survivors' reports in therapy groups. *Journal of Marital and Family Therapy, 24*(4), 473–485.

Post, R.M., Weiss, R.B., & Leverich, G.S. (1994). Recurrent affective disorder: Roots in developmental neurobiology and illness progression based on changes in gene expression. *Development and Psychopathology, 6,* 781–813.

Post, R.M., Weiss, S.R.B., Smith, M., Li, H., & McCann, U. (1997). Kindling versus quenching: Implications for the evolution and treatment of posttraumatic stress disorder. In R. Yehuda & A.C. McFarlane (Eds.), *Psychobiology of posttraumatic stress disorder* (Vol. 821, pp. 285–295). New York: New York Academy of Sciences Press.

Pouissant, A., & Alexander, A. (2000). *Laying my burden down: Unraveling suicide and the mental health issues among African Americans.* Boston: Beacon Press.

Prior, S. (1996). *Object relations in severe trauma.* Northvale, NJ: Jason Aronson.

Prochaska, J.O., DiClemente, C.C., & Norcross, J.C. (1992). In search of how people change: Applications to addictive behaviors. *American Psychologist, 47,* 1102–1114.

Purcell, D., & Hicks, D. (1996). Institutional discrimination against lesbians, gay men, and bisexuals: The courts, legislature, and the military. In R. Cabaj & T. Stein (Eds.), *Textbook of homosexuality and mental health* (pp. 763–782). Washington, DC: American Psychiatric Publishing.

Putnam, F. (1989). *Diagnosis and treatment of multiple personality disorder.* New York: Guilford Press.

Putnam, F. (1995a). Negative rebuttal. *Journal of the American Academy of Child and Adolescent Psychiatry, 34,* 963.

Putnam, F. (1995b). Resolved: Multiple personality disorder is an individually and socially created artifact: Negative. *Journal of the American Academy of Child and Adolescent Psychiatry, 34,* 960–962.

Putnam, F., & Tricket, P. (1997). Psychobiological effects of sexual abuse: A longitudinal study. In R. Yehuda & A. McFarlane (Eds.), *Psychobiology of posttraumatic stress disorder* (Vol. 821, pp. 150–159). New York: New York Academy of Sciences Press.

Pynoos, R.S., Steinberg, A.M., Ornitz, E.M., & Goenjian, A.K. (1997). Issues in the developmental neurobiology of traumatic stress. In R. Yehuda & A.C. McFarlane (Eds.), *Psychobiology of posttraumatic stress disorder* (Vol. 821, pp. 176–193). New York: New York Academy of Sciences Press.

Pynoos, R., Steinberg, A., & Wraith, R. (1995). A developmental model of childhood traumatic stress. In D. Cicchetti & D. Cohen (Eds.), *Manual of developmental psychopathology: Risk disorder, adaptation* (pp. 72–95). New York: John Wiley.

Rabin, C., & Nardi, C. (1991). Treating post-traumatic stress disorder couples: A psycho-educational program. *Community Mental Health Journal, 27*(3), 209–224.

Racker, H. (1968). *Transference and countertransference.* Surrey, England: Meadway Press.

Rampage, C. (1991). Personal authority and women's self-stories. In T.J. Goodrich (Ed.), *Women and power: Perspectives for family therapy* (pp. 109–122). New York: W.W. Norton.

Rauch, S.L., van der Kolk, B.A., Fisler, R.E., Alpert, N.M., Orr, S.P., Savage, C.R., et al. (1996). A symptom provocation study of posttraumatic stress disorder using positron emission tomography and script-driven imagery. *Archives of General Psychiatry, 53,* 380–387.

Reichelt, S., & Sveaass, N. (1994). Therapy with refugee families: What is a "good" conversation? *Family Process, 33,* 247–262.

Renzetti, C. (1992). *Violent betrayal: Partner abuse in lesbian relationships.* Newbury Park, CA: Sage.

Richman, N. (1998). Looking before and after: Refugees and asylum seekers in the west. In P.J. Bracken & C. Petty (Eds.), *Rethinking the trauma of war.* New York: Free Association Books.

Riggs, D. (2000). Marital and family therapy. In E.B. Foa, T.M. Keane, & M.J. Friedman (Eds.), *Effective treatments for PTSD* (pp. 280–301). New York: Guilford Press.

Riggs, D., Byrne, C., Weathers, F., & Litz, B. (1998). The quality of the intimate relationships of male Vietnam veterans: Problems associated with posttraumatic stress disorder. *Journal of Traumatic Stress, 11*(1), 87–101.

Rivera, R. (1991). Sexual orientation and the law. In J. Gonsiorek & J. Weinrich (Eds.), *Homosexuality: Research implications for public policy* (pp. 81–100). Newbury Park, CA: Sage.

Roche, D.N., Runtz, M.G., & Hunter, M.A. (1999). Adult attachment: A mediator between child sexual abuse and later psychological adjustment. *Journal of Interpersonal Violence, 14*(2), 184–207.

Rolland, J. (1994). *Families, illness, & disability: An integrative treatment model.* New York: Basic Books.

Rosenbloom, D.J., Pratt, A.C., & Pearlman, L.A. (1999). Helpers' responses to trauma work: Understanding and intervening in an organization. In B.H. Stamm (Ed.), *Secondary traumatic stress: Self-care issues for clinicians, researchers, and educators* (rev. ed.). Baltimore: Sidran Press.

Rosenheck, R., & Fontana, A. (1998). Warrior fathers and warrior sons: Intergenerational aspects of trauma. In Y. Danieli (Ed.), *International handbook of multigenerational legacies of trauma.* New York: Plenum Press.

Rothschild, B. (2000). *The body remembers: the psychophysiology of trauma and trauma treatment.* New York: W.W. Norton.

Rustin, J. (1997). Infancy, agency, and intersubjectivity. *Psychoanalytic Dialogues, 7*(1), 43–62.

Rutter, M. (1985). Resilience in the face of adversity: Protective factors and resistance to psychiatric disorder. *British Journal of Psychiatry, 147,* 598–611.

Rutter, M. (1987). Psychosocial resilience and protective mechanisms. *American Journal of Orthopsychiatry, 57*(3), 316–331.

Rutter, M. (1993). Resilience: Some conceptual considerations. *Journal of Adolescent Health, 14*, 626–631.

Ruzek, J., Polusny, M., & Abueg, F. (1998). Assessment and treatment of concurrent post-traumatic stress disorder and substance abuse. In V. Follette, J. Ruzek, & F. Abueg (Eds.), *Cognitive–behavioral therapies for trauma* (pp. 226–255). New York: Guilford Press.

Ryff, C., Singer, B., Deinberg-Love, G., & Essex, M. (1998). Resilience in adulthood and later life: Defining features and dynamic processes. In J. Lomranz (Ed.), *Handbook of aging and mental health: An integrative approach.* New York: Plenum Press.

Saakvitne, K.W. (1995). Vicarious traumatization: Countertransference responses to dissociative clients. In L. Cohen, J. Berzoff, & M. Elin (Eds.), *Dissociative identity disorder* (pp. 467–492). Northvale, NJ: Jason Aronson.

Same-Sex Marriage? (2003). Retrieved November 19, 2003, from *www.cnn.com/2003/LAW11/18/samesex.marriage.ruling.*

Scarf, M. (1987). *Intimate partners: Patterns in love and marriage.* New York: Ballantine Books.

Schamess, G. (1996). Ego psychology. In J. Berzoff, L. Melano Flanagan, & P. Hertz (Eds.), *Inside out and outside in: Psychodynamic clinical theory and practice in contemporary multicultural contexts* (pp. 67–101). Northvale, NJ: Jason Aronson.

Scharff, D., & Scharff, J. (1987). *Object relations family therapy.* Northvale, NJ: Jason Aronson.

Scharff, D., & Scharff, J. (1991). *Object relations couple therapy.* Northvale, NJ: Jason Aronson.

Scharff, J.S. (1989). Object relations theory and its application to family therapy. In J.S. Scharff (Ed.), *Foundations of object relations family therapy* (pp. 11–22). Northvale, NJ: Jason Aronson.

Schechter, S. (1982). *Women and male violence: The visions and struggles of the battered women's movement.* Boston: South End Press.

Schnarch, D. (1991). *Constructing the crucible: An integration of sex and couple therapy.* New York: W.W. Norton.

Schoenewolf, G. (1993). *Counterresistance: The therapist's interference with the therapeutic process.* Northvale, NJ: Jason Aronson.

Schore, A.N. (1997). A century after Freud's project: Is a rapprochement between psychoanalysis and neurobiology at hand? *Journal of the American Psychoanalytic Association, 45*, 841–867.

Schore, A.N. (1998). Early trauma and the development of the right brain. In P. Gilbert & B. Andrews (Eds.), *Shame, interpersonal behavior, psychopathology, and culture* (pp. 57–77). New York: Oxford University Press.

Schore, A.N. (1999) *The development of a predisposition to violence: The critical roles of attachment disorders and the maturation of the right brain.* Unpublished invited presentation, Children's Institute International Conference, Understanding the roots of violence: Kids who kill. Good Samaritan Hospital, Los Angeles, CA (March).

Schore, A.N. (2000). Attachment and the regulation of the right brain. *Attachment and Human Development, 2*(1), 23–47.

Schore, A.N. (2001a). The effects of a secure attachment relationship on right brain development, affect regulation, and infant mental health. *Infant Mental Health Journal, 22*(1–2), 7–66.

Schore, A.N. (2001b). The effects of early relational trauma on right brain development, affect regulation, and infant mental health. *Infant Mental Health Journal, 22*(1–2), 201–269.

Schore, A.N. (2003). Early relational trauma, disorganized attachment, and the development of the predisposition to violence. In M.F. Solomon & D.J. Siegel (Eds.), *Healing trauma: Attachment, mind, body and brain* (pp. 107–167). New York: W.W. Norton.

Sedlak, A., & Broadhurst, D. (1996). Executive summary of the third national incidence study of child abuse and neglect. Washington, DC: U.S. Government Printing Office.

Sgoifo, A., Koolhaas, J., De Boer, S., Musso, E., Stilli, D., Buwalda, B., & Meerlo, P. (1999). Social stress, autonomic neural activation and cardiac activity in rats. *Neuroscience and Biobehavioral Reviews, 23,* 915–923.

Shapiro, D.L., & Levendosky, A.A. (1999). Adolescent survivors of childhood sexual abuse: The mediating role of attachment style and coping in psychological and interpersonal functioning. *Child Abuse and Neglect, 23*(11), 1175–1191.

Shapiro, F. (1995). *Eye movement desensitization and reprocessing: Principles, protocols and procedures.* New York: Guilford Press.

Shapiro, F. (2001). *Eye movement desensitization and reprocessing: Basic principles, protocols and procedures* (2nd ed.). New York: Guilford Press.

Shapiro, F., & Maxfield, L. (2003). EMDR and information processing in psychotherapy treatment: Personal development and global implications. In M.F. Solomon & D.J. Siegel (Eds.), *Healing trauma: Attachment, mind, body and brain* (pp. 196–220). New York: W.W. Norton.

Shapiro, J. (1995). *Eye movement desensitization and reprocessing: Principles, protocols, and procedures.* New York: Guilford Press.

Shapiro, J., & Appelgate, J. (2000). Cognitive neuroscience, neurobiology and affect regulation: Implications for clinical social work. *Clinical Social Work Journal, 28*(1), 9–21.

Sharpe, S. (1997). Countertransference and diagnosis in couples therapy. In M. Solomon & J. Siegel (Eds.), *Countertransference and couples therapy* (pp. 38–71). New York: W.W. Norton.

Sharpe, S. (2000). *The ways we love: A developmental approach to treating couples.* New York: Guilford Press.

Sheehan, P. (1994). Treating intimacy issues of traumatized people. In M.B. Williams & J.F. Sommer, Jr. (Eds.), *Handbook of post-traumatic therapy.* Westport, CT: Greenwood Press.

Sheinberg, M. (1992). Navigating treatment impasses at the disclosure of incest: Combining ideas from feminism and social constructionism. *Family Process, 31,* 201–216.

Sheinberg, M., & Fraenkel, P. (2001). *The relational trauma of incest: A family based approach to treatment.* New York: Guilford Press.

Shin, L.M., McNally, R.J., Kosslyn, S.M., Thompson, W.L., Rauch, S.L., Alpert, N.M., et al. (1999) Visual imagery and perception of posttraumatic stress disorder: A positron emission tomographic investigation. *Archives of General Psychiatry, 54,* 233–241.

Siegel, D.J. (1999). The developing mind: Toward a neurobiology of interpersonal experience. New York: Guilford Press.

Siegel, D.J. (2003). An interpersonal neurobiology of psychotherapy: The developing mind and the resolution of trauma In M.F. Solomon & D.J. Siegel (Eds.), *Healing trauma: Attachment, mind, body and brain* (pp. 1–56). New York: W.W. Norton.

Siegel, J. (1991). Analysis of projective identification: An object-relations approach marital treatment. *Clinical Social Work Journal, 19*(1), 71–81.

Siegel, J. (1992). *Repairing intimacy: An object relations approach to couples therapy.* Northvale, NJ: Jason Aronson.

Siegel, J. (1997). Applying countertransference theory to couples treatment. In M. Solomon & J. Siegel (Eds.), *Countertransference in couples therapy.* New York: W.W. Norton.

Sodomy laws. (2003). Retrieved August 20, 2003, from *www.sodomylaws.org/lawrence/lawrence.htm.*

Solomon, M. (1989). *Narcissism and intimacy: love and marriage in an age of confusion.* New York: W.W. Norton.

Solomon, M. (1997). Countertransference and empathy in couples therapy. In M. Solomon & J. Siegel (Eds.), *Countertransference and couples therapy* (pp. 23–37). New York: W.W. Norton.

Solomon, M. (2003). Connection, disruption, repair: Treating the effects of attachment trauma on intimate relationships. In M. Solomon & D. Siegel (Eds.), *Healing trauma: Attachment, mind, body, and brain* (pp. 322–345). New York: W.W. Norton.

Solomon, Z. (1988). The effect of combat-related posttraumatic stress disorder on the family. *Psychiatry, 51,* 323–329.

Solomon, Z. (1998). Transgenerational effects of the holocaust. In Y. Danieli (Ed.), *International handbook of multigenerational legacies of trauma* (pp. 69–73). New York: Plenum Press.

Spanos, N. (1996). *Multiple identities and false memories: A sociocognitive perspective.* Washington, DC: American Psychological Association.

Spero, M. (1997). Cross–cultural and multiethnic assessment of trauma. In J. Wilson & T. Keane (Eds.), *Assessing psychological trauma and PTSD.* New York: Guilford Press.

Spiegel, D. (1997). Trauma, dissociation, and memory. In R. Yehuda & A.C. MacFarlane (Eds.), *Psychobiology of posttraumatic stress disorder* (Vol. 821, pp. 225–237). New York: New York Academy of Sciences Press.

Spitz, R. (1956). Countertransference: Comments on its varying role in the analytic situation. *Journal of the American Psychoanalytic Association, 4,* 256–265.

Sprenkle, D. (1994). Wife abuse through the lens of systems theory. *Counseling Psychologist, 22,* 598–602.

Spring, J.A. (1997). *After the affair: Healing the pain and rebuilding trust when a partner has been unfaithful.* New York: Harper Perennial.

Sroufe, L.A. (1996). *Emotional development: The organization of emotional life in the early years.* New York: Cambridge University Press.

Sroufe, L.A. (1997). Psychopathology as an outcome of development. *Development and Psychopathology, 9,* 251–268.

Stamm, B.H. (Ed.). (1999). *Secondary traumatic stress: Self-care issues for clinicians, researchers & educators.* Lutherville, MD: Sidran Press.

Staub, E. (1989). *The roots of evil: The origins of genocide and other group violence.* New York: Cambridge University Press.

Staub, E. (2003). *Psychology of good and evil: Why children, adults and groups help and harm others.* New York: Cambridge University Press.

St. Clair, M. (1996). *Object relations and self psychology: An introduction* (2nd ed.). New York: Brooks/Cole.

Stern, D. (1985). *The interpersonal world of the infant.* New York: Basic Books.

Straus, M.A., Gelles, R.J., & Steinmetz, S.K. (1988). *Behind closed doors: Violence in the American family.* Newbury Park, CA: Sage.

Streissguth, A.P., Sampson, P.D., Carmichael Olson, H., Bookstein, F.L., Barr, H.M., Scott, M., et al. (1994). Maternal drinking during pregnancy: Attention and short-term memory in 14-year-old offspring—A longitudinal perspective study. *Alcoholism: Clinical and Experimental Research, 18,* 202–218.

Stromwall, L. (2002). Is social work's door open to people recovering from psychiatric disabilities? *Social Work, 47*(1), 75–83.

Sutker, P.B., Vasterling, J.J., Brailey, K., & Allain, Jr., A.N. (1995). Memory, attention, and executive deficits in POW survivors: Contributing biological and psychological factors. *Neuropsychology, 9,* 118–125.

Sveaass, N., & Reichelt, S. (2001). Engaging refugee families in therapy: Exploring the benefits of including referring professionals in first family interviews. *Family Process, 40*(1), 95–114.

Talmidge, L., & Wallace, S. (1991). Reclaiming sexuality in female incest survivors. *Journal of Sex and Marital Therapy, 17*(3), 163–181.

Tatum, B. (1992). Talking about race, learning about racism: The application of racial identity development theory in the classroom. *Harvard Educational Review, 62*(1), 1–24.

Tatum, B. (1997). Racial identity development and relational theory: The case of black women in white communities. In J. Jordan (Ed.), *Women's growth in diversity: More writings from the Stone Center* (pp. 91–106). New York: Guilford Press.

Tatum, B. (2000). The complexity of identity: Who am I? In M. Adams, W. Blumenfeld, R. Castaneda, H. Hackman, M. Peters, & X. Zuniga (Eds.), *Readings for diversity and social justice.* New York: Routledge.

Teicher, M.H., Ito, Y., & Glod, C.A. (1996). Neurophysiological mechanisms of stress response in children. In C.R. Pfeffer (Ed.), *Severe stress and mental disturbances in children* (pp. 59–84). Washington, DC: American Psychiatric Publishing.

Terr, L. (1999). Childhood traumas: An outline and overview. In M. Horowitz (Ed.), *Essential papers on posttraumatic stress disorder* (pp. 61–81). New York: New York University Press.

Terry, W. (1984). *Bloods: An oral history of the Vietnam war by black veterans.* New York: Ballantine Books.

Thompson, R., & Lamb, M. (1986). Infant–mother attachment: New directions for theory and research. In P. Baltes, D. Featherman, & R. Lerner (Eds.), *Life-span development and behavior* (Vol. 7, pp. 1–41). Hillsdale, NJ: Lawrence Erlbaum.

Tower, L.E. (1956). Countertransference. *Journal of the American Psychoanalytic Association, 4,* 224–255.

Trepper, T., & Barrett, M. (1989). *Systemic treatment of incest: A therapeutic handbook.* New York: Brunner/Mazel.

Trepper, T., & Neidner, D. (1996). Intrafamily child sexual abuse. In F. Kaslow (Ed.), *Handbook of relational diagnosis and dysfunctional family patterns* (pp. 394–406). New York: John Wiley.

Trop, J. (1997). An intersubjective perspective of countertransference in couples therapy. In M. Solomon & J. Siegel (Eds.), *Countertransference in couple therapy* (pp. 99–109). New York: W.W. Norton.

Tully, C. (2001). Domestic violence: The ultimate betrayal of human rights. *Journal of Gay and Lesbian Social Services, 13*(1/2), 83–98.

Turner, S. (1993). Psychological sequelae of torture. In J.P. Wilson & B. Raphael (Eds.), *International handbook of traumatic stress syndromes.* New York: Plenum Press.

Turner, S., McFarlane, A., & van der Kolk, B. (1996). The therapeutic environment and new explorations in the treatment of posttraumatic stress disorder. In B. van der Kolk, A. McFarlane, & L. Weisaeth (Eds.), *Traumatic stress: The effects of overwhelming experience on mind, body, and society* (pp. 537–558). New York: Guilford Press.

United States Bureau of Citizenship and Immigration Services. *Statistics.* Retrieved March 10, 2003, from *www.immigration.gov/graphics/aboutus/statistics.*

van der Kolk, B. (1994). The body keeps score: Memory and the evolving psychobiology of posttraumatic stress. *Harvard Review of Psychiatry, 1,* 253–265.

van der Kolk, B. (1996). The body keeps score: Approaches to psychobiology of posttraumatic stress disorder. In B. van der Kolk, A. McFarlane, & L Weisaeth (Eds.), *Traumatic stress: The effects of overwhelming experience on mind, body and society* (pp. 214–241). New York: Guilford Press.

van der Kolk, B. (2003). Posttraumatic stress disorder and the nature of trauma. In M.F. Solomon & D.J. Siegel (Eds.), *Healing trauma: Attachment, mind, body and brain* (pp. 168–195). New York: W.W. Norton.

van der Kolk, B., Burbridge, J.A., & Suzuki, J. (1997). The psychobiology of traumatic memory: Clinical implications of neuroimaging studies. *Annals of the New York Academy of Sciences, 821,* 99–113.

van der Kolk, B., & McFarlane, A. (1996). The black hole of trauma. In B. van der Kolk, A. McFarlane, & L. Weisaeth (Eds.), *Traumatic stress: The effects of overwhelming experience on mind, body and society.* New York: Guilford Press.

van der Kolk, B., Pelcovitz, D., Roth, S., Mandel, F., McFarlane, A., & Herman, J. (1996). Dissociation, affect dysregulation and somatization: The complex nature of adaptation to trauma. *American Journal of Psychiatry, 153(7),* 83–93.

van der Veer, G. (2000). Empowerment of traumatized refugees: A developmental approach to prevention and treatment. *Torture, 10(1),* 8–11.

Verbosky, S., & Ryan, D. (1988). Female partners of Vietnam veterans: Stress by proximity. *Issues in Mental Health Nursing, 9,* 95–104.

Vicary, D., Searle, G., & Andrews, H. (2000). Assessment and intervention with Kosovar refugees [Electronic version]. *Australasian Journal of Disaster and Trauma Studies, 2.* Retrieved from *www.massey.ac.nz/~trauma/issues/2000–2/vicary.htm.*

Vogel, W., & Lazare, A. (1990). The unforgivable humiliation: A dilemma in couples' treatment. *Contemporary Family Therapy, 12(2),* 139–151.

Walker, L. (1979). *The battered woman.* New York: Harper & Row.

Walker, L. (1984). The battered woman syndrome. In G.T. Hotaling, D. Finkelhor, J.T. Kirkpatrick, & M.A. Strauss (Eds.), *Family abuse and its consequences* (pp. 139–148). Newbury Park, CA: Sage.

Wall, J.C. (2001). Trauma and the clinician: Therapeutic implications in clinical work with clients. *Clinical Social Work Journal, 29(2),* 133–145.

Waller, N., Putnam, F., & Carlson, E. (1996). Types of dissociation and dissociative types: A taxometric analysis of dissociative experiences. *Psychological Methods, 1,* 300–321.

Walsh, F. (1996). Partner abuse. In D. Davies & C. Neal (Eds.), *Pink therapy: A guide for counselors and therapists working lesbian, gay, and bisexual clients* (pp. 188–198). Buckingham: Open University Press.

Walsh, F. (1998). *Strengthening family resilience.* New York: Guilford Press.

Walsh, F. (Ed.). (2003). *Normal family processes: Growing diversity and complexity* (3rd ed.). New York: Guilford Press.

Weaks, K.A. (2000). Effects of treating trauma survivors: Vicarious traumatization and style of coping. *Dissertation Abstracts International, 60,* 9B, p. 4915 (UMI No. AAI9944511).

Weil, S.M. (2003). The extramarital affair: A language of yearning and loss. *Clinical Social Work Journal, 31(1),* 51–62.

Weingarten, K. (1991). The discourses of intimacy: Adding a social constructionist and feminist view. *Family Process, 30,* 285–305.

Weiss, R. (1982). Attachment in adult life. In C. Parkes & J. Stevenson-Hinde (Eds.), *The place of attachment in human behavior.* New York: Basic Books.

Werner-Wilson, R., Zimmerman, T., & Whalen, D. (2000). Resilient response to battering. *Contemporary Family Therapy, 22(2),* 161–188.

West, M.L., & Sheldon–Keller, A.E. (1994). *Patterns of relating: An adult attachment perspective.* New York: Guilford Press.

Westerlund, E. (1992). *Women's sexuality after childhood incest.* New York: W.W. Norton.

Wheeler, R.E., Davidson, R.J., & Tomarken, A.J. (1993). Frontal brain asymmetry and emotional reactivity: A biological substrate of affective style. *Psychophysiology, 30,* 83–89.

White, M. (1995). *Re-authoring lives: Interviews and essays.* Adelaide, Australia: Dulwich Center Publications.

White, M., & Epston, D. (1990). *Narrative means to therapeutic ends.* New York: W.W. Norton.

Wilkinson, D. (1997). Reappraising the race, class, gender equation: A critical theoretical perspective. *Smith College Studies in Social Work, 67*(3), 261–276.

Willi, J. (1982). *Couples in collusion.* New York: Jason Aronson.

Williams, C., & Williams, T. (1987). Family therapy for Vietnam veterans. In T. Williams (Ed.), *Post-traumatic stress disorders: A handbook for clinicians.* Cincinnati: Disabled American Veterans National Headquarters.

Williams, M.B., & Sommer, J.F. (1995). Self care and the vulnerable therapist. In B.H. Stamm (Ed.), *Secondary traumatic stress: Self-care issues for clinicians, researchers, and educators* (rev. ed., pp. 230–246). Baltimore: Sidran Press.

Wilson, D., & Mitchell, V. (1998). *Extramarital affairs in mid-life: The splintered mirror.* Presented at the 1998 Self Psychology Conference, San Diego, CA.

Wilson, J.P. (2001). An overview of clinical considerations and principles in the treatment of PTSD. In J.P. Wilson, M.J. Friedman, & J.D. Lindy (Eds.), *Treating psychological trauma and PTSD* (pp. 59–93). New York: Guilford Press

Wilson, J., & Keane, T. (Eds.). (1997). *Assessing psychological trauma and PTSD.* New York: Guilford Press.

Wilson, J.P., & Lindy, J.D. (1999). Empathic strain and countertransference. In M.J. Horowitz (Ed.), *Essential papers on posttraumatic stress disorder.* New York: New York University Press.

Wilson, K., & James, A. (1992). Child sexual abuse and couple therapy. *Sexual and Marital Therapy, 7*(2), 197–212.

Winkelman, M. (2001). Ethnicity and psychocultural models. In I. Susser & T. Patterson (Eds.), *Cultural diversity in the United States.* Malden, MA: Blackwell.

Winnicott, D.W. (1956). *The maturational processes and the facilitating environment.* Madison, CT: International University Press.

Winnicott, D.W. (1958). *Collected papers: Through paediatrics to psychoanalysis.* London: Tavistock.

Winnicott, D.W. (1965). *The maturational processes and the facilitating environment.* London: Hogarth Press.

Winnicott, D.W. (1971). The use of an object and relating through identifications. In D.W. Winnicott (Ed.), *Playing and reality* (pp. 86–94). London: Tavistock.

Winnicott, D.W. (1975). Hate in the countertransference. In *Through pediatrics to psychoanalysis* (pp. 194–203). New York: Basic Books.

Winnicott, D.W. (1992). *Through paediatrics to psycho-analysis: Collected papers.* New York: Brunner/Mazel.

Woodcock, J. (2001). Threads from the labyrinth: Therapy with survivors of war and political oppression. *Journal of Family Therapy, 23,* 136–154.

Woods, M., & Hollis, F. (1990). *Casework: A psychosocial therapy.* New York: McGraw-Hill.

Yassen, J. (1995). Preventing secondary traumatic stress disorder. In C. Figley (Ed.), *Compassion fatigue: Coping with secondary traumatic stress disorder in those who treat the traumatized* (pp. 178–208). New York: Brunner/Mazel.

Yehuda, R., & McFarlane, A. (1999). Conflict between current knowledge about posttraumatic stress disorder and its original conceptual basis. In M. Horowitz (Ed.), *Essential papers on posttraumatic stress disorder.* New York: New York University Press.

Yellow Horse Brave Heart-Jordan, M. (1995). The return to the sacred path: Healing from historical unresolved grief among the Lakota. *Dissertation Abstracts International, 56,* 09A, p. 3742.

Yerkes, S., & Holloway, H. (1996). War and homecomings: The stressors of war and of returning from war. In R. Ursano & A. Norwood (Eds.), *Emotional aftermath of the Persian Gulf War: Veterans, families, communities and nations.* Washington, DC: American Psychiatric Publishing.

Ying, Y.W. (2001). Psychotherapy with traumatized Southeast Asian refugees. *Clinical Social Work Journal, 29*(1), 65–78.

Young, A. (1995). *The harmony of illusions: Inventing post-traumatic stress disorder.* Princeton, NJ: Princeton University Press.

Zimmerman, J.L., & Dickerson, V.C. (1994). Using a narrative metaphor: Implications for theory and clinical practice. *Family Process, 33,* 233–245.

Zinner, J. (1989). The implications of projective identification for marital interaction. In J. Scharff (Ed.), *Foundations of object relations family therapy* (pp. 155–173). Northvale, NJ: Jason Aronson.

Zinner, J., & Shapiro, R.L. (1972). Projective identification as a mode of perception and behavior in families of adolescents. *International Journal of Psychoanalysis, 53,* 523–530.

Zur, J. (1996). From PTSD to voices in context: From an "experiencefar" to an "experience-near" understanding of responses to war and atrocity across cultures. *International Journal of Social Psychiatry, 42*(4), 305–317.

INDEX

Page numbers for entries occurring in figures are followed by an *f* and those for entries in tables are followed by a *t*.

abandonment, fear of, 30, 98
abandonment anxiety, 99, 101, 102
Abdulkhaleq, H., 326
abreaction, 166, 299, 300
acupuncture/acupressure, 166
Adams, J., 38
adaptation, 134
adrenaline, 71, 72
Adult Attachment Interview, 117–18, 129
affairs, 172, 195–201
affect balancing, 82–84
affective changes, 149
affective disorders, 166
affect regulation, 12, 32, 155, 166, 242–43; attachment theory on, 114, 116, 119, 120, 121, 123, 125–26, 129; biopsychosocial assessment of, 149; coregulation, 120; intergenerational patterns in, 174; in Ken and Janet clinical vignette, 125–26; in military couples and families, 291–92, 300; neurobiological effects in, 18–20, 81, 82–84; neurophysiological effects in, 134; overregulation, 116; right-brain disruption and, 73–76, 78; underregulation, 116
Afghanistan war, 285–86
African Americans, 9; gender identity in, 48; intergenerational family theory on, 57, 59; in the military, 288–89, 294–95; parenting issues and, 189; racial identity development in, 42; sexual orientation and, 50. *See also* Pelim and Dorothy (clinical vignette); Rod and Yolanda (clinical case illustration)

aggression: countertransference, 222, 224–27; in military couples and families, 294–96; objects to modulate, 92, 110; right-brain disruption and, 75; Winnicott on, 92, 110, 112. *See also* violence
agreements, 268, 269–70
Ainsworth, M., 115–16
Akhtar, S., 325
Alaskan Natives, 59
Alex and Ivan (clinical vignette), 62
Alexander, A., 7, 305, 319
Alexander, P. C., 188, 190
alexithymia, 79, 87, 170
Alice and Sam (case example), 200–201
Allen, I. A., 7, 9
Allen, J. G., 115, 116, 189
alliance-building techniques, 29
alpha bias, 39, 53, 160, 183, 186, 303
ambiguity, 64–65
ambitendency, 98, 102
ambivalent attachment, 115–16, 117t, 118, 157; correlation with adult version, 119t; couple systems and, 122; in Rod and Yolanda clinical case, 263, 266
American Army Medical Corps, 22
American Indians, 43, 57, 59
American Psychiatric Association, 23, 304
American school of object relations theory, 93
amnesia, 77
amygdala, 71–72, 74, 75, 77, 79, 83
Anderson, C. L., 188, 190
Andrews, H., 325

Angela (case example), 162
annihilation anxiety, 96, 99, 102, 261
anorexia, 82
anthrax threat, 24
antidepressant medication, 268
anti-libidinal ego, 92, 106, 107–8, 153, 262
antipsychotic medication, 323
anxiety, 99–100; abandonment, 99, 101,
    102; annihilation, 96, 99, 102, 260; fear
    of bodily harm (castration), 100; loss of
    love of the object, 99, 102
Applegate, J., 19
armed conflict, 56, 57–61. *See also* war- and
    combat-related trauma
Asch, A., 49
Asian-American immigrants, 318
attachment injury, 122–23
attachment style, 114, 148; ambivalent (*see*
    ambivalent attachment); avoidant,
    115–16, 117t, 118, 119t, 122; dismissing,
    117–18, 119t, 153; disorganized, 117–21,
    122, 153; disorganized/disoriented (*see*
    disorganized/disoriented attachment);
    phase-oriented therapy and, 157–59;
    preoccupied, 117–18, 119t, 153; right-
    brain disruption and, 73, 74–75, 78; in
    Rod and Yolanda clinical case, 263, 266;
    secure (*see* secure attachment);
    traumatic memory retrieval and, 137
attachment theory, 11, 113–29, 134, 161; adult
    classifications, 117–18; applied concepts,
    123–29; child classifications, 115–16, 117t,
    118; correlation of child/adult
    classifications, 119t; couple systems and,
    121–23; foundation concepts of, 114–21;
    in Ken and Janet clinical vignettes (*see*
    Ken and Janet [clinical vignettes]);
    object relations theory and, 92; phase-
    oriented therapy and, 155, 165; in Rod
    and Yolanda clinical case, 275
autism, 94, 95–96
automatic thought records, 274
autonomic nervous system, 72, 73–74, 75,
    295
autonomy, 52, 110, 111
Autonomy phase of racial identity
    development, 45, 255
avoidant attachment, 115–16, 117t, 118, 119t,
    122

Bader, E., 100
Baker, W. L., 71
Balcolm, D., 27–28, 41

Balint, Michael, 94
Banyard, V. L., 189
basal forebrain, 72
Basham, K., 32, 303, 305
BASS model, 150
Beavers Systems Model, 180
Becker, D., 324
Beebe, B., 71, 95
benevolent helper role, 192
Benjamin, L. R., 190
Benjamin, R., 190
Bennet-Baker, A. A., 241
Bergman, A., 91, 94–98
Bernstein, M. M., 58
beta bias, 39, 53, 160, 183, 303
Bettinger, M., 304
binging and purging, 82
biofeedback, 166
biological theories, 242
biopsychosocial assessment, 33, 133–53, 156;
    factors in phase-oriented model, 139t;
    in Rod and Yolanda clinical case,
    247–66. *See also* institutional factors;
    interactional factors; intrapersonal
    factors
bipolar disorder, 119, 205
bisexual couples. *See* gay, lesbian, bisexual,
    and transgendered (GLBT) couples
Black, M., 93, 94
Blakely, T., 71
Bob and Linda (clinical vignette), 228
body (somatic) memories, 78, 87
body–mind approaches, 81, 87, 136, 164,
    166, 300
Boehnlein, J. K., 320
Bograd, M., 186
Bookheimer, S. Y., 74
borderline personality disorder, 75, 97, 120
Bosnia, 7
both/and thinking, 51, 64–65, 66, 187
boundary violations, 220–21, 222;
    countertransference and, 224, 229–31;
    between couples, 145–46, 259
Bowen, M., 198
Bowlby, J., 94, 113, 114, 115, 120
Bracken, J., 18
Brad and Frances (clinical vignette), 55
brain, 18–20, 134. *See also* neurobiological
    effects; neurophysiological effects;
    specific regions of the brain
breathing exercises, 83, 85, 126, 194
Brende, J., 26
Briere, J., 220

British Psychoanalytic Society, 105, 109
British school of object relations theory, 93–94, 109
Broca area of the brain, 77, 78, 87, 170
Brown, S., 198
Bui, H., 325–26
Buist, A., 188
Burkett, L. D., 190
Burkitt, I., 40
Buttenheim, M., 190

CAGE questions, 151
capacity to be alone, 92, 110, 111
CAPS. See Clinician-Administered PTSD scale
Carter, R., 41
Cassidy, J., 117
castration anxiety, 100
catatonic states, 150
catecholamines, 71
catharsis, 136, 166
Catherall, D., 239
central ego, 106
Chan, C., 39
Charcot, J. M., 20, 21
Charihn and John (clinical vignette), 321–22
Charles and Barbara (clinical vignette), 290–91
chemical and biological weapons, 4, 23, 24, 285, 297
chemotherapy, 207
Child Protective Services, 3
Chilean refugees, 323
Chrepanov, E., 325
Christopher, J., 40
Chu, J., 220
Circumplex Model, 180
clergy, sexual abuse by, 203
Cliff and Sonya (clinical vignette), 235–36
clinical case illustration. See Rod and Yolanda (clinical case illustration)
clinical vignettes: Alex and Ivan, 62; Bob and Linda, 228; Brad and Frances, 55; Charihn and John, 321–22; Charles and Barbara, 290–91; Cliff and Sonya, 235–36; Dave and Janet, 224–27; Emily and Holly, 313–14; guidelines for, xiii; Jacob and Sarah, 234–35; Jane and Carlita, 310; Jim and Cathy, 229–31; Joanne and Jill, 231–33; John, Marie, Pat, and Cherise, 182; Johnnie and Jeannie (see Johnnie and Jeannie

[clinical vignettes]); Judi, 238–39; Ken and Janet (see Ken and Janet [clinical vignettes]); Kirk and Wayne, 305–6; Lara and Vitos, 184–85; Margaret and Peter, 53–54; Margaret and Tom, 199–200; Maria and Paolo, 327–29; Maria and Ramon, 228–29; Maureen and Alice, 79–80; Nancy and Ed (see Nancy and Ed [clinical vignettes]); Olga and Boris, 178; Paula and Colette, 66–69, 308; Paul and Janet, 107–8; Pelim and Dorothy, 55–56; Rachel, Seth, and Ben, 59–61.63; Rosa and Joan (see Rosa and Joan [clinical vignettes]); Sally and Deirdre, 311–12; Sam and Anna, 292–93, 295–96, 300–301; Stephen and Michael, 308–9; Susan and Barry, 193–94
Clinician-Administered PTSD scale (CAPS), 148
clinician responses, 212–41; idealization of the survivor, 221; to immigrants and refugees, 330; to infidelity, 196; institutional factors in, 140–41, 214–16; personal characteristics in, 214; in Rod and Yolanda clinical case, 254–57; sociocultural factors in, 214–16. See also countertransference; vicarious traumatization
coexisting disorders, 202–7
cognitive–behavioral therapy, 5, 12, 30–31, 81, 155, 242, 266; attachment theory and, 123, 126; for immigrants and refugees, 326–27; infidelity and, 199, 200; in Phase I of therapy, 136, 164, 165, 166, 171; psychophysiological responses and, 87; for rage storms, 83; in Rod and Yolanda clinical case, 273–74; for sexual abuse survivors, 194
cognitive distortions, 12, 243, 274
cognitive science, 114
cognitive theories, 237–38
Cohen, M., 38–39
Cole, P., 190
Coleman, E., 312
combat neurosis, 16
combat stress reaction, 22
Combat Veterans Anonymous, 26
commitment, building, 299
communication, 146; in Phase I of therapy, 164, 170–71, 273–74; specific skills in, 180
compartmentalization, 149–50, 207, 209

compassion fatigue. *See* vicarious traumatization

complementary identification, 217

complex posttraumatic stress disorder (PTSD), 3, 8, 26, 162, 185; biopsychosocial assessment of, 148–49, 153; cultural issues in, 10; in immigrants and refugees, 326; neurobiology of, 73, 76; object relations theory and, 32; Phase I of therapy and, 136, 165, 166; in Rod and Yolanda clinical case, 260, 266, 271–72, 275; substance abuse and, 151, 202, 204, 206; terrorism and, 23–24; torture and, 7

Compton, J., 30–31

compulsive behavior, 82, 149

concordant identification, 217

conditioned fear responses, 78

confidentiality, xiii, 163, 164, 181, 182, 270

Conformity phase of racial identity development, 43, 45

Consolidation. *See* Phase III of therapy

constructivist theory, 238. *See also* social constructionist theory

Contact phase of racial identity development, 44

container function, 127, 160, 176, 199, 268

control systems theory, 114

conversion states, 22

Cook, D., 43–45, 255

coping, 134

Cornell, S., 46

cortical section of brain, 19, 74

corticotropin releasing factor (CRF), 71

cortisol, 72

countertransference, 143, 161, 162, 212–14, 216, 217–36; aggression and, 222, 224–27; boundary violations in, 224, 229–31; in couple therapy, 223–24; cultural, 38, 219; definitions of, 218–19; detachment responses, 224, 228–29; eroticized, 141, 224, 231–33; evolution of the concept, 217–18; helplessness in, 224, 234–35; in individual therapy, 220–23; objective, 219; passive indifference, 224, 227–28; personal, 219; reaction formation, 141, 224, 235–36; in Rod and Yolanda clinical case, 250, 255–57, 263, 278; traps, 104, 140–41, 168, 183, 220, 223, 255–57; vicarious traumatization compared with, 237, 237t

couple, composition of, 180–85

couple systems: attachment theory and, 121–23; separation–individuation themes in, 100–105; separation–individuation theory and, 98–100

couple therapy, 24–33; countertransference in, 223–24; current issues and future trends in, 32–33; for immigrants and refugees, 324–29; indications for, 25; for military couples, 296–302; models of, 25–32; neurobiological effects and, 81–82; practice model, 4–6; Winnicott's principles and, 111–12. *See also* phase-oriented couple therapy model

Courtois, C., 29

Crandell, L. E., 122

CRF. *See* corticotropin releasing factor

critical interaction, 299–300

Cross, W., 59

cross-cultural therapy, 32–33, 37, 140, 160, 247, 269, 278

cultural competence, 38

cultural congruence, 156–57, 172, 173, 175, 278, 300

cultural counterresistance, 219

cultural countertransference, 38, 219

culturally congruent paranoia, 250

culture: composition of the couple and, 181; identity and, 38–39; of immigrants and refugees, 315, 325; military, 286–89; power relationships and, 55–56; PTSD diagnosis and, 9–10; separation–individuation theory and, 95; trauma sanctioned by, 7–8; traumatic memory retrieval and, 136–37. *See also* cross-cultural therapy; ethnocultural factors; sociocultural factors

cumulative trauma disorders, 7

Dalenberg, C., 220

Danaher, G., 40

Daniel, E. V., 319, 320, 324

Daniel, J., 7, 42

Dave and Janet (clinical vignette), 224–27

Davies, J. M., 220, 222, 223

daymares, 77

DBT. *See* dialectical behavioral therapy

declarative memory, 72, 77, 78

decompensation, 136

deconstructionism, 51

defender role, 84, 85, 88, 168

delusion of a common boundary, 96

demographic data: on physical, sexual, and emotional abuse, 3, 4; on substance abuse, 202–3
Department of Social Services (DSS), 136, 165
depersonalization, 150, 291
depression, 12, 22, 97, 155; attachment theory on, 119; in immigrants and refugees, 323; physical health and, 206; in Rod and Yolanda clinical case, 261, 263, 266, 268, 271; substance abuse and, 205; theories appropriate for, 242–43; in torture victims, 319
derealization, 150
DESNOS. *See* disorders of extreme stress not otherwise specified
destructive impulses, fear of, 30
detachment, 149–50, 207, 209; in countertransference, 224, 228–29
detoxifying of sites, 200–201
developmental histories, 244–46
developmental moments, 95
developmental themes, 213
developmental theories, 238
Diagnostic and Statistical Manual of Mental Disorders, 3rd edition (DSM-III), 20, 22
Diagnostic and Statistical Manual of Mental Disorders, 3rd edition Revised (DSM-III-R), 304
Diagnostic and Statistical Manual of Mental Disorders, 4th edition (DSM-IV-TR), 8, 9, 58, 271
dialectical behavioral therapy (DBT), 6, 81, 166
Dicks, H., 106
DiClemente, C. C., 204
DIDs. *See* dissociative identity disorders (DIDs)
differentiation, 52, 96, 97, 110, 111, 112, 152, 262
DiNicola, V., 18
disability, 49, 143, 254, 297
disciplinary power, 40
Disintegration phase of racial identity development, 44
dismissing attachment, 117–18, 119t, 153
disordered action of the heart, 22
disorders of extreme stress not otherwise specified (DESNOS), 8
disorganized attachment, 117–21, 122, 153
disorganized/disoriented attachment, 74–75, 78, 116, 118, 121, 129; behavior

associated with, 117t; correlation with adult version, 119t
disowned attributes, 158, 175, 262
dissociation, 5, 8, 21, 146, 207–11, 312; biopsychosocial assessment of, 149–50; defined, 149, 209; dereification of, 209–10; fragmentation versus integration, 210–11; memory lapses in, 165, 208–9; in military personnel, 298; in Nancy and Ed clinical vignette, 86–87; neurobiology of, 72, 73, 75–76, 81, 83, 86–87; parenting and, 190; in sexual abuse survivors, 192, 194; substance abuse and, 205
Dissociative Experience (assessment tool), 150
dissociative identity disorders (DIDs), 16, 190, 207; controversy over, 150; in Dave and Janet clinical vignette, 224–25; dereification, 209–10
Dissonance phase of racial identity development, 43
distancing, 145, 262
diversity, 155
diversity themes, 139, 164; overview of, 141–43; in Rod and Yolanda clinical case, 247, 249–53
domestic violence. *See* violence
dreams, 10. *See also* nightmares
drive theory, 93
DSM. *See Diagnostic and Statistical Manual of Mental Disorders*
DSS. *See* Department of Social Services
dual-trauma couples, 10, 184
Dubrow, N., 18
Dutton, D. G., 122
dyad, defined, 10
Dyche, L., 38

East Asian culture, 39
eating, compulsive and excessive, 82, 261, 273
eating disorders, 82, 166, 207
EEG. *See* electroencephalography
ego, 105–7; anti-libidinal, 92, 106, 107–8, 153, 262; central, 106; libidinal, 106, 107
ego dystonic homosexuality, 304
ego-enhancing work, 29
ego fragmentation, 149
ego psychology, 165
ego strengths, 152, 153
ego-supportive interventions, 136, 164

Ehrenreich, B., 47
elderly: abuse of, 143; immigrant and refugee, 318, 326
electroencephalography (EEG), 74
Elsass, P., 238, 319, 321
EMDR. *See* eye movement desensitization reprocessing
Emersion phase of racial identity development, 43, 44–45, 249, 255, 282
Emily and Holly (clinical vignette), 313–14
emotional abuse, 215; attachment theory on, 122; demographic data on, 3; narrative therapy and, 66; in Rod and Yolanda clinical case, 259; type II trauma from, 7
emotional container function, 127, 160, 176, 199, 268
emotionally focused therapy, 31–32
empathic attunement, 126–27, 136
empathy, 102, 123
empowerment, 5, 25, 155, 161, 205, 269
endopsychic structure, 105
engulfment, fear of, 98
Epston, D., 51
Erichsen, J., 20, 21
eroticized countertransference, 141, 224, 231–33
ethnicity, 46, 142
ethnocultural factors, 17–18
ethology, 114
Evans, K., 151
exciting object, 106
existential dilemma, 319
experience-distant/-near response to trauma, 320
explicit memory. *See* declarative memory
exposure, fear of, 30
eye movement desensitization reprocessing (EMDR), 5–6, 81, 166, 201

Fairbairn, W. R. D., 91, 92, 94, 105–8, 153, 262
Falicov, C., 317
false memories, 5, 16, 216
family histories, 244–46
family loyalties, 61–62
family of origin, 137, 138, 159, 169, 272–73, 276
family theory, 51–69. *See also* feminist family theory; intergenerational family theory; narrative theory and therapy
family therapy: for immigrants and refugees, 324–29; for military families, 296–302

fathers, 52
faulty attributions, 83, 84, 86
fear of bodily harm anxiety, 100
fears, 149; of abandonment, 30, 98; of attack, 30; conditioned responses, 78; of destructive impulses, 30; of engulfment, 98; of exposure, 30; of merger, 30
F-E-A-R-S (mnemonic device), 148–49
Feeney, J., 120
fees for therapy, 161, 162–63, 164, 270
Feldman, S., 299
Felsen, I., 58
feminist family theory, 51, 52–56; gendered beliefs and roles in, 53–54; offender responsibility in, 56; power relationships in, 54–56
feminist family therapy, 52
feminist theories, 5, 12, 16, 24, 49, 133, 242, 247; phase-oriented therapy and, 155, 161, 165; on use of language, 65
fight/flight response, 73, 79, 84, 88, 149, 165, 295, 297
Figley, C. R., 6–7, 299, 300, 324
Fine, M., 49
Fisher, J. V., 122
Flanagan, M., 98
flashbacks, 149, 165, 201; in military personnel, 290, 291, 296; neurobiology of, 77; in sexual abuse survivors, 28, 192
flooding, 136
Follette, V., 30–31, 193
Fonagy, P., 116, 119, 121, 122, 127
Foucault, M., 40, 52
framing the problem, 299
Frawley, M. G., 220, 222, 223
freeze response, 75–76, 79, 295
Freud, A., 94
Freudian theory, 20, 21, 93–94, 105
Friedman, M., 17
frontal lobe, 78
Frye, M., 311
funding sources, 163–64. *See also* fees for therapy

gambling, compulsive, 82–83
gay, lesbian, bisexual, and transgendered (GLBT) couples, 142–43, 181, 183, 303–14; clinical implications for, 309–14; historical bias against, 304; identity and, 50; institutional factors and, 305–9; parenting and, 190, 312–14; social policies and, 307–9; violence in, 185–86, 216, 309–10. *See also* gay male

couples; lesbian couples; sexual orientation

gay male couples, 293, 294, 304, 312; Kirk and Wayne, 305–6; Stephen and Michael, 308–9

Gelinas, D., 16, 20–21

gender: feminist family theory on, 53–54; identity and, 48–49; immigrant experience and, 318; PTSD and, 18; sexual abuse and, 4, 203, 215. *See also* women

gender roles, 39, 142; cultural differences in, 181; feminist family theory on, 53–54; in military couples and families, 293–94; in Rod and Yolanda clinical case, 253–54

generalized anxiety states, 22

genocide, 7, 9–10, 56, 57–61

genograms: for Paula and Colette, 67f; for Yolanda and Rod, 245f

Gergen, K., 64

Gerrity, E., 17

Glass, S. G., 200

GLBT couples. *See* gay, lesbian, bisexual, and transgendered (GLBT) couples

Glod, C. A., 74

glucocorticoids, 76

glutamate, 71

Goffman, E., 41

going-on-being, 110

Goldberg, A., 197

Goldner, V., 48, 187

Goldstein, E., 93, 97, 107

good-enough clinicians, 160

good-enough mothering, 92, 109, 110

Goodwin, J., 148

Gorman, W., 326

Gottman, J., 180–81

Graham-Bermann, S. A., 188, 189

Green, R. J., 304

Greenan, D., 312

Greenberg, J., 92, 95, 107, 110

Greene, B., 48, 50

Grinker, R., 22

guided imagery, 201

Gulf War, 23, 24, 27, 285, 292–93, 296, 297

Guntrip, H., 94

Hairi, A. R., 74

Hanna, E., 217, 218

Hare-Mustin, R., 39, 51, 53, 303

Harris, M., 25

Hartmann, D., 46

Hartmann, H., 93

hate crimes, 309

Hazan, C., 122

healing theory, 299

Health Insurance Portability and Accountability Act (HIPAA), 163

Helms, J., 43–45, 255

helplessness in countertransference, 224, 234–35

Herman, J., 7, 16, 21, 22, 23, 24, 32, 214

heterosexism, 50, 183, 186, 190, 303, 305–6, 310–11; defined, 305; in the military, 308; parenting and, 312–13, 314

Higginbotham, E., 48

Hindy, C. G., 122

HIPAA. *See* Health Insurance Portability and Accountability Act

hippocampus, 72, 76, 77, 78

historical family perspective, 12, 243

historical ghosts, 201, 301, 308, 310, 311, 329

historical review, 15–33; of ethnocultural factors, 17–18; of neurobiological research, 18–20; of psychiatric concepts, 16–17; of trauma theory, 20–24

holding environment, 92, 109, 111, 112, 127, 160, 163, 164, 176; dissociation and, 210; infidelity and, 199; in Phase I of therapy, 268

holidays, 146–47

Hollis, F., 197

Holloway, H., 23

Holocaust, 5, 7, 57, 58, 234

Homeland Security Office, U.S., 24

homeostasis, 95, 105

homophobia, 183, 186, 190, 203, 303, 305–6, 309; defined, 305; in the military, 287, 308; parenting and, 313, 314

Horner, A., 97

HPA. *See* hypothalamic–pituitary–adrenocortical axis

hyperarousal, 87, 149, 166; in military personnel, 291, 297; neurobiology of, 73, 76, 81, 82; in Rod and Yolanda clinical case, 260, 272

hypermnesia, 77

hypersexuality, 83, 146, 149

hypervigilance, 71, 88, 149, 165, 166

hypnotherapy, 81, 166

hyposexuality, 83

hypothalamic–pituitary–adrenocortical (HPA) axis, 71, 76

hypothalamus, 72, 75

hysteria, 16, 20, 21, 22

iconic memory, 77, 78, 79–80, 81, 167
idealization of the survivor, 221
ideal object, 106
identified client, 27–28, 184, 192, 209–10, 215
identity, 39–42; ability/disability in, 49; ethnicity and, 46; gender and, 48–49; religion/spirituality and, 47; sexual orientation and, 50; shame and (*see* shame); social construction of, 37, 38–39; socioeconomic status and, 47–48; stigma and, 37, 39–42, 204–5
identity development theory, 8, 242
Immersion phase of racial identity development, 43, 44, 255, 281
immigrants, 48, 315–30; clinical implications for, 319–23; experience of, 317–18; GLBT, 308–9; interventions for, 323–29; in the military, 289; by source area to Canada, 316t; by source area to the United States, 316t
Impact of Event Scale, 288
implicit memory, 77, 78, 79–80, 81, 167
impulse control, 19, 75
individual factors, 139t, 148–52; in Rod and Yolanda assessment, 248t, 260–61; in vicarious traumatization, 240–41
individual therapy, 25, 220–23
individual treatment stage model of trauma therapy, 32
Indochinese culture, 320
infants, 8; attachment theory on, 114–15; bond with mother, 109–11; neurobiological effects in, 70–73; separation–individuation theory on, 95–96
infidelity, 172, 195–201
insight-oriented therapy, 158, 179
insomnia, 149
institutional factors, 139–43; clinician responses and, 140–41, 214–16; diversity themes (*see* diversity themes); for GLBT couples and families, 305–9; in Rod and Yolanda assessment, 247–57, 265t; in vicarious traumatization, 239–40
insurrection of subjugated knowledge, 52
Integrated Awareness phase of racial identity development, 43
integrative therapy models, 10–13, 206, 210–11
interactional factors: overview of, 143–47; in phase-oriented therapy, 139t; in Rod and Yolanda assessment, 248t, 257–60, 265t

intergenerational family theory, 51, 56–63, 133; on loyalties and secrecy, 61–62; rituals in, 62–63; in Rod and Yolanda clinical case, 253, 258, 266; on transmission processes, 57–61
intergenerational patterns, 4–5; in Rod and Yolanda clinical case, 275–79; transmission processes, 57–61; of victim–victimizer–bystander dynamic, 174–77, 275–79
Internalization phase of racial identity development, 43, 249
internal saboteur, 92, 106, 107–8, 153, 262
interpersonal exchange, enhancement of, 123, 128–29
interruption of negative exchanges, 84–85, 162, 170, 268, 270
intersubjectivity, 140, 142, 143, 160–61; countertransference and, 218; identity and, 38; in Rod and Yolanda clinical case, 256–57, 263
intimacy, 30; attachment theory on, 114; phase-oriented therapy on, 174, 191–95; in Rod and Yolanda clinical case, 279–81
intrapersonal factors: overview of, 148–53; in phase-oriented therapy, 139t; in Rod and Yolanda assessment, 248t, 260–63, 265t. See also intrapsychic factors; individual factors
intrapsychic factors: overview of, 152–53; in phase-oriented therapy, 139t; in Rod and Yolanda assessment, 248t, 261–63
Iranian refugees, 327
Iraq war, 4, 23, 24, 208, 285–86, 289, 295, 302, 308
Israeli veterans, 26–27
Ito, Y., 74

Jacob and Sarah (clinical vignette), 234–35
Jacobs, C., 12–13
Jacobson, E., 93
Jane and Carlita (clinical vignette), 310
Jane and Maria (case example), 145
Janet, P. M. F., 20–21
Janoff-Bulman, R., 237–38
Japanese-American internment, 7, 58, 147
Jehovah's Witnesses, 55
Jenkins, J., 18
Jewish culture, 47, 181; Jacob and Sarah, 234–35; Rachel, Seth, and Ben, 59–61, 63. See also Holocaust
Jim and Cathy (clinical vignette), 229–31

Joanne and Jill (clinical vignette), 231–33
John and Marie and Pat and Cherise
    (clinical vignette), 182
Johnnie and Jeannie (clinical vignettes), 138,
    297–98; dissociation, 208–9; support
    systems, 169
Johnson, D., 299
Johnson, S. M., 31–32, 113–14, 122–23
Johnson, T., 312
journals, 270
Judi (clinical vignette), 238–39

Kanninen, K., 319
Kaplan, N., 117
Kardiner, A., 22
Kaufman, J., 188
Kaye/Kantrowitz, M., 47
Kemp, S. P., 190
Ken and Janet (clinical vignettes), 123–27,
    129; affect regulation, 125–26; empathy
    and mentalization, 126–27
Keren, M., 312
Kerewsky, S. D., 312
Kernberg, O., xii, 93
Khan, M., 109
kindling states, 71
King Keenan, E., 40
Kinzie, J. D., 320
Kira, I. A., 7, 319, 320, 321, 324, 326
Kirk and Wayne (clinical vignette), 305–6
Klein, M., 93–94, 103, 153
Knudsen, J. C., 319, 320, 324
Ko'ach (veteran assistance program), 26–27
Kobak, R. R., 118, 122
Kosovar refugees, 325

labeling, 204–5
Lachman, F., 95
Langston, D., 47
language, use of, 56, 65, 160
Lansky, M., 41
Lara and Vitos (clinical vignette), 184–85
Larson, N. C., 190
Lazare, A., 41
Lee, E., 318
Lee, R., 41
lesbian couples, 303–4; African-American,
    50; Emily and Holly, 313–14; Jane and
    Carlita, 310; Joanne and Jill, 231–33;
    Maureen and Alice, 79–80; in the
    military, 293, 294; narrative therapy
    and, 66–69; parenting and, 313–14;
    Paula and Colette, 66–69, 308; Rosa
    and Joan (see Rosa and Joan [clinical
    vignettes]); Sally and Deirdre, 311–12;
    violence in, 309, 310. See also gay,
    lesbian, bisexual, and transgendered
    (GLBT) couples
Levendosky, A. A., 188, 189
Leverich, G. S., 73
Lewis, M., 41
libidinal ego, 106, 107
libidinal object constancy, 98
limbic system, 19, 71, 72–73, 74, 79
Lindy, J., 220
Liotti, G., 190
listening skills, 180
Liu, P., 39
locus of control, 155, 159, 161, 253, 269
logical memory, 72
Lorber, J., 48
loss of love of the object anxiety, 99, 102
loss of object anxiety, 99, 101, 102
Lubin, H., 299

McCann, I. L., 238
McCarthy, B. W., 192
McFarlane, A., 221
McGoldrick, M., 38
magnetic resonance imaging (MRI), 70, 74
Mahler, M., 91, 93, 94–98, 100, 152
Main, M., 116, 117
Makarec, M., 74
Maker, A. H., 190
Maltz, W., 28, 193, 238
mandated reporting of abuse, 216
Maracek, J., 51
Marcenko, M. O., 190
Margaret and Peter (clinical vignette), 53–54
Margaret and Tom (clinical vignette),
    199–200
Maria and Paolo (clinical vignette), 327–29
Maria and Ramon (clinical vignette),
    228–29
Marsella, A., 17
Massachusetts Supreme Judicial Court, 307
massage, 166
mastery, 134
Maureen and Alice (clinical vignette),
    79–80
Mazziota, J. C., 74
Mederos, F., 186
media, 23, 49, 196
meditation, 83, 126, 166, 201, 271
memory, 12, 21, 76–80, 134, 155; body
    (somatic), 78, 87; declarative, 72, 77, 78;

memory (*continued*)
 dissociation and, 165, 208–9; explicit,
 72; false, 5, 16, 216; iconic, 77, 78,
 79–80, 81, 167; logical, 72; semantic, 77.
 See also traumatic memory retrieval
mentalization, 114, 116, 119, 121, 123, 126–28,
 129
merged object relations, 152
merger, fear of, 30
meta-monitoring of interactional cycles, 122
metaphor, 30, 154, 171, 270
Miehls, D., 28–29, 32, 43, 93, 103–4, 192,
 197
Miliora, M., 42
military couples and families, 4, 285–302;
 aggression and violence in, 294–96;
 clinical interventions for, 296–302;
 culture of, 286–89; GLBT in, 307–8;
 unique themes relevant to, 289–94; value
 base of, 289–91. *See also* war- and
 combat-related trauma
Miller, D., 33, 312
Mitchell, S., 92, 93, 94, 95, 107, 110
Mitchell, V., 197
Mock, M., 318–19, 325
Modell, A., 19
Moffatt, K., 40
moment of illusion, 109
mothers: attachment to, 115–16; bond with
 infant, 109–11; feminist family theory
 on, 52; good-enough, 92, 109, 110;
 neurobiological dysfunction caused
 by, 71
motivational interviewing approach, 204
MRI. *See* magnetic resonance imaging
Munro, K., 194
Munroe, J., 239
Muslims, 7, 47, 55–56, 181
mutism, 77, 80, 87
mutuality, 114

Nader, K., 18
Nagata, D. K., 58
Nancy and Ed (clinical vignettes), 81–82;
 dissociation, 86–87; psychophysiological
 responses, 88–90; rage storm, 84–86
narcissistic envy, 102
narcissistic pathology, 97
narcissistic vulnerability, 41
Nardi, C., 26–27
narrative theory and therapy, 12, 51, 63–69,
 133, 243; complexity and ambiguity in,
 64–65; multiple perspectives in, 64;

narrative transformation in, 66–69;
 phase-oriented therapy and, 155; in Rod
 and Yolanda clinical case, 253, 258, 266;
 use of language in, 65
National Clearinghouse on Child Abuse
 and Neglect, 3
Native Americans, 43, 57, 59
Nelson, B., 27
neocortex, 19, 72, 79, 84
neurasthenia, 22
neurobiological effects, 18–20, 75–90;
 clinical implications for therapy, 19,
 81–82; in dissociation, 72, 73, 75–76, 81,
 83; research related to, 70–73
neurophysiological effects, 12, 133–34, 148,
 155; of complex PTSD, 260; in Rod
 and Yolanda clinical case, 260, 263;
 self-care and, 165, 166. *See also*
 psychophysiological responses
neurotransmitters, 76
neutralizing of sites, 200–201
nightmares, 76, 77, 149, 291. *See also*
 dreams
Nijenhuis, E. R. S., 73
Nokai and Edward (case example), 147
nonrelational trauma, 70, 71
Norcross, J. C., 204
norepinephrine (noradrenaline), 71, 76
normative development theory, 105, 109
Northcut, T., 47
Norwood, A., 23, 27
numbness, 87, 149, 165, 167, 272; in
 military personnel, 291, 297;
 neurobiology of, 72, 76, 79, 81, 82
nurture-sorrow neural circuits, 83, 84

object constancy, 8, 91, 92, 101t, 112, 157; in
 Rod and Yolanda clinical case, 262–63;
 traumatic memory retrieval and, 137
objective countertransference, 219
object relating, 110, 111
object relational capacity, 123, 148, 153, 175;
 in military couples and families, 300;
 phase-oriented therapy and, 157–59,
 173; in Rod and Yolanda clinical case,
 263, 266; traumatic memory retrieval
 and, 137
object relations theory, 11, 28–29, 32, 91–112,
 134, 152, 161, 238; American school of,
 93; British school of, 93–94, 109;
 defined, 92; phase-oriented therapy
 and, 155, 165, 166; in Rod and Yolanda
 clinical case, 275; synopsis of, 92–94.

See also Fairbairn, W. R. D.; separation–individuation theory; Winnicott, D. W.
object usage, 110, 111
oedipal issues, 197, 213
offenders, responsibility assigned to, 56, 169
Ofshe, R., 16
Ogden, T. H., 103
Olga and Boris (clinical vignette), 178
on-the-way-to-object-constancy, 96, 98
opiates, endogenous, 76, 83
orbitofrontal cortex, 74, 75
Ortner, S., 48

Papadopoulos, R. K., 330
paralysis, emotional/physical, 79
paranoid-schizoid position, 153
parasuicidal behavior, 83, 167
parasympathetic nervous system, 72, 73–74, 75, 295
parenting: clinician responses to, 216; GLBT families and, 190, 312–14; intergenerational family theory on, 57; phase-oriented model on, 188–91; in Rod and Yolanda clinical case, 275–77, 281
partnership status, assessment of, 171–72, 274–75
part-object relations, 100, 152, 172, 179, 210
passive indifference countertransference, 224, 227–28
patriarchy, 48–49, 142, 215, 216; feminist family theory on, 52; homophobia and, 305; in military couples and families, 293; violence and, 185, 186
Paula and Colette (clinical vignette), 66–69, 308
Paul and Janet (clinical vignette), 107–8
Pearlman, L., 219, 220, 221, 238, 239, 240
Pearson, P., 100
Pelim and Dorothy (clinical vignette), 55–56
Pérez-Foster, R. M., 38, 219
Perry, B. D., 19, 71, 72, 74
Persinger, M. A., 74
personal countertransference, 219
personality disorders, 93
PET. *See* positron emission tomography
phallic exhibitionism, 213
phallic-ornamentation, 197
Phase I of therapy, 81, 134, 154, 156, 157, 164–72; attachment and, 123, 165; collaboration with other sources, 164–65; communication in, 164, 170–71, 273–74; for GLBT couples and families, 310, 311; goals of, 135–36; for immigrants and refugees, 325, 326; for military couples and families, 297, 300; object constancy in, 91; partnership status assessment in, 171–72, 274–75; physical health assessment in, 166–68, 271; in Rod and Yolanda clinical case, 265t, 267–75; safety in, 135, 164, 165, 267–70; self-care in, 136, 165–66, 270–72, 275; support systems in, 168–70, 272–73; time limitations and, 159
Phase II of therapy, 81, 134, 154, 156, 157, 158, 172–79; attachment and, 123; goals of, 135t, 136–37; for immigrants and refugees, 326–27, 328; meaning of intimacy in, 174; meaning of trauma narrative in, 172–73; object constancy and, 91; in Rod and Yolanda clinical case, 265t, 275–81; time limitations and, 159
Phase III of therapy, 81, 134, 154, 156, 157, 179–80; attachment and, 123; goals of, 135t, 137–38; for immigrants and refugees, 326, 327, 329; for military couples and families, 300–302; object constancy and, 91; in Rod and Yolanda clinical case, 265t, 281–82; time limitations and, 159
phase-oriented couple therapy model, 11, 154–211; agreements in, 268, 269–70; biopsychosocial assessment factors in, 139t; central themes in, 180–201; clarity of structure, 162–63, 268–69; coexisting disorders and, 202–7; collaboration with other sources, 163–64, 270; composition of the couple in, 180–85; decision-making processes in, 156–59, 264–66; fees in, 161, 162–63, 164, 270; frequency and length of sessions, 161–62, 270; goals of each phase, 135t; infidelity addressed in, 172, 195–201; initial meeting, 161; intimacy issues and, 191–95; overview of, 133–38; parenting issues in, 188–91; professional stance in, 160–62; relationship building in, 160–64; in Rod and Yolanda clinical case, 263–82; sexuality issues and, 191–95; time limitations and, 159; violence and, 135, 165, 181, 185–88, 193. *See also specific phases*
phobic states, 22

physical abuse, 215; attachment theory on, 122; demographic data on, 3; narrative therapy and, 66; right-brain disruption and, 74; in Rod and Yolanda clinical case, 246, 259, 261, 262, 272, 276–77; shame and stigma attached to, 41; type II trauma from, 7

physical health assessment, 148, 149, 166–68, 271

physical illness, 242; mental health disorders and, 206–7; in Rod and Yolanda clinical case, 271

physioneurosis, 22

Piastro, D., 49

Pinderhughes, E., 7, 59

Pine, F., 91, 94–98

polarizations, 144, 163, 175, 262, 273, 274, 277

political and social advocacy, 138, 159, 179

Pollard, R., 71

positron emission tomography (PET), 70

Post, R. M., 73

postmodernism, 38, 51, 66, 218

posttraumatic stress disorder (PTSD), 3, 8, 24, 27, 201, 215, 319; biopsychosocial assessment of, 148–51, 153; cultural relativity of, 9–10; dissociation and, 207, 209; ethnocultural factors in, 17–18; historical review of, 16–17, 20, 22, 23; in immigrants and refugees, 323, 324; intergenerational family theory on, 58; in military couples and families, 285, 286, 288, 289, 290, 291–93, 294, 295, 296, 297–99; neurobiology of, 19, 73, 76, 78; Phase I of therapy on, 136, 165, 166; right-brain disruption and, 74, 75, 78; in Rod and Yolanda clinical case, 266, 271–72, 275; substance abuse and, 151, 202–3, 204. See also complex posttraumatic stress disorder (PTSD)

Pouissant, A., 7, 305, 319

poverty, 190

power, 39, 143, 145, 176; disciplinary, 40; feminist family theory on, 54–56; gender roles and, 293–94; immigrant experience and, 318; in military couples and families, 293–94; violence and, 185

practicing, 96, 97, 152

practicing themes, 101t, 102

pragmatic experiential therapy, 84

Pratt, A. C., 239

precontemplative stage, 204

prefrontal cortex, 75, 78

prefrontolimbic system, 74

pregnancy, 71, 109

preoccupied attachment, 117–18, 119t, 153

pre-oedipal theories, 96–97

prisoners of war, 58

probation officers, 136, 165

Prochaska, J. O., 204

projective identification, 8, 140, 148, 152, 175, 218, 224; aggression countertransference and, 227; detachment countertransference and, 228; developmental themes in, 213; helplessness in countertransference and, 234; insight into, 158; object constancy and, 92; objective countertransference and, 219; object relational capacity and, 157; in Rod and Yolanda clinical case, 252, 256, 261–62, 263, 275, 277–78; separation–individuation theory and, 103–4; in sexual abuse survivors, 192

Pseudo-Independence phase of racial identity development, 44

psychiatric constructs, 16–17

psychoanalytic principles, 114

psychodynamic theories, 52, 134

psychoeducational approach, 5, 81; to dissociation, 209–10; for immigrants and refugees, 325; for military couples and families, 297; in phase-oriented therapy, 136, 158, 164, 165, 171, 268; problems with, 27–28; to psychophysiological responses, 87; review of, 26–28

psychoimmunologic function, 76

Psychological Birth of the Infant, The (Mahler et al.), 94

psychopharmacology, 81, 205. *See also specific drug types*

psychophysiological responses, 76, 81, 87–90. *See also* neurophysiological effects

psychosexual themes, 213

psychosomatic reactions, 22. *See also* somatization

psychotic disorders, 166, 323

PTSD. *See* posttraumatic stress disorder

Punamaki, R. L., 319

Quiche (indigenous people), 9–10

Rabin, C., 26–27

Rachel, Seth, and Ben (clinical vignette), 59–61, 63

racial identity development, 12, 37, 41–45, 133, 142; Autonomy phase of, 45, 255; of clinician, 140; Conformity phase of, 43, 45; Contact phase of, 44; Disintegration phase of, 44; Dissonance phase of, 43; ego schemas of, 43–45; Emersion phase of, 43, 44–45, 249, 255, 282; Immersion phase of, 43, 44, 255, 281; Integrated Awareness phase of, 43; Internalization phase of, 43, 249; phase-oriented therapy and, 155, 161, 165; Pseudo-Independence phase of, 44; Reintegration phase of, 44; in Rod and Yolanda clinical case, 247, 250, 253, 255, 281–82

racial issues, 3, 7, 42, 142; immigrants and, 318; in the military, 287–89, 294–95; parenting and, 190; in Rod and Yolanda clinical case, 246, 249–53, 261, 278. *See also specific racial groups*

Racker, H., 217

rage, 170; in military personnel, 297; right-brain disruption and, 75; road, 146; Winnicott on, 110, 112

rage storms, 147, 165, 322; biopsychosocial assessment of, 148, 149; in Nancy and Ed clinical vignette, 84–86; neurobiology of, 79, 83–86

RAMC. *See* Royal Army Medical Corps

rapprochement, 96, 97–98, 152

rapprochement themes, 101t, 102–5

reaction formation countertransference, 141, 224, 235–36

Rebecca and Harry (case example), 145

reconstructing meaning, 320–21

reenactment of trauma. *See* trauma reenactment

reflection, 157–58, 159, 161, 300; attachment theory on, 121, 123, 127–28; on trauma narrative (*see* Phase II of therapy)

reframing, 30, 299

refugees, 48, 315–30; clinical implications for, 319–23; defined, 316; experience of, 318–19; interventions for, 323–29; by source area in Canada, 317t; by source area in the United States, 317t

Reichelt, S., 320

Reintegration phase of racial identity development, 44

rejecting object, 106

relational models, 134, 299–302

relational trauma, 70–76

relaxation exercises, 126, 166, 194, 271

religion/spirituality, 17, 18, 142; gender roles and, 181; GLBT couples and families and, 307; identity and, 47; Phase I of therapy and, 136, 164, 169; power relationships and, 55–56; in Rod and Yolanda clinical case, 244, 254, 261, 273; substance abuse treatment and, 206; vicarious traumatization and, 241

rescuer role, 141, 222–23, 227, 256

resilience, xii, 4, 8, 9, 15, 33, 152, 155, 281; family theory on, 51; of immigrants and refugees, 325; intergenerational family theory on, 57–58, 59; in military couples and families, 286, 289–90; neurobiological factors in, 19; in women, 17

Richman, N., 325

right-brain disruption, 73–76, 78, 79

rituals, 146–47; intergenerational family theory on, 62–63; in Phase II of therapy, 177–78, 279; in Rod and Yolanda clinical case, 259–60, 279

Rivers, W. H. R., 21

road rage, 146

Rod and Yolanda (clinical case illustration), 14, 37, 144–45, 152–53, 242–82; biopsychosocial assessment, 247–66; developmental and family histories, 244–46; goals of therapy, 265t, 266–67; parenting issues, 275–77, 281; phase-oriented therapy, 263–82; presenting issues, 244; racial issues, 246, 249–53, 261, 278; sexuality issues, 261, 263, 271, 279–81; strengths of, 264–66; support systems, 272–73

Rosa and Joan (clinical vignettes), 173; intergenerational patterns, 174–77; intimacy, 174; physical health problems, 167

Rosenbloom, D. J., 239

Royal Army Medical Corps (RAMC), 21–22

Rwanda, 7

Saakvitne, K., 219, 220, 221, 238, 239, 240

safety, 135, 162, 164, 165, 267–70

St. Clair, M., 95

Sally and Deirdre (clinical vignette), 311–12

Salvadoran immigrants, 327–29

Sam and Anna (clinical vignettes), 292–93, 295–96, 300–301

Sansei, 58

SASSI. *See* Substance Abuse Subtle Screening Inventory

Scarf, M., 197
Sceery, A., 118
Schamess, G., 99
Scharff, D., 99, 197, 224
Scharff, J., 99, 197, 217, 224
Schiratz, T., 40
Schoenewolf, G., 219
Schore, A. N., 73, 75, 120
Schwarz, J. C., 122
SCID. *See* Structured Clinical Interview for
    DSM
Scurfield, R., 17
Searle, G., 325
secondary trauma, 291. *See also* vicarious
    traumatization
secrecy, 61–62, 324, 326
secure attachment: adult classification,
    117–18, 119t; child classification, 115–16,
    117t, 119t; couple systems and, 121–22
Selective Serotonin Reuptake Inhibitors
    (SSRIs), 268, 280
self, 39–42; fluid, 64; spoiled, 41; tainted,
    37, 48; use of professional, 160–62. *See
    also* shame; stigma
self-awareness, 240–41
self-care, 31, 148; for military couples and
    families, 297; in Phase I of therapy, 136,
    165–66, 270–72, 275; vicarious
    traumatization and, 240
self-definition/identification, 65, 137,
    158–59, 179, 204–5, 282
self-disclosure, 180
self-esteem, 74, 261, 263, 272
self-injury/mutilation, 83, 138, 298
self-medication, 151, 203, 291–92
self-parts, 210
self psychology, 237–38
self-regulation, 120, 121
self-soothing, 166, 261, 272, 273
semantic memory, 77
sensation focus exercises, 83, 85, 89
sensorimotor memory, 77, 78, 79–80, 81, 167
separation–individuation theory, 91,
    94–105; couple systems and, 98–100;
    main critiques of, 94–95; themes in
    couple systems, 100–105
September 11 terrorist attacks, 3, 23–24, 47,
    213
serotonin, 76
sexism, 216
sex therapy, 28–30
sexual abuse, 25, 48, 65, 146, 162, 192–95; in
    Anna and Ivan clinical vignette, 62; in

Ann and Boris clinical vignette, 178; by
    clergymen, 203; in Dave and Janet
    clinical vignette, 224; demographic data
    on, 3, 4; distancing and, 145; Freudian
    theory on, 21; gender and, 4, 203, 215;
    GLBT couples and families and, 311–12;
    infidelity impact on survivors, 198; in
    Joanne and Jill clinical vignette, 231; in
    Margaret and Peter clinical vignette,
    53–54; in Nancy and Ed clinical
    vignette, 82, 88–89; narrative therapy
    and, 66; parenting abilities and, 190,
    191; in Paula and Colette clinical
    vignette, 68; psychophysiological effects
    of, 88–89; right-brain disruption and,
    74; in Rod and Yolanda clinical case,
    244, 271, 276; sex therapy for survivors,
    28–30; shame and stigma attached to,
    41; in Susan and Barry clinical vignette,
    193–94; type II trauma from, 7
sexual history, 192
sexuality: attachment theory on, 114; in
    GLBT couples, 310–12; hyper-, 83, 146,
    149; hypo, 83; issues for the clinician,
    216, 222, 224, 231–33; in Nancy and Ed
    clinical vignette, 88–89; phase-oriented
    therapy and, 191–95; in Rod and
    Yolanda clinical case, 261, 263, 271,
    279–81
sexual orientation, 142–43, 183; cultural
    factors and, 39; identity and, 50. *See also*
    gay, lesbian, bisexual, and transgendered
    (GLBT) couples
sexual violence, 16
shadow (traumatic memory), 299
shame, 37, 39–42, 61; in clinicians, 220;
    story of, 63, 66
Shapiro, J., 19
Sharpe, S., 100, 104, 197
Shaver, P., 122
Sheehan, P., 30
Sheldon-Keller, A. E., 122
shell shock, 22, 285
shopping, compulsive, 83
Siegel, J., 104, 217–18
Simon Rosser, B., 312
simple phobia, 288
single-trauma couples, 10, 184
slavery, 59
social constructionist theory, 6, 12, 51, 56,
    133, 155, 165, 242, 247
social construction of identity, 37, 38–39
social learning theory, 238

social policies, 307–9
social theory, 33, 37–50, 134, 161; ability/
    disability and, 49; ethnicity and, 46;
    gender and, 48; identity construction
    in, 37, 38–39; of racial development
    (*see* racial identity development);
    religion/spirituality and, 47; sexual
    orientation and, 50; shame and stigma
    in, 37, 39–42; socioeconomic status and,
    47–48
sociocultural factors, 155; in biopsychosocial
    assessment, 247–49; clinician responses
    and, 214–16; GLBT couples and
    families and, 305–9
socioeconomic status, 4, 47–48, 143
sociopathic personality disorder, 75
sodomy laws, 307
Solomon, J., 116
Solomon, M., 123, 197, 223
somatic (body) memories, 78, 87
somatization, 149, 263, 271, 291, 319, 323
Sommer, J. F., 240
South Americans, 320
Southeast Asian refugees, 323
speechless terror, 76, 77
Spiegel, J., 22
Spinhoven, P., 73
splitting, 98, 105, 106, 107, 163, 168, 261,
    262
Sroufe, L. A., 120
SSRIs. *See* Selective Serotonin Reuptake
    Inhibitors
stage model of treatment, 28, 31–32
Stamm, B. H., 18
startle response, 87, 88, 149, 165; in military
    personnel, 291, 298; neurobiology of, 71,
    76, 83; in Rod and Yolanda clinical case,
    263, 272
Stephen and Michael (clinical vignette),
    308–9
Stern, D., 95–96
stigma, 37, 39–42, 204–5
stimulus barrier disturbances, 291
Strange Situation Experiments, 115–16, 118
stress hormones, 74
stress reduction techniques, 166, 271
Stromwall, L., 49
Structured Clinical Interview for DSM
    (SCID), 148
substance abuse, 25, 82, 146, 148, 155,
    202–6; attachment theory on, 119;
    biopsychosocial assessment of, 149,
    150–52; clinical issues, 203–6;

demographics of, 202–3; dependence
    versus, 203–4; integrative therapy
    models for, 206; in Jim and Cathy
    clinical vignette, 229–31; labeling and,
    204–5; in military couples and families,
    291–92, 297; paradox of powerlessness,
    205–6; Phase I of therapy and, 166, 168;
    traumatogenic theory of, 151, 203; use of
    medications and, 205
Substance Abuse Subtle Screening
    Inventory (SASSI), 151
suicidal behavior, 19, 149, 167, 268, 298
suicide, 295
Sullivan, J. M., 151
support systems, 168–70, 272–73
Supreme Court, U.S., 307
survivor guilt, 61
Susan and Barry (clinical vignette), 193–94
Sveaass, N., 320
switching behaviors, 190
symbiosis, 96, 152
symbiotic themes, 100–102
sympathetic nervous system, 71, 72, 73–74,
    75, 295
synthesis, 10–13
systems theory, 52

Tager, J., 41
tainted self, 37, 48
Tatum, B., 42
Teicher, M. H., 74
television coverage of war, 23, 285
terrorism, 3, 4, 7, 23–24, 47, 213
testimony, 323–24
Teti, L., 188, 190
thalamus, 79, 80
therapists. *See* clinician responses
torture, 8, 315, 321, 326; defined, 7;
    intergenerational family theory on,
    59; resilience of victims, 289; shame
    and stigma attached to, 41; traumatic
    memory retrieval and, 136; typical
    sequelae of, 319; vicarious
    traumatization and, 237
touch, recoil from, 88, 146, 260, 261, 263
transference, 161, 212–14, 218, 220, 250, 252,
    263. *See also* countertransference
transgendered couples. *See* gay, lesbian,
    bisexual, and transgendered (GLBT)
    couples
trauma: constructs of, 6–9; defined, 6–7;
    factors influencing aftereffects of, 8;
    nonrelational, 70, 71; relational, 70–76;

trauma (*continued*)
  secondary, 291; type I, 7, 8; type II, 7, 8; type III, 7–8, 305, 319
trauma narratives, 155; meaning of, 147, 172–73, 259; reflection on (*see* Phase II of therapy); retelling of, 157, 327; in Rod and Yolanda clinical case, 259, 266
trauma reenactment, 7, 149; countertransference and, 220, 223, 227; infidelity as, 198–201; in Lara and Vitos clinical vignette, 184–85; in military couples and families, 286, 300. *See also* victim–victimizer–bystander scenarios
trauma theory, xi–xii, 70–90, 242; evolution of, 20–24; in Phase I of therapy, 165; and right-brain disruption, 73–76, 78, 79; in Rod and Yolanda clinical case, 275; sociopolitical context of, 16–20. *See also* neurobiological effects
traumatic bonding, 298
traumatic memory retrieval, 21, 157, 216; immigrants and refugees and, 321; military personnel and, 299, 300; Phase I of therapy and, 166; Phase II of therapy and, 136–37, 172, 173
Traumatic Neuroses of War, The (Kardiner), 22
traumatogenic theory of substance abuse, 151, 203
trust, 96, 320, 324
Tunnell, G., 312
Turner, S., 221, 319
twelve-step programs, 205, 206
type I trauma, 7, 8
type II trauma, 7, 8
type III trauma, 7, 305, 319

United Nations High Commissioner for Refugees, 316
universality, 160, 183
Ursano, R., 23, 27

vagal tone, 72
van der Kolk, B., 16–17, 19, 78, 202, 221
Vanderlinden, J., 73
Veterans Administration (VA), 150, 202
vicarious traumatization, 140, 213, 214, 236–41, 291; antidotes to, 239–41; countertransference compared with, 237, 237t; defined, 236–37; in Rod and Yolanda clinical case, 247, 255
Vicary, D., 325

Victimology Olympics, 184
victim–victimizer–bystander scenarios, 87, 88, 143–45, 146, 147, 152, 158, 163, 184; attachment theory and, 124; countertransference and, 140–41, 143, 162, 212–13, 214, 217, 220, 221, 224, 227, 228, 233, 234, 235, 256, 257; dynamics of, 8–9; family loyalties and, 61; in GLBT couples and families, 312; in immigrants and refugees, 322, 323, 326, 328, 329; infidelity and, 195, 198, 201; intergenerational patterns of, 174–77, 275–79; labeling and, 205; in military couples and families, 294, 297, 298, 300, 301; narrative theory and, 65; Phase I of therapy and, 165–66, 167, 168, 169, 170; Phase II of therapy and, 137, 172, 173, 174–77; Phase III of therapy and, 137, 138, 179, 180; power inequalities and, 54; in Rod and Yolanda clinical case, 256, 257, 258, 259, 267, 272, 275–79, 280, 281; separation–individuation theory and, 101; in torture victims, 321
Vietnam Veterans Against the War, 23
Vietnam war, 16, 24, 208, 215, 285, 292, 296; Charles and Barbara clinical vignette, 290–91; influence on trauma theory, 22–23; intergenerational family theory on, 58; intimacy issues for veterans, 30; Johnnie and Jeannie clinical vignette, 297–98; psychoeducational approach for veterans, 26; racial issues in, 288–89, 294–95; violence in veterans of, 295
Vigilante, D., 71
violence, 7, 16; attachment theory on, 122; clinician responses to, 215, 216; in GLBT couples and families, 185–86, 216, 309–10; in military couples and families, 294–96; parenting affected by, 189–90; phase-oriented therapy and, 135, 165, 181, 185–88, 193; sexual, 16. *See also* aggression
Vogel, W., 41
Vojvoda, D., 324

Walsh, F., 181
war- and combat-related trauma, 18, 23–24, 27, 202, 203, 208; dissociation, 208; intergenerational effects, 56, 57–61. *See also* military couples and families; *specific wars*
weapons of mass destruction, 4, 24, 286
Webb, J., 40

Weber, L., 48
Weil, S. M., 196–97
Weine, S., 324
Weiss, R. B., 73
Werner-Wilson, R., 17
West, M. L., 122
Whalen, D., 17
White, M., 51
whole-object relations, 152, 173
Wilkinson, D., 41
Williams, C., 27
Williams, M. B., 240
Williams, T., 27
Williams-Keeler, L., 31–32
Wilson, D., 197
Winkleman, M., 46
Winnicott, D. W., 92, 94, 109–12, 127, 153, 160
women: identity issues for, 48–49; as immigrants, 318; PTSD in, 203; resilience in, 17; substance abuse in, 150–51, 202, 203, 205. *See also* gender

Women for Sobriety and Rational Recovery, 206
Woodcock, J., 324, 327
Woods, M., 197
Woolger, C., 190
World War I, 21–22, 285
World War II, 7, 21–22, 58, 147, 285
worry circuit, 74
wraparound services, 7, 324, 326
Wright, D., 27

Yassen, J., 240, 241
Yerkes, S., 23
Ying, Y. W., 323, 330
yoga, 83, 166, 201, 240, 271
Young, A., 20, 21, 22

Zacks, E., 304
Zayas, L., 38
Zigler, E., 188
Zimmerman, T., 17
Zur, J., 9, 320